FAMILY SECRETS

The Case That

Crippled

the Chicago Mob

JEFF COEN

CHICAGO
REVIEW
PRESS

The Library of Congress has cataloged the hardcover edition as follows:

Coen, Jeff.
    Family secrets : the case that crippled the Chicago mob / Jeff Coen.
        p. cm.
    Includes index.
    ISBN-13: 978-1-55652-781-4 (cloth)
    ISBN-10: 1-55652-781-0 (cloth)
    1. Mafia—Illinois—Chicago.   2. Outfit (Organization).
3. Organized crime—Illinois—Chicago—History.   4. Criminals—
Illinois—Chicago—Biography.   5. Murder—Illinois—Chicago—Case
studies.   6. Trials (Murder)—Illinois—Case studies.   I. Title.

    HV6452.I32O874 2009
    364.152'30977311—dc22   2008040135

Cover design: Rachel McClain
Interior design: Pamela Juárez
Map design: Chris Erichsen

Jacket photographs courtesy of the U.S. Department of Justice

FRONT COVER
Top row: Joseph Hansen, Frank Calabrese Sr., Angelo "the Hook" LaPietra, Michael Spilotro
Row 2: Frank "Gumba" Saladino, collection receipt
Row 3: Joey "the Clown" Lombardo (1974)
Row 4: William "Butch" Petrocelli, John Fecarotta
Row 5: George Jay Vandermark, Frank Calabrese Jr., Frank "the German" Schweihs,
    James "Jimmy Light" Marcello
Row 6: Ortiz/Morawski crime scene photo, Joey "Doves" Aiuppa, Gerald Scarpelli

BACK COVER
Top row: Cagnoni crime scene photo, government exhibit #1: the "Last Supper" photo
Row 2: unidentified mug shot from FBI photo array
Row 3: fingerprints on Ford LTD title application, Ortiz/Morawski crime scene diagram

First hardcover edition published 2009
First paperback edition published 2010
Published by Chicago Review Press, Incorporated
814 North Franklin Street
Chicago, Illinois 60610
ISBN 978-1-56976-545-6
Printed in the United States of America
5 4 3 2 1

This only have I found:
God made mankind upright,
but men have gone in search of many schemes
                                        —ECCLESIASTES

CONTENTS

AUTHOR'S NOTE

S ource material for this book consists primarily of court transcripts, interviews with central players in the case, trial exhibits, and notes taken while I covered the Family Secrets trial for the *Chicago Tribune* during the summer of 2007.

Many of the quotations in the book were taken from transcripts, most notably in chapters that cover the trial testimony of Nick Calabrese and Joey "the Clown" Lombardo. Accounts of conversations recorded at the federal prison in Milan, Michigan, also were taken from transcripts of the actual discussions. The government prepared printed versions of the Milan conversations, which became trial exhibits.

Many documents and photos used in this book and shown to the jury during the trial were made available to the public by the U.S. Attorney's Office in Chicago.

Other reference material included stories from the archives of the *Chicago Tribune* and the *Chicago Sun-Times*. Prior to the time I covered the case for the *Tribune*, many detailed stories on Family Secrets were produced by *Tribune* reporters Matt O'Connor and Todd Lighty, former *Tribune* reporter Rudolph Bush, and *Tribune* columnist John Kass. Reporter Steve Warmbir covered the case and the trial for the *Sun-Times*, and his work is widely respected as well.

Reuters coverage of the Las Vegas case involving the Spilotros and the "Hole in the Wall Gang" was reviewed, as were stories by the late John O'Brien, a legendary *Tribune* scribe whose colorful stories are still remembered at the Tribune Tower and the Dirksen U.S. Courthouse in Chicago.

One final important note: The narrative accounts of murders included in the book were taken from the testimony of trial witnesses and case documents. Most of the descriptions of homicides included in the case and repeated here were provided to the government during debriefings of Nick Calabrese, and later by Nick himself to the Family Secrets jury, which was not able to unanimously assign blame for all of the killings.

1

A KILLING
BETWEEN FRIENDS

Taking a life was like a riddle to be solved or a puzzle to be slowly pieced together, and by 1986, Nick Calabrese was a pretty patient guy.

He was hardly the bruising movie version of the mob hit man, some beefcake with a machine gun and a chiseled jaw who bursts into a restaurant in a pinstriped suit to flatten someone, sending plates of ravioli and a checkered tablecloth flying. There was no swagger or bravado about him. You could walk toward him on the street and pass by without a second thought or glance.

He had an everyman appearance to be sure, but many would have been wiser not to be fooled. Nick was a deadly and cool technician. He would stalk his victims, trailing them and learning as he watched them move. Sometimes his hit squads would lurk for weeks, looking for the best way to strike and then escape detection.

Follow the target long enough and a pattern would emerge; eventually a weak spot in his daily routine could be recognized and then efficiently exploited. There was almost always a time when the victim's guard would be down or he could be found in an opportune spot. Trickery and deceit were preferred to the daylight ambush. Making a good kill was about guile and cunning and surprise, and not always blasting in and then out if need be. Finding the right angle or lure usually made all of that unnecessary.

The idea, of course, was not to get caught. So the Chicago Outfit liked to take its victims to secret places, such as garages or basements, closed businesses, or empty buildings. Its killers appeared like phantoms and vanished quickly.

For the least accessible victims, maybe a bomb was the answer, as the Outfit took every step to try to keep the advantage. Men like Nick were responsible for figuring out how the killing should be accomplished and then doing what had to be done and disappearing—though sometimes they would stop for coffee when they were through. There was no bragging and no returning to the scene of the crime to take it in.

Most of the time it was only later that the sinister handiwork would turn up: a body in a gulley or stuffed mostly naked in a trunk, tied up and contorted with a gaping wound to the neck.

In many ways that layer of mystery was better when the goal was keeping Chicago's criminal underworld in line, sending a constant threatening chill over the streets. For some the threat of being killed was always there and felt as if it could come from any direction. That was good business for the mob, keeping Outfit associates and customers alike looking over their shoulder. Break the Outfit's rules or don't pay who you're supposed to pay, and that could be it. The next time anyone sees you, there's a group of cops standing over your corpse, with flashes going off while your picture is taken for the file.

Bosses in the Chicago Outfit marked many for death to protect the organization, sometimes from a witness who might talk to the feds and sometimes to punish a member who stepped out of line or brought too much heat. Sometimes it was just to make a bloody example out of an enemy, and Nick was among the trusted few called upon to do the ugliest of jobs.

Nick was a weapon, although a mostly reluctant one.

He had allowed himself to begin down the dark path, never having the courage to make it all stop. He had been in the navy and had held real jobs. He'd been a union ironworker and had a family. None of that had involved digging holes or lying in wait for the unwary with a rope or a gun.

Maybe he could have found the courage to tell them he was through. But once in the Outfit, there was no deciding to quit, no retirement parties, no turning away and deciding you'd had enough. He'd wanted to run, but where was he supposed to go? There was really only one way out—death—and Nick was afraid of that consequence.

It was an oppressive fear, a fear that had a name and a face that stayed with him—as close as a brother.

It was Frank Calabrese Sr., a successful Outfit loan shark, who had started Nick's slow sink into the Chicago syndicate. It had been almost harmless at first, after all. Nick would help Frank Sr., a member of the mob's Chinatown street crew, make sense of scrawled loan notes and betting slips. He would collect envelopes and track what debtors owed, parking out of sight and walking to meet them where he could take their tribute. He would help run sports bookmaking and hold his brother's many agents accountable. It was a way for Nick to make a little extra cash, above and beyond what he could make doing his legitimate work.

The quiet Nick was a paper-and-numbers guy—at least at the beginning—not a vicious killer.

In 1970, the first time he watched his brother plunge a knife into someone's throat, he wet himself he was so scared. It was dark and his pants were grimy with the dirt of the South Side construction site where they would hide the body in a small pit, so neither his brother nor his brother's henchman had noticed.

He had started as the ride-along, the spare hand.

But some sixteen years later, he was the kind of soldier those in command of the Outfit valued, no matter his reasons for being a part of it. He asked no questions and caused no trouble, a trait appreciated by the harsh men in charge. They needed to give an order and have it carried out with merciless determination. Nick was given a job, and in a Chicago lunch-bucket kind of way, it got done. He would return with a quick word or make a coded phone call where he talked about having soup or something, and the mob's business could go on. His brother passed an order from the bosses, and Nick was in, fearing what might lie in store for him if he said no. There were mobsters with more bluster, intense men who would yell and threaten and instill fear, but it's the quiet ones you never see coming.

That's not to say that things always went perfectly when Nick was told to take a life. Sometimes the adrenaline would kick in too strong and force mistakes. When the heart raced too fast, it could be hard to stay focused. In the dark, with a begging, struggling victim, things could get confusing quickly.

There was the time Nick helped kill another mobster lured from a neighborhood club, placing the beaten, strangled, and stabbed man in his car and leaving it parked on a residential street. When it was over, his street crew's capo, or captain, had demanded that the body and the car be burned, so Nick went back and doused the man's corpse in Zippo lighter fluid in the backseat and lit it. But in his haste he left all the windows rolled up and snuffed out the flames when he shut the car door. Only a fresh snow covered that error, at least for a few weeks.

And there was the time in Phoenix Nick had pulled a grand jury witness into a van and shot him in the head. It had taken two trips to Arizona and weeks of careful planning to finally execute him, but one of his guns clumsily fell into the tarp on the floor of the van as he rolled up the body to dispose of it.

Nick had been far from home for that hit, traveling on the nastiest kind of business. But a member of the Chicago mob finding himself that many states away for a killing was not an outlandish idea at the time. The Outfit that he worked for in the 1970s and 1980s was a ruthless organization of extraordinary reach, a hidden evil at the pinnacle of its strength. Its bosses ruled an empire of gambling that stretched to Las Vegas and made untold millions through extortion and high-interest "juice loans." Nick's brother alone had hundreds of thousands of dollars on the street at a time, ordering his minions out to make collections.

Their Chicago was a dense mass of rail and truck yards, warehouses, insular neighborhoods, grit, steel, and vice, and the mob drained it wherever it could. Outfit muscle collected street taxes and protection money from porn shops and legitimate businesses alike, and the syndicate held sway over everything from trucking to strip clubs. The city's lifeblood—money—flowed under the Outfit's watchful eye.

Unlike La Cosa Nostra, the fractured Mafia of the East Coast, organized crime in Chicago had been unified for much of the century, since the days of the infamous boss Al Capone. He had molded the factions into a singular, menacing organism that would go on to thrive in the 1940s under Paul "the Waiter" Ricca. Instead of tearing itself apart through infighting, the Outfit acted as a united force for decades under one "Old Man," a shadow mayor of sorts.

With Chicago under its thumb, the Outfit began to concentrate on expansion, tapping into vast labor union pension funds that it used to build glittering casinos—which it then skimmed—in the Nevada desert.

At home in Chicago, both the businessman who couldn't get a legitimate loan from the bank and a sucker needing to cover a mounting gambling tab would find themselves accepting Outfit loans that required interest payments of 5 percent per week. A pornographer wanting to open a city sex shop was wise to get permission from the Outfit and then give it a cut to avoid facing its wrath. Burglars were expected to pay a percentage, too, and in some neighborhoods even a hot-dog stand would require a blessing before it could open.

The Outfit's influence seeped into the Chicago Police Department, corrupting street cops who looked the other way or, worse, warned the mob when the police were moving against its interests. One officer who became a chief of detectives was even found to be running a massive jewelry-theft ring with a nod from Chicago bosses. And in 1977 the mob bought an acquittal in a murder case in court in Cook County, crossing a barrier that few believed could be breached.

The Chicago Outfit of the day included six street crews around the city and suburbs: Elmwood Park, Melrose Park, Chinatown, Grand Avenue, Rush Street, and Chicago Heights. But they weren't so much geographic territories as seats of power. Nick and Frank's Chinatown organization, also known as the Twenty-Sixth Street crew, had gambling agents as far away as Rockford, sixty miles northwest of Chicago. The crews were made up of handfuls of individuals working closely to make money, which was passed up the chain and into the Outfit's hierarchy. Crew members worked bookmaking rings together, gave out juice loans, and collected extortion payments. And when necessary, they became murder squads.

Nick knew them all and had threatened, bombed, and killed with many.

There was Johnny "Bananas" DiFronzo, later known as "No Nose," in Elmwood Park. Vince Solano and Frankie Belmonte of the Rush Street crew, and Al Pilotto in Chicago Heights. There was Joey "the Clown" Lombardo, a gangster known for his humor and eccentricity, leading the Grand Avenue crew on Chicago's North Side, and there was James "Jimmy Light" Marcello in Melrose Park, a crew that had Sam "Wings" Carlisi as its capo.

Yet another group of mobsters had banded together under Joe Ferriola into what became known as the Wild Bunch, including feared hit man Harry Aleman, Gerald Scarpelli, and William "Butch" Petrocelli.

And at the top of the entire food chain were "Number One" and "Number Two," boss Joey "Doves" Aiuppa and his second in command, Jackie Cerone. They demanded absolute loyalty and could impose their will with just a look or a gesture.

But of more immediate concern for Nick was the capo of the Chinatown crew on the South Side. Angelo "the Hook" LaPietra was in command, and Nick's brother Frank Sr. and his juice operation were among his chief moneymakers. The crew had the reputation of being the Chicago mob's real enforcers, the arm that leaders went to when others weren't able to get a killing done. They were the worst of the worst, men who took pride in their refusal to give up on a stubborn job even where others had failed.

In some years Nick found himself bringing LaPietra's cut of the crew's action to the capo's garage in the Italian stronghold of Bridgeport, on the South Side, where Nick and his brother had come to be connected to the Outfit. Nick would stuff the cash in a barbecue mitt hanging on the wall—sometimes $20,000 at a time—flipping it over so the thumb would alert LaPietra that his payment was there.

Frank Sr. had been plugged into the Outfit years before Nick, beginning as an auto thief in the chop shop business and eventually moving into making juice loans. He was a bit of a natural, and his success eventually was noticed by LaPietra, who didn't get his menacing nickname "the Hook" for nothing. Frank soon was whistled in, or summoned, for a meeting and was told in no uncertain terms that he would work with the mob. Even though the brothers had grown up with immigrant parents in the West Side Italian neighborhood around Grand and Ogden avenues—known as "the Patch"—with Frank Sr. the eldest of seven children and Nick smack in the middle, they found themselves key members of the South Side crew.

In later years when LaPietra was headed to prison, he informed the Calabreses that his brother, Jimmy LaPietra, would take over as capo, muttering in Italian in a restaurant meeting and letting the Calabreses know he was handing over daily control.

In fact, in the days before September 14, 1986, it was "Brother Jimmy" who had given the order for Nick to kill his next victim. A simple "Go ahead" was all that had been said after Frank Sr. had taken his grievances about the target to mob leaders.

Soon Nick was driving a stolen blue four-door Buick that Sunday evening on the Northwest Side, taking the car, which he'd lifted from a suburban train station, to a bowling alley to meet up with his friend, fellow hit man John Fecarotta. Nick had stolen some license plates from another car and put them on the Buick himself. Like many Outfit "work cars," the Buick would be used solely to commit a crime and then promptly dumped.

Fecarotta, a mobster known as "Big Stoop," had been with Nick on jobs a number of times, including the killings of the mob's leader in Las Vegas, Anthony "the Ant" Spilotro, and his brother Michael, which for a time would be one of the city's most notorious unsolved gangland slayings. The Spilotros had been lured to their deaths with promises of promotions in the organization, killed, and buried in an Indiana cornfield.

But as it turned out, Fecarotta wouldn't be helping Nick this time.

Outfit bosses had become displeased with Fecarotta's seemingly endless money problems, and he had made the very serious misstep of leaving the Arizona killing before it had been completed. On that trip Fecarotta had also taken a gambling excursion, and when he'd won $2,000 at a Bullhead City casino, he had asked Nick to sign paperwork for the winnings when they were supposed to be keeping a low profile. His fate was sealed when he became involved in a dispute over a juice customer with the forever-plotting Frank Sr., the kind of loan shark who wasn't accustomed to letting such things slide.

The man who had been making payments on his Outfit debt to Frank Sr. was suddenly told to start coming up with Fecarotta's house payment instead. So it wasn't long after the money dried up that Frank Sr. paid a visit. He pulled the debtor close and held a knife near his crotch, telling him it would probably be best for him if he settled with the Calabreses before listening to that idiot Fecarotta. The man quickly agreed with the angry loan shark and his blade, and the bully of Chinatown released his hold without doing any long-term damage.

Fecarotta knew he was on bad paper with Frank Sr. and those above him, so he had been "on point," or alert, in the weeks leading up to the Sunday bowling alley meeting with Nick, his old pal.

Catching another hit man unaware would be difficult enough and would take a very clever ruse for Nick, but a hit man who already feared that his time had come and that he was going to get hurt was an especially hard target. There had been too many disputes with Frank Sr. and other mobsters, like John "Johnny Apes" Monteleone, for either of them to get close to Fecarotta. It would take Nick and his relationship with his trusting friend to put Fecarotta at ease and catch him in a weak moment. Fecarotta, a seasoned hit man, would expect a lot of things, but not that Nick would be the one to take him out.

So with the trap set, Nick watched from his stolen car as Fecarotta was dropped off near their meeting point. But Nick didn't drive up right away. Appearing instantly might make Fecarotta think Nick had been eyeing him, activating the suspicious hit man's intuitive sense that he was in some kind of danger. Instead, Nick drove around the block, relaxing the energy around the situation and waiting to make sure that the person who had dropped Fecarotta off was gone before he approached. It was better to let things develop at a normal pace and keep the situation from feeling forced.

After pulling up, Nick parked and slid over into the passenger's seat.

Fecarotta's skills as a wheelman in this kind of Outfit work were widely known and respected, so he would have expected to drive. Fecarotta had been told that he and Nick would go together from the meeting to an alley near Austin Boulevard and Belmont Avenue on the Northwest Side. In the alley was the back door of the offices of a dentist who did union work, the story went, and the dentist had to be sent a fiery message from the mob.

At Nick's feet was a brown paper bag he had pulled from a garbage can, containing what looked like the kind of makeshift bomb they'd used a number of times before—four sticks of dynamite with a fuse and a blasting cap. But the device was as phony as the job that had Fecarotta in the car that evening. It was just four road flares wound together with duct tape to look like a typical toss-and-run explosive.

And also in the bag, out of sight, was a .38-caliber revolver, Nick's hardy weapon of choice.

The careful Fecarotta might check the glove compartment for a gun, his cohorts knew, so Nick had taken care of that, too. He had placed an older gun there after disabling it by filing down the firing pin. If something went wrong and Fecarotta happened to go for it during their drive, it would be of no help to him. Everything was covered. And if that wasn't enough insurance, Nick had a third gun in the car, a spare .38, tucked into the waistband of his pants.

The men already had taken the ride once or twice, going past the dentist's office to scope it out and work out precisely where they would park and how it would be approached. It would look and feel like a typical job, and Fecarotta wouldn't have been made suspicious by any obvious lack of their typical planning and preparation.

It was getting dark as they arrived, but they couldn't move in right away. There was a man working nearby as they rolled up. They could see him moving around in an open garage, so they would have to circle back to the alley after a few minutes. Fecarotta drove his friend around again for another pass, his friend Nick with the bag at his feet and a pair of pistols at the ready.

The next time the scene was clear. Whoever the man in the garage had been, he was nowhere in sight. Fecarotta found the spot where they had planned to park; the time had arrived to go ahead. Nick, wearing the tight black golfing gloves he often wore on such jobs, reached into his bag as if to light the bomb's fuse.

Instead, he gripped the revolver.

Maybe Fecarotta didn't hear the exact sound he expected. Maybe the expression on Nick's face suddenly changed or he tightened his jaw in a way that caused alarm. But whatever it was, the game was up. Fecarotta had "caught the play" and made a frantic move for Nick. He was going to try to save himself.

As Nick brought the gun up in his right hand, the men were already beginning to struggle. Nick cleared his legs with the .38 and got off a shot toward Fecarotta's side, firing across his own body toward his surprised friend. The pair who had killed together so many times before were now fighting to the death.

Fecarotta grabbed at the gun, getting hold of it and trying to pull it from Nick's grasp. As they grappled with each other, the gun tilted and the cylinder of the revolver fell open, spilling its bullets into the front seat with the wrestling hit men.

That might have sent a wave of relief over Fecarotta for just an instant, but Nick wasn't done with him yet. His adrenaline pumping, Nick reached to his waist, taking hold of the spare handgun. The bleeding Fecarotta jerked backward, jumping from the car to make a final desperate run for it.

A thought flashed through Nick's mind. Allowing Fecarotta to get away was not an option, for failure to finish this kind of task meant only one thing. He had heard the warning with his own ears countless times. If the target eludes you, "you'll take his place," Nick and others always had been told. Punishment would come swiftly, and it might not be the quick death that Nick was now trying to dish out.

As he opened the passenger door in pursuit, he thought of two other mobsters who had recently messed up their work and wound up in a trunk. Nick had to catch Fecarotta, he said to himself. He had to catch him and he had to finish him off; there was no doubt about that.

Fecarotta ran, leaving a trail of blood from the Buick and up the alley as Nick stepped from the car and pursued him. Fecarotta was making for a bingo parlor on the north side of Belmont. Behind the men the car was still running, both of its front doors left wide open in the alley.

In a matter of seconds Nick closed in on his wounded prey, reaching Fecarotta as he approached the bingo hall's door. Nick came up quickly from behind; there would be no escape now. This time he raised the extra .38 and took steady aim at nearly point-blank range. He squeezed the trigger, sending a bullet crashing through Fecarotta's skull. His friend went limp, and it was over. Nick turned and walked away.

He stepped over a guardrail and across the alley toward Austin Boulevard. Somewhere nearby, Frank Sr., his brother, was supposed to be in a trail car, watching for the police and calling out warnings with a walkie-talkie. Frank Sr. was supposed to pick up Nick, whisking him safely away before the cops could respond. But Frank was nowhere to be seen.

Nick continued walking south, trying to stay calm as he watched for his brother. He knew he needed to keep moving away from the alley, since the shot had echoed across the neighborhood. He needed to move away from witnesses who would soon be starting to gather around Fecarotta's body, if they weren't already.

It was only then that he realized something was wrong.

With the frenzy of the killing fading, there was pain, along with warmth and moisture. There was blood.

It was the first shot, he said to himself. As he had fired toward Fecarotta, his own left arm must have gotten in the way. The bullet had passed through it, leaving a shard of bone sticking through his skin. There was blood on his clothes and on the gloves. He knew he needed to take them off in a hurry. It was only September—not that cold—so gloves would look odd to someone passing by. He pulled them off to put them in one pocket and slid the .38 into another. He looked again for Frank Sr., but still his brother wasn't there.

Nick turned off Austin and onto a side street, deciding just to head for his own car, which he had parked earlier before switching to the stolen Buick. It was best not to be carrying the pistol, so he pulled it out and dropped it through a sewer grate. He would head home hurt but having accomplished his latest job. It was Fecarotta who would be going to the morgue, not him.

He kept walking, hastily, getting nearer to his car with each step. Nick needed to get his wound clean and needed to talk to his brother. He needed to tell Frank Sr. what had happened, how Fecarotta had put up a fight, but he had finished him off. He had managed to kill his own friend without losing his nerve.

But as he walked, he didn't notice the small crumpled shapes on the sidewalk behind him, or that both of his pockets were now empty.

No, things didn't always go perfectly for Nick. And there, left in the growing darkness, lay two black gloves.

2

THE SURPRISE LETTER

"I am sending you this letter in total confidentiality," the single sheet of paper read, with a message that looked as if it had been tapped out on an electric typewriter. "It is very important that you show or talk to nobody about this letter except who you have to. The less people that know I am contacting you the more I can and will help and be able to help you."

The message, dated July 27, 1998, had been sent without warning from the federal correctional institution in Milan, Michigan, to FBI organized crime supervisor Tom Bourgeois at the bureau's headquarters in Chicago. It was from Frank Calabrese Jr., the son of loan shark Frank Calabrese Sr. and Nick's close nephew. He had once been considered new blood in the Chinatown crew, part of a new generation that would help ensure the Outfit survived into the future. But with his letter, Frank Jr. was letting the government know that he wanted to cooperate with them, to flip and help them investigate the Chicago mob and his father. Then entering his midthirties, he'd had it with his father's abusive ways and broken promises. He wanted a face-to-face talk with the FBI, apparently ready to fill them in on what he knew about his father's crimes, the street crew, and the murder of John Fecarotta almost a dozen years earlier.

"NOBODY not even my lawyers know I am sending you this letter, it is better that way for my safety," the letter continued. "Hopefully we can come to an agreement when and if you choose to COME HERE.

"Please if you decide to come make sure very few staff at MILAN know your reason for coming because if they do they might tell my father and that would be a danger to me," it read. "The best days to come would be TUES. OR WEDS. Please no recordings of any kind just bring pen and lots of paper. This is no game. I feel I have to help you keep this sick man locked up forever."

FBI agents weren't focused on the Calabreses when they received Frank Jr.'s message. The bureau already had come down on the family and their associates a few years earlier, in 1995, for a time breaking up their loan-sharking operation. After an investigation supervised by Bourgeois, a grand jury had indicted nine people, including Frank Sr., Nick, Frank Jr., and another of Frank Sr.'s sons, Kurt. The Calabreses were accused of collecting juice loans and taking over the auto repair business of one customer who had become an informant. Their street crew was able to get a service contract with a large suburban car dealership, Celozzi-Ettleson Chevrolet in Elmhurst, and then began overbilling.

The four Calabreses had pleaded guilty. Frank Sr. got almost ten years in prison, and Nick almost six years. They had been bagged and would be locked up for a while, so federal prosecutors and the FBI had moved on.

When the letter from Milan was delivered to Chicago, Michael Maseth was a new FBI agent, just twenty-seven, a native of Pittsburgh who had given up a career as a defense lawyer when his mother urged him to apply to the bureau. Having been in the city for just a few months, he had been assigned to the case of a mobster and union official named Jimmy "Poker" DiForti, who had been charged the prior year with shooting a man named William Benham. Benham had refused to pay a $100,000 juice loan and threatened to become a rat.

Bourgeois told Maseth that the bureau was about to conduct a wiretap at a prison and sent Maseth and Special Agent Michael Hartnett to debrief the younger Calabrese and hear what he knew about his father's ring of associates, and about John Fecarotta.

Frank Jr. and Nick had created a good relationship in the violent orbit of Frank Sr., sometimes doing their mob work together. When Frank Jr. was barely old enough to drive, they had collected juice payments from customers and visited pornography shops, the kind of businesses where men would slip coins into a box to watch a few minutes of an X-rated film, to take the Outfit's due.

Frank Jr. had more than enough information to be dangerous to the Outfit and his family. He had worked on a city sewers crew for part of the 1980s, and his uncle had asked him to retrieve the handgun that he had dropped through a grate on the street as he walked from where he had killed Fecarotta. Frank Jr. also knew that his uncle had been shot and injured during the hit, a fact he shared with Maseth and Hartnett. In addition, his father had mentioned more murders in the past, including the high-profile killings of Anthony and Michael Spilotro, though sometimes Frank Sr. spoke in code, making the details a bit murky. Still, there was enough information for agents to quickly become very interested in what Frank Jr. was offering.

For Frank Jr. to record his father, he would use a listening device hidden in plain sight—in a pair of headphones like the kind circulating at the prison in Milan, for music listening. When Frank Jr. talked to his father in the prison yard, leading him through long discussions and taping his secrets, the headphones would simply be hanging around his neck.

The enthusiastic Frank Jr. was eager to get started. His father was looking to have a discussion with him, he wrote in another note to the FBI that December, so it was urgent to be ready to record him soon.

"I need to do it ASAP, because he wants to have this long talk and walk with me," Frank Jr. wrote. "He keeps saying, 'Lets walk—I need to talk to you.'"

And Frank Jr. said he was willing to go further to keep his father incarcerated, if the FBI desired. If they would move him to the Metropolitan Correctional Center in downtown Chicago, Frank Jr. wrote, "I will also do my uncle if you can put us together."

FBI agents and federal prosecutors knew they had a rare opportunity, but no one was exactly certain where things might lead. It's not every day that the son of a "made" member of the Chicago Outfit—meaning the member was brought into the Outfit's inner circle in a secret ceremony after having killed for the organization—drops a note out of the blue offering to put members of his family away.

Maseth and Hartnett were at the prison as Frank Jr. started making his secret recordings, but they had no way of listening in to what was happening or reacting if there was a problem. As the son taped his father, he would be on his own, exposed to any punishment Frank Sr. or any of his associates at Milan might hand out on the spot if they discovered the recording device.

"We just thought if they find it, the next thing we're going to hear is sirens going off," Maseth said. "It was a dangerous situation for him."

The taping began, and by late winter FBI agents were starting to collect material they could use to build a case. On Valentine's Day, 1999, father and son met in the prison yard at Milan, with Frank Jr. wearing the special headphones agents had given him. He was ready to do what he had promised.

"Sit down, son, I don't think anybody's here," the elder Calabrese said. He was a stout and pugnacious man, with a very quick temper. He was "good with his hands," as the Outfit phrase went, and his son knew it. The thick, powerful neck of his youth was chubbier now that he was in his sixties, but anger could still bring an intense glare to his face. He was largely uneducated as far as traditional schooling went and could barely read. What he did have were street smarts and a head for numbers. And he was a good student of the human animal—able to read people and manipulate them.

Frank Jr. was a taller version of his father and balding, just like him. He was gentler in appearance but had his father's eyes and furrowed forehead. The men had had their differences in the past, with Frank Jr., while addicted to cocaine and broke, once stealing several hundred thousand dollars from his father to try to open a Chicago restaurant. It was that theft and Frank Sr.'s reaction to it that had pushed the son toward sending his letter to the FBI. His own father had held a gun to his son's face and threatened to kill him. The son's bitterness had grown against his father after Frank Sr. had gone against his word to leave his mob life. Frank Jr. had told the FBI he felt as though his dad was a pretend father and that he had no love for his son. Still, he obviously had some deep feelings about what he was doing.

"He was emotional at times about it—it wasn't easy for him," Maseth said later. "He wasn't businesslike about it."

As Frank Sr. spoke to his son with the tape rolling, he was clearly hoping he could restore the relationship to what it had been earlier in the son's life. Frank Sr. was willing to trust his son again, and that was about to become his undoing.

The men began by making small talk, but Frank Sr. quickly switched to what was really on his mind. There was the possibility that DiForti, the mobster whose case Maseth was assigned to, was a snitch. He had worked alongside the Calabreses for years in the Chinatown crew. He had committed murders with them and could hurt them deeply if Frank Sr.'s worries were proven true.

The month before the father and son spoke, in January 1999, authorities had begun to pull old evidence from the Fecarotta murder from the Chicago Police Department's storage warehouse, and it was a move that had not gone unnoticed. The Outfit had its own network of spies, and its moles inside the police department had informed Frank Sr. that the murder file had been reopened and evidence was being reviewed. Nick had pulled the trigger, but Frank Sr. had helped plan the hit. And while Frank had never been able to hook up with his brother immediately after the shooting, he had in fact been in the lookout car nearby when Fecarotta was killed, making him just as culpable.

Frank Sr. was left trying to put two and two together while sitting in prison, considering all the variables and trying to figure out what made the most sense about why the feds suddenly were interested in Fecarotta's killing. He had no idea that it was actually the FBI's discussions with his own son, talking with him now, that had led them to go to Chicago police to pull the old evidence.

What Frank Sr. did know was that DiForti had been released on bond in the Benham murder not long before, and suddenly the FBI seemed to be concentrating on the Fecarotta homicide, a killing from 1986 that many had forgotten about.

"See what happened here, when Jimmy come out; he come out, a week later, they pulled all his stuff on the [Fecarotta] case," Frank Sr. told his son.

The FBI would later learn that Nick Calabrese also had gotten word about the Fecarotta murder file being reopened, and that he too may have suspected DiForti. "Poker," so nicknamed for his love of the card game, had always been a weak link in Nick's mind.

Agents did nothing to use informants to feed the street network false information that DiForti was a turncoat, but certainly they did nothing to alter that perception. In fact, investigators saw the mobsters' suspicions as another lucky break in an investigation that was starting to develop very well.

"These guys started things along those lines, and it was just fortunate for us," said supervisory FBI agent John Mallul, who would come to lead the investigation in its final stages. "It gave Junior a tremendous amount of cover."

The incorrect suspicions about Fecarotta and DiForti essentially kept Frank Sr. distracted while the real informant—his son—stayed right in front of him. And it provided a convenient platform for the men to discuss old crimes on Frank Jr.'s tapes. As Frank Sr. talked about what he didn't want authorities to know, he was playing right into their hands.

The FBI really had no way to react to the belief about DiForti anyway. They couldn't just interrupt the prison discussions and tell Frank Sr. he was wrong about his hunch. Agents would never deliberately circulate lies implicating someone as an informant; that would have put DiForti in very real danger of being violently eliminated. In fact, Maseth would meet DiForti in a parking lot at that stage of the investigation, telling him that rumors were flying that he was cooperating. But DiForti was uncaring, Maseth remembered.

"He basically said, 'I don't have anything to say about anybody,' and that was it," Maseth said.

As Frank Sr. and his son talked, the mobster decided it would be best if they kept some of their discussions coded. You never knew who could be listening in. He would be monitoring the DiForti situation from then on, Frank Sr. promised, and DiForti would be referred to by a nickname.

"So what we're gonna call him, remember this name, 'Tires,'" Frank Sr. said, reminding his son that DiForti used to have a shop in Chicago where he sold automobile tires.

"So remember that—call him Tires," Frank Sr. said. "Tires went home and it wasn't a week later everything was taken out."

The code extended to Nick, too. Frank Sr. called him "Joy," the name of Nick's first wife, and referred to him as a "she" in conversation. Instead of his brother, Nick became Frank Sr.'s "sister." The street network was crackling with information that Nick, or Joy, was suspected by the FBI in the Fecarotta hit, the father told the son.

"They think that Joy did the guy, and they've taken a sample off of a glove," Frank Sr. said. But Frank Sr. wasn't clear on whether the glove could be his brother's. He had never known exactly what had happened to Nick's gloves and may not have fully realized what an exposure they truly represented for Outfit leaders.

"But why would've she left it over there, Frank?" Frank Sr. said to his son. Maybe the gloves could have been Fecarotta's, he guessed, speculating that police would have taken any gloves Fecarotta was wearing when they processed the crime scene.

"They took [Fecarotta's] gloves at the time," Frank Sr. said, sounding like he was trying to convince himself that it must be true. "They took everything that they wanted—all his clothes and everything, they took it."

Investigators would be looking for forensic evidence, Frank Sr. said, as his son recorded every word. Investigators would be looking for blood, though in the old days it might have been hair.

"They did that; they did that back in the seventies," he told his boy. "That's why, if you remember, we used to wear our hat under the hood, so that when you pull the hood off, your head is still covered. Remember what I used to do? Wash my hair before I'd go anyplace? So nothing, there would be no loose hair."

Anyway, Frank Sr. said, it should take only a few days to get some answers. His police contacts were due to pay him another visit soon, he told his son. They were men with access to the right information.

"They're gonna tell me some more."

With that conversation on tape, the FBI believed it had enough for the investigation to progress and quickly went to court to get permission for broader eavesdropping in the case. A surveillance camera bubble on the ceiling of a visiting room at Milan was equipped with a directional microphone sensitive enough to pick up particular conversations happening anywhere in the room. Agents could watch and listen if anyone did come to speak with Frank Sr.

As it turned out, they wouldn't have long to wait. Five days after the Valentine's Day conversation with his son, Frank Sr. was in the room meeting with the visitors he had expected.

Arriving to see him in the prison were Cook County sheriff's officer Mike Ricci, a former Chicago police officer, and Anthony "Twan" Doyle, a broad-shouldered Chicago cop whose name had been Passafiume before he'd changed it to join the police department. At the time of the visit, Doyle worked at the subterranean evidence storage area underneath the bustling Cook County Criminal Courts Building, a sprawling old courts complex at Twenty-Sixth Street and California Avenue on the city's Southwest Side. He had access to a computer that could show where old evidence was in the police warehouse, who had removed it, and when it was removed. Authorities believed Ricci had long supplied Frank Sr. with inside information from law enforcement. They had owned at least two businesses together, a hotdog stand and a go-go lounge.

Twan—who had gotten his nickname from the way his Italian mother shouted, "An-twan-y!" from the family's porch over the old neighborhood at dinnertime—had known Calabrese for years. The men sat in a circle in the crowded prison visiting room, with the FBI watching and recording from the security camera above their heads.

"Rotie, Rotie," Frank Sr. said, mindful of his code word for DiForti, playing off the Italian word *rote*, or "tires," as he had planned.

"The guy with the—that—ah . . . we ah . . . we were concerned about might have been doing," he said.

"Tires" might have been talking to friends of the men, Frank Sr. was trying to say, but he told his visitors he was more concerned with what DiForti might have been saying to *Scarpe Grande*. It was another of Frank Sr.'s code words—"big shoes," or "wing tips"—and it meant the FBI. The three in the visiting room began to review the chain of events as they knew it, attempting to figure out what kind of information DiForti might be able to provide. They worked what they knew of the time line backward, with Frank Sr. finally asking Doyle when the "purse" had been taken, using code to inquire when the sample from the gloves had been pulled from storage. It had been about a month earlier, Doyle told Frank Sr.

"And it never, the purse never ever came to our unit," Doyle said, telling Calabrese that the gloves had never physically been present at the evidence storage area where he worked under the courthouse, but had been taken from long-term storage and turned over for testing.

"It stayed at the crime lab till the thirteenth of January '99, when somebody named Lorri Lewis withdrew it from the crime lab," Doyle said. "It never come down to our warehouse, where it was supposed to go."

Frank Sr. noted that the date Doyle had gotten from the police computer was about the time that Ricci had been talking to one of their associates, who in turn had been talking to DiForti.

"It stinks, don't it," Frank Sr. said.

The men talked about who spoke to whom and when, and about how Nick—calling him "the Sibling" and "the Sister"—might be holding up while incarcerated. There was a feeling among many they knew that the Sibling might not be able to take "the sickness," meaning prison, Frank Sr. said.

"Fragile," Doyle agreed. "She's fragile."

The men decided they should get a message to James Marcello, who was imprisoned at the time with Nick at the federal facility in Pekin, Illinois. Marcello should be told to keep watch, Frank said, and monitor Nick's attitude. Marcello, the leader of the Melrose Park crew, had been sentenced in 1995 to more than twelve years in prison in a racketeering case that also had snared Sam Carlisi and Anthony Zizzo. Some at the FBI believed Marcello was in fact the day-to-day boss of the whole mob. If DiForti were to cooperate, Nick might too, Frank Sr. reasoned, and Nick could do damage to Frank Sr. and Marcello as well.

DiForti might tell the FBI that Nick was to blame for the Fecarotta murder, and it might not take much from there for Nick to break down and point to Frank Sr. and others.

"If she's gonna start to becoming a prostitute, the other one will, automatic, there wouldn't be a doubt in my mind after what . . . what's taken place," is how Frank Sr. phrased it for his guests.

"Nobody wants to see a prostitute in the family," Ricci answered.

Marcello definitely should be watchful of his prison mate, Frank confirmed. "Somebody has to watch, because if not, that one sister can hurt the whole family," Frank Sr. said. He continued, saying that a message should be given to Marcello's brother, Mickey, who was on the outside. Mickey should go to Pekin to tell James Marcello to start paying attention. The Outfit needed to raise all of its antennae to consider the emerging threat.

"The message should be given to the brother to tell the brother exactly that there is something [that] stinks, that the Sister should be watched," Frank declared. "The Sister should be watched real strong.

"Nobody's concerned about what's really taking place here, and how this thing could mushroom," Frank Sr. told the visiting cops. "First of all, the one sister that, that, that could be the big prostitute is the one that could hurt her whole family . . . you know what I mean by 'her whole family'? All the brothers and all the sisters," he said as he reasoned that the situation was growing increasingly threatening and serious.

"Pick up the Bible sometimes," Frank Sr. told the visiting cops. "Pick it up and read it. And it tells you, 'Brother, don't hurt your brother, 'cause it'll come back to haunt you.'"

There was, Frank Sr. told the men, something in his mind that told him "the Sister," Nick, could snap. Their past hadn't always been rosy, he said.

But unbeknownst to Frank Sr., Marcello already was well aware of the problems between the brothers and already had taken a few steps to try to insulate himself.

Nick and Marcello had grown friendly while incarcerated together at Pekin and spoke often. They had been meeting, and Nick had been airing his complaints about Frank Sr. to Marcello since shortly after arriving there in October 1997 to serve his sentence after pleading guilty in the loan-sharking case. They had spoken regularly about Outfit business and their plans when they were released. Nick complained about how shabbily his brother had treated him, and Marcello had welcomed Nick to join his crew instead of working with Frank Sr. once they were out. Nick said his brother and the organization were doing nothing to help Nick's wife while he was in prison, breaking what amounted to an Outfit tradition.

Marcello had then agreed to provide Nick's family with $4,000 a month, knowing better than to leave Nick, with all of his knowledge of past crimes, feeling neglected and abandoned.

Back at Milan, Frank Sr. remained unaware of just how much Nick had complained, but he knew Marcello should be warned about the new coincidences and how investigators had taken a sudden interest in the Fecarotta murder. Someone should give "the Sister" encouragement, Frank Sr. and his visitors agreed.

But there could be other solutions, too. Maybe Joy needed to see "a psychiatrist" to help with her mental state, Frank Sr. joked.

"Shock treatment," Doyle said.

Right, Frank Sr. answered, "Not only that, but a psychiatrist would be able to determine if she needed shock treatment, or a . . . prodder up her ass."

It was two days later when Frank Jr. went back to his father in the prison, again wearing his recording device hidden in headphones.

Frank Sr. was even more open this time, telling his son about the 1979 murder of his friend, Tony Borsellino. He and Nick had gotten word it was going to happen, and Frank Sr. had been unable to convince his capo, Angelo LaPietra, to help save Tony. The brothers were sitting and talking on Nick's father-in-law's porch in Norridge, a suburb near O'Hare International Airport, around the time they knew Tony was to have been killed.

"Oh, it bothered me; I loved that guy," the elder Calabrese told his son.

The killing had been the idea of Borsellino's rival, he said, William "Butch" Petrocelli of the Wild Bunch. Petrocelli was a "big mouth" who would brownnose bosses to get his way, Frank Sr. said.

He had always hated Petrocelli, who had once used his connections to Outfit leaders to freeze the Chinatown crew out of some betting parlors.

Maseth and Hartnett had talked to Frank Jr. about a few general areas of interest, but he hadn't specifically been coached on how to explore key areas. The operation had begun mostly as a trolling expedition, with agents simply curious about what Frank Sr. might say to his son on tape. They weren't totally aware of the full extent of their target's past—and neither was Frank Jr., for that matter. When the son was successful in getting Frank Sr. to talk about his history in the Outfit, it was a testament to his own ability.

"Frank Jr. knows his father," Maseth explained. "You can't put too many words in a guy's mouth; it would seem unnatural."

The father and son went on that day to discuss which other mobsters had made good money in their careers and which had been smart about trying to cross over into legitimate businesses in attempts to keep free of government attention. Some had gotten involved in car dealerships and some in restaurants. Many in the old guard were either dead or in prison, so the mob's leadership on the street had shrunk lately to a few key people, Frank Sr. said.

In fact, if someone wanted to, he could take over everything with just a handful of good men, the elder Calabrese pointed out.

"You have to nail about six, seven guys," Frank Sr. said matter-of-factly.

"That's all?" his son answered.

"So you can clean house," Frank Sr. said. "That's all; them are the ones with the brains and the balls."

Among the other mobsters Frank Sr. told his son he had known were the Spilotro brothers, Anthony and Michael. Frank Sr. said he had taken a liking to Michael and had told his brother he would have brought Michael into his organization if Michael hadn't been spoken for. Michael was a good kid, the elder Calabrese said, but Anthony had ruined him.

"Tony, he had [Michael] believing that he was the boss, which is something Butch would do," Frank Sr. said of the Wild Bunch gangster he had called a big mouth. "Butchie had a big party at the

Ambassador [Hotel], a Christmas party . . . and he's telling people up there that he is going to be the new boss."

Such boasting was one of the things that had doomed Anthony Spilotro, Frank Sr. told his son as the FBI's recording continued to roll.

Boss Joey "Doves" Aiuppa and capos Joey "the Clown" Lombardo and Angelo LaPietra were going to jail in 1986, after being convicted in a colossal skim at the Stardust Casino in Las Vegas. Before Aiuppa went in, he had ordered Anthony Spilotro "knocked down," Frank Sr. said. "I don't care how you do it—get him," he recalled Aiuppa saying. "I want him out."

So the Spilotros had been lured to a house where about fifteen men were waiting for them, including "you know who," Frank Sr. said of his brother Nick. "They thought they were being made when they walked in."

Suddenly the full promise of the investigation came more sharply into focus for FBI agents and federal prosecutors. The Spilotro murders were unsolved and ranked as the most high-profile mob slayings in Chicago and one of the most infamous gangland killings in the nation's history. The murders were the stuff of mob myth, with many in the public believing the men had been buried alive. The 1995 film *Casino* had portrayed the men's deaths, showing them being beaten with baseball bats in a cornfield. Being able to charge someone with those murders would be a very big score, indeed, for the FBI.

A few minutes later Frank Jr. continued to try to lure his father down the right path. There was more mob business to discuss, more about his uncle Nick.

"Fecarotta was his friend, too, wasn't he?" Frank Jr. asked, keeping things going, asking what his uncle had been capable of and what kinds of things his uncle had had difficulty with.

Well, there was one killing, Frank Sr. said, when he and Nick and DiForti had been plotting a bombing, and a blasting cap had gone off in their car. The men had rigged up a bomb to detonate by remote control, with a blasting cap wired to a receiver. It wasn't yet wired up to the bomb when their car had inadvertently driven past something that was transmitting the same signal as the remote they had planned to use, which was a new device at the time and was used to start a car from a distance. That set off the blasting cap as Frank Sr.'s hand was on it. Luckily for those in the car it was only the blasting cap.

"We'd have been in little pieces," Frank Sr. told his son. "But it's not in—my hand is there and I'm holding it in my hand, but there's a bag there, a canvas bag," he said. "It blew my fuckin' door off, blew the bag up, you know there was blood squirting out all over."

Nick had panicked, Frank Sr. remembered, and he told his son he had had to slap his brother to get him to calm down and get the car moving again. "And he's going, 'I'm sorry,' and I says, "No, 'I'm sorry I had to do that, but you were panicking,'" Frank Sr. said of the smack.

He had been the one to bring Nick into the family business in the first place, Frank Sr. reminded his son, meeting Nick for fish at a place called Slicker Sam's late in 1969. His juice loan business was going well, Frank Sr. said. Nick was still working as a Teamster but had asked to get involved. No one had pushed him.

"'Well, Nick,' I says, 'but this is not all peaches and cream,'" Frank Sr. remembered saying, after telling his brother, who had shown up in a leisure suit, that he could work with him.

Time went on, Frank Sr. said, and Nick was asked whether he was willing to do anything besides the numbers and some collections for their mob crew. "Yeah," Frank Sr. said his brother had answered. "He says I'll do whatever I have to do."

When the father and son met again less than a month later, Frank Sr. still had his brother Nick on his mind. Twan and Ricci would be coming to see him again soon and would hopefully have more information about the gloves and what investigators might be looking for. Frank Sr. still was trying to convince himself that Nick couldn't have left the gloves behind after killing Fecarotta.

Nick eventually had shot Fecarotta in the head, but on the first shot he had fired across his body into his victim's side, he told Frank Jr., with his son again recording the conversation. As he had thought more about it, Frank Sr. said, he thought he remembered that the glove on Nick's left hand had to be cut off because of the gunshot wound to his arm.

"I'm 99 percent sure," Frank Sr. told his son.

Nick had stuffed his jacket into a garbage can, he remembered.

"Maybe that's where he threw the gloves," Frank Jr. said to his father.

"I'm not a hundred percent sure on that," Frank Sr. answered. "I know the gloves were gone."

So the men walked themselves through the shooting yet again, with Frank Jr. leading his father through what he thought he knew. Frank Sr. showed his son how Nick had fought with Fecarotta and how and where he had been shot.

"Do you think, any chance he mighta taken one of the gloves off on the car anywhere and touched the car?" Frank Jr. asked.

"No," the father answered. "Because there's too much excitement going on."

He had been nearby, Frank Sr. admitted, "riding around like a fucking donkey" looking for his brother after the shooting was to have gone down.

Again calling Nick "she," he said his brother had never called to say he was in position. Mistakes were made, and now, probably because of DiForti talking, Frank Sr. said, they just might wind up getting caught for it.

Frank Jr. continued to pull his father along, telling him he was somewhat worried about the plan to have James Marcello watch Nick at the prison in Pekin. Once someone is told to watch someone in case they are acting funny, the mind wanders and suspicions grow on their own, he said.

But his father was having none of it.

"Frank. Remember one thing," the unmoved Frank Sr. answered. "When you make your bed, you better sleep in it."

Nick had been doing a lot of talking out of turn, Frank Sr. said, speaking of what he knew of Nick's increasing complaints. The father reminded his son that in an earlier conversation, Frank Jr. had told him Nick believed Frank Sr. was responsible for killing a woman in a hit. Frank Sr. had come to believe that Nick was doing his best to turn his boys against him.

"When I had nothing in my hand and he says that I even did the wife," Frank Sr. said angrily.

Well, the son asked, what if Nick did decide to become a turncoat? What if he wanted to go ahead and also tell authorities that Frank Sr. had killed that woman? If he were cornered on the Fecarotta murder, maybe he would try to give the feds something in return.

"I don't think he's that smart," Frank Sr. answered, adding that Nick could lean on Marcello if things got tough in prison. "I don't think he's that smart to do that."

It had been in 1970, almost thirty years earlier, Frank Sr. began to remember, when the brothers had done their first murder together. That was a spot that Nick might be able to take the FBI to if he ever decided to turn.

There was a construction site in the Bridgeport area near Chinatown. They had placed a body in a hole there, and it had remained undiscovered. Eventually, the building that had been built was replaced, and the area was turned into a parking lot for the White Sox ballpark, but Frank Sr. had checked afterward to see if the grave had been disturbed. The bones must have been dug up in the project, he told his son, because he had remembered exactly where it was by recalling a spot on a brick wall.

"And it was faded in color in the brick here, and right there was the spot on the other side," he said. "Now, now that brick was all taken down, lower."

OK, Frank Jr. said, but Nick also claimed to know about the killing with the woman, "the Dauber one."

"Don't even mention that name," his father quickly answered.

William Dauber was a mob hit man who had decided to become a federal informant, and he was targeted to be killed by Outfit bosses. After the Wild Bunch had been unsuccessful in trying to take him out, the Chinatown crew had been pressed into service, too. When Dauber and his wife, Charlotte, left a court date in Will County on July 2, 1980, their car was chased down by a mob work car and a van.

The van had pulled alongside their car at high speed, its door had opened, and men had fired. The Daubers' car wound up off the road, with the murder squad finishing off the couple at close range. It was another high-profile murder that had never been solved. Nick hadn't been there, Frank Sr. agreed, but had gone ahead and told the story to others and "made it sound like I purposefully went after [Dauber's] wife."

"I mean, Frank, I wasn't even in that vehicle," Frank Sr. repeated as his son's hidden recorder picked up the admission. "I was in the lookout vehicle."

Federal prosecutors and the FBI could know that Nick was weak, Frank Sr. went on to say, and might make a strong attempt at turning him. If Nick panicked, his life could be in danger from a vengeful Outfit, the father said.

"I don't wanna see nothing happen to him, but I'm gonna tell ya something," he said. "If somebody feels that it's . . . it's either them or him, he's gone. That's the bed he made."

If Nick did turn, Frank Sr. said, he had alibi witnesses lined up to say he was with them the evening Fecarotta was killed, and also that he wasn't at the Dauber killing. Anyway, there were still reasons to be optimistic, he said. It was already a month after the gloves supposedly had been removed from evidence, and there hadn't been any information circulating about a DNA match. That probably meant authorities had come up with nothing, Frank Sr. speculated, and that the gloves had been Fecarotta's after all.

Frank Jr. reminded his father that he would be out of prison before long, and he wondered whether someone might come after him if it was learned on the street that his uncle Nick actually was cooperating, as they were starting to fear. If someone wanted to do away with Nick, wouldn't they come after him, too? Wouldn't the mob take them all, worrying that the younger Calabreses would seek revenge if something happened to Nick?

"No . . . in fact, if something did, I will send my blessing," Frank Sr. said ominously.

For much of that spring, the father and son continued to talk, but hearing no more hints of trouble, Frank Sr. had decided not to stir the pot by issuing a full alarm to Outfit bosses on the outside. It might be too early to open Pandora's box when the only thing certain for Frank Sr. was that nothing was certain.

Even if DiForti were cooperating, Frank Sr. reasoned, DiForti couldn't say who was at the Fecarotta murder because he wasn't there himself. There would be plenty of room to just deny any involvement. The FBI would need more, the father told the son, and it would be hard for them to get it.

There were murders that DiForti and Frank Sr. had done together, though, Frank Jr. reminded his father on April 10, 1999, sowing more seeds of worry and leading him perfectly into yet another part of his past. There was one with an innocent victim, Frank Jr. recalled, one his father had mentioned before. The innocent man was Polish, and the murder was in Cicero—the town that had once been Al Capone's headquarters—with his father at the wheel of the work car. Maybe DiForti would mention that one to the FBI, the father and son thought, but maybe he wouldn't. He wasn't free of blame, because he had been a triggerman in that hit along with Nick.

"I was the one talkin' to them," Frank Sr. said, laughing at the memory of yelling at DiForti and his brother to jump out of their car and open fire. "All right guys, here's what you gotta do here. OK, now, out. Out. Out. Get out."

The hit squad had known that the passenger in the car was innocent and was simply in the way. It was the July 1983 killing of Richard Ortiz and Arthur Morawski, two men who were gunned down as they sat in a car in Cicero outside Ortiz's bar. Ortiz, who once had been under the thumb of John "Johnny Apes" Monteleone, had begun handing out juice loans on his own. The pair had been at the horse track that day, and Morawski just happened to be with his friend as the killers moved in on them.

Some who knew the men had even been sitting across the street at the time of the hit, Frank Sr. remembered.

"They couldn't even describe the car," Frank Sr. told his son. "Because you see how confusing things are when people get scared?"

The elder Calabrese described in detail how he pulled up at an angle behind Ortiz's parked car, blocking him in on busy Cermak Road. There was no car next to the work car, so the killing team could make a fast getaway. Frank had ordered his brother and DiForti out, both armed with shotguns, and each had walked up on a side of Ortiz's car, aiming through it toward Ortiz in the driver's seat.

"But what happened was, this one," Frank Sr. said, motioning with his hand, "which was Joy, from this window wound up hittin' the other one, too."

The men had used double-aught buckshot shells, the father remembered, almost fondly.

"Big, big bearings," Frank Sr. said. "So them, them will fuckin' tear half your body apart."

"And you want me to tell you something?" he continued. "The Polish guy that was with 'em was a nice guy. OK? But he happened to be at the wrong place."

By June 1999, Frank Sr. was giving thought to his son's release, which was only a few months away. Frank Jr. promised his father he would come back to visit.

The elder Calabrese said he had no doubt about that, because he felt like he had grown closer to his son while they were in prison together. Some of the past friction finally seemed to have eased. All of the long talks had improved their relationship, Frank Sr. said. And once they were all out together, they would be a family again.

What was left unresolved was Nick.

It wasn't a certainty whether he was holding up under pressure that the Outfit wasn't fully aware of or whether his "weakness" was causing him to go the other way. Frank Sr. was still trying to decide how to approach the problem and how to get Nick a message telling him to hold tight and keep his problems to himself.

Maybe he would send Doyle and Ricci, his cop pals, he told his son.

"I wish he gets outta this fucking stupor he's in," Frank Sr. said of his brother. "The hatred. OK? He's trying to blame everybody for what he did himself. Listen. If we wanna stand there and blame, we can all look in the mirror. We're all guilty, aren't we?"

"We gotta put somebody in a hole"

"Come on, take a ride with me," Frank Sr. said to Nick. "We gotta put somebody in a hole."

It was July 1970. Nick had decided to join his brother in the juice loan business, a decision that had been blessed by Angelo LaPietra of the mob's Chinatown crew. Nick thought his brother must be kidding about the hole, but went along anyway without so much as even asking to know who Frank Sr. might have been talking about.

Around the South Side of Chicago they drove, looking for a suitable spot for the supposed victim. Up and down streets of the city's grid, watching out the windows for lots where new buildings might be going up. His brother couldn't be serious about burying a body, Nick continued to tell himself.

Maybe it was just some kind of test of his loyalty.

Soon they came to a multitenant building that was under construction. Maybe that would work. So the brothers walked to the edge of the site, peering down to where the basement of the three- or six-flat would be going in. It might have been a good place a few weeks earlier, but by the time the Calabrese brothers were there, workers already had prepared the lower area for a cement pour. Frank knew that wouldn't do. A disturbance of the ground there would be noticed for sure. So the brothers temporarily gave up. Finding the right site would have to wait, giving the unsuspecting target a little more time above ground.

It would be a few weeks before they would come across an ideal location. It was in the Bridgeport neighborhood—home base for the

Outfit crew. Almost in the shadow of Comiskey Park there was a factory going up.

Late on a Friday afternoon it was deserted for the weekend, with its foundation walls standing to provide a screen from the street. Look up and you saw only the sky, with the building's roof yet to be put in place. Look down and it was only dirt, with the floor yet to be fully leveled and covered over in concrete. This was right, Frank Sr. decided, so the pair left, heading off to get a shovel and some lye.

Still Nick didn't really believe they would be going through with leaving someone there. It must be his brother wanting to see if he had a backbone and gauge how he would react under pressure. He was fairly new to the Chinatown crew. Did he have the nerve for this kind of thing? Or would Nick try to talk his brother out of it before they had even begun?

As they returned, Nick went along with it, even going so far as to take turns digging with his brother. One would push the shovel into the packed gray clay over and over until he tired, then passing the tool off to the other. Sitting nearby was the lye, waiting for a later moment.

More than four feet down the brothers dug, finishing the job by pulling a piece of plywood over the hole to hide it from anyone who might happen by and then making their way out of the partly finished building.

Sending out subpoenas that year was the Illinois Crime Investigating Commission, collecting data on juice racketeers and mob figures for a public report. It had worried Frank Sr. so much when he got his that he had decided he needed to duck out of town for a time, taking a trip to Arizona to lay low. Others had gotten them, too, including one of Frank Sr.'s collection agents, a man who had made the mistake of saying out loud that if he ever went to jail, he wouldn't be going alone.

The next night one of Frank Sr.'s most trusted crew members, Ronnie Jarrett, would attempt to pick up the mouthy collector in a car he'd stolen. He would drive him to meet the Calabrese brothers if the plan developed right, telling him he needed to take him for a talk. Jarrett had stolen a Chevy for the task, taking the step of yanking out the dome light so they would stay hidden in the dark if they opened a door.

Frank Sr. would sit in the backseat behind Jarrett, and Nick would get in behind the passenger, who would be next to Jarrett in the front, the plan went. Things would seem normal to the victim, even as the brothers put their hands down between their feet in front of them and silently slipped on their gloves.

It was starting to seem as if maybe there would be a killing after all, though it wouldn't be that Saturday night. The collector couldn't make it to see Jarrett, but that was fine. Frank Sr. had waited most of the summer to erase this threat. He could wait another twenty-four hours.

On Sunday, Jarrett did pick up Frank Sr.'s quarry and brought him to where the Calabreses were waiting to meet up with them. Frank Sr. sat down in the backseat behind Jarrett, and Nick slipped in behind a man whose name he still didn't know. Just a few blocks away was the unfinished building.

It took almost no time to get there, with Frank Sr. chatting with his collector to keep him from suspecting that this was his very last ride.

They drove to the construction site, never letting on that their trap was in place. Nick had only one job. When Jarrett put the car in park and turned the ignition off, he was to reach forward and grab the man's right arm, the one closest to the door, pulling it backward and holding it there. Now the victim was sitting right in front of him, and he just might have to do it, with his brother making small talk in the dark.

As Jarrett parked and turned the car off, it happened. The three men jolted toward the man in the passenger seat, and he was caught by surprise. Nick grabbed his right arm and kept it in place as best he could as Jarrett pulled the victim's left arm away from him and across the front seat, leaving him squirming and defenseless. Then, lurching forward from the shadow of the backseat were Frank and a rope, which the angry loan shark quickly looped over the man's head, pulling it back across his neck as hard as he could and cutting off his air.

The three men pulled as their victim fought. It may have seemed like forever to Nick, but the man gave out, leaving Jarrett and the

Calabreses to dispose of him. Michael "Hambone" Albergo wouldn't be going to jail or taking anyone with him, as it turned out, and he wouldn't be answering any subpoenas either. In a few moments he was pulled from the car and laid on the pile of dirt that the brothers had left as they dug two days before.

Take off his pants, Frank Sr. told his brother, and throw them at the other end of the building.

Nick, out of sorts, did as he was told, carrying the pants as he walked to a much larger pile of dirt at the other end of the site. He tossed them up on the mound and returned to his brother and Jarrett—and the body of the man he had just helped them to strangle.

"What did you do with them?" Frank Sr. asked.

The answer about the pants wasn't good enough, and his brother sent Nick back for them with a command to take them farther away and throw them up on a set of raised rail tracks nearby. As before, Nick did what his brother said to do, retrieving the pants from the dirt hill, walking farther, and tossing them up and out of sight.

Then he returned again to the corpse, this time to find that Jarrett had left with the car. But his brother was still there. He stood in the night with a knife. Albergo was still lifeless, but Frank Sr. leaned down and sliced through his victim's neck just to make sure there would be no unfortunate miracles. With his throat opened up, Albergo was dropped into his waiting grave, with the lye falling on him a moment later to speed his decomposition. In too went the bag that had contained the lye, and the brothers hastily filled the dirt in on top of their victim.

Nick was terrified. There in the darkness as they quickly buried Albergo, Nick had lost control of his bladder. But his brother said nothing. It was hard to see, and Nick's pants already were filthy from the dirt and the shoveling.

Here Albergo would stay, waiting for a layer of concrete to seal him in the makeshift tomb.

The deed done, the brothers walked to a nearby gas station for Jarrett to come back around to pick them up and take them to his mother-in-law's garage. It wasn't far away, just a quick ride through the Bridgeport neighborhood from Thirty-Third Street to 2820 South

Lowe Avenue, a house about eight blocks from that of Chicago mayor Richard J. Daley, through the low-rise ethnic neighborhood shared by Italian and Irish immigrant families.

The three would change their clothes in the garage before going their separate ways for the night.

It was some time later that Nick would pick up the Crime Commission's *Juice Racketeers: Report on Criminal Usury in the Chicago Area*. A curious Frank Sr. had gotten hold of one of the booklets with the bright orange cover. Nick was flipping through it when he suddenly came face-to-face with Albergo, the look of the victim burned in his memory. For the first time he learned Albergo's name. He was a balding man with arched eyebrows, staring back at him from page twenty-seven—the man in the hole.

As they would come to do whenever there had been a killing, the brothers would nickname Albergo's murder in case they ever needed to talk about it in front of others. When they needed to refer to the collector and what had happened, when they had to talk about the digging and the rope and the lye, they would simply call him "It."

3

WITNESS OF A LIFETIME

Nick's routine in the federal prison in Pekin, Illinois, was broken one morning in 1999 by directions from a unit officer.

"They want you at medical," the officer had said, puzzling Nick.

It was an unusual request at 9:30 in the morning, especially since Nick hadn't complained to anyone about his health. Why would they want him there?

He arrived to find several of his fellow inmates waiting to see a doctor, but a nurse soon stepped into the waiting area and immediately told everyone to leave. Everyone but Calabrese, the nurse said, letting Nick know for sure that something was up. And sure enough, in a few minutes he was summoned in, only to find not the doctor but two FBI agents waiting to see him. It was Michael Hartnett and Tom Bourgeois, whom Nick knew from his 1995 case. They had a warrant, and Hartnett was soon leaning toward him with what looked like a giant Q-tip swab, wiping the inside of his mouth for a DNA sample. The worst fears of the Outfit and his brother were now materializing.

And the agents weren't finished. They had a warrant for photo evidence, too, and directed a technician to X-ray both of Nick's forearms.

The image of his left one would provide a telltale clue: splinters of bone left over from an old injury. It was evidence that corroborated what the FBI already was piecing together on the Fecarotta murder.

Not long after the DNA collection, Hartnett returned to the prison, along with Chicago police detective Robert Moon, who was on loan to the FBI to work organized crime cases. The pair told Nick it might be time for him to consider cooperating. But he wasn't ready.

For one thing, Nick wasn't particularly fond of either man. Hartnett was the one who had swabbed him, effectively ending Nick's life in the mobster's mind, and the agent had been with Bourgeois when he'd done it. Nick knew Bourgeois as the supervisor on the racketeering case that had put him in prison in the first place. Nick had a grudge against Moon, too: he had once arrested him in a gun case.

Nick was quiet and introverted but still had a strong personality. It wasn't enough that he was cornered; he was the kind of guy who would let himself go down just because he didn't really get along with the people who were coming to meet with him. He actually would cut off his nose to spite his face, as they say.

Nick had told the agents that he would not be helping them for any reason until after his daughter graduated from high school in June 1999, wanting to spare her any embarrassment. And even after his daughter did graduate, he told the investigators that he had a lawyer, effectively ending negotiations with them.

That left the FBI to tell Nick's attorney in January 2000 that the DNA testing had been a match. The DNA sample taken from Nick's mouth had inextricably linked him to the Fecarotta crime scene, matching a sample taken from blood on the pair of gloves left on the sidewalk the night the hit man had been killed. He would not be getting out of prison as expected in 2002.

When Jimmy "Poker" DiForti died in 2000 of natural causes, Frank Sr. had breathed a sigh of relief. The death of a man he suspected was an informant for the FBI was proof that God was in control of his situation, he told his son.

Frank Sr. didn't spend as much time worrying about Nick, either, hearing less about his brother and simply going about his business. He spent some of his time writing coded letters directing associates from inside the federal correctional facility at Milan. The elder Calabrese would pass messages out, telling Frank Jr. and others how money from juice loans should be collected and where it should be placed.

But in reality Frank Sr. should have been more worried about his brother than ever.

Near the end of 2001, the FBI prepared a proffer letter for Nick's new attorney, John Theis. If Nick would tell the agents what he knew, they wouldn't use his statements against him in court. Nick was getting the message: You are through, and your only hope is to cooperate. He would die in prison unless he decided to turn against his brother and the Chicago Outfit.

Nick, who had been moved to a federal prison in Ashland, Kentucky, agreed to a preliminary meeting held at the FBI's office in the town on January 15, 2002.

Maseth, Hartnett, and Bourgeois were there, along with Mitch Mars, chief of the Organized Crime Division of the U.S. Attorney's Office in Chicago. Mars was widely regarded as one of the sharpest minds in his office, a prosecutor hardened by years of making cases against Chicago wiseguys.

The men waited for a time as Nick spoke with Theis in another room, until finally Nick chose to meet with them.

"Initially it was touch and go," Maseth said. "Nick had spent much of his life not wanting to sit in a room with a bunch of FBI agents. He's been trained to keep his mouth shut."

Nick still wasn't a fan of Bourgeois and wasn't fully connecting with the all-business Hartnett either. But he had made up his mind and started telling the agents what he knew.

"He started by saying Fecarotta is basically where it ends," Maseth recalled. "He said, 'Let me tell you about the stuff I did to get to Fecarotta.'"

There was surprise at the table, Maseth remembered, as the soft-spoken man sitting with them began to describe murder after murder. They were sitting with an unassuming Outfit soldier who had been tapped to carry out the mob's judgment time and time again.

For the FBI and prosecutors, their efforts were converging perfectly. It was a combination of good police work and sheer luck, but Operation Family Secrets was well on its way to becoming the most significant case against the Chicago mob in decades, with the help of a man who was promising to be the witness of a lifetime. Nick, a made member of the mob, was lifting the shadow on the Chicago mob in a way that no one had before him.

Later in 2002 there would be a changeover in the personnel dealing with Nick. Hartnett was the supervising agent over Frank Jr., and a logistical decision was made to bring someone else on to talk with Nick. Maseth and Hartnett spoke and thought that Mallul, who would eventually take over as supervisor for the retiring Bourgeois, would be a good fit to permanently join Maseth on the visits. Mallul was closer in age to Nick, who was by then fifty-nine, and had spent two decades investigating organized crime in Chicago. He was a steely veteran agent who could easily talk to Nick about things that had happened in the 1980s.

In fact, one of Mallul's first assignments in the FBI after leaving a life as a public defender in Michigan was investigating a tip on the then-missing Spilotro brothers. He was sent to a local junkyard after information surfaced that the bodies of the pair might be hidden there.

The new team worked exceptionally well with Nick, who became less short with the agents when they pressed him, and he was heavily debriefed well into spring 2003, providing details on a long list of Outfit killings.

Nick was afraid of getting the death penalty for killing Fecarotta and the others. But even so, "51 percent" of his decision to cooperate was resentment toward his brother, Mallul said. Frank Sr. had paid Nick little during his time working the books and making collections on juice loans. He had pushed him around and mocked him. In later years Frank Sr. had accused him of trying to steal the affection of his two sons, Frank Jr. and Kurt.

"He called him stupid; he shortchanged him financially," Mallul said. "Frank Sr. gave Nick garbage to do, and Nick never doubted for a moment that his brother would have killed him if he had to."

In one murder in particular, the killings of Richard Ortiz the bar owner and his friend Arthur Morawski in Cicero, Frank Sr. had aimed a carbine rifle at DiForti and Nick after ordering them out of the car. If Nick hadn't fired his shotgun at the victims, he told the FBI, he knew his brother would have shot him and left him right there in the street.

"If Frank Sr. had been a good brother to him, I have no doubt at all that Nick would have continued to tell us to screw off," Mallul said. "He would have done life in prison. I really believe that."

By early 2003 the FBI was also involved in a separate investigation of James Marcello, the rising mob leader and Nick's former prison mate, and his brother Michael, known as "Mickey." James Marcello had been sentenced to prison for racketeering and had been Sam Carlisi's driver and top lieutenant. The latest investigation of him centered on a business the Marcellos ran that placed video poker machines in bars and restaurants around some of Chicago's scruffy inner suburbs.

The machines were supposedly only for amusement, since such gambling was illegal in Illinois. But regular customers who were known to the owners of the tavern could actually build up credits and collect winnings. If the bartender didn't know you, then sorry— the machines were only for fun. But paying out or not, they were well used, and the business was earning the Marcellos a very hefty payday. Between 1996 and 2003 alone, authorities estimated the company had underreported its income by more than $4 million. So, the $4,000 a month that James Marcello was giving Nick and his family to keep Nick quiet and happy was pocket change.

As its investigation moved ahead, the FBI was monitoring Michael Marcello's telephone on the outside and was making recordings inside prison of James, who eventually had been moved to the prison at Milan. The same equipment that had recorded Frank Sr. was used again, this time to capture conversations involving the Marcello brothers.

In December 2002 the FBI and IRS moved to serve subpoenas at some of the businesses where M&M Amusement, the company owned by the Marcellos, had its video poker machines running. Federal agents paid visits to three Cicero spots and a pizzeria in Berwyn, a pair of towns just west of Chicago.

The FBI was making recordings as M&M employee Thomas Johnson called Michael Marcello with an update.

"Um, so far it looks like just records," Johnson said of the subpoenas.

"Is that what they asked for?" Michael asked in a worried tone.

"Yeah," Johnson answered. "Paperwork, I got paperwork."

A month later, on January 9, 2003, Mickey was at Milan to visit his brother. The feds had started to subpoena licensing records from the village halls of the towns where the brothers had the machines. The men could be seen on video, seated next to each other and leaning against a back wall in the visiting room. They faced the same direction, surrounded by others who were oblivious to their conversations. James was short and balding but had a piercing gaze.

James asked Mickey how things were looking for him and whether anyone would tell agents that Mickey knew about the illegal collections being made on the equipment.

"I still own the joint," Michael said. "You know."

The men talked for a while about what things were like on the street, with James clearly frustrated about his situation. They spoke in heavy code about how things had come apart. At times they whispered or talked with their hands covering their mouths, and at times they gestured to each other in an attempt to thwart anyone who might be trying to listen to them.

"Everybody that got protected is still out there," an irritated James said. "Everybody that shouldn't have been wound up in here. . . . Is it a joke? I hope they don't think it's a joke when I come home, pal."

Later on in the conversation, the men turned for the first time to Nick, and wondered whether he could be turned under federal heat. James was continuing to pay Nick's family, and knowing Nick's disillusionment, was eager for updates about him. Nick was supposed to have been released already, so the Marcellos had been trying to keep tabs on him through one of Nick's friends, Frank Giudice, a man the brothers referred to in code as "the Drywall Guy" because of his vocation.

"So you ain't heard nothing, nothing else from the Drywall Guy, huh?" James asked his brother.

Mickey shook his head as James asked again.

"He said he can't believe it," Michael said of Giudice. "He says 'the last time I was there, [Nick] told me "well I'm glad you come one more time before I come home."'"

Nick's wife had been calling him, too, Michael said, right up to the time he was supposed to be getting out.

"Then all of a sudden, nothing."

Nick was supposed to have gotten out in November 2002 but had never made it home. Instead of going back to Chicago to be with his wife, he had simply disappeared. It had never been confirmed for the Marcellos and the rest of the Outfit, but Nick actually had been in witness protection since the summer, since he had started cooperating in earnest with the FBI.

Before they ended the visit, Michael promised he would call Giudice again. But James said there was no reason yet to panic. In fact, don't call, he said; just leave him alone. No news was still good news.

Unless Giudice called for a meeting, James said, nothing was to be done.

Then, on January 30 came the first serious indication for the FBI that the brothers had started to figure out that Nick actually was cooperating. In another prison talk, Michael began talking to James about "Tipper, you know, that brother."

Someone had been sent in to look at something, Michael said vaguely. He was doing his best to hide what the men were discussing but could be heard telling his brother: "All your names are on that shit."

Well, James wanted to know, what does the Drywall Guy say?

Not much, Michael answered. Giudice still claimed to know nothing, and Nick's wife was telling friends that she was in the dark, too, Michael said.

"She hasn't talked to him since, uh, October," Michael said. "He's out in the cold."

As the men continued to speak, it would become clearer that the Marcellos knew what the FBI was investigating. Someone was sneaking them some very sensitive and specific information.

"The big thing with them is the Zhivago deal," Michael told his brother.

Agents later pieced together what the code name meant. During another visit, when the brothers discussed an article that had been in the *Chicago Tribune* the day before, Michael mentioned that the story discussed "Zhivago and his brother." There was no mention of any brothers in the story the men discussed but Anthony and Michael Spilotro.

The brothers had a source who knew for certain that Nick was cooperating. And James was surprised to hear that the person they were using for information had said Nick mentioned Zhivago, or Spilotro. He thought the investigation was aimed elsewhere, at Frank Calabrese Sr. or Joey "the Clown" Lombardo. Neither of those men had taken part in the Spilotro murders.

Not every detail of what Nick was saying to authorities was known, Michael told his brother, "but, I'm telling you, you're in there."

"You know, how far, whatever. I don't know," he continued. "The guy can only do what he can do."

Federal authorities would later allege that "the guy" was a U.S. marshal assigned to Nick's security detail. Nick had been named in a sealed indictment in October 2002 and had been brought to Chicago that month to be arraigned in the growing conspiracy case ahead of the date when he was supposed to have been released from prison. While in the city, he had stayed in a secure facility of the marshals' witness security program, or WITSEC, and in a filing cabinet where he was housed were documents detailing his background, names of men he had discussed with the FBI, and summaries of the murders he had mentioned. One marshal in particular had been a part of the night watch at the building.

"Mm hmm," James Marcello said. "I mean that's all he saw was names?"

"The guy had the notes," Michael answered, holding his hands out as if he were writing something. "Everything he was writing down."

The source was going in to look at what he could every chance he had, Michael was telling his worried brother.

Well, Nick could say what he wanted, the two decided, but it seemed that the FBI would need to corroborate his accounts. They wondered to each other whether Frank Calabrese Sr. might even be another target for the feds to try to turn. If he were to cooperate, maybe then the FBI would have a case against the Outfit.

Still, Michael said, Nick had apparently been talking, and talking a lot.

"He admitted to being involved in nineteen of them things," he said, meaning murders, though he did not have the number exactly right.

"And he named them, one by one by one, I guess," he said.

By then, Mallul, Maseth, and the FBI had been meeting monthly with Nick and had been debriefing him "in gross detail," as Mallul would later say. Nick had finally come around and been mostly honest with agents, providing details on sixteen murders, including fourteen he had committed, and offering information that he had heard about another twenty-two killings, including the murder of former Outfit boss Sam Giancana in suburban Oak Park. For the FBI it was a bonanza. It was a detailed account of Outfit activities in Chicago over the prior quarter of a century and beyond.

Agents had kept Nick in the dark about what they were trying to investigate, allowing him to bring pure information to them without any taint. They avoided asking him leading questions and contaminating his account. To throw specific names and crimes at him might have steered his statements, so they let Nick take the lead.

"We did that on purpose," Mallul said later. "This is what made it so good. We never went to him and said, 'We can't corroborate something; can you think of another way?' And we knew he was being truthful. We talked to him over and over again, and it would have been impossible for him to have manufactured it and lied about it and kept every little detail and variable straight."

For example, in one murder, Nick told the agents that a car used to dispose of a man's body was stolen the same day at a local mall. Agents went back and checked police records, and verified that the car the man's body was found in had in fact been stolen from a Chicago shopping center.

The first public indication that Nick Calabrese was talking in heavy detail to the FBI came on February 21, 2003. *Chicago Tribune* columnist John Kass penned a column stating that Calabrese had vanished instead of being released from prison the prior fall. He was apparently in witness protection, Kass wrote, telling readers that sources had told him that Nick was cooperating. It was a major coup to say the least, the columnist told readers.

"Investigators are being given a road map through crime and time," Kass wrote, "including unsolved Outfit murders going back over decades.

"This must aggravate some folks, including imprisoned Chicago street boss Jimmy Marcello, convicted of bookmaking and loan sharking," he continued. "Marcello hopes to be released from a twelve-year federal prison term in a few months."

The column went on to name the murder of the Spilotros specifically, as well as those of Fecarotta and the Daubers. And the murder in 1974 of federal witness Daniel Seifert was in the column, too, a brazen killing in front of his wife and young son in which Lombardo had long been a suspect.

If someone was interested in using the column to rattle Marcello's cage and fire a shot across the mob's bow, the message was received. When a friend came for a visit at Milan a few days after the Kass column appeared, James Marcello was again asking what was going on that he needed to know about.

"Just what I read in the newspaper and what I hear from . . . anybody," said the friend, Nicholas Vangel.

"Uh-huh," James answered.

The FBI quickly went on the move, swabbing mobsters across Chicago for DNA samples, and before long it was James's turn.

One evening in early March, he was in the prison library when he was approached and asked his name. He was told to follow and found himself headed to the medical offices.

"I thought it was gonna be a piss test," he told his brother Michael in a recorded conversation the next day.

"I went in; there were two guys that were here that come from Pekin that time for Slim," James said, using a nickname for Nick and speaking of the time Nick's DNA had been collected.

After five minutes and six swabs, his visit to medical was over. He deliberately made no attempt to get cocky with the agents, he told his brother. He just took the subpoena they handed him and put it in the mail to his attorney.

Who on the outside had gotten a similar visit? James wanted to know.

"Just, uh, Pagliacci," Mickey answered, using the Italian word for "clowns," which the Marcellos used as code for Lombardo.

"Flapjack" had gotten swabbed too, Mickey added, using a nickname for a mobster who owned a pancake house on North Avenue, as had "Hitler," a nickname for feared hit man Frank "the German" Schweihs, who long had been known as Lombardo's muscle.

Also getting a visit was "this guy," Michael said as he touched his nose. It was code for John "No nose" DiFronzo.

But all the activity didn't worry James, at least not outwardly. It was almost as if the FBI seemed desperate, he thought, as though they didn't have enough for a case. Even though the brothers had an inside source, it seemed to them like the feds were just crawling along, swinging wildly.

Fair enough, but some of the targets might not wait around to find out what the results could be, Michael answered, including "Pagliacci."

"Skip, hop, he's gone," Mickey said of Lombardo.

"Well, could you blame him?" James answered. "I wish the fuck I had the opportunity."

The other guy, James added, touching his nose again, DiFronzo, ought to go ahead and do the same thing.

"Now, what are you waiting for?" James said of DiFronzo. "You think this is a high school prom or something?"

Nearer to the end of March, the brothers would meet again in the visiting room at Milan, and they would begin to say too much about their source, a man they had begun referring to as "the Babysitter" in their coded talks. It was a reference to the source's job watching over Nick while he was in Chicago.

Michael Marcello unwittingly began filling in gaps for the FBI during another taped conversation on March 24, telling his brother that the middle man for the information had been in Marion Prison Camp in Illinois with "this guy," again waving a hand toward his nose. Mickey mentioned "the Marquette 10," a famous Chicago police scandal from the 1980s that involved officers taking bribes from drug dealers, and he told his brother that the source's father was a part of the case.

"This kid's father was with them," he said of the rogue cops, providing what turned out to be the key that agents would need to solve the puzzle of the alleged leaker.

"On that beef and everything," Marcello said of the source's father. "He went down with them. He died, though."

It wasn't much, but FBI agents reverse-engineered the brothers' exchange. The variables pointed to one person, they said: John Ambrose, a decorated U.S. marshal who had a sterling reputation as one of the best fugitive hunters in Chicago. Ambrose had been on Nick's security detail. His father, Thomas Ambrose, was among the Chicago police officers convicted in the Marquette 10 case and had died in prison in Texas in 1986. Another of the convicted officers was William Guide, a sort of father figure to Ambrose who had gone to prison at Marion in 1994. While he did his time there, John "No Nose" DiFronzo also had been housed at Marion.

Ambrose eventually was charged with passing information, which authorities said went to Guide and then to the mob. It was a shock to the law enforcement community in Chicago, since Ambrose in many ways had come to be one of the faces of the marshals in the city. He was a ten-year veteran, had friends in the Chicago Police Department and across all the federal agencies, and was very well respected. When the U.S. marshals found themselves in a big case, it was a guarantee that Ambrose, a married father of four, was right in the middle of it. When he was arrested, he was a supervisor in the Great Lakes Regional Fugitive Task Force and was known for tracking the fugitives that no one else could find. He had made front-page news when leading an effort to track a ranking Chicago gang member who was hiding out while working at a Wisconsin cheese factory.

The U.S. Attorney's Office called it another example of the mob's tentacles stretching into law enforcement, alleging that Ambrose was "the Babysitter" and had confessed when confronted with what federal agents had learned. His fingerprints were found on a sensitive file that had been kept with Calabrese at the witness security facility, prosecutors said, contending that Ambrose had wanted to impress Guide with the fact he was involved in such a high-profile case. For his part Ambrose denied passing anything sensitive to Guide, arguing that the Kass column and other media reports already were surfacing. If Guide passed damaging information, it must have come from somewhere else, Ambrose and his lawyer said.

But back in the spring of 2003, Ambrose's identity was still unknown and more media reports were surfacing about where the FBI might be going in its investigation. Well-known Chicago TV news reporter Carol Marin wrote a piece that appeared in the *Tribune*, outlining murders authorities were looking into.

And in April the brothers again were in the Milan visiting room and could be seen and heard reacting to the newest press accounts. Mickey mentioned the Marin article to his brother.

"A lot of guys with problems," he said of the story on the expanding federal investigation. "Uh, but mostly leaning towards, uh, Emmett Kelly," referring in code to Joey Lombardo by naming the famous circus clown.

There were other murders mentioned, too, Michael said, including "Zhivago" and the "guy with his old lady," an apparent reference to the killing of William Dauber and his wife, Charlotte.

Still James wasn't impressed. To him it appeared that the feds had the word of one person and were otherwise grasping. The investigation seemed unfocused.

"This is what they got," he said, making a zero with his left hand.

But unknown to the brothers, the FBI's work actually was accelerating. Agents continued to work through Nick's stunning account of Outfit murders, and Nick was returned to the city the following month in an attempt to show agents where some of the killings had taken place. He led them to Bensenville and other nearby suburbs, searching for the neighborhood where the Spilotros had gone, thinking they were going to get their promotions. He looked out the window as agents drove him around a suburb in the flight path to and from O'Hare, hoping that something would jog his memory from almost seventeen years earlier. And he was taken to a parking lot near the new home of the Chicago White Sox, U.S. Cellular Field. It was here, Nick told agents, that he and his brother had killed a man and thrown his body in a hole at what was once a construction site.

Ambrose again was on Nick's overnight security detail, and in June, Michael was recorded again filling his brother in.

"They were driving him all over the city," Michael said of Nick. Among the places Calabrese went was an area "where 'the Knee' was," Michael told his brother, resting a hand on his knee.

It was code for Angelo LaPietra, who had a bad knee, and showed that the Marcellos knew Nick had been taken to a site in the Bridgeport area, which was controlled by LaPietra's old Chinatown crew. Nick had called his wife while in Chicago, the brothers had learned, but their source had seen no paperwork that suggested the investigation was moving "in this direction," Michael said, pointing at James as they spoke.

As Nick had worked with the FBI, he had in fact not linked James Marcello to "Zhivago," deliberately keeping James out of the murder because of the payments the mob leader was continuing to make to his family. The $4,000 a month was being delivered without fail, and the consideration had bought Nick's silence at least on that point.

"I told you," James said. "That was the best investment. . . . Believe me."

"I hope so," his brother answered. "I hope it works out that way, buddy."

The payments should continue, the men decided, since there was no hint that Nick had yet turned on James.

"'Cause you know they're trying to push him," Mickey said.

Later in the conversation James wondered if something along the same line shouldn't be done for their source of information, "the Babysitter." Michael said he knew what his brother meant, rubbing his thumb and fingers together.

But actually, Michael said, Ambrose had refused any payment for his information.

"The guy said no," he said. "Just leave it like it is."

The FBI kept on watching and recording as their efforts against the Chicago Outfit continued to merge into a monster case.

And unknown to the Marcellos, their effort to buy Nick's silence would not last. He would walk into a meeting with agents with something on his mind. It was typical of his personality that he would broadcast with his body language when he had something new to tell them. And on that particular day, he had walked toward Maseth with a purpose, the agent recalled, sitting down in his chair without so much as a "hello."

"He says, 'I have to tell you something. I lied to you,'" Maseth said, remembering he answered Nick with a puzzled, "OK, about what?"

"Jimmy was at the Spilotro murders," Nick had answered.

Up to that point he had been telling investigators that Fecarotta picked him up on the day of the Spilotros' murder and drove him to the Bensenville subdivision where they were killed. But Nick was now changing that part of the story. He had made it to the murder scene and helped kill the Spilotros, Nick said, but it was James Marcello who had taken him there.

"Don't make any plans"

Nick was living in the basement of a building his brother owned in suburban Elmwood Park when Frank Sr. stopped by one night in 1976 with a warning.

"Don't make any plans, because we're going to be busy," he said.

Angelo LaPietra and other Outfit bosses wanted a twenty-seven-year-old ex-convict named Paul Haggerty questioned about his dealings with a mobbed-up suburban jewelry store, and then they wanted him killed. LaPietra had gotten an address for a halfway house on Indiana Avenue on the South Side where Haggerty had been staying. The Wild Bunch had first been tapped to eliminate Haggerty, but the job had languished.

So Nick and other members of the Chinatown crew soon found themselves on stakeout. Nick cased the halfway house off and on for months, occasionally watching to see when Haggerty came and went. He regularly took a bus to work, so the crew watched to see whether they could notice a pattern in his movements.

Frank Sr., Ronnie Jarrett, Nick, and Frank "Gumba" Saladino all took turns in the surveillance, communicating with walkie-talkies, with Nick sometimes parking nearby in his own car to watch.

Sometimes the men would sit for long spells and never see their target. Other times he'd walk into view, and the crew would note his path and what time it was. One morning Nick followed him on foot as he left the halfway house, watching as he walked through two large empty lots to make it to a Michigan Avenue bus headed north.

Still another time, Nick followed him all the way onto the bus, trying not to stand out as the unaware Haggerty rode it downtown and walked to a building on Jewelers Row on Wabash Avenue. Nick followed him right into the building, going so far as to get on an elevator with him. Haggerty had never seen the man who was stalking him before in his life, so he would have had no idea how close death was.

When Haggerty stepped off, so did Nick, first walking in the opposite direction in a hallway, but doubling back to see that the man he was following had stepped into a door with the Marshall Field's department store name on it. Now the crew knew where Haggerty was working.

But they were still indecisive on just how to catch Haggerty in a position where he could be taken. Jarrett, sometimes called "Jeff" or "the Little Guy" by his cohorts, had thought about purposefully "bumping into" Haggerty someplace and striking up a friendly conversation. That would allow him to roll up on him in a car at some later time and motion to him from the window with a friendly hello. That might lead Haggerty to unwittingly come closer to a vehicle that contained his killers.

Weeks after Nick had followed the murder squad's prey to his job, he again found himself sitting outside the halfway house, watching. It was June. He had his walkie-talkie, and a police scanner to listen for any dispatch to the block if someone called in a suspicious car. If a police officer did happen upon him, he would simply say he was reading the paper, and the crew might break off their effort for a time.

It was morning again as Nick waited, the rest of his crew nearby and determined to strike this time.

Suddenly, Haggerty appeared. Nick picked up his radio to tell his brother and the rest of his team that he was on foot and on the move. Nick was to lurk behind the others, who were in a separate car that would be used in the kidnapping. If anyone came up from behind, Nick would be the blocking car so those ahead might escape.

Haggerty was walking in front of Nick when it finally happened. A blue Oldsmobile driven by Jarrett raced up, and Saladino, a tall, imposing three-hundred-pound man, got out and started trying to drag Haggerty into the car. He put up a fight, desperately grabbing at the roof of the Oldsmobile as Saladino pulled on him and punched him. Soon Frank Sr. was out of the car, too, as Nick watched, also pounding on Haggerty until they could stuff him into the backseat.

All of it took just a few seconds, and soon the Oldsmobile was moving again. Nick came up from behind the lead car for the drive to Jarrett's mother-in-law's garage in Bridgeport. It was the same garage they had gone to when they needed to change their clothes after taking out "Hambone" Albergo.

It was then that Nick noticed a small Chevy approaching quickly. Thinking it could be trouble, he grabbed his walkie-talkie again to tell his brother, in the car ahead, to watch out.

"No," his brother answered. "That's Cheech," using a nickname for mobster Frank Furio. With the murder about to go down, a third car had been used as a lookout, which was news even to Nick.

Before long they were in the neighborhood, so Nick went to park a couple of blocks away and walk back to where he knew Haggerty had been taken. Jarrett had backed into the garage, and by the time Nick got there, Haggerty already had been cuffed.

Frank Sr. dismissed Saladino for the day and told Nick that he and Jarrett would be leaving for a few minutes to get someone. So Nick sat in the garage with the cuffed Haggerty, whose mouth and eyes were covered with duct tape.

When Frank Sr. returned, he had LaPietra and mob capo James "Turk" Torello with him. The faithful Frank Sr. had done his job, delivering to the bosses the man they had been looking to question. Torello peeled the tape from Haggerty's mouth.

Did he know a jewelry store in Elmwood Park called Esposito's? Had he sold some jewelry there?

There were answers, but they weren't the ones Torello wanted, and soon the desperate Haggerty had his mouth taped again. As before, Nick found himself alone with the victim. LaPietra and Torello had left, and Frank Sr. and Jarrett were off to a mall to steal a car to use to get rid of Haggerty.

Nick sat in the garage with the twenty-seven-year-old for what seem like a long time, watching him. Haggerty had to go to the bathroom, so Nick helped him relieve himself. Haggerty was thirsty, too, so Nick gave him some water.

When Frank Sr. and Jarrett returned, they had a yellow Chevy with a black top, freshly pulled off the street. The pair had waited at the mall, near its movie theaters, looking for someone to park and head inside to see a show. That would give them plenty of time to do what they had to do and get away before the vehicle was reported stolen. They pulled the Oldsmobile out of the garage and parked it nearby, bringing the disposal car in and popping its trunk with a hammer and screwdriver.

What mercy there had been for Haggerty was at an end.

Nick stood by as his brother again took a length of rope, put it over his victim's head and around his throat, and pulled as hard as he could. Still cuffed, Haggerty was unable to struggle free, and soon his ordeal was over. Frank Sr. took a plastic bag and placed it over Haggerty's head, cutting his throat with a knife and catching as much blood as he could.

With Haggerty's body in the trunk, Frank Sr. and Jarrett left the yellow Chevy on Ashland Avenue, returning to the garage a short time later to pick up Nick and drive to a meeting with Angelo LaPietra at a Chinatown restaurant.

Frank Sr. needed to let LaPietra know that the job was finished and that the Outfit could expect no further problems from Haggerty.

Nick and his brother would come up with a code name for this murder too. It was "do-be-do," though years later, Nick couldn't even remember why.

4

UNITED STATES VS. THE CHICAGO OUTFIT

When Joey "the Clown" Lombardo left prison in 1992, he had served years behind bars and found himself needing to reduce his profile a little.

He was already a Grand Avenue legend and a Chicago original, a figure with an impressive crime boss resume. It included being convicted along with other mob leaders in the landmark conspiracy to skim $2 million from the Stardust Casino in Las Vegas, and he had been found guilty of attempting to bribe Senator Howard Cannon of Nevada in a bid to have a trucking deregulation bill defeated. He would have been tried in the 1970s in a Teamsters pension fund fraud case, but the only witness against him, Daniel Seifert, had been gunned down by a hit team in 1974 before he could testify. The mob was in control of men who could deliver loans from the union's Central States Pension Fund, and Seifert, whose business was used to launder the money from one of the takes, had the potential to blow the lid on the scam and send some of the principals to prison. Lombardo, also known as "Lumpy" or "Lumbo" inside the Chicago syndicate, had drawn a paycheck from Seifert's fiberglass company, but he had avoided being charged in that murder despite law enforcement's belief that he was responsible for eliminating the threat to the Outfit's golden goose.

So, in a bid to stay out of the limelight after regaining his freedom, Lombardo took the unusual step of taking out a classified newspaper ad officially announcing that he had never taken any blood oath to the mob involving "guns and daggers" and that he would have nothing to do with the Chicago Outfit. Anyone who saw him socializing with other mobsters should go ahead and call his probation officer or contact the FBI, he said in the ad. It was an odd move for an odd guy who already had a reputation as one of the city's most colorful mobsters.

He had grown up among ten brothers and sisters, sometimes delivering papers or working as a shoe shine boy, another son of immigrant parents. From his humble beginnings as a common thief and local tough guy, he became a driver for boss Joey "Doves" Aiuppa and then a powerful mob chieftain. And despite climbing to a seat as an Outfit capo and Las Vegas supervisor, he never left his old Grand Avenue neighborhood. He was part of its fabric, having even coached kids' baseball there. He chose to remain in a house on Ohio Street, hanging out in his favorite restaurants.

Never without a wisecrack, Lombardo was a charmer whose sense of humor was well known. If it weren't for the real-life violence that seemed to follow him around, he could have come straight from the pages of a gangster comic book. He'd gone to trial in the early 1960s for beating a man who owed the mob, but he was acquitted by a jury after it was realized that police had originally picked up the wrong guy. In the 1980s he was arrested after a gambling raid carrying a notebook of jokes, and he did nothing to shed his nickname when he left a court date in Chicago with an eye hole cut out of a newspaper to avoid having his picture taken by photographers. He walked out peeking through a story in the *Chicago Sun-Times* about the White Sox signing catcher Carlton Fisk.

If Nick Calabrese was an unassuming character, more comfortable blending in than calling attention to himself, Lombardo was just the opposite. A classic, brassy mobster who backed down from no one, Lombardo looked and acted the part. For many, just hearing his name conjured up 1980s TV news images of Lombardo sweeping in or out of court in a trench coat and fedora. He could deliver a menacing glare, and all joking aside, crossing him was not a good idea.

When agents came to swab him for DNA in 2003, he was still doing his best to lay low. He was spending many of his days at a machine shop on Chicago's West Side, doing repairs on equipment that sharpened masonry blades. He liked working with his hands, so he would keep up with the machines and hang out playing chess with friends. He was aging but still as clever as they came.

The feds made a number of big cases against the Chicago Outfit in the 1990s, but Lombardo had stayed out of them. He wasn't publicly running anything, even though authorities still believed he had "consigliere" status over his old Grand Avenue street crew and the Chicago Outfit as a whole. It was a sort of senior adviser role that meant his opinion still had a lot of weight among younger, more active Outfit members who handled everyday business. He was the wise old figure behind the curtain.

Lombardo was still going to the machine shop two years after authorities came for his DNA, but he wasn't there on Monday, April 25, 2005.

The indictment in the Family Secrets case had been expected as bits of the investigation had started to become more public, but by the time the government had dotted all the i's and crossed all the t's, it still went off like nuclear warhead.

The scale of the case was unprecedented, for the first time naming the Chicago Outfit itself as a criminal enterprise under federal anti-racketeering laws and alleging a conspiracy that was born with Al Capone and flourished from the 1960s forward. The case included fourteen defendants, eighteen murders, and decades of bookmaking, loan sharking, extortion, and violence. The Calabrese and Marcello investigations had come together, with Nick's account of his Outfit life as a centerpiece.

"At the times material to this indictment there existed a criminal organization which is referred to hereafter as 'the Chicago Outfit,'" the document declared. "The Chicago Outfit was known to its members and associates as 'the Outfit' and also was known to the public as 'organized crime,' the 'Chicago syndicate,' and the 'Chicago mob.'"

That cloaked group of criminals had affected interstate commerce, it continued, and the organization existed to generate income for its members. The Outfit collected street tax and ran bookmaking operations and video gambling machines. Those who were a part of it had collected juice loans and had threatened, intimidated, and killed.

That ambitious scale and structure of the indictment, with the entire Chicago mob being accused as a criminal enterprise, allowed prosecutors to create a sprawling super case. Mitch Mars and his partner John Scully, another seasoned organized crime prosecutor, were the architects, deciding that a host of targets could be included and handled together under the conspiracy umbrella. First the government would prove that the Outfit itself was a working illegal organization, and then those charged would be plugged back into it. The murders themselves were just another part of what the Outfit did.

"The murders and the violence really were meant to protect the organization and keep it going," said William Paulin, a top mob investigator for the IRS and the agency's case agent on Family Secrets. He retired a few months after the trial ended. "Murder just allowed the money-making parts of the enterprise to continue and to prosper."

For Mars and Scully the case was the culmination of more than twenty-five years of work put together by prosecutors who had dedicated their professional lives to organized crime cases. It took their institutional memory to make the cases that paved the way to Family Secrets, the biggest organized crime case Chicago had seen in decades.

Momentum for it really had begun in the early 1980s with the federal Organized Crime Strike Force, when Mars had been involved in the prosecution of prolific burglar Paul "Peanuts" Panczko, one of a trio of burglar brothers who were crooks in the grand Chicago tradition. He had tried to go legit and drive a cab in Chicago's Gold Coast, but Mars got him ten years on a gun possession case in 1985.

"I never got a break in my life," Panczko told longtime *Tribune* reporter John O'Brien after his sentencing that year. "All my sentences have been max, max, max."

A few years later the feds were engaged in Operation Safebet, a large investigation of prostitution and police corruption involving suburban brothels and payoffs that depended on a credit service laundering credit charges from the illicit businesses. Dozens were convicted, including Victor Spilotro, brother to Anthony and Michael, and Cook County sheriffs who protected the businesses. The case also had grounded a suburban madam, Doris "Dolly" Fischer, who ran an extensive escort service by phone from her Buffalo Grove home. She had a cutting-edge business for the time, keeping computerized client lists. And she also happened to be Panczko's love interest.

In 1986, a little more than a year after getting his ten years, the longtime thief wanted out to be with Dolly. To accomplish this, he decided to make himself available to help the government in any way he could. He wrote the judge in his case, informing him he was helping Scully make cases, and he planned to testify against his brother Joseph "Pops" Panczko that year when Pops went on trial for boosting a trunkload of jewels from a traveling salesman in Indiana.

"I have changed my whole life since I met this woman," he reportedly wrote that year.

And Peanuts had plenty to spill. Among the capers he told Scully and the FBI about was a 1983 attempted heist at the Balmoral Park Racetrack in Crete, outside Chicago. A burglary gang featuring Panczko himself had crept into the track through an abandoned rail tunnel and after cutting their way in, they had tied up a pair of guards and took a torch to a safe containing $600,000 in cash. But the gang hadn't counted on a shift change taking place at that exact moment, and they gave up on their effort to avoid getting caught by the new guards arriving for work.

The attempted job had been unsolved for five years, but the lovesick Peanuts would change that. Seven men were indicted, including two City of Chicago employees and James "Duke" Basile, a noted bank robber. Panczko had worn a wire to trick Basile into discussing a number of jobs he had pulled over the years.

Prosecutors continued working up the criminal food chain, eventually convincing Basile to cooperate too and tell them what he knew about the city's underworld. Basile slipped into witness protection after giving up information about mob leader Joseph Ferriola and hit man Gerald Scarpelli, a member of Ferriola's Wild Bunch. Basile's assistance against Scarpelli included wearing a wire and recording conversations with him for more than a year, a victory for the feds that was considered a major infiltration of the Outfit.

In the summer of 1988, Scarpelli was arrested and charged with planning thefts and possessing a machine gun. Agents had been listening in when Basile and Scarpelli had discussed a gold heist.

Prosecutors and agents continued to roll ahead, with Scarpelli eventually deciding that he too would flip to help himself. He had information on a few mob murders, he told authorities, including the chase and shootings of William and Charlotte Dauber. The killings had been the work of a couple of Outfit crews working together, he told authorities.

Scarpelli would eventually try to recant his statements, but a judge had decided they could be used against him. But before that happened, Scarpelli smothered himself with plastic laundry bags in a shower at Chicago's downtown federal jail. It would be recorded, officially, as a suicide, though the death has always left some wondering whether someone could have "helped" Scarpelli take his own life.

His case was over; however, before his attempt to take back his admissions, Scarpelli had mentioned some names in his cooperative moments, including one in particular. It was Frank Calabrese Sr., and Scarpelli had placed him and Chinatown crew member Ronnie Jarrett at the Dauber killing. Prior to that information, Frank Sr. had been known to authorities only as a juice guy. His name had come up in previous mob cases, but he was considered a thuggish loan shark and had never been on the radar as a major player or a killer.

Not any longer. Federal interest was now piqued, and by the late 1980s into the early 1990s prosecutors and agents were beginning to gather information on the Calabrese loan business. They developed an undercover cooperator—an auto-repair shop owner named Matthew Russo who was under federal pressure for an insurance scam involving the sale of "stolen" cars—to get inside the organization. Russo had borrowed large amounts of money from Frank Sr., whose crew wormed into Russo's business, and had signed over his auto repair shop to help pay his debt. He agreed to begin taping crew members talking about cheating Celozzi-Ettleson Chevrolet for work and about juice loans. The case was made through both his cooperation and efforts by the feds to get the cooperation of Phil Tolomeo, a former Chicago cop who was involved with the Calabrese crew until bailing out of Chicago and making off with some of the organization's funds. It would become the case that saw Frank Sr., Frank Jr., Kurt, and Nick Calabrese plead guilty in the mid-1990s.

The long-term strategy employed by career prosecutors and agents continued to blossom next when Frank Jr. had finally had it with his father and his mob life late in the decade. His father had promised to leave the Outfit but had always gone back on his word. Frank Jr.'s marriage was failing, and his father was a wedge between himself and his wife. He had wanted a real dad and a grandfather for his children, not an abusive mobster determined never to let go.

"Frank Jr. decided he wanted to have a life for himself, and it wasn't going to be with him," FBI agent Maseth said. "It was a choice he made for his family."

Growing up in a tidy Italian American neighborhood in Elmwood Park, west of Chicago, a place where you're likely to see nice Christmas decorations during the holidays and lots of vanity license plates featuring names ending in vowels, Frank Jr. and his brothers had gone to good schools and been involved in sports just like other kids. The family had a veneer of normalcy, but behind closed doors Frank Sr. was physically abusive. Other Outfit guys had seen to it to take care of their sons, with many trying to keep their kids out of the mob altogether and even sending them to college. Frank Jr. was bitter and hurt and resentful. So he wrote his letter to someone he thought he could trust, Tom Bourgeois, the FBI supervisor who had handled the case involving his father, brother, and uncle.

Frank Jr.'s cooperation had set the Family Secrets case in motion, leading to the taping, the testing of the glove samples, and the turning of Nicholas Calabrese, whose murderous past was another surprise.

Nick had been thought of by FBI agents and prosecutors as a relatively nice guy. He was soft spoken and had been honorably discharged from the navy, just like Scully, as a matter of fact. Investigators thought he had gotten involved in the juice business because his brother had bullied him and knocked him around. They had had no idea that the man who seemed like the reluctant, quiet person standing on the sidelines was actually an efficient Outfit executioner.

Now Nick was the lynchpin in the broad Family Secrets case, a made guy who was the nexus of the investigation. He was the central link between the three main defendants in the conspiracy, his brother Frank Sr., James Marcello, and Joey "the Clown" Lombardo, who were leaders of three different Outfit crews.

Eight others also were charged with racketeering, including Mickey Marcello, Frank "the German" Schweihs, Paul "the Indian" Schiro, and Anthony "Twan" Doyle and Michael Ricci, the two officers who had been taped talking with Frank Sr. in prison.

Chicago's U.S. attorney Patrick Fitzgerald called the case "a hit on the mob" while announcing the charges at a crowded press conference, where FBI leaders praised the agents who had tackled the case.

"What makes this indictment significant to us is for the first time we have the heads of multiple crews in one indictment," said Robert Grant, special agent in charge of the FBI's Chicago office. Grant was quoted in the *Tribune* as calling the mob "a bunch of murderous thugs."

Frank Sr. was accused of committing thirteen killings, including that of "Hambone" Albergo, Haggerty, and Fecarotta. He was blamed for the Dauber homicides and the shootings of Ortiz and Morawski in Cicero. He was accused of killing William "Butch" Petrocelli, the hit man he had always hated, and with helping a hit team blow up Hinsdale businessman Michael Cagnoni, whose Mercedes had exploded on a Chicago-area highway in 1981. And Nick hadn't stopped there in his FBI conversations. His brother had killed Henry Cosentino, who had been found hog-tied in a trunk, Nick said, as well as burglar John Mendell, a thief murdered when the mob went on a killing spree as revenge for a break-in at the home of boss Tony "Big Tuna" Accardo. He had killed Vincent Moretti, too, Nick told the FBI, another thief, and Moretti's friend Donald Renno.

For good measure, Frank Sr. was charged with one count of extortion for collecting street tax from a restaurant, Connie's Pizza, and with conducting an illegal gambling business for the operation of his bookmaking ring.

James Marcello was named in the Spilotros murders, his bid to give Nick hush money having crumbled under the weight of his own recorded words. And Nick told authorities that he had also been with James at an earlier slaying, the killing of mob lieutenant Nicholas D'Andrea, who was lured to a warehouse and bludgeoned by a group of Outfit hit men.

"Jimmy Light" was also charged with operating an illegal gambling business for running the video poker operation and with obstructing a criminal investigation. Michael Marcello was hit with those charges, too, and three employees of M&M Amusement also were named.

Authorities knew Lombardo was then seventy-five and in questionable health, and their window to bring him back to court was closing. So they finally named him as committing the Seifert murder, along with his trusted henchman Schweihs. Nick had informed authorities he had been told that Lombardo and Schweihs had personally taken part in the slaying.

Nick also told the FBI that he had been aided in the murder of Emil Vaci in Phoenix by Schiro, another Chicago mobster, and by Schweihs. Schiro, who was serving a prison sentence after being convicted along with William Hanhardt, a Chicago police chief of detectives who ran a mob-connected jewelry-theft ring, had helped Nick stalk and kill the grand jury witness in June 1986, the Family Secrets indictment alleged.

As they were preparing to make their announcement, authorities had fanned out making arrests, taking Schiro into custody in Arizona, and James Marcello at his home in the western Chicago suburb of Lombard. Frank Sr. was easy to find because he had never made it out of prison, and Schiro too was incarcerated.

Doyle, the cop who had given Frank Sr. information about the gloves, was arrested at his Arizona home. Michael Marcello was brought in, as were his employees who had collected the take from the video poker machines.

But not everything had gone exactly as expected. One indicted defendant, Frank "Gumba" Saladino, the mob enforcer known for his hulking frame who had helped kill Haggerty and others, was found dead of natural causes in a hotel room on the outskirts of the metropolitan area when agents went to arrest him. Schweihs wasn't at his Florida home and was considered a fugitive. And the recorded words of Michael Marcello had proven prophetic when it came to Lombardo. Chicago's infamous clown had indeed skipped, hopped, and disappeared, apparently led into hiding by his considerable network of friends. The FBI would be criticized for letting him slip away, but agents had been unable to watch him around the clock for fear that they would be detected and more of their targets would get nervous and scatter.

Mars would lead the prosecution, relying on all of his experience through decades as a thorn in the Outfit's flesh. In addition to the string of cases leading directly to Family Secrets, he had the prosecution of mobsters Albert Tocco and Ernest Rocco Infelice (also known as "Rocky") in his background. He wasn't tall or someone you'd look twice at on the bus, but he was a methodical investigator and a bulldog in court. More than once his name would be mentioned by syndicate guys who were being taped, speculating in recordings that it was Mars who was behind their troubles. And more often than not, they were right.

To call Mars beloved in his office would be an understatement. In many ways, if the U.S. Attorney's Office had been asked to choose one of its own who best represented what the office is all about, it would have been Mitch. In addition to his smarts, he was dedicated. He could have left the office for good in the morning and had a high-paying job at a private firm by lunch, but that wasn't what he was about. He was a Chicago native who loved his city and took it personally when organized crooks wormed their way into politics and business and everyday life. He had the talent to deal with it, and he was not going to sit idly by. He was undaunted by highly complicated mob investigations that required years to organize and months of working around the clock to get ready for trial. His personality—constantly making jokes and laughing mostly at himself—made working with him a plum assignment. Taking on a case with Mars could mean weeks with little time for family or free time, but those who got to work with him were happy to do it, and many found that they would never learn more in their professional lives than when they were on a case with him.

Mars graduated from the Georgetown University Law Center and joined the staff of the U.S. House of Representatives in 1977, getting tapped to work as a researcher for the House select committee that investigated the assassinations of John F. Kennedy, Robert F. Kennedy, and Rev. Martin Luther King Jr. By 1980 he was back in his home town, joining the government's Organized Crime Strike Force before it merged with the U.S. Attorney's Office in 1990. He became chief of the Organized Crime Division in 1992 and led the prosecutions of south suburban mob leader Tocco, Infelice, and former Cicero town president Betty Loren-Maltese.

Scully would join Mars as a sure right-hand man, focused, earnest, and steadied by his own deep experience. He was educated at the historic U.S. Naval Academy at Annapolis, Maryland, and was active in the navy for almost a decade. He had joined the Department of Justice's Strike Force in Chicago as well in 1982, moving to the U.S. Attorney's Office with Mars in the merger. His past cases also included the prosecution of Hanhardt, the jewel-thief cop with whom Paul "the Indian" Schiro had been imprisoned.

And also on the team was Markus Funk, at thirty-nine, a younger assistant than his partners and among his office's rising talents. He didn't have a wealth of experience taking it to Outfit street crews, but he was certainly up to the task. He had a Ph.D. from Oxford University and had taught there from 1997 to 1999 before joining the U.S. Attorney's Office in Chicago. Once there he had traveled to Kosovo for the Justice Department as an adviser for two years. He was a well-published writer, having penned articles on everything from archaeology to juvenile justice. Among his early experience in Chicago as a federal prosecutor was a case against an abusive priest, and he had been assigned to the case of a 450-pound identity thief who jumped on a victim and killed him as he watched *The Wizard of Oz*. The plan had been to fake his own death using that man's body, but he didn't think ahead and realize the victim was barely half his own weight. He died in prison before Funk had a chance to take him to trial.

*

Joey Lombardo apparently spent many of his weeks on the lam in a basement in Oak Park, a historic suburb just west of Chicago known for its Frank Lloyd Wright architecture and leafy streets.

Speculation grew that Lombardo had rigged an escape plan all along, and that he might have made it to a Caribbean hideout or to Europe. But in reality he huddled in his below-ground apartment, growing a wild beard. There was a kitchen, a shower, a bed, and a television set. Avoiding arrest meant staying put, as the FBI made catching up with him a top priority and cast a wide net.

As his codefendants began appearing in court, Lombardo wasn't there. He was staying out of sight. But true to his nature, he wouldn't stay quiet for very long.

After a couple of weeks, Chicago got a shock. Lombardo wrote a letter to U.S. district judge James Zagel, who was handling the case, declaring himself an innocent man.

"I am writing you a letter to let you know that I am not hiding to avoid the charges against me," he had scrawled.

Lombardo said he would turn himself in if he could be released on a $50,000 bond and have his own trial apart from the other defendants. He had no part in any racketeering conspiracy with those he had been charged with, he claimed, and what's more he didn't even know them.

"There is not one defendant in this case that I received 1 penny or did I give them 1 penny," Joey spelled out in capital letters.

He knew nothing of the murders in the case, either, and said his two prior trials were unfair. He hadn't been in on the casino skim and hadn't tried to bribe a congressman at all. Just think, there were many people convicted in Illinois and sent to prison who were innocent, he wrote, and DNA evidence had proven it.

He called himself a seventy-six-year-old with a heart condition who just wanted to live out his remaining years in peace. He was not a violent man and promised he had no weapons. If the FBI were to come and find him, he would offer no resistance and accept his fate.

There were a few postscripts.

"Like they say, they could indict a hamburger [for] murder and get a conviction" was one.

"Judge, with the prepublicity I do not have a chance" was another. "The media made me a ten-headed monster. How does [an] innocent person defend himself?"

And finally, there was a "PSSS," again asking for a separate trial and offering an apology.

"Excuse the mispelt [sic] words and also my grammar," Joey "the Clown" asked of Zagel. "English was my worst subject in school."

The letter had been mailed to Lombardo's lawyer, Rick Halprin, a real veteran of Chicago's legal scene who gave the distinct impression that whatever block you could name, he had been around it at least twice. He was a onetime marine with a booming courtroom voice. A Vietnam War wound to his back forced him to walk somewhat stiffly, but he could more than command an audience. He was proud of a former life as a semipro hockey player, with his white number 12 jersey still hanging in his office.

Halprin had defended everyone from El Rukn gang members to crooked cops to players in the On Leong gambling case out of Chicago's Chinatown. There wasn't much he hadn't seen, but still many of Lombardo's antics left him shaking his head.

The letter was a bizarre communication, and the judge was hardly impressed.

Zagel at the time was approaching his twentieth year as a federal judge. He was a Reagan appointee and was perceived as one of the brighter and wiser jurists on the federal bench in Chicago. He had a calm demeanor and kept an orderly courtroom with his well-spoken directions, even if he did operate by his own clock. Some who gathered often in his courtroom, only to find themselves waiting for him to take the bench, joked about ZST, an abbreviation for "Zagel Standard Time."

A white-haired man with glasses who seemed very comfortable in his seat, Zagel was in his middle sixties. He was a former director of the Illinois State Police who had once been married to noted Chicago TV reporter Pam Zekman and had even written a novel about a robbery plot against the Federal Reserve Bank. He was rarely ruffled, and in fact his confidence would leave some female reporters who covered the Family Secrets proceedings in his courtroom with a bit of a schoolgirl crush on him.

In short, Zagel wasn't new to the game, either, and he wasn't about to be pushed or bullied into some strange agreement with a mobster who wouldn't even appear in his courtroom. Lombardo was a fugitive, and he would remain one until he came to court, shackled or otherwise.

In the meantime, other defendants in the case were appearing before Zagel. Nick appeared in a nonpublicized hearing away from the press to plead not guilty to a single count of racketeering conspiracy, though eventually he would admit to taking part in fourteen gangland killings. His brother, Frank Sr., appeared in another hearing, limping and hunched over to plead not guilty and complain about his health problems.

"I'm in my sixty-ninth year," he would say to Zagel, telling the judge he had heart trouble and needed back surgery. He was on nine medications, he said, then stopping himself to quickly add a tenth.

Calabrese's lawyer was no less a character than Halprin—or some of his mob clients, for that matter. Born and raised in Chicago, Joseph Lopez had been doing Outfit cases since 1986, involved in defending mobsters such as Anthony "the Hatch" Chiaramonti, a mobster on James Marcello's bad side who was gunned down in 2001 in the vestibule of a chicken restaurant with a list of names of M&M Amusement customers in his pocket. He'd been on the case of Eddie Pedote, Mikey "the Bomber" Swiatek, and Daniel Bambulas, a trio that recruited an undercover ATF agent to drive a getaway van when they'd gone to pull a jewelry heist on South Wabash. He'd even defended a Mafioso discovered working in Elmwood Park as a waiter in an extradition case.

Lopez was so plugged into the network that he considered Michael Marcello a pal. When Marcello's phone was tapped, Lopez had been captured on it making small talk. He was unafraid of his links to the mob world, talking freely about trips he'd taken with reputed mobsters to Wisconsin resorts where he'd eaten steak and lobster and had a great time.

Lopez was known for his almost nonstop joking and for his sharp suits, and he relished his "Shark" nickname. With slicked-back hair, pointy shoes, pink socks, and a love of Italian restaurants and cooking, he was more than in his element when it came to Outfit cases. He'd been attracted to the law in the first place by watching *Perry Mason,* and by reading *The Godfather,* remembering the line that a man could make more money with a briefcase than with a gun.

Lopez worked out of a small office in the historic Monadnock Building just south of the Dirksen courthouse, in a room decorated with courtroom sketches of himself and a huge sailfish that he had captured in Acapulco mounted on the wall.

"He opened his mouth and that's why he got caught, see?" he would say. "That's the lesson to be learned from that fish."

He rejected Frank Jr.'s version of the family events. Nobody from the neighborhood would come to court to say Frank Sr. was a bad dad. Had he slapped Junior around? Maybe once or twice after catching his son smoking crack. They'd gone on nice vacations, attended private schools. The kids had cars and clothes and whatever else they wanted, Lopez said. Their father wasn't a tyrant; he was a good provider.

He wasn't afraid to eventually argue that Frank Sr. should be released on bond before trial. Never mind that his client was a convicted mob loan shark and had been accused of more than a dozen violent killings by his own brother.

"I feel like I'm trying to get Ray Charles a driver's license," Lopez quipped.

Frank Sr. wouldn't flee because he knew he'd just get caught, Lopez said. Frank Sr. wanted nothing more than to be at the trial; he wanted to face his brother and son and look them in the eye before making his way to the great beyond, Lopez argued. Frank had been alone when the reality of Nick's and Frank Jr.'s cooperation had started to sink in. He, too, was summoned to a medical area in prison, with agents executing a search warrant for X-rays of his hand, telling him that someone close to him had let the FBI know about the time in the car when the blasting cap had gone off and injured him.

All of these experiences had made him more grounded, Lopez said. Frank Sr. had become a Bible reader while he was behind bars, the lawyer told the judge, especially the early books with the vengeful God, what his client referred to as "the First Testament."

"Whatever it is—at least he read it," Lopez said.

Zagel was unmoved, siding with Mars, who argued Frank Sr. was one of the most devious criminals he'd seen. It was hard to imagine how he would be able to explain the taped conversations made by his son, the judge said. Plus, the Outfit was about following orders to protect itself, and Frank Sr. was accused of being a made member of the charged enterprise.

"If released, there is a distinct possibility that he will attempt to deprive the prosecution of as many living witnesses as he can to comply with such orders," Zagel said.

For Joey Lombardo, the clock ticking away his last moments of freedom had begun to run out in January 2006, after nine months of hiding and moving to try to stay ahead of authorities.

His lifelong friend Dominic Calarco got a knock on the door of his Elmwood Park home one evening that month. Calarco was supposed to have been cooking for his social club, where he would go mingle with pals each night of the week. Without warning he found himself staring at an uninvited guest. It was a bearded man he thought maybe he knew.

He looked a little closer, but it wasn't until he heard the man's voice that he knew who it was. He had once lived in an apartment house with him.

"I got no place to go," Joey Lombardo said to him. "Can I say here for a couple of weeks?"

Calarco, an eighty-five-year-old World War II veteran, couldn't turn his friend away, believing the case against him was none of his business. He told Joey he could stay, though he soon urged the bearded fugitive to give it up and turn himself in. It would be easy, after all, since Calarco's place was just a quick walk to the Elmwood Park police station. But Joey was reluctant, even though his friend kept pointing out that he was not a well man. There were nights when Joey would cry because he missed his family.

He would turn himself in the next day if he thought he could get bond, Joey told Calarco, but he had a few more things to do. One of them was to try to see a dentist for an abscessed tooth that was killing him. If he could see his dentist, Dr. Patrick Spilotro, after hours, maybe he could be cared for without being recognized by a stranger and turned in. As the name suggests, Spilotro was another brother of Anthony and Michael Spilotro, and he had never gotten over their murders. He had Outfit clients, including Joey and Nick Calabrese, but he had continued to see them in the hopes of gathering information about what had happened to his brothers. He agreed to see Joey at his practice in the northwest suburbs of Chicago even though Joey was a wanted man, and he had "the Clown" come after his practice had closed for the day. Joey went with Calarco, entering through a parking garage after dark and under a hood so there would be no chance he might be noticed.

Patrick Spilotro, who occasionally would tip the FBI when he learned something related to the killing of his brothers, knew Joey was dodging the Family Secrets case and decided it might be his best chance to press him again for real answers. Joey had always told him that if he hadn't been in prison on the casino case in 1986, he would have interceded for the brothers, and their murders most likely wouldn't have happened. This time, however, his answer changed.

Instead of the line about saving the dentist's brothers, Joey gave the pleading dentist a focused response about what it really meant to be in the Outfit.

"Doc," he said, "you get an order, you follow that order. If you don't follow the order, you go, too."

And when the work on his tooth was finished, Joey left Spilotro's office. He returned to Calarco's home, leaving the dentist behind.

A few days later, though, he scheduled a return appointment for more work. He needed a bridge adjusted this time, and the runaway mobster arranged for what he thought would be another secret visit. Again he arrived with Calarco. But this time the FBI was alerted by Spilotro, who had finally had enough of Joey's games. Agents would surprise the men in Calarco's silver Lincoln in an alley behind Calarco's home.

Just as he had written to Zagel, Lombardo didn't have any weapons when the FBI finally caught up with him, just some cash and his own driver's license. He had long hair and a full beard, looking like a crazed mountain man or Saddam Hussein in his spider hole.

Before he knew it, he was clean shaven and appearing before Zagel, who appointed Halprin to represent him. Now shackled, wearing a jail jumpsuit, and declared indigent, Lombardo, like many of his codefendants, complained about health issues.

Well, the judge asked, when was the last time he had seen a doctor?

"I didn't see my doctor since nine months ago," Lombardo answered. "I was—what do they call it? I was unavailable."

There would be no bond for Lombardo, and none for James Marcello, either, despite Marcello's pledge to put up more than $12 million in property and cash to secure his release.

Marcello was represented in court by a pair of defense lawyers, also veterans of Chicago's courthouses. Marc Martin and Tom Breen were just as comfortable street fighting in the Wild West of the Criminal Courts Building as they were in the more civilized environs of federal court downtown. Martin had stood up for everyone from R&B superstar R. Kelly to corrupt media baron Conrad Black and had been an opponent to Mitch Mars in the Loren-Maltese case. Breen routinely won tough cases, and even many reporters covering the proceedings would joke that if they ever got in trouble, they'd probably call Breen first.

Martin and Breen called for a separate trial for Marcello, reasoning that jurors could be prejudiced by all of the murder evidence in the case that had nothing to do with him. The lawyers wouldn't get lost in the vast conspiracy charges, choosing instead to hit specific weak points as if Marcello were trying to beat a murder charge in state court. And the jury should be kept from seeing too many shocking photos of crime scenes, they argued.

Actually, each defendant wanted his own trial, but Zagel wouldn't bend. No one wanted to be on the same side as Frank Sr. when his family blew up in his face, and some of the defense lawyers feared they'd spend as much time cleaning up after one another as they did defending their own clients. They bickered and fought as the trial approached.

All of the attorneys worked to limit as much of the testimony against their clients as possible, but Zagel again wasn't inclined to give them much ground. The judge would allow the daughter of Michael Spilotro to testify that Marcello, a man she knew as "Jim," had called her family's Oak Park home to summon her father the day he disappeared. And he would allow James Wagner, head of the watchdog group Chicago Crime Commission, to testify for jurors about the history and capabilities of the Chicago Outfit.

Frank Sr. and Marcello failed in bids to convince the appeals court that the case represented double jeopardy for them. They argued they'd already been convicted of racketeering activity in the 1990s and now the government was recycling the same conduct in the Family Secrets case.

And Zagel limited Lombardo's plan to argue he had an alibi for the morning Seifert was killed. Halprin had wanted to fully explore his client's claim that as Seifert was being gunned down, Lombardo was dealing with Chicago police to report a stolen wallet.

Lopez's defense plans were curtailed as well, with Zagel not allowing the lawyer to get too far into his contention that Frank Jr. actually was plotting to keep his father locked up because he had stolen money and cars from him. Lopez would have to try to draw it out of the younger Calabrese or Nick once he got either of them on the witness stand. He had wanted to argue directly that Frank Jr. had pitted his uncle against his father by telling Frank Sr. all of the things Nick said he had done. Lopez wanted the jury to think Frank Jr. used information from Nick to set up the father—to get him bragging about what a tough guy he was and saying too much on the recordings.

A tough case was growing ever tougher for the defense, but their uphill climb would grow steeper still. Zagel even agreed with prosecutors that it should be an anonymous jury that heard the case, believing that juror safety could be an issue. That plan especially rankled defense lawyers, who would now argue before a jury that thought their clients could harm them.

"Now, of course, the jury can infer that these must be pretty nefarious people," Doyle's lawyer, Ralph Meczyk, said at the time. Meczyk too was an experienced lawyer in Chicago. Among his most notable clients was David Dowaliby, a suburban Chicago man found guilty of killing his seven-year-old stepdaughter in a high profile case that ended with an appeals court overturning his conviction. But Meczyk's favorite case might have been one he took to trial a few years earlier, when he defended a man from charges of attempted murder and solicitation of the attempted killing. When prosecutors opted to drop the attempted murder count just before the proceedings started, Meczyk beat the solicitation charge by having his client testify on the stand that he had done the shooting himself. In defending Doyle, he would be assisted by two up-and-coming young lawyers from his firm, Darryl Goldberg and Damon Cheronis.

As the Family Secrets trial approached, the number of defendants who would actually face the jury thinned. Most pleaded guilty, including Michael Marcello, and Joe Ferriola's son, Nicholas, a member of the Twenty-Sixth Street crew who was accused of helping Frank Sr. communicate from prison and of operating a bookmaking business. Michael Ricci died after having heart surgery. And Frank Schweihs, who had eventually been tracked to a small Kentucky town where he and a girlfriend were paying cash for a townhouse, was found to be too sick to have his day in court. He was slated for a later trial by himself. By June 2007 only five defendants remained: James Marcello, Joey Lombardo, Frank Calabrese Sr., Paul Schiro, and Anthony Doyle. A single jury would hear a conspiracy case against all of the men and then would deliberate a second time to decide whether to assign blame for the murders in the case. Only Doyle was not accused of murder, but any of the remaining four defendants found guilty in the conspiracy and also found to have committed a murder could face life in prison.

With the indictment as sweeping as it was, the case seemed to come at the defendants and their lawyers from every direction at once. The government would show that the men had acted to further the conspiracy through any number of acts, including gambling, extortion, and murder. Defense lawyers were left either trying to take their clients out of the Outfit or trying to show that acts they were accused of were done without the goal of advancing mob interests. Neither option was a particularly good one. Each defendant but Schiro was on tape somewhere, and Frank Sr. already had pleaded guilty to some of the activities that jurors would hear about.

In past cases the government had "shown all of this thuggery," Halprin said before the trial began, and then would ask jurors to believe that certain things had been done for the Outfit. But in Family Secrets, the government would begin by essentially proving that organized crime existed and then try to show that all manner of illicit acts were done in an effort to advance the mob.

Prosecutors would show that "there was this evil," Halprin explained. "This case says that these guys controlled everything in one capacity or another and it was all done in this structured way."

Lopez decided he would try to remove at least some of the murders from the mob pipeline. For the government to be right, it would have to prove that orders for the killings flowed down through a chain of command, just as Nick was going to claim. Sure there had been murders, but Lopez would argue that prosecutors couldn't definitively show that the killings had been committed to protect the Outfit and were specifically ordered by bosses.

"People get killed for a variety of reasons," he would say before the trial.

Lopez would try to chop away at the government's case with the Ortiz and Morawski murders, in particular. There were witnesses interviewed by police at the time who gave a different account from the one that prosecutors would present, and if authorities were wrong about that murder being a mob hit and if Nick could be proven a liar, then the whole case might disintegrate.

As for his client, Frank Sr. was in business for himself, Lopez would argue. He gave out loans, sure, but not by order of any mob leader. He made a lot of money on his own terms and didn't kowtow to any Outfit boss. His brother was the mobster, Lopez said, making up stories about Frank Sr. now that he was caught himself.

Schiro's lawyer, Paul Wagner, agreed, as did Martin and Breen, Marcello's attorneys. There was no proof that what Nick was saying really happened, they would argue. And it was Nick's blood on the gloves, after all, not any of their clients' DNA.

Despite not being accused in a murder, Doyle had his own hurdle. He was on tape seemingly aiding the imprisoned Frank Sr. as the convicted mobster tried to figure out who was cooperating against him. Meczyk would try to convince the jury that his client was just visiting an old friend and not purposefully giving away protected investigative information.

Having failed in his bid to get Lombardo his own trial, Halprin would do his best to set Joey apart as much as possible. He would option to withhold his opening statement until the start of the defense case, many weeks into the summer. And he also planned to have Joey take the stand, hoping at first that he would be the only one with the guts to take that extreme risk. Halprin would try to show that his client was a working man who only had ties to big shots who ran in Outfit circles. His links to mob-connected businessmen confused the picture when it came to Lombardo, he would argue. Lombardo essentially was an errand boy for people such as Irwin Weiner, a high-rolling bail bondsman, and labor racketeer Allen Dorfman, who ran an insurance agency that did business with the Teamsters. When he was convicted with Dorfman in the attempt to bribe a member of Congress, it had created the misunderstanding that Lombardo was some mob overlord, Halprin planned to argue. The truth was Lombardo had been a hard worker from his days as a youth in the Italian neighborhood around Ogden and Grand avenues, Halprin would say. He had pulled himself up from humble beginnings and had worked hard at real jobs. Halprin, assisted by lawyer Susan Shatz, would try to get the jury to see Joey as a blue-collar guy who had gotten roped into his mob problems, carried along and catching big cases. He once worked in trucking and had gotten his hands dirty in the fiberglass business with Seifert.

For the government's case to work, Joey would have to be shown as a leader, giving orders and setting plans in motion for the Outfit.

Anyone could take a look at his life and see that he wasn't that, Halprin said. He didn't drive fancy cars or live in a house in River Forest, an upscale suburb that was home to the likes of Tony "Big Tuna" Accardo. To win, the government would have to put Joey in the mob's hierarchy, and the defense attorney wasn't ready to give in and admit there was enough proof. Lombardo wouldn't go down without fighting back.

So maybe he ran a dice game, Halprin said, but Joey wasn't sitting in darkened restaurants at corner tables, ordering people to their death with a word or a nod.

"He was a minor, minor player."

And Lombardo would keep one extra card up his sleeve. If the jury decided they wanted to believe that "the Clown" was part of the conspiracy, Halprin also planned to argue what is known as the "withdrawal defense." It's a viable strategy to argue that a defendant withdrew from a conspiracy if the withdrawal was more than five years before the indictment in the case. That allowance would let Halprin argue that if the jury thought Lombardo was a mobster in the 1970s and '80s, his newspaper ad in 1992 was effectively a retirement announcement.

"You do it"

In December 1977 a band of burglars had the bright idea to break into the home of Tony "Big Tuna" Accardo, hoping to retrieve jewelry and other items that they themselves had first taken from a Chicago store.

Among the ringleaders was a master thief named John Mendell, a burglar with a knack for disabling alarms and landing the tough scores. It had been his plan to take the valuables from the well-known Levinson's Jewelry, which had connections to Accardo, the Chicago mob's retired "Number One." Mendell had pulled the job, an unsanctioned theft that had angered mob bosses, leaving Mendell to try to hide the loot in the rafters of his business for safekeeping. It didn't work. The jewels and silver were restolen from the hiding place and were stored away in a place where no one would be foolish enough to attempt to get them back.

Mendell was skilled and had turned down mob work in the past. He didn't want to take part in working for the syndicate, he told some who knew him, and he didn't want to pay any Outfit street tax on what he stole. But now he just wanted his stuff back, so he led a crew that reclaimed the jewelry from a walk-in vault in the basement of Accardo's residence.

It was an incredibly daring move. Mendell had basically pulled a job at the White House of Chicago crime.

The longtime boss of the Outfit had once been a driver and personal bodyguard for Al Capone, and he had not risen to his rank by being a nice guy. The Outfit would have its revenge, and it was no longer about the stolen trinkets. Involved in the break-in or not,

Chicago burglars began turning up dead as the mob took a scorched-earth approach to dealing with Mendell's great sin.

It was a few weeks later, around the time of the Super Bowl in 1978, that Nick got another foreboding warning from his brother, Frank Sr.

"We got to go down to Bridgeport," Frank Sr. had said. "Down to the neighborhood. We got something to do."

By now Nick had an idea of what that "something" was likely to be, but he went along and did as he was told. Ronnie Jarrett had stolen with Mendell in the past, so it would be Jarrett who would lure the burglar in. He told Mendell he had some hot merchandise for him to have a look at. Jarrett would pick up Mendell and bring him to a secure place where he could be dealt with. Things fell through on the first night of their attempt, but the very next evening, Mendell was free to meet with Jarrett.

Nick and his brother were the first to arrive at the garage of Jarrett's mother-in-law on South Lowe, the site of other Outfit work of this kind. It was the same place where ex-convict Paul Haggerty had been taken and where Nick had found himself after the Albergo killing. The Calabrese brothers were soon joined by Frank "Gumba" Saladino, the hulking enforcer who had helped punch Haggerty into a car during the earlier kidnapping.

It wasn't too long before they heard the back gate open and then heard Jarrett walking up as he talked to someone.

The three gloved men tensed up in the darkened garage. Nick leaned against one wall, and Gumba hid against another near a workbench. Frank Sr. stood in the shadows just in front of his brother. The door opened, and in walked the unsuspecting ace burglar.

In a blur, the men had jumped him.

Gumba and Frank Sr. shoved him against a car and began punching him in the abdomen, landing deep, bruising blows. With the two muscular men slugging him over and over, it took only seconds for the hit squad to gain control of Mendell, but Frank Sr. didn't strangle him immediately. Mendell wouldn't live to tell anyone about it, but this was meant to be a message about picking the wrong house to burglarize.

So with Nick and Gumba holding the battered Mendell down, Frank Sr. straddled his legs and leaned forward. He swung one arm back and delivered several heavy slaps to Mendell's head and face, beating him with an open hand as he lay sprawled on the concrete floor.

Only then, with that extra pain and punishment delivered, did Frank Sr. go for his rope. He pulled it over Mendell's head and around his neck. He pulled hard, choking and eventually killing him.

With the dead man lying on the floor, the men moved the car that was in the garage outside, and Jarrett left to get Mendell's car from the street for the disposal of his body. They pulled off Mendell's clothes and lifted him into the trunk of his car.

It was time to ensure that Mendell would stay dead, so Frank Sr. put a black plastic bag over Mendell's head and again produced a knife. But this time there would be a twist.

"You do it," Frank Sr. said, handing the knife to his brother.

Nick would be the one to slit Mendell's neck open, as Frank Sr. continued to guide his brother's descent into Outfit life. Nick was slowly graduating into his brother's sinister world, and there was already no turning back. He took the knife, did as he was told, and held the knife out for his brother to take back.

The trunk was closed, and Jarrett went to the driver's seat to back the car out and get rid of it. The Calabrese brothers followed in another car, watching from behind as Jarrett drove to a spot on the South Side to leave Mendell's body for authorities to find in the trunk. The city's burglars would be getting yet another grisly message to respect the rulers of Chicago's underworld—or face the brutal consequences.

Jarrett parked Mendell's car as the Calabreses waited around a corner for Jarrett to walk up. It would be a month before the body would be found in the car in the 6300 block of South Campbell. Mendell's mouth was taped and his wrists were bound. His Adam's apple and vocal chords were gashed.

With the car parked, there was nothing to do but to drive back to Chinatown. To find Angelo LaPietra waiting in a restaurant and to report that the job was finished.

"Dirty shorts" is what Nick and his brother would call the killing of Mendell.

5

THIS IS NOT *THE SOPRANOS*

Joey Lombardo was pushed into the courtroom in a wheelchair, his mouth turned down in a scowl and his short hair pushed forward in a Caesar cut. He took a quick look around the room before rising with the help of a cane and then slowly lowering himself into a chair at the defense table near Rick Halprin.

The room Lombardo saw was completely full. There was a group of tables in the well of the ceremonial courtroom on the twenty-fifth floor of the Everett M. Dirksen U.S. Courthouse, one for each of the defendants. The men sat with their lawyers, chatting and occasionally looking at papers or glancing up to see who was in the crowded gallery. The rows of benches were divided into three sections, with a herd of Chicago reporters sitting closest to the jury box. A wide middle section had its first few rows set aside for leaders of the Chicago office of the FBI and the U.S. Attorney's Office, who sat in dark suits surveying the room, as well as for family members of the victims in the case. Dozens of the simply curious filled in the rows behind them, and those of a smaller third section. Courtroom sketch artists argued over the best angles for trying to capture the scene.

The prosecution table was closest to the judge and the jury. The ceremonial courtroom had a large dais that arched the length of the front of the room, with no space for a traditional witness stand. When witnesses testified, they would be seated fairly near the defense tables—and virtually at eye level with the defendants. There might be only ten yards between Nick Calabrese and his brother when he was finally called to testify.

Behind the witness box was a seat for the court reporter, and above her, seated near the end of the dais, was Judge Zagel, looking down upon the whole room. It was a commanding perch, granted even more authority by more than sixty black-and-white portraits of current and former federal judges ringing the room. The robed men and women stared down from the rich wooden walls, and at times it looked almost as if Zagel had stepped down from among them.

A nervous buzz melted away as all in the courtroom stood for the jury's entrance. The jurors, their names unknown, filed in one by one, walking under Zagel and turning to their right to fill in rows of padded chairs and arrange notebooks in their laps. They were welcomed, and the attorneys again introduced themselves after having selected them a few days earlier. Each defense team also introduced its client, and the defendants nodded toward the jury.

"Good morning," Joey chirped in his raspy voice after Halprin said his name. He and James Marcello were the farthest from the jury, with Paul Schiro and Anthony Doyle seated below the midpoint of the dais. Just in front of the middle of the gallery, and just behind the table where prosecutors Mitch Mars, John Scully, and Markus Funk sat with FBI and IRS case agents, was the table for Frank Calabrese Sr. and Joseph Lopez.

Soon, with all of the last-minute objections and motions addressed, and the introductions made, there was nothing left to do but begin. Scully rose from his chair and approached the podium carrying a black three-ring binder. The prosecution team knew it wanted Mars, who was quick on his feet, to do the closing rebuttal argument. Scully, with his experience and ability to handle heavy loads of facts, would do the opening statement.

As Scully began to speak, there was more than a hint of anger in his voice. He had labored for years to help bring this case, and much of the emotion attached to his life's work seemed to be welling up in him. There was a sense of indignation on behalf of an entire city.

There were five men on trial, he told the jury, including four who were Outfit killers of the most elite order, called upon to commit brutal crimes on behalf of the Chicago mob. He turned and walked away from the jury, and as he passed the defense tables, he called out each man's name, pointing at each one as he did so.

"The Outfit is a decades-old criminal organization," Scully said. "With the same structure, the same criminal activities, and a common language throughout those years."

Calabrese, Lombardo, Schiro, and Marcello were long-term members of that organization, he said, and Doyle was a corrupt cop who helped them.

But there was something Scully wanted to get out of the way for the jury right from the start. They should reject the popular, sanitized, and romanticized image of organized crime that Hollywood loved. Forget what you know about organized crime from TV, the prosecutor told the jury; they were going to hear about terrible deaths at the hands of vicious men.

"This is not *The Sopranos*; this is not *The Godfather*," Scully said. "This case is about real people and real victims."

His voice lowered, and there was tension on his face. Nothing about the Outfit is glamorous, he told the jury.

"It is corrupt. It is violent. It is without honor."

From there Scully addressed the crimes of the defendants, naming them and explaining to the jury what each had been accused of.

Frank Calabrese Sr. was a made member of the Outfit who had killed thirteen people on its behalf and had directed his brother Nick to help him. His son Frank Jr. and his brother helped him in his bookmaking and loan-sharking businesses and helped him collect tribute for the mob.

James Marcello was one of the Chicago syndicate's top bosses, Scully told the jury. He had killed three people, including the Spilotro brothers.

"He lured Michael and Anthony Spilotro to their deaths at a location where representatives of most of the Outfit crews were present, and beat them to death," Scully said.

Joseph Lombardo was an Outfit killer with decades in the organization who ran the Grand Avenue street crew, Scully told jurors next. Lombardo had been involved in the 1974 killing of federal witness

Daniel Seifert, a man who had become a threat to him. His finger-print had been found on a title certificate for one of the getaway cars used in the Seifert killing.

When the indictment came down, Lombardo had taken great steps to avoid responsibility, the prosecutor said.

"He ran on this case."

Paul Schiro was next. Scully told jurors he was another Outfit killer, and he was associated with the Spilotros and Lombardo. In addition to being involved in the overall conspiracy, he had taken part in the killing of his friend Emil Vaci in Phoenix. Like Seifert, Vaci was a threat to rat on the Outfit, having been called to tell a grand jury what he might know about the mob's efforts to steal from casinos.

And there was Anthony Doyle, Scully told the panel. He had once been a worker for Frank Sr., collecting on juice loans. Later he had become a Chicago police officer, a corrupt one who helped the Outfit get information from inside law enforcement.

There would be evidence on eighteen murders in all, and Scully moved next to introduce the jurors to the victims they would come to hear so much about. One at a time, on a large screen set up on the dais, the face of each victim appeared larger than life. Off the screen and out of Chicago history they stared. They were men who in different ways had become enemies of the Chicago Outfit, and they had been erased as a result. There was only one woman, Charlotte Dauber, who looked out over the courtroom with tousled hair and eyes wide open.

It was a stark presentation, using mugshot-type photos and plain text on a white background. Prosecutors had deliberately avoided fad-ing colors and slick PowerPoint graphics. This wasn't a corporate pre-sentation, and the jury didn't need arrows flying in from the left and right to be impressed by what they were being told. The information was dramatic enough in its very basic form.

Scully gave the jurors a quick description of each murder and who was accused of carrying it out. He began with Michael Albergo, the man buried at the construction site. Then Daniel Seifert, executed at close range in front of his family. Paul Haggerty, brought to the South

Lowe garage for "questioning" by mobsters. Henry Cosentino, stalked and killed and left in a trunk. John Mendell, strangled and stabbed in retaliation for the Accardo burglary. Vincent Moretti and Donald Renno, attacked by a gang of men while a jukebox played after they were lured to the scene of their murder. Charlotte and William Dauber, husband and wife, killed in their car. William Petrocelli, the braggart whose throat was cut. Michael Cagnoni, the businessman killed by a bomb that scattered parts of his body across a suburban tollway. Nicholas D'Andrea, a mobster suspected of participating in a failed hit on an Outfit boss that hadn't been approved by mob leaders. Richard Ortiz and Arthur Morawski, the men shot in a car outside the bar. Emil Vaci, hunted in Phoenix. Anthony and Michael Spilotro, brothers killed because Anthony's violent ways were disrupting Outfit business in Las Vegas, the Chicago mob's lucrative western outpost.

And finally, John Fecarotta. He appeared on the screen in a sport coat and striped tie, with emotionless eyes and no smile. It was a turf battle with Frank Sr. that did him in, Scully said, lured to his death by a man he trusted, Nick Calabrese. But the plan to kill him had gone awry, and Nick had left his gloves behind.

"The Chicago Outfit almost got away with this murder," Scully said.

The Outfit was "the charged business here," he said as his review continued. "It's in the business of making money."

The men on trial sat mostly still as Scully ran down their list of crimes and began explaining the Outfit's structure to jurors, who scribbled notes with blue pens as he spoke. Frank Sr. would occasionally smirk or lean to his left to whisper something to Lopez, who sat at the table in a suit with a bright pink shirt. Lombardo leaned back in his chair, staring toward Scully from behind his oversize, tinted glasses.

Scully explained the system of street crews to the jury and how proceeds of the mob's activities were passed up the chain of command, from soldiers to made members to bosses. To be "made" in Chicago required that the member was 100 percent Italian, Scully said, and had committed at least one murder. The making ceremony was one of the closest-held events in what Scully called the "secret organization hidden in the shadows." And becoming a made member allowed one to collect a greater share of proceeds from illicit gambling, juice loans, and street taxes.

After Scully promised jurors they would be getting an inside look at the organization, hearing from both Nick and Frank Calabrese Jr. as well as others who had been controlled by the organization over the years, the prosecutor was finished. The concise opening statement had lasted about fifty minutes, surprising some observers with its brevity. Scully and his team had wanted focus, choosing to eliminate a lot of extra detail as they had gone over and over what Scully would say. They had decided that a pared-down statement was better, simplifying things for the jury without overwhelming them on the first day. It would be hard enough for jurors to listen to weeks and months of evidence that lay ahead, but now the panelists knew the core of what the government was seeking to prove.

Prosecutors had told jurors the trial was deadly serious, but the idea that it wasn't going to be like some TV show had only a few seconds to sink in before Lopez stood up in his pink shirt and socks and did his best to pull it back in the direction of HBO.

The whole city would be watching, he declared. That didn't mean the case should be tried in the *Tribune* or the *Sun-Times*, he said, less than convincingly. Jurors would have to become "mini-judges," deciding what the facts would be.

"You'll be able to take note of my wardrobe," he said, smiling. "You might think I'm getting out of line with somebody, but I'm just doing my job."

Listen, jurors, to the little voice in your head telling you that the men on trial are innocent, he urged. The case was built only on finger-pointing, he said. It would be up to them, the jury members, to decide whether a witness simply saying that someone else had done something would be enough to convict.

"That's why that flag is there," Lopez said, raising a hand toward the Stars and Stripes over Zagel's shoulder. "That's why they kicked all that tea into Boston Harbor."

To find the men guilty—especially his client—the jury would have to believe that certain acts weren't done independently of whatever the supposed enterprise in the case was, Lopez told them. And to the extent that there was an organization or an enterprise, they should remember that Nick was a respected leader who was himself a boss. When Nick was in prison, Outfit crew members went to see him, not Frank Sr., Lopez argued.

Frank Sr. sat at his table nearby, stuffed into a powder-blue sport coat and leaning forward to catch everything Lopez was saying. He nodded slightly when Lopez promised the jury that what they had really walked into the middle of was a quality family feud.

Frank Jr.'s mother, Lopez continued, was his client's first wife, and Frank Sr. had since remarried. Jurors were looking at a man who loves his family, believes in God, and has medical issues, he said.

"You're gonna hear that he's not a rotten father, no matter what his son tells you," Lopez said. "Frank's not the killer. Nick is the killer."

Nick had been in the armed forces and knew how to handle a weapon. He had even once worked at Wrigley Field, the lawyer said, and had used a rifle with a silencer to shoot birds off the hand-operated scoreboard above the center-field bleachers. Whatever Frank Sr. had been a part of in his past, Lopez said, it had ended in the 1980s. Frank Sr. had stepped to the back of the theater, while his brother had stepped to the front.

And even when Frank Sr. had made street loans, he would negotiate with the customers who were late on payments, not beat them up or kill them, Lopez said, his voice going up and down in a bit of a nasally Chicago accent.

Anything Frank Jr. said about his father should be taken with a grain of salt. The son was addicted to cocaine and had stolen hundreds of thousands of dollars in cash from his father and jewelry from a neighbor. Frank Jr. had appeared in the bars and clubs on Rush Street in Chicago in years past, throwing his weight around like a wannabe thug, Lopez said mockingly,

"It was good for him then, and now he's saying his father was rotten," Lopez said as his client continued to lean forward to hear.

In fact, the entire case was a put-on by Frank Jr., Lopez went on. The son's plot was to get rid of his uncle and father so he could continue to take his father's money. He had stolen from any family member he could, Lopez said, even his own grandmother.

Frank Jr. had brought his grandmother to Arizona to buy a house, the lawyer said, and had sent her home penniless.

Listen to the tapes made by the son, Lopez told the jury; listen to Frank Jr. lead his father through the subjects that the FBI chose. Listen, too, when Nick testified; listen to a brother who hates his brother. There was no proof that Frank Sr. had killed anyone, he continued, and there were many people who might have wanted someone like the Daubers dead, for example. There were witnesses to the Ortiz and Morawski slaying, and they would tell of a killing with different facts than what Nick would testify about.

Now Lopez was rolling, jumping from subject to subject as many in the courtroom tried to follow him. Frank Sr. and his son weren't getting along because Frank Jr.'s wife drove a wedge between them; it wasn't the father driving apart the son and his wife. Nick also had accused his brother of destroying his first marriage, Lopez said. That wife was "a little kooky" anyway, the lawyer said.

"She sewed his zipper shut because she didn't trust him."

Even those seated at the prosecutors' table exchanged glances after that comment.

To see his points, Lopez urged jurors to look at pictures of Nick's second wedding. Such Outfit heavyweights as John "Johnny Apes" Monteleone were there, attending because Nick was a boss. Nick got permission from no one to do what he wanted to do, the lawyer continued, and when he got caught by physical evidence that pointed to him and him alone in the slaying of Fecarotta, he tried to save himself from life in prison by dragging others into his crimes.

In closing, Lopez asked jurors to think of the saying that went something like "The truth is somewhere between the clouds." And with that he turned to walk back to his table as the courtroom tried to absorb what he had said.

It had been a fairly unorthodox opening statement to say the least, but little about the case was average. Much of the personality of the lawyer and his client had come through, and Lopez had thrown a lot of pasta against the wall in the hope that some might stick.

Marc Martin had a tough act to follow, rising from his back table to speak for James Marcello. He certainly lacked the flash of a Joe Lopez, but he was going to continue his camp's strategy of working the evidence as in any tough murder case. He was going to attack what the government didn't have.

"Physical evidence, physical evidence, physical evidence," Martin said, telling jurors to remember those words if they heard him at all. "Where is the physical evidence with respect to James Marcello? Where is the corroboration? Where is the proof?"

There was no DNA pointing to Marcello's guilt in the Spilotro murders, and no hair or fibers, either.

The law says the government's evidence is to be tested at trial, Martin continued, and no one should be convicted based on innuendo. "Competent, believable, credible evidence." In fact, he said, waving a hand toward the large screen towering over the room, make the chart as big as you want.

"That is not going to hide the hole in this case," Martin said, raising his voice with the kind of classic Chicago accent that makes the city's name sound like "Chi-caw-go."

James Marcello had been in prison for the eleven years between 1992 and 2003, time he had done like a man, Martin said. Now he welcomed his trial day, "away from rumor and speculation," he said, in an obvious reference to Nick.

Even the FBI's wiretap on James while he was at Milan had given the FBI precious little beyond garbled noise, Martin contended. There was definitely no bragging from his client about murdering anyone. Almost anything could be extrapolated from the coded conversations.

But what jurors would hear for sure on the tapes was a man worried about an investigation.

"Of course he talks to his brother about that," Martin said. "He knows government informants will lie and put people in offenses they didn't commit."

And when it came to the alleged gambling business, it was Mickey Marcello running it, not James, Martin stated. The men were recorded talking about work that James had had no part of for years.

While Mickey was out talking to his men in the field, James was sitting in prison.

What was actually happening in the case was the Calabrese family was imploding, Martin said, and James Marcello was being caught up in it. Nick was testifying to save himself and grabbing anyone he could to try to improve his situation. James Marcello's only crime was being unlucky enough to find himself in the federal penitentiary at Pekin with a man who was about to be crushed by a murder case and eager to find any way to avoid death by lethal injection. Nick was just like any jailhouse informant, a man whose word shouldn't be trusted. There was no evidence that James had killed the Spilotros or Nicholas D'Andrea, Martin said, just the word of a desperate man.

"The government has made a deal with the devil," he told the jury.

After a weekend break Paul Wagner gave his statement, telling jurors that his client, Paul Schiro, was a seventy-year-old Chicago native who was friends with Anthony Spilotro. And it was through Spilotro that Schiro had met Joey Lombardo, the only man among his four codefendants with whom Schiro had ever been acquainted.

Schiro had moved from Chicago to Phoenix in the 1960s and had stayed there since. It was "vitally important" for jurors to consider the evidence against Schiro as an individual, said Wagner, a bearded and somewhat soft-spoken lawyer. His client didn't know most of the men charged in the case. There would be waves of evidence jurors would hear that had nothing to do with Schiro, who sat nearby in a green jacket as his attorney spoke, his expression giving away no hint of what emotions might be churning inside him.

Throughout the trial, Schiro kept the best poker face of all the defendants. As the others on trial with him reacted to testimony or were animated as they whispered to their lawyers, Schiro maintained an almost lizardlike calm. He could just as easily have been watching a boring movie on TV as an Outfit trial in which his own future was at stake.

Wagner told the jury that his client was accused in the Vaci murder, a charge that Schiro "vigorously denies." He had considered doing nothing to defend him, because he had nothing to prove. There would be no fingerprint or DNA tying Schiro to anything, the lawyer contended.

There were hours and hours of recorded conversations in the case "but not of Mr. Schiro," Wagner said. There would be no evidence that he was involved in collecting street tax, loan sharking, or running a video gambling business, some of the central allegations the government would use to argue that there was a conspiracy.

In the Vaci murder, law enforcement in Arizona had investigated Schiro years before and had declined to prosecute him.

"Now, twenty-one years later, the federal government has prosecuted Mr. Schiro," Wagner said. The primary reason for that, of course, was the cooperation of Nick Calabrese.

Nick was a confessed murderer and "stone-cold killer" the lawyer told the jury. Nick had been committing crimes for the mob for some thirty-five years. In addition to killing, he had collected on juice loans and on gambling debts and had been involved in dynamiting a trucking firm and a theater.

There would be nothing for jurors to use to connect Schiro to the Vaci killing but Nick's own words, and even then, Nick would tell the panel that he had pulled the trigger himself. It was Nick waiting for Vaci in the back of a van in Phoenix, and Nick who had fired a .22-caliber pistol twice before dumping Vaci into a canal. Schiro supposedly was in a lookout car nearby, monitoring a police scanner with Jimmy "Poker" DiForti. Watch Nick Calabrese, Wagner said, and consider the tremendous benefit he would receive in exchange for cooperating and bringing down whomever he could for the government.

Wagner spoke for just twenty minutes, underscoring his view that Schiro didn't really need to do much to get out of the way of the Family Secrets juggernaut. It was up to the government and Nick Calabrese to convince jurors that their version of events was true, and they would have little hard evidence to back up that view.

With Rick Halprin waiting to deliver his opening statement weeks down the road, that left Ralph Meczyk to make his statement for Anthony Doyle. Meczyk was a short, bespectacled man who was passionate about defending Doyle, even if he didn't always seem like he was in complete control. Much of his hesitation came from the fact that the judge in the case was giving him precious little traction. He had gotten on Zagel's bad side, and there seemed to be little he could do to recover the situation, despite a constant stream of apologies.

Meczyk did, however, score early points when he convinced the judge to allow him to bring a full-size street sweeper's cart into the courtroom for his opening statement. Doyle had worked for the city's Department of Streets and Sanitation when he was nineteen in the 1960s, a time when Nick Calabrese contended Doyle was really a juice collector. It was a demonstrative prop, the attorney argued, and Zagel eventually had said he would allow the jury to see it.

Meczyk strode toward the jury box at midmorning, mustering as much conviction as he could.

"You can call him 'Anthony,' or you can call him 'Twan,'" Meczyk said. "But what you will not be able to do is call him guilty."

What Doyle was, the lawyer told the jury, was a fiercely loyal friend to Frank Calabrese Sr., a *paisan*. He was the son of Italian immigrant parents who was raised in a small Bridgeport flat to become a decorated Chicago police officer.

Doyle had never knowingly helped a criminal, Meczyk promised jurors, and had never dishonored his oath to uphold the law.

"The only Outfit he was a member of was the Chicago Police Department," he said. Any allegation that Nick would make about him being muscle for his brother, Frank Sr., was false, Meczyk said.

Nick was the hardened criminal, the lawyer went on; in fact, he was a serial killer and a serial liar. He was a pitiful man trying to avoid spending the rest of his life in jail.

And with that, Meczyk retreated up an aisle of the courtroom to get the cart. It was yellow and boxy, with CITY OF CHICAGO BUREAU OF SANITATION printed on its side in black letters. Meczyk struggled with it for a moment, trying to get it pointed back toward the front of the room, bumping a row of seats as he moved.

"It's a good thing I'm a lawyer and not an usher in a theater," he said to no one in particular as he tried to push the cart ahead through a velour rope strung between two posts at the front of the courtroom.

Finally he got it going, and its metal wheels squeaked as the cart moved toward the jury box.

This is the kind of job Anthony Doyle had as a youth, Meczyk said. The cart would have held a shovel and a broom for the worker to use to sweep the streets of the city. Every block would have one, which would be tied to a lamppost when the day was through.

Doyle would humbly push his cart around, stopping now and again to fetch a stray piece of trash. Maybe even an empty juice carton.

"That's when he dealt in juice, ladies and gentlemen of the jury," Meczyk said.

In the Bridgeport neighborhood near Chinatown, organized crime was a way of life. The streets were mean, and nearly everyone knew someone who was part of the Italian mob. No one asked anyone what he did for a living, Meczyk said.

Anthony Passafiume lost his father to a robber's gun when he was eighteen months old. He grew up in the wrong crowd, going to kindergarten with the likes of Ronnie Jarrett, fighting his way to respect on the block and getting thrown out of schools. At Tilden High School he had become an athlete, earning wrestling accolades but failing to graduate. To earn a few extra bucks, he would sweep the local pool halls and card rooms, looking up to men he saw at the Italian social clubs. Among them was Frank Calabrese Sr., who was a little bit older than Passafiume, and had nice clothes and a car. The two would become friends, hustling and playing handball.

But while young Anthony was comfortable looking like a greaser on the street corner, he had a secret wish. He wanted more than anything to be a police officer, Meczyk told the jury. In the flat next door was the local Irish beat cop, Officer Doyle, who filled his young neighbor's head with stories of life behind the star. It was that officer whose name Anthony Passafiume had adopted as his own, becoming Anthony Doyle.

But the young Doyle didn't go from street tough to a job with the department overnight. His first legitimate work was a union job at the McCormick Place exposition center, which his friend, Frank Sr., was able to get for him, Meczyk said. He studied to pass a high school equivalency exam and went to talk to his local precinct captain about getting a good word with the right person to make his police dream a reality. It was the precinct captain who would get Doyle the work with the pushcart.

Still, he didn't give up, Meczyk said, achieving his goal of wearing the Chicago police uniform in 1980. Among his early duties was the mass transit detail, where he would work undercover, riding "L" trains and watching and waiting for muggers to move in on someone. He made hundreds of arrests, Meczyk said.

"Now they have the audacity to call it corrupt?" the lawyer said, raising his voice for effect.

Doyle wound up seeing Frank Sr. in prison at Milan only through a network of friends. One of his pals was a cousin of Aldo Piscitelli Jr., another mob figure also imprisoned there, Meczyk said. Piscitelli and Frank Sr. spoke often in prison, talking about the old days, and Doyle's name had come up. Word got back to Doyle that his friend from long ago would like to see him, Meczyk told jurors, and he was just happy that an old pal still remembered him.

Doyle would soon learn that Mike Ricci, a retired Chicago police detective who had become a Cook County sheriff's officer, also was heading to see Frank Sr., so the two made arrangements on a whim to travel together. Their visit would just be a reunion, Meczyk said. Doyle was working at the time in the police evidence and recovered property section, but he went to Milan only to gossip, not pass sensitive information.

Before the men made their way to Michigan, it was Ricci who had called Doyle and asked him to look up the status of evidence in the Fecarotta killing, Meczyk said. Doyle didn't even know why.

And when they finally sat down with Frank Sr., it was the mobster who slipped into the heavily coded language, leaving Doyle unable to keep up. Doyle didn't want to be rude, so he had just played along and feigned interest, his attorney told the jury. It was Ricci who did most of the talking, with Doyle only acting as if he knew what was happening. When it became clear that Ricci was delivering the information

Doyle had looked up, Doyle chimed in and told Frank Sr. the date that evidence was pulled.

"He figured it is innocent, worthless information," Meczyk said. And then Doyle had gotten up to get his friend a sandwich—chicken cordon bleu on a kaiser roll. Meczyk reasoned that if a grand jury would indict a ham sandwich, as the old saying goes, then in Doyle's case they might have indicted a man for giving someone a sandwich.

The lawyer's next move would leave some of his fellow defense attorneys cringing. Meczyk didn't have to defend his client from murder accusations, but the other defense attorneys did. All they could think about was the photos the jury was going to see of shot, slashed, tied-up, burned-up, and blown-up bodies of the victims in the case, and they weren't thrilled with Meczyk's emphatic wrap-up. Meczyk told jurors that, in the end, there should be only one thing they would want to do with the Family Secrets indictment when the trial was over. With that he stepped back over to his prop and tossed a copy of the thick document over the side. Jurors looked on as it landed with a loud "whump" in the bottom of the street sweeper's cart.

6

TESTIMONY AND TAPES

To begin building its case, the government would start with a bit of a history lesson. The first person called to the witness stand was the expert dubbed "the mobologist" by the defense lawyers, the president of the Chicago Crime Commission and a former FBI Outfit fighter named James Wagner.

Wagner walked purposefully to the witness stand in a dark, pin-striped suit. He had gray, swept-back hair, and wore a red tie, looking not unlike a politician who might have carefully selected his clothing for a big speech or a televised debate.

Wagner was sworn in, and Mitch Mars began his questioning. Was he aware of an organized crime family known as the Chicago Outfit?

"Yes, I am," Wagner said, telling jurors he had been with the FBI since June 1969. He had gotten his start at the bureau's Little Rock, Arkansas, office handling mostly general crimes, such as bank robberies. But he had also been involved in investigating the Ku Klux Klan and had gone undercover to go to a rally.

Before long he was off to New York, beginning his career investigating organized crime with an assignment to a unit that worked against the Genovese and Gambino families. Among his duties was working undercover at a racetrack to watch Mafia activity, and he sometimes was involved in the debriefing of confidential informants. There was a term used in the FBI, he said, the "top-echelon informant," a description of a provider of information who had a position in the upper hierarchy of organized crime. Wagner had interviewed "a dozen or so" of these rare turncoats and had used surveillance and other methods to learn how organized crime operated, both before and after he arrived at the FBI's Chicago office in 1976.

Mars continued to walk Wagner through his impressive credentials, and Wagner answered with the tone and manner of a college professor. He had in fact given lectures on subjects such as labor racketeering, both in the United States and in Europe, and after his FBI career ended, he had been a deputy administer of investigations for the Illinois Gaming Board.

Wagner's status as an expert established, it was time for the jury to hear one of those lectures. Wagner began with Prohibition in 1920s Chicago. The city was a morass of competing criminal gangs, representing virtually every racial and ethnic group that had arrived on the shores of Lake Michigan. They fought with the law and fought with each other, trying to establish themselves. It was chaos, but it would last for only so long. One event had brought unity, Wagner explained to the jurors, who were writing as fast as he was talking, seemingly realizing they might need this material as a reference later on.

"The entrance of a Mr. Capone brought a change in the way that was organized," Wagner told them. Under his harsh leadership rose a multifaceted but singular syndicate, the Chicago Outfit, a crime family that set up crews responsible for prostitution, gambling, and juice loans in different parts of the city. The crews passed a portion of their take back up the food chain, and mob leaders grew very wealthy. In turn, Wagner said, mob leaders used their vast sums of money to make it easier for the Outfit to operate, by corrupting politicians and law enforcement.

Had that organization survived and prospered until the present day? Mars asked.

"It certainly has," Wagner answered.

The Chicago crime family, still known as the Outfit, had continued under a system of one overall boss. Beneath him was an underboss, who handled some of the day-to-day disputes, and under him were the street crew capos, each responsible for their own crew of soldiers to do the mob's dirty work.

Wagner then outlined for the jury the Chicago street crews, describing how it would be the capos' job to keep individual soldiers in line, and the task of higher-ups to mediate arguments between crews. And there were a few specialized jobs, too, including being a driver for a boss. Such a spot often put the trusted member in line for a future promotion, since he was often around the leaders at meetings.

In addition to mob soldiers, there were mob associates, which could be a term applied to anyone who ran in certain circles and offered the Outfit assistance. And out of the teams of soldiers, the best could rise to become "made" members, a title given in a secret ceremony. It was most often a requirement that made members be of Italian heritage, that they had performed at least one murder, and that they had been recommended to bosses by other made members. The title earned the average solider more respect and a chance to receive a greater portion of what his crew earned. If a made member was imprisoned, his family was still expected to be paid his share in his absence.

The soldier had to swear absolute allegiance to gain this status, and it would never leave him, even if he wished it would.

"There are no provisions for getting out once you're in," Wagner said.

With Chicago's rackets firmly in its control, the Outfit had turned its attention to "open cities" such as Las Vegas, Phoenix, San Diego, and Miami, establishing outposts to bring money back to Chicago. The mob from Chicago would mediate disputes among local criminal rings, Wagner told the jury, and would typically leave one of its own members in place to represent Chicago.

Fueled by labor racketeering, the Las Vegas arm had grown especially prosperous, Wagner went on. The Outfit had infiltrated the unions decades earlier, he said, steering loans from Teamsters pension funds to individuals who were under its control. The large loans were used to construct the city's gleaming casinos, and the mob had little trouble skimming profits from them.

In Chicago the Outfit made millions in street tax, taking fees from bookmakers, chop shop owners, and others in illicit businesses in exchange for allowing them to operate, Wagner said as he continued his primer. At least one juror, a man who would become the jury foreman, had said during the selection process that he was a mob buff who had read books on the subject. Others, such as a young woman who said she was a secretary for a suburban church, seemed to need more help.

So Mars had Wagner go on to explain how juice loans worked, and how the Outfit would charge up to 10 percent a week in interest. It was a steep price to pay for fast cash, but the price of not paying what was owed was even higher. Customers knew the mob backed up its threats, he said.

"Ultimately their true collateral is their body, and they understood that," Wagner testified.

The first to cross-examine Wagner was Tom Breen, one of the attorneys for James Marcello. Breen had a very comfortable way in the courtroom, and he asked questions in almost a casual tone, trying to take on the role of an extra juror. Breen said he wanted to clear up a couple of terms. What was the difference between a *cooperating witness* and an *informant*?

Well, Wagner answered, an informant offers information and can become a cooperating witness once he is willing to testify in court about what he knows. Breen continued to elicit information clearly designed to make jurors think early and often about what kind of benefits a man such as Nick Calabrese might be getting for flipping.

Cooperating witnesses could be placed in the witness protection program and might get a reduction in their own sentence if they were responsible for crimes. All of it was negotiable with the government, Wagner admitted. There were many incentives for top-echelon informants to come forward and even to testify, the men agreed. Couldn't one of those reasons be to get even with someone else? Hadn't informants given false testimony on purpose? Breen asked.

Yes, they had, Wagner said.

Rick Halprin was next, also using Wagner to pave the way for points he wanted to make about Joey "the Clown" Lombardo.

Back to the term *associates*, couldn't those be any people, even those involved in otherwise legitimate businesses, who help the mob? That was correct, Wagner said again.

Wasn't Allen Dorfman, an insurance man who had been given control of the Teamsters Central States Pension Fund, a high-ranking associate? Wagner had been part of the Operation Pendorf case—short for "penetrate Dorfman"—and knew that Dorfman had an office below Teamsters official Roy Williams. Both men had been convicted in 1982 of trying to bribe U.S. senator Howard Cannon of Nevada.

How about bail bondsman Irwin Weiner, a businessman who orbited the mob for years—in the FBI's view, wasn't he an associate, too? Halprin asked, trying to lead Wagner and create a question in the jury's mind. Halprin wanted eventually to lump Lombardo in with such men, painting him as someone who had powerful allies in the Outfit but was not a member himself. But that would be enough for now.

Joseph Lopez was next, asking whether Wagner had spoken to either Nick or Frank Calabrese Jr. when he mentioned he had debriefed informants in the past. No was the answer; he had not spoken to either.

Well, what about this secret "making" ceremony? Jurors were supposedly going to hear about mobsters pledging lifelong membership while a holy card burned in their hand. Was it like the blood oath Huck Finn was supposed to take to get into Tom Sawyer's gang? Lopez asked with a slight smile.

"It's a little more serious than that," Wagner responded, returning a mild smirk.

Anyway, Outfit members would stick together, Lopez said he assumed. So when a crew leader got married, would other capos make it there?

"Normally they would," Wagner said, "depending on the influence of the person putting on the wedding."

And lots of alleged Outfit guys were involved in legitimate business, right? Lopez wanted to know. Maybe they invested in restaurants, bars, or car washes, he said. Maybe they were "actually working."

Some might even be paying taxes, Lopez said.

"I think several are paying taxes," Wagner answered.

Before Wagner's testimony was finished, Mars and Halprin would take turns probing the Dorfman issue. Mars asked whether it was true that organized crime was really giving the directions about what should be done with Teamsters money. In another case, Operation

Strawman, it was revealed that Teamsters funds were misused in schemes to build casinos and skim from them.

Right, but Dorfman had contacts at the highest levels, Halprin returned. Dorfman, the associate, knew what was expected of him. The defense lawyer was playing a card. Wagner was called only as an expert witness and had been instructed by the judge not to testify on what he knew about any of the individual defendants. He was only to inform the jury in generalities, but Halprin decided it was as good a time as any to front Lombardo's history while trying to make a point.

Regardless, Mars was about to act on the offer.

Who else was convicted in the attempt to bribe Cannon? the prosecutor wanted to know.

"It was Joseph Lombardo," Wagner answered firmly, so the jury could hear.

With Wagner finished, prosecutors called former IRS agent Robert Pinta to the stand, for the sole purpose of admitting into evidence what would become known as Government Exhibit 1. It was known more generally as the "Last Supper" photo and included ten mob figures seated or standing at a table. There are drinks and plates atop a red tablecloth, and a painting of a couple looking over a coastal terrace appears on the wall behind the men. Pinta had found the photo in a raid of a suburban home in 1980, noting that someone had written 1976 in pencil on the back of it. Tony "Big Tuna" Accardo was seated front and center, with his heir Joseph "Doves" Aiuppa near him. Standing in the back was underboss Jackie Cerone, and standing just to his left was a grinning Joey "the Clown" Lombardo in a gray suit and a silvery blue tie. The gathering had all the appearances of an Outfit summit, with all the members of the old guard and a few up-and-comers as well. It was the first of dozens of times that the jury would see the photo, so Halprin took the opportunity to try to show that his client really didn't belong.

Pinta agreed that nine of the ten men were dressed fairly casually, wearing open, collared shirts and slacks. Lombardo stood out.

"Mr. Lombardo is in fact wearing a three-piece suit, isn't that right?" Halprin asked.

To introduce jurors to the world of the Chicago Outfit, prosecutors looked far and wide for witnesses in their stable who had crossed paths with the mob and some of the men on trial. They would call to the witness stand bookies, gamblers, burglars, henchmen, hit men, juice collectors, safe crackers, and pornographers. It promised to be a parade of characters from the dark corners of the city's recent past, and leading that unseemly march was William "Red" Wemette, who went to get permission from the Outfit when he wanted to open an adult bookstore called the Peeping Tom near downtown on Wells Street in the early 1970s.

Wemette certainly looked the part of a mob-connected porn peddler. He waddled into court wearing a dated gray suit and a smarmy mustache. Relocated because of his help to the government, Wemette seemed more than a little uncomfortable, taking deep, audible breaths on the witness stand and staring around the courtroom through his large glasses. He didn't actually stop to fan himself, but stress rippled over him. In his world you tried not to do something like testify against Joey Lombardo, with him sitting at a table twenty feet away.

Did Wemette know what street tax was, and had he ever paid it?

"I was required to," he told Mars. "Basically it's permission to be in a business without being hurt by someone or possibly being burned down."

Wemette had run his store in the 1300 block of North Wells from 1974 until 1988 and had begun paying his street taxes to Lombardo, Wemette said. Over the years he had been a paid FBI informant, allowing agents to record some of his business dealings and providing information on crimes when he could.

At the beginning, when Wemette realized how lucrative opening a porn shop in Chicago could be, he had gone to a man he had worked for named Curt Hansen to ask about starting one. He had been a bit of a "go-fer" for Hansen, getting him coffee and feeding the horses he kept in the suburbs. If Wemette would do the work, Hansen, who was associated with mobster Jimmy "the Bomber" Catura, would find the money.

But Catura was more of a South Side guy. The Wells Street location was outside his territory, up on the North Side, closer to Grand Avenue.

"The instructions were, 'Go and see Joey; he's a good boy,'" Wemette said. "'He'll take care of you.'"

Wemette knew Lombardo by his other nicknames, "Lumpy" or "Lumbo." He and Kurt met Lombardo at a restaurant to discuss their arrangement, with Lombardo choosing to say nothing directly to Wemette. The front of the store would sell merchandise, and the back of the store, the more profitable half, would feature peep shows, where men could drop a quarter into a slot for a few minutes of entertainment. The back of the store would be split *menza-menza*, Lombardo had said, using slang for 50-50.

It was a steep cut of the business, but Wemette knew it was the proverbial offer he couldn't refuse. Lombardo was a powerful man, and there would be consequences for not paying him what he wanted. Wemette wasn't looking to have an "accident," he said.

"It was expected if you didn't, you might have a problem," Wemette told the jury as Lombardo looked on nearby.

Because the store was under construction, two men had come by to have a look around. They were Marshall Caifano, a member of Joey's crew, and one of the crew's worker bees, Alva Johnson Rodgers, a lanky Texan who was Caifano's right-hand man.

"They walked around like they owned the place," Wemette said. "I was told not to give them any problems."

The business opened its doors after Labor Day in 1974, he said, and he began paying between $250 and $500 a week in street tax. Rodgers would come and pick up an envelope filled with cash.

And things went smoothly for about five years, with other representatives of the Grand Avenue crew coming around to collect. But around 1979, there was another knock on the door, and Wemette had a curious invitation from a man he knew as "Pete the Greek" to "join the neighborhood association." Wemette knew what that really meant, but he was already paying street tax. He believed it was the Rush Street crew trying to horn in on the Grand Avenue crew's action and his business. So he reached out for Frank "the German" Schweihs, Lombardo's muscle. He was a fearsome hit man who even other mobsters wanted absolutely nothing to do with. If you saw him coming for you, there would be no talking your way out of it.

By the late 1980s, Wemette had decided to become an FBI asset. He was tired of the business and needed a way out, so the feds wired up his apartment and watched as Schweihs came around on Lombardo's behalf to talk about turf disputes and other issues surrounding the porn shop.

By the way, Mars interrupted, did Wemette see Lombardo in court that day?

"He just stood up," Wemette said, putting a hand to his chin as Joey got to his feet at the table near Halprin.

Then Mars showed Wemette a mug shot of Joey from thirty years before, where the playful mobster was staring up, off the frame of the image and out into space.

"He looked a lot better then than he does now," Wemette said, drawing a chuckle from the courtroom gallery.

Jurors next saw and heard for themselves what it was like to do business with the Chicago mob, watching on a screen as prosecutors played grainy recordings from a hidden video camera that had been placed in Wemette's dingy apartment. Schweihs could be made out walking around in some of them dressed in a casual shirt and ball cap and in others sitting on a couch.

By the fall of 1987, it was Schweihs who would be collecting from the shop, letting Wemette know in no uncertain terms that he was not to pay anyone else. His last Outfit contact was to be ignored from then on because he was "gonna open up a hot-dog stand in Alaska." Jurors watched as Schweihs paid a visit to the apartment, barking orders at his obviously intimidated host. Had the man Schweihs was replacing called that month?

No, Wemette answered as the video camera picked up the conversation.

"And he ain't gonna never call you again, and if [he] does, should ever call ya, say look it, don't call me; I made other arrangements," Schweihs snarled. "That's all you tell the motherfucker, OK, Red? Nothing else."

"When's the last time . . ." Wemette started to say.

"He is not to fucking come here," Schweihs interrupted.

The enforcer was firm about his having control.

"I don't give a fuck who comes here and talks to you," Schweihs repeated. "Don't get smart, just say, 'Listen, I'll get back to ya. I'm spoken for.' That goes for any motherfucker on this street, anywhere in this city. OK."

Schweihs would need to straighten out the mess his predecessor had left, skipping collections and leaving the books confused. Wemette's business had reached a point where he was paying around $1,100 a month in street tax.

The men could be seen counting out hundreds, until Wemette had made sure there were twenty-two of them.

"So, what I'm getting off you now cleans you up for the month of September and the month of October," Schweihs told Wemette. "You are not due now until November."

November was only a few days away, but don't worry, Schweihs said, he wouldn't be coming around until sometime around the middle of the month. Fine, Wemette said; it would almost be better if there weren't a set pattern. He had never liked the schedule in his prior situation.

"OK, anyway, fuck him; he's history," Schweihs answered.

The two went back and forth about other shops in the area and who was behind them. Schweihs wanted to know whether Wemette was having any trouble with the guy who owned a business next door. The man had bothered Wemette previously in some dispute, but Schweihs had stamped out that trouble.

There hadn't been any problems since, Wemette assured his guest.

"OK, then I don't have to make a believer out of him, that we're for real," Schweihs said.

So Schweihs continued to appear for his collections, with the FBI taping and gathering evidence in an effort to build an extortion case against him. The enforcer eventually was convicted in 1989 of shaking down the business, based on Wemette's efforts. But in the spring of 1988, agents were looking to strengthen their material even more. They had Wemette tell Schweihs that a rival had been coming around, someone who may or may not have been sent by Rush Street gangster Mike Glitta.

Wemette told Schweihs that he had felt threatened. The made-up story was that a man they didn't know had come into the shop demanding to know who Wemette did business with. Schweihs asked whether it could have been an undercover cop, but Wemette told him he didn't think so.

The feds wanted to see how Schweihs would react, and needless to say, he blew his stack.

It was none of the mystery man's business who Wemette was in business with, Schweihs said, and when was this guy supposedly coming back anyway? If he did return, he'd be getting something he wasn't looking for.

Wemette should simply say that it wasn't his business to know who Wemette was associated with, and he could take that information wherever he wanted. That might flush out who was really behind sending him. If the visitor had been a cop, that was the end of it, and if he was "a wiseguy," he would have to go back and tell a boss, and that would flush out who was behind it.

Mike Glitta and Rush Street were supposed to know that the business was spoken for, Schweihs could be heard to say as he began to steam. Wemette said he thought Glitta had been told by Lombardo that his business was off-limits.

Right, Glitta was supposed to know better, Schweihs said.

"And I don't think he would be that stupid to try and step on my fuckin' prick, or the people I'm affiliated with. Do you understand?" he continued. "So this jagoff that come here has to be some fuckin' half-ass wiseguy that's just going around trying to arm joints."

If it were Glitta behind the visit, it would be a serious problem. Well, Wemette said, maybe it could be someone that supplied his store?

"Why sure, they'd get their ass knocked off, Red," Schweihs answered. "They know that. Chicago's got the worst reputation in the

United States. Them fuckin' New Yorkers don't want to come here and fuck around. They know better."

But Schweihs wasn't finished. If the unknown visitor returned, remember the plan: just say it was none of his business who was behind the shop, and that would be that.

No one would win a battle with the Grand Avenue crew.

"There is no one has the right to come in and fuck in our domain," Schweihs declared to the furiously agreeing Wemette.

"If it's Al Capone's brother and he comes back reincarnated, OK? This is a declared fuckin' joint."

Lombardo had gone to prison for the casino skim, but that changed nothing on the streets of Chicago. Wemette's business was Grand Avenue's forever. Glitta should know that.

"Mike never liked me here," Wemette said, stoking the fire perfectly and nearly sending Schweihs into a full rage. If it did turn out to be Glitta, Schweihs promised to go straight to his boss and do what had to be done.

"He ain't going no-fuckin'-where!" Schweihs shouted. "I hope the fuck he did send the guy here. What do you think of that?"

Wemette watched the spectacle of Schweihs exploding in front of him. He laughed nervously.

"I'm gonna be looking at the obituaries," he chuckled.

"Let's just say it's an act of God, whatever happens to him," Schweihs said.

Most of the jurors in Zagel's courtroom had stopped taking notes early on in the videotaped tirade, choosing instead to watch it unfold and give one another a few amazed looks. Others in the courtroom had traded glances and nods, too, impressed with the blazing avalanche of expletives and threats shooting from the video.

Wemette sat on the witness stand in his gray suit. So, Mars asked, had he ever considered not paying up under those conditions?

Um, no.

"Something would've happened to me," he answered. "I feared death."

On cross-examination, Halprin tried to take a swipe at Wemette and federal agents by asking about another time the dirty bookstore owner had been a witness. He had lived off and on with Curt Hansen and his brother, Kenneth. He had spent a lot of time with Kenneth, who eventually confessed to him that he had assaulted and killed young brothers John and Anton Schuessler and their friend Robert Peterson. It was a 1955 triple murder that had rocked Chicago to its core, and it had gone unsolved for decades. The boys' naked bodies had been found discarded in a forest preserve, and many credited the homicide with peeling away whatever innocence Chicago might still have had at that point in its history.

Halprin said he understood that Wemette had the information on Hansen and the Schuessler-Peterson killings as long ago as 1968; was that true? The government objected repeatedly.

Didn't you testify against Hansen at the Criminal Courts Building at Twenty-Sixth and California almost thirty years later? Wemette moved his hands in front of him, almost as if he didn't understand.

"Don't bother waving your hands around; just listen to the question," Halprin demanded.

Was it not accurate that he had told law enforcement about the confession for the first time in 1993, Halprin asked, protecting a child killer?

Actually, Wemette finally answered, he had told an FBI agent about what Hansen had told him back in 1971.

Now Halprin turned the revelation on its head. Maybe it was the FBI suppressing information to preserve its precious informant that was helping to bust the Outfit.

He had told an agent that Ken Hansen had told him that he had killed the boys, Wemette said again, "and some other information."

Halprin pressed on. Hadn't Wemette previously been asked in state court why he had waited until 1993 to come forward?

"My answer was, the people I did speak to about it were really not interested in what I had to say," he answered.

So, Halprin continued, the FBI hadn't done anything about it? Judge Zagel had had enough, sustaining objections by prosecutors no matter how the defense lawyer phrased the question. Halprin was out of string.

But when it came to "the Peeping Tom," could what Wemette kept referring to as "street tax" really have just been a business arrangement not with Lombardo but with Alva Johnson Rodgers? Wemette had previously signed statements that said Rodgers was to supply the peep shows with projectors.

And Wemette had never received any money directly from Lombardo, nor given him any. Wasn't that right, the lawyer asked? Rodgers didn't look anything like that guy, Halprin said, pointing over at his client, who leaned back in his chair with his head cocked, his mouth still turned downward.

The opening stretch of the trial was becoming "Lombardo week," as Halprin would come to call it, with the government concentrating the early presentation of evidence on the wisecracking mobster.

And it would continue as prosecutors called to the witness stand another former FBI man, Art Pfizenmayer, who had been part of the investigations into the Chicago Outfit's expansions into Las Vegas. The bureau had run surveillance around Allen Dorfman and in the late 1970s was intercepting phone calls at his Chicago-area office. On April 4, 1979, he watched once after Dorfman was summoned to a restaurant meeting with Outfit leaders, picking up the location from a phone call. Dorfman was to report to an eatery on North Avenue in Northlake called the Golden Horns. Pfizenmayer went to the location, parked, and noticed that another car was arriving, with Joey Lombardo at the wheel as the driver for boss Joseph "Doves" Aiuppa, the leader of the Outfit.

Pfizenmayer wanted to act naturally, so he got out of his car, took off his coat, and made his way toward the restaurant's door. Aiuppa and Lombardo were now heading that way, too, and by coincidence the undercover agent and the mobsters hit the door at the same instant.

"I just motioned with my hand that they could go ahead of me," Pfizenmayer told the jury.

A manager came over to help Aiuppa as the men entered. Dorfman was already inside, the agent said; he had his coat folded over his shoulder and was staring at the floor.

The agent took a spot at the bar, trying not to look like he could be listening in as the three men sat in a booth about twenty-five feet away. Dorfman was in the middle, Pfizenmayer said, with Aiuppa on his left and Lombardo on his right. The animated Aiuppa was doing most of the talking, at times jabbing his finger into the table to make his points. Dorfman seemed to be trying his best to answer questions.

"Dorfman kind of sat there with his hands in his lap," Pfizenmayer said. The conversation lasted about 90 minutes, before Dorfman left first.

The FBI was picking up Lombardo everywhere, catching a phone conversation a week later between "the Clown" and Grand Avenue crew member Louis "the Mooch" Eboli.

"OK, do we know a massage parlor on 83 and Touhy?" Lombardo could be heard to ask as prosecutors began playing the tape for the jury.

Eboli didn't know the name but didn't think the crew had anything to do with it.

"We don't, no, but them other guys might have it, Joe, something," he said. There was another club up that way, but it was "Joe Nick's," Eboli said, using a nickname for Joe Ferriola.

Well, there was now another club virtually next door, the men discussed, a business that apparently had opened without getting clearance from anyone. Ferriola was complaining and wanting to know if it was backed by Grand Avenue.

It wasn't, and Lombardo told Eboli that the place would have to close.

"Because, if he don't close up, he'll get fucking flattened," Lombardo said. "We'll flatten the joint."

Someone named Frank Orlando allegedly had given the operators the OK to open, but that wasn't good enough, Lombardo said. No one in authority had said the other parlor could open and now it was in conflict with an Outfit property.

Eboli was concerned because he had juke boxes and games in the business. Well, too bad, Lombardo repeated.

"You better take them out," he warned. "Because they're going to flatten the fucking joint . . . if they don't move."

It was a month later that agents again were listening as Lombardo took care of his business. The FBI had bugged Dorfman's offices, and Lombardo was there discussing a St. Louis mob lawyer, Morris Shenker, who Dorfman and the mob thought owed money for a Teamsters loan that was financing Las Vegas projects for Shenker.

Dorfman brought Lombardo in to help get his point across to the attorney, who was withholding the kickback. Shenker had made promises but had not delivered. The men would be meeting with Shenker later that day and were discussing how to approach him.

"You see, my statement to him today is going to be, listen, Morris, where is my 25 percent of the holdings that Hoffa and I are supposed to have?" Dorfman said, mentioning Teamsters Union president Jimmy Hoffa, who had given Dorfman the purse strings to the Central States Pension Fund.

Dorfman said he had been expecting 25 percent cuts in various projects, including the Dunes Hotel, of which Shenker was part owner.

"I says, all I know is we ain't got a fucking thing," Dorfman told Lombardo. "That's all I'm going to say to him. Now where the fuck we goin'?"

From one development alone, the men decided, Dorfman and the Outfit might be owed some $2.5 million. The total might have been well over ten times that. It was money the men wanted right away, Lombardo decided, and he would be making the demands. Shenker might panic and go for help to his contacts in St. Louis, but he would find them telling him the matter was out of their hands. Shenker was going to get a threat, Lombardo told Dorfman. If the mob couldn't spend that money, then Shenker wasn't going to get to either. Shenker would be given thirty days to come up with a payment plan, or else.

Shenker could even go to the FBI with it, Lombardo said, but it wouldn't matter because he had an army behind him. The mob didn't want trouble; it just wanted its due, and Lombardo, the Outfit's liaison to the Teamsters, was going to get it.

Before long Shenker arrived, and Lombardo went to work.

"Morris, the reason why I'm here—you don't know who I am," he began. "My name is Joey."

Shenker said he assumed Lombardo was all right because he was with Allen. That's right, Lombardo replied.

"Allen belongs to Chicago," he said. "Now you know what I mean when he belongs to Chicago? I was sent here to find out what the story is. When they talk to Allen, he says he don't get this, he don't get this, he got this, he got this coming."

Everybody belongs to somebody, Lombardo reminded the lawyer, including him. What Dorfman had coming, Chicago had coming.

Shenker began to try to explain the structure of one of the deals in question, offering that some of the money put into certain projects might not have been connected like Lombardo thought. Shenker had done much of his business with Hoffa, whom he had once represented, he said. That was all well and good, Lombardo said, but Dorfman had a number he believed he was owed, and that meant Shenker was on the hook for it.

Shenker had some decisions to make.

"You say you're seventy-two, and you defy it; all you can do is send a guy like me to jail—one guy," Lombardo said, as Shenker promised he wasn't going to send anyone to jail.

"But you ain't gonna send the system to jail," Lombardo said, beginning to raise his voice. "I'm just tellin' ya, if they come back and tell me to give you a message and if you want to defy it, I assure you that you will never reach seventy-three."

The mob had nothing coming from him, Shenker said. But Lombardo made it plainer: Dorfman did have something coming from Shenker, and the mob had a piece of Dorfman.

"If Allen can't get it, they'll reach out and get it for him," Lombardo continued. "Allen's not that type of guy, but the people that got a piece of him are that type of guy. Allen is meek and Allen is harmless. But the people behind him are not meek and harmless. Do you know what I mean?"

"This is a robbery"

Daniel Seifert was already afraid for his life when the masked gunmen finally came for him on September 27, 1974.

He had been telling family members that he planned to testify against his former friend, Joey "the Clown" Lombardo, at an imminent pension fraud trial. He'd had a falling out with Lombardo, and he was going to tell a jury what he knew about a scheme to steal funds from the Central States Pension Fund of the Teamsters. He had armed himself, strategically placing guns at his home and workplace, and he was looking over his shoulder.

Also a defendant in the case was Irwin Weiner, the mob-connected bail bondsman. He had negotiated a $1.4 million loan from the fund through his friend Allen Dorfman. Seifert had been friends with Weiner, too, having done carpentry work for him, and Weiner had put up money for Seifert's start-up business, International Fiberglass in Elk Grove Village, northwest of the city.

Investigators had traced part of the bad loan to the business, when the money was originally to have gone to another firm, ostensibly for the manufacture of work pails. Seifert's company supposedly was contracted to produce four molds for those pails, but they didn't seem to exist. Federal agents had followed the money and had found checks written from International Fiberglass to Lombardo, where the reputed capo worked, at least on paper. The feds believed they had discovered a case of the mob laundering funds it had extracted from the pension fund, and the discovery of checks being written from International Fiberglass to Lombardo seemingly closed the loop for them.

Federal authorities were confident that with Seifert's testimony, they could get convictions. He was the only witness to the transactions involving Lombardo, so his cooperation would be essential.

Seifert, then twenty-nine, hadn't led a perfect life, but he was ready to put his peripheral association with the Chicago Outfit behind him. He had tried to break off contact with Lombardo, and he had a new business in Bensenville, Plastic-Matics Products, running out of fifteen hundred square feet in a small suburban office park. A number of businesses rented space there in a group of buildings ringing a parking lot, with two driveways leading to Foster Avenue. Seifert and his wife, Emma, did most of the work there, with Emma running the office and helping with manufacturing.

The couple arrived early that Friday, with their four-year-old son in tow. They had left their house and pulled up in front of the glass door to their business before 8:30 A.M.

There was a single concrete step up to the doorway, cut out of the brick front wall. Inside was a small entryway, with another entry to the business's office, which had a kitchen area. Through a second door at the back of the office was a space for storage and the shop where the manufacturing took place.

The Seiferts unlocked the door and went into the office area, with Daniel bringing in an armload of toys for his son to play with. His son, Joseph, had been named for Lombardo.

Emma Seifert began to make coffee in the small kitchen as Daniel walked back out through the entryway and to the family car to get a vacuum cleaner he wanted to bring in. It was at that moment that Emma was startled by two men with rifles bursting through the other office door, the one that led to the shop.

"This is a robbery," one of the men lied.

The men must have entered through the business's back door and laid in wait. They wore ski masks and demanded Emma's husband.

Unaware of what was happening inside, Daniel started to make his way back into the business when he was met by one of the men in the entryway. The man struck him with the gun, knocking him to the ground. There was a gunshot.

Somehow, Daniel made it back to his feet, and he was running. He bolted away from the front door and across the blacktop parking lot. He went as fast as he could go, trying to get to the building opposite his own.

But waiting for him there was another member of the hit team, a stocky man in a ski mask, carrying another rifle. His job apparently was to cut off any possible escape, the exact scenario that was now unfolding.

Seifert made it across the lot, went around the corner of the building, and began to run across a stretch of mowed grass. His pursuer, though, was too close.

There was another shot, and a round struck Seifert in the knee as he ran. He grabbed at it but went down in a heap.

In the grass now too was the gunman. He came up to where the bleeding Seifert was crumpled and stood over him. The brief chase was over. The man pointed his shotgun straight at Seifert's head, the muzzle of the gun hovering just behind Seifert's left ear as he lay there. The gunman fired, killing his victim instantly and sending a spent shell flitting through the air.

Their cold mission accomplished, the murder team piled into a pair of getaway cars, forgetting to pick up a pair of handcuffs that one of them had dropped near the door of the business. The first car was a brown Ford LTD, and the second was a blue Dodge Challenger, turning out onto Foster and rocketing away toward Illinois Route 83 to head south for Elmhurst.

The cars made it to a Pontiac dealership in that western suburb not far from Route 83, where the men removed a few things from the LTD, left it, and took off again in the Challenger. A police alert had been issued for a shooting in Bensenville, along with a description of the vehicles.

Happening by was a police trainee at the wheel of an Elmhurst squad car, with a senior officer in the passenger's seat. They had watched as the car switch was made, and they started a pursuit.

The Challenger turned right and began weaving through commuter traffic on Grand Avenue, even bumping cars out of its way, then accelerating and putting some distance between the men and the Elmhurst cruiser.

The trainee made it where the Challenger had turned south onto York Road, but the driver of the muscle car ahead of him had put his foot all the way to the floor. It was vanishing as the Elmhurst squad's siren blared futilely. The officers sped up, but the Challenger ducked into a residential area, accelerating again as it raced toward a Lake Street frontage road and the Cook County line. A few moments later it was lost, disappearing for good as it arrived in Northlake.

Back at the dealership, investigators would begin to have a look at the 1973 brown Ford the hit men had abandoned.

It was a true mob work car, outfitted with heavy shocks and a police scanner, and its motor had been boosted to allow for greater air intake. On the dashboard were extra black boxes, with switches that could allow for the car's tail and brake lights to be disabled. The car could move with stealth in the dark. Its rear license plate was held in a bracket on a hinge that could tilt the frame forward, letting someone switch out the plate for another in a hurry if necessary. It even had a siren and a red emergency light, which could be placed on top of the dash to make it look like an unmarked police car.

Investigators found the masks apparently worn by the shooters and were able to save a few strands of hair from them, but they dusted surfaces all over the car for fingerprints and came up empty.

7

ALVA AND EMMA

William "Red" Wemette would be a tough act to follow, but Alva Johnson Rodgers would be up to the task.

If the Family Secrets trial had been a movie, Rodgers would have been played by David Carradine. He loped to the front of the courtroom to be sworn in, a career criminal with a Texas twang, a drawn face, and hollow eyes. As he swore he'd tell the truth, he raised his left hand, quickly catching that error and holding up his right.

Rodgers settled in on the witness stand in a dark suit, peach shirt, and gray tie and proudly announced that he had been born in Eldorado and had spent twenty-five of his seventy-eight years on earth in prison.

John Scully calmly led him through his record, a veritable national road show of crime that would take some time to get straight.

There were three car thefts as a juvenile in Arkansas, federal auto theft cases in California and Arizona, and an escape in Arkansas, a burglary in Texas, and a bank robbery in New Jersey. "Armed with a pistol," Rodgers interjected.

There was the counterfeiting case in New Orleans and, of course, the possession of the stolen stock certificates in Florida. He'd also been part of a plan to bring "a boatload" of marijuana up from South America, though he hadn't been prosecuted for that one.

Rodgers wasn't exactly a tough mark for prosecutors. "I always pled guilty to everything I got charged with," he said, telling the court he'd been in witness protection twice.

Scully asked whether Rodgers realized he'd be testifying with a grant of immunity, meaning he had to be truthful and the only thing he could be charged with as a result of his testimony was perjury. Right, the gray-haired Rodgers said, having to lean toward Scully slightly to hear what he was asking.

"I have a recent letter to that effect, yes."

So it was back to the beginning. How had Rodgers come to Chicago in the 1970s?

He had been in federal prison in Atlanta, where he had an unusual cellmate. It was Marshall Caifano. The men would work prison jobs together and play handball in the yard, Rodgers told the jury.

Rodgers was a bit of a jailhouse lawyer, so he did some research in the law library and pointed out there might be a flaw in the way Caifano had been sentenced. It turned out he was right.

"The appellate court agreed with us and turned him loose," Rodgers said.

Not one to forget a favor, Caifano, when on the outside, paid for a lawyer, who was able to spring Rodgers, too, and then invited him to come up to Chicago. Rodgers did, and soon found himself employed by Caifano and his friends, including Joey "the Clown" Lombardo.

Scully asked him to pick Lombardo out in court that day, and Lombardo obliged by getting to his feet again. "Yeah, I see him," Rodgers said.

Lombardo sat back down but leaned forward with a hand on his chin as if he was growing more interested in where this was going.

Rodgers said he spent more than four years in Chicago, hanging out with Caifano almost constantly. The Outfit put him up in an apartment that was normally set aside for visiting members of the Teamsters, he told jurors, until he settled into a more permanent place above the garage of the father-in-law of Vincent "Jimmy" Cozzo, a member of the Grand Avenue crew. How much did he have to pay for it?

"Nothin'," he said.

As Rodgers adjusted to life in Chicago, Caifano showed him around the territory his income was derived from, Rodgers said. It was centered on Grand Avenue, running east to around Rush Street.

Caifano would occasionally meet with Lombardo, he added, just to catch up with what was going on. Some of the meetings were at Rose's Sandwich Shop on Grand, the same location where Richard Cain would be killed in December 1973, a killing some attribute to Lombardo. Cain had been a chief in the Cook County sheriff's police and a driver for mob boss Sam "Momo" Giancana.

Early in Rodgers's time in Chicago, both Caifano and Lombardo were up for a promotion when capo Sam Battaglia, the crew street boss, died, and Lombardo was tapped for it.

"Everyone behind his back called him 'Lumpy,'" Rodgers said, adding that he sometimes drove Lombardo around.

The mobster liked to keep a police scanner in his car, and at one point Rodgers and Lombardo realized they were listening to radio traffic about their own police tail. The pair could hear officers talking about where they were driving as they moved around.

"Apparently they considered him to be "the Clown" and me "the Rabbit," Rodgers said. "We were laughing about it."

Around the start of 1974 there was a proposal for Rodgers involving pornography, Rodgers stated. He and Caifano would be allowed to take over some of the city's smut trade, Lombardo had told them. Rodgers could do what he wanted, he said Lombardo had decreed, but should stay away from an adult bookstore owner named Robert Harder.

"I've got a crew on him," Rodgers said Lombardo had told him. "And if we get a chance, we're gonna take him down."

Harder was in fact killed a few weeks later, and Rodgers began to get set up to go into business. He got a bank account, he said, and the Outfit gave him some starting capital.

Over at the defense table, Lombardo continued to look on, with a curious look on his face and his head tilted to the side.

Rodgers said he started to invest in peep show equipment and built a handful of projector booths. Drop in a quarter and the booth would show thirty seconds or so of a porno movie, he said. Rodgers even managed to have a couple of employees. There was some guy named "Cowboy Mirra" and another one called "the Greek."

"I don't even know his name," Rodgers said. "I never called him anything but 'the Greek.'"

That worker lasted only as long as it took for him to make his first theft attempt, Rodgers recalled.

Lombardo showed up a couple of times, including with Anthony Pellicano, who would become a celebrated Hollywood private investigator and who would be caught up in a high-profile wiretapping case. Rodgers told Lombardo he had gotten a lease for a storefront where he could set up the peep show booths.

Lombardo thought that was fine, until he learned that the spot was just a few blocks from a Catholic church. That would mean a change of plans, Lombardo said, telling Rodgers there was a store being set up on Wells Street that could be a replacement. It was Red Wemette's new place.

The agreement was Rodgers's booths would go in the back of "the Peeping Tom," with Rodgers getting $500 a week from them and Caifano getting another $500.

"It was in quarters," Rodgers said, and there came a point where he didn't think he could scratch out a living on it anymore. Maybe there was a way to maximize his position.

So Rodgers said he plotted to take over the wholesale pornography business in Chicago by burning down a giant warehouse owned by a company called Capital News. There was more than $2 million in merchandise in that warehouse, and it was obvious that was where the real money was. But the plan never came off.

Eventually, Outfit leaders placed Rodgers under Pellicano, which didn't make Rodgers particularly happy. The henchman even threatened to skip out of town and head back to Florida, though he testified that he did wind up doing a few jobs for his new mob contact. Pellicano, who has always denied Outfit connections, paid him $5,000 to blow up a house in Chicago's northwest suburbs, but he managed to severely burn an arm, a hand, and a leg in the process, sprinting across a golf course to get away.

That pretty much signaled the twilight of Rodgers's less-than-top-shelf organized crime career in Chicago, since Lombardo was mad about the house job and Caifano had changed into someone he didn't recognize as his old friend. Rodgers said that before he left town for good, he was selected to go out west to a few film companies and encourage them to "join the association."

But before Scully finished questioning him, Rodgers said he did recall one conversation he overheard between Lombardo and Caifano. It was at a golf driving range, not long after Daniel Seifert had been gunned down. The two Outfit men were laughing about it, Rodgers said.

"Joey said, 'That son of a bitch won't testify against anybody now, will he,'" Rodgers told the jury.

When he got his chance, Halprin couldn't wait to get up to lay into the guy. He waved back to Lombardo to make sure Joey could hear and then asked if he could begin.

Sure, Rodgers said.

"I'm asking the judge," Halprin said. "I'm glad it's OK with you."

The lawyer asked if it was only Caifano and Lombardo talking when Rodgers supposedly heard the Seifert remark. That was the case, Rodgers answered. And Halprin asked about Rodgers's decision not to pay taxes during one fifteen-year stretch, and some of the legitimate jobs he had held. Those included laying brick and being a mechanic, Rodgers said, continuing to lean forward over the witness stand.

"I know I'm not the government, so maybe you should lean back," Halprin said mockingly.

Hadn't Rodgers had a pretty unimpressive record, even for a career criminal? He had spent decades in prison for a bunch of relatively minor offenses, Halprin said, right?

"You were just a bust-out loser?" Halprin asked, adding that he didn't mean to be insulting.

"I did eleven years in prison for that bank robbery," Rodgers answered, his feathers ruffled.

"I'm glad you're not modest," Halprin shot back.

So, being such a low-rent criminal, where exactly was Rodgers planning to get $2 million to replace the pornography he wanted to burn in the big warehouse?

"Your good credit?" Halprin asked, trying not to laugh as he thought out loud about Rodgers going to get the loan. "Oh, and I met Joey Lombardo in a sandwich shop?"

The dealings with Wemette weren't on behalf of the mob, Halprin suggested. Wasn't it true that Rodgers was just a good friend of Wemette's? Hadn't he driven a car of Wemette's to California?

No, Rodgers said, that was a stolen car; it just had Wemette's license plates on it. That answer even had jurors laughing.

Emma Seifert was in the prime of life when her husband was shot and killed. She took the witness stand at the Family Secrets trial as a poised woman in her early sixties, with short blond hair, and wearing a dark pantsuit. She looked as though she had gone over and over this moment in her head and was going to do everything she could to stay composed.

She looked at the government exhibit known as Seifert 1 on a video screen in front of her by staring down through her glasses.

"That was my husband," she said.

The photo showed a brown-eyed Daniel Seifert sometime not long before he died in 1974. He was wearing a goatee and appeared to be sitting in some kind of wicker chair with a curtain behind him. He looked youthful, with long sideburns.

She recounted for the jury how International Fiberglass had gotten off the ground in around 1968 with the help of Irwin Weiner and Felix "Milwaukee Phil" Alderisio, a hit man who would go on to die in prison.

Lombardo showed up a few times a week but never really did any work, she said. He would hang out and use the phones or spar on a boxing bag he had hung at the business. He wasn't exactly an integral part of what was going on there. Still, everyone got along fine, until her husband and Lombardo had a falling out sometime in 1972.

Things got strained in a hurry, and Seifert remembered a time she saw Lombardo driving by her house twice on the same day.

"It was midafternoon," she told the jury, recalling that she was standing in the doorway of her Bensenville home. It wasn't a through-street. She already knew her husband was starting to talk to authorities about International Fiberglass.

"I saw a car drive by. Mr. Lombardo was driving; there was a passenger in the car, and they drove by slowly."

She called her husband, she said, who told her to keep their children inside and keep the doors to the house locked, reminding her that there were guns there.

Watching in the courtroom gallery that day were Seifert's two sons, Nick and Joseph. It was Joseph who had been present as a child when his father was killed and who carried Lombardo's name. He bore a significant likeness to his father, especially around the eyes, and he wore a goatee, too.

Emma Seifert said that her husband had acquired a number of weapons as he started to worry about Lombardo, including one in the office desk at his new business. He was extremely cautious in the months leading up to his death, she said. He worried constantly and always reminded her about protecting the children.

Joseph the preschooler wasn't even supposed to be with his parents on that day in 1974, when they packed up some toys for him and a vacuum and drove to the plastics company on Foster Avenue early that Friday. The boy had been feeling a little sick, so his mother and father decided to have him come along with them to the office. The men who attacked the couple were likely surprised to find a child there, though they certainly didn't break off the killing once it began.

The two men who surprised her as she started to make coffee didn't seem concerned there was a boy there, she said.

"Two men wearing ski masks came through with guns pointing at my son and myself," she said on the stand, her voice dropping off as the courtroom became completely still. But just as quickly she composed herself and continued recounting the frightening seconds, which she seemed to be viewing again in her mind as she described them.

"I believe they said, 'This is a robbery, and where is . . .' and I don't know if they said my husband or 'that S.O.B.,'" she added.

At that moment Daniel was starting to come back through the door, and Seifert remembered yelling out to warn him as she moved toward the desk to get the pistol her husband had stashed there.

"I screamed but obviously not loud enough, because Daniel didn't hear me," she said.

One of the men went toward her husband in the entryway and smashed the butt of his gun into the area of Daniel Seifert's eye, knocking him down.

Scully worked a laser pointer on a map of the layout of the business as Seifert recalled what happened. At his table Lombardo watched the screen and then dropped his head to look at Seifert, then up again at the screen, and back down at Seifert. Once he even scratched his head, looking confused about what she was saying.

One man came back from the entryway, Seifert said, and shoved her to the floor. Her son was still in the room with his toys, confused, and not knowing what to do, she said, her voice dropping again.

So the man herded her and the boy into a bathroom off the office, she remembered. He still had a gun.

"He told me to be quiet and not to worry," she said.

There was a gunshot, and the man suddenly left her side. For a second or two, she froze and listened. But there were no other sounds, she testified, so she recalled telling Joseph to stay in the bathroom.

And she stepped out.

Her gaze went to the front door, and then outside it. Daniel was running. He was fleeing across the parking lot outside. There was the building across the blacktop, and Daniel was heading in that direction. She remembered seeing him heading toward the corner of the building, near where its loading dock was.

But there was another masked man in that direction. He held a sawed-off shotgun, she said. It must have been chrome-plated, she remembered, because in the seconds her husband was running, she noticed that it was giving off a glint in the sun.

And then her husband was around the corner of the building across the way, she said, running out of her life.

"That was the last time I saw him," she said.

Was she able to get an idea of the races of the men, Scully asked, even though they were masked and wearing gloves?

The skin that she could see was light, Seifert answered, but there was more.

She couldn't be absolutely positive, she told the jury, but she had the distinct feeling that one of the men who ambushed her family that day was Lombardo himself. She thought it because of the way he moved.

One of them was built like Lombardo, a man she had been around a few times a week for years. She had been in the same room with him, up close, countless times. She had seen him hop around the heavy bag in the International Fiberglass building, slugging it from a fighter's stance.

"He was light on his feet," she remembered. "He was agile in his day. He was a boxer."

"It just struck me that that's who it was."

Lombardo's defense team would be in the unenviable position of attacking the very sympathetic Seifert, but they had a little room to do so. The first time her belief that Lombardo was present showed up anywhere in the case file, it was in notes of an FBI interview in 2003, while the Family Secrets investigation was heating up. She had gone almost thirty years apparently telling no one her thought. So Shatz approached her cross-examination the best way she could, by asking Seifert when she supposedly had mentioned her suspicions the first time. Had she ever told Bensenville police her thought that Joey Lombardo was there? And Seifert had testified under oath about the killing once before, at an inquest soon after her husband's death, and she hadn't said anything then, either.

Seifert said she hadn't told the local police because she was afraid for her family at the time. She'd been scared to mention Lombardo's name, she said. But 2003 wasn't the first time she had mentioned it, she contended. She told Shatz she had told FBI agent Peter Wacks her suspicion in the weeks after her husband died.

Shatz had an interview report from September 30, 1974. It was six pages long, single-spaced, and there was no mention of any belief that

Lombardo was a masked gunman. Well, she had told Wacks, Seifert insisted, though she was unsure whether he had written it down. Lombardo's defense would have to call Wacks and put him under oath to get to the bottom of things.

When Daniel Seifert's older brother, Ronald, took the stand the same day, he backed up Emma Seifert's contention that she had been telling people she thought Lombardo was there. She had told him, he said, and he took it a step further.

"What she told me is that she knew it was Joey that held her in the washroom," Seifert said. "Her and her son Joey."

Ronald also was an employee of International Fiberglass. His brother ran the place, he said, dealing with customers and giving directions to everyone else about their jobs. How about Lombardo, Scully asked; did he give any directions or appear to be working?

No, Seifert said, Lombardo was rarely on the work floor, where machines used molds to shape fiberglass into products the company could sell. But there were photos of Lombardo in what looked like work clothes, holding rollers and appearing to be a valuable employee. There was Government Exhibit 33D, which seemed to show Lombardo wearing some kind of work hat and an apron.

Those had been taken by his brother, Seifert said.

"They took the picture and they went back," to the front office, he said. "It was kind of funny. My brother said, 'This is Joey's excuse that he's a hard-working guy.'"

A number of mob so-and-sos were known to visit the building. Seifert said he saw Anthony Spilotro and Frank Schweihs there. Eventually, as others had described, Daniel Seifert had a falling out with Lombardo and Irwin Weiner. When suspicions were building that his brother might work with the feds, Lombardo called Ronald at home, Seifert told the jury.

"He said I'd better straighten Danny out, or 'You know what's going to happen to him,'" Seifert said, remembering that he talked to his brother about it.

"He was pretty mad," Seifert said. "He said, 'To hell with them, I'm gonna testify against them.'"

He would go visit Plastic-Matics when Daniel and his wife were running it in Bensenville, and he remembered his brother's fear. He had hidden guns everywhere and had said that Lombardo and Anthony Spilotro, a longtime Lombardo associate, were out to kill him.

Lombardo even visited the business, Ronald Seifert recalled. It was a couple of months before Daniel Seifert was attacked there.

"'Guess who stopped by the place today,'" Ronald Seifert told jurors his brother had said. "'He was just casing the place out.'"

As for Emma Seifert's statement to him that she thought Lombardo was there at the time of her husband's death, it had come the same day as the murder, he testified. He saw her at his mother's house, Seifert said, and she told him that she knew Joey Lombardo had been with her for those terrifying seconds in the bathroom.

The brown 1973 Ford LTD left at the Pontiac dealership in Elmhurst as Daniel Seifert's killers got away was thoroughly examined for evidence, with investigators cataloging everything they took from it. They found hairs in the masks left by the shooters, but by 2003 there was insufficient DNA left to make any comparisons.

And detectives in 1974 gathered anything else they could pull together on the unusual car, sending an FBI agent from the bureau's offices in Springfield, Illinois, to the Secretary of State's records department in the state's capital city.

More than a dozen documents were pulled, including a very ordinary Application for Certificate of Title, which showed that the car had been purchased new in December 1973 in Chicago's south suburbs.

Applying for the title was the very generic-sounding Acme Security Service, which gave its address as 2350 W. Grand Avenue in Chicago. And on the line for the written signature of the owner was again written, in large off-kilter cursive: Acme Security Service.

The FBI agent retrieved the documents and sent them off to an FBI crime laboratory for examination.

On the receiving end there was Roy G. McDaniel, an agent who would come to make a forty-year career out of examining fingerprint evidence.

McDaniel sat before the Family Secrets jury as a thin, white-haired retiree, who said with a hint of a Southern accent that he was currently occupying himself with "a little bit of farming." He had been a supervisor at the lab for years, running two teams of specialists, and he had worked plane crashes and other disaster events for the FBI.

In the DNA age of the television show *CSI* and computerized sweeps of millions of genetic profiles, McDaniel was a throwback. As late as 2002 his concentration was the outline of friction ridges left on objects when touched by a human being.

It could be hard for "the nekkid eye," to pick them up, McDaniel said.

As old-fashioned as fingerprints might be, they remained a key tool for making identifications, he said. No human fingerprint has a duplicate anywhere on the planet, and they are permanent throughout one's life, never changing.

"All your ten fingers are different from each other," he told the jury. "You have them before you were born, and you will have them until you decompose after death."

McDaniel himself had made untold thousands of comparisons and had testified in court more than ninety times. In October 1974, he said, he found himself working on the title application for the Ford LTD from the Seifert homicide.

He sprayed it with an anhydrous solution and worked it over with steam from an iron to look for latent prints. And he found one.

There just under the *Ser* in the loopy signature for Acme Security Service was what appeared to be a usable print. He circled it and began comparing its characteristics with those of fingerprints in FBI files. There were a number of suspects that investigators were looking at, including Joey Lombardo, whose prints had been taken and kept on file card 673515E.

Some jurors stared at the print on television screens that had been set up near the jury box, and others looked up at the large screen over the dais, where the Ford's title application appeared several feet across.

There was a match with the Lombardo card, McDaniel said. Lombardo's left middle finger had left the print on the document—he was sure.

"Only that one finger of everybody in the world could've made that particular print," he said.

Halprin got up from the defense table and walked around the back of the prosecution table, his back typically hunched over, and purposefully making faces as he stepped over the tangle of cords running across the floor of the courtroom and powering all of the screens and equipment all over the room.

He made it to the podium and looked toward McDaniel.

"I know they tell you in the FBI to look at the jury when you testify," Halprin said, and McDaniel had in fact been speaking to the panel when he answered questions from Mitch Mars. "I'll work with that," Halprin said.

The original of the document no longer exists, Halprin pointed out, and McDaniel said that was his understanding, too. The evidence survived only in copies and photographs.

Halprin wanted to know exactly whose prints had been compared with the print on the application; wasn't it just subjects in the pension fraud matter? Men such as Irwin Weiner and Anthony Spilotro? There was no wide examination, the attorney pointed out, no national inventory of possible suspects. There were other prints on other documents related to the car.

"I'm just following procedures," McDaniel offered.

"Right," Halprin answered in his trademark deep voice. But there were a number of employees in Weiner's bail bond office at American Bonding who were never looked at. There was a notary public working there, processing all kinds of paperwork.

No matter, Mars tried to show as he got the chance to question the witness again. There had been only one print found on the document that was suitable for comparison with anyone. And, Mars asked again, whose print was it?

"Objection—asked and answered; he said Lombardo," Halprin said loudly.

As for the 2350 W. Grand Avenue address, investigators found that it was the home not of a security company but of Menotti Plumbing & Heating, owned by a Lombardo friend.

Lombardo leaned back in his chair through much of the day's testimony, resting his head back and watching the witnesses. He kept that pose as the government began calling former employees of a Chicago store called C.B. Center of America to the witness box in the well of the courtroom.

They were asked to look at receipts from the business, which sold CB radios and mobile scanners, including the one found in the brown Ford, which investigators tracked to the store through its serial number.

Mark Rokicki remembered working there when he was in his midtwenties, between 1973 and 1975, and recalled his best customer. It was a company that called itself Advanced Towing and Services, or AT&S, and paid cash for everything.

Three men had walked in the first time on behalf of AT&S, asking about the capabilities of different scanners. They needed them to listen for police calls about car accidents, so they could show up and get business, they claimed. They wanted equipment only from the upper end of the store's product lines.

"Most people wouldn't have been able to afford it," Rokicki said. And the AT&S guys came back repeatedly for purchases, spending hundreds of dollars. He could get them a discount, but they would have to fill in some basic information on a credit application.

"They weren't interested," he said, they only gave him a contact phone number that didn't work. When they would come in, a couple of guys would wait over by the store's windows, Rokicki told the jury, while he dealt with a third up at the counter.

Investigators had come to ask Rokicki about the purchases in 1974 and wanted to see if he could pick out the man to whom he sold the scanners, sometimes five or more at a time. The customer was a man who would sign the sales slips "Savard." Rokicki recognized him in the group of photos he was shown, pointing out a mug shot of Joey "the Clown" Lombardo.

But it wasn't Rokicki who had sold the actual scanner found in the Ford. Paperwork showed it was purchased on September 7, 1974, the same month Seifert was killed. AT&S was the purchaser, paying more than $150 in cash for the scanner along with a cigarette lighter jack and a crystal.

The FBI had asked an employee named George Rusu to pick out the man he sold the scanner to from an array of twenty-five photos, which had included shots of Frank "the German" Schweihs and Anthony Spilotro, and Rosu had chosen two images of Lombardo, including the picture of him staring off the frame.

When Halprin got his chance to question Rusu, he asked about a description of the man that he had first given investigators. He had said the man who bought the scanner had "long brown hair."

Lombardo's hair touched his collar and covered his ears in a shaggy 1970s sort of way. Halprin had him look at the photo again.

"I'm not a hair person, but it looks long," Rusu said.

Halprin pressed on. Rusu couldn't remember the name of the person who had bought the scanner, or seemingly which photo he had pointed to back in 1974. But it seemed safe to assume he had picked the Lombardo photos, seeing as how he was testifying at Lombardo's trial in 2007, the attorney said.

"That would appear to be correct," Rusu said.

"That was your best guess then, and you have no guess now," Halprin finished.

Witnesses had been able to catch the plate of the blue Dodge Challenger that fled the Seifert murder scene, KK 6014. Investigators tracked down its paperwork, too. It was a 1973, bought almost exactly a year before Seifert's shooting and sold to a "Henry Corona."

Agents could find no Henry Corona but did work the address on North Dearborn Street that went along with the fictional name. Frank Mendoza, who owned a dry cleaning store, was the landlord there; he was a longtime friend of Schweihs, Mendoza said, and he and Lombardo gave each other slight waves as he testified.

No, he confirmed, no one named Henry Corona had lived in his building in Apartment 104 in the early 1970s.

But, he answered when asked by a prosecutor, he did remember Schweihs's wife from his cleaning business. Her name was Anita Savard.

Lombardo week had drawn to a close. And with the jury out of the room, another witness was summoned to the box in the well of the courtroom. The government was shifting its focus back to the Calabreses.

The witness was Joel Glickman, seventy-one, a career bookie who took a seat wearing a black short-sleeve collared shirt. Funk wanted to know whether he had paid street taxes to Frank Calabrese Sr. so he could run his gambling operation.

"I respectfully refuse to testify," Glickman said calmly, repeating the statement no matter what the prosecutor asked.

Judge Zagel reminded Glickman that he had been granted immunity and was to testify in the case. "I order you, Mr. Glickman," he said.

But the bookie wasn't going to take the gamble. He would stay silent, and Zagel decided to give him a weekend in Chicago's federal jail to think about it before calling him to the stand again.

Glickman would relent days later, but after court, Frank Sr.'s attorney, Joseph Lopez, acted puzzled before the TV news cameras that had gathered in the lobby of the Dirksen courthouse. The relationship between Glickman and his client, such as it was, had ended decades earlier. Glickman didn't have any reason to fear Frank Sr., Lopez said.

"No reason whatsoever."

"Strangers in the Night"

Frank Sr. and Nick were on the floor of a closed restaurant in Cicero, pulling as hard as they could on opposite ends of a rope that was wound around the neck of a fifty-something thief named Vincent Moretti.

The Outfit was still collecting scalps for the burglary at Tony Accardo's house in River Forest, and this would be another one.

Nick was pulling so hard that he was bracing himself by planting his foot on the side of Moretti's head as he held tight. Nearby, a thirty-one-year-old friend of Moretti's who had just happened to come with him to the restaurant was being strangled, too. Donald Renno had decided to tag along thinking maybe he could sell some pizza boxes to the place.

It was January 31, 1978, just a couple of weeks or so after the brothers had killed the burglar John Mendell in a garage.

Things had started the day before with Ronnie Jarrett calling Nick at home. He wouldn't say what was going on over that phone line, but as they often did, he gave Nick the number of a pay phone. Nick walked to another pay phone and called the number from there to make sure their conversation was secure. Still, the men spoke in code.

"Listen," Jarrett said. "We gotta go to a party tomorrow, so don't make any plans."

Someone was going to be killed, Nick knew, so he asked, did he need to bring any gifts? Maybe a nice bracelet, Jarrett said, meaning a set of handcuffs.

When he saw his brother next, Nick told him something was up, and the older Calabrese left to get the specifics on where to go and when.

The next day Frank Sr. drove Nick to Cicero, and the restaurant on Twenty-Second Street at Laramie, a place owned by a guy named Tony "the Head." But the Calabreses didn't park right in front; Frank Sr. parked a few blocks away, and the brothers walked there together.

Johnny "Apes" Monteleone unlocked the door. And there was Jimmy LaPietra, listening to a police scanner to try to make sure no one had been followed. Joe Ferriola was there with Wild Bunch gangster William "Butch" Petrocelli. Tony Borsellino was there, too, and Frank "Gumba" Saladino and Ronnie Jarrett arrived a short time later.

John Fecarotta would be bringing the two men who would be jumped, so they would need plenty of extra hands.

Monteleone left the door unlocked so the men could just walk in, and someone turned on some of the lights and the jukebox. From the street the place wouldn't look closed or foreboding. The men would walk up, hear music, and think nothing was suspicious.

Nick peeked out through a small window in the door, watching in order to see when the men were approaching. As he looked through the glass, he had no idea whom Fecarotta was bringing to their death. Behind him the group of Outfit men waited with their gloves on to do what had to be done.

Moretti had called Renno's house as his mother was making dinner, asking him for a ride to a pizza place. Renno, having known Moretti from their neighborhood around Grand and Harlem avenues on the Northwest Side, said that would be fine. Renno was expecting to be gone for an hour or two at the most and left to pick up Moretti in his grandfather's light green Cadillac.

Before long, the men appeared with Fecarotta, pushed open the door, and walked in a few steps in the direction of the kitchen in the back. In seconds their killers were on them.

Nick turned from where he was standing, still near the door, to see the men on the ground. His brother and Gumba had started strangling Moretti. Gumba got up, and Nick took over, pulling on the rope as his brother leaned away on the other end. Gumba, the biggest man there, began jumping on Moretti's chest. Up and down the enforcer jumped, bringing the weight of his hulking frame down on the older man, who was losing his struggle.

Others had a rope around Renno's neck. And LaPietra kept his ear to the police scanner to make sure everything was still clear.

Soon both victims were dead.

Someone went through Renno's pockets and found his car keys, which Jarrett took to go get the man's car. He pulled the Cadillac convertible around through an alley alongside the building. Moretti and Renno were taken outside and placed in the backseat. Borsellino took a butcher's knife from the kitchen to the car so everyone could be certain the job would stay done. Jarrett would take the car somewhere, again leaving it for someone to make an unpleasant discovery.

With the two men loaded into the car, the hit team was beginning to scatter. Nick was leaving as Gumba was, and the men decided they should go grab a cup of coffee. Up to North Avenue they went, spending a few minutes together without talking about what had happened and then going their separate ways.

It was later that Nick would learn that Moretti too had been killed as part of the message to Chicago area burglars that you don't screw up and burglarize the wrong house. He was sitting down with his brother and Fecarotta when they recalled the killing spree. A few burglars had been saved by their Outfit connections, but by and large any mob member who knew a burglar at the time was doing his best to lure that burglar someplace to be killed. Fecarotta had known Moretti, so he had been the one used to lure him to the restaurant. Renno, the younger guy, was just interested in trying to sell some pizza boxes and had been unlucky enough to be hanging out with the wrong guy that day.

The Cadillac would be found abandoned in the working-class suburb of Stickney with the men inside. Both had signs of being strangled. Renno had been stabbed in the neck three times and Moretti once.

Frank Sr. and Nick would have a code name for this murder, too. It was "Strangers in the Night," the song that was playing on the jukebox as they pulled on the rope.

8

A SON AGAINST HIS FATHER

It would be hard to live in the Chicago area for very long and not have heard of Connie's Pizza, known for its deep-dish pie and heated delivery trucks that zip around on local streets. It's been billed as the official pizza of Wrigley Field on the North Side and the White Sox on the South Side, a small chain that made good and became a Chicago brand.

James Stolfe was its founder, selling his 1962 Oldsmobile Starfire to buy a little pizza place on Twenty-Sixth near Chinatown. He worked a county job by day and made pizza at night. Connie was the aunt of an early partner, and the name stuck.

When Stolfe appeared on the stand at the Family Secrets trial more than forty years later, he was a soft-spoken sixty-seven-year-old with white hair and a dark pinstriped suit, and his business had seven locations.

One day in the early 1980s, two men walked into one of Stolfe's restaurants as he was making pizzas and demanded to talk to him. Sorry, he replied, no time. He'd never seen the two before and figured they were probably salesmen.

"Find time," one of the men said gruffly, and the pair walked to the dining room to wait for him.

When Stolfe went out to meet them, he got a surprise.

"They told me I was being shaken down," Stolfe told jurors. "They wanted $300,000."

Suddenly he wasn't feeling very well, Stolfe remembered, telling the men he wouldn't be paying. He left the table and headed out of the room.

Strangely enough, Frank Calabrese Sr., a man Stolfe knew but had not seen for several years, had just come in to his office maybe ten minutes earlier. And Frank Sr. was still there as the goons left the restaurant. Stolfe had a suspicion that Frank Sr. had some involvement in organized crime, so he mentioned what had just happened. Don't worry, Frank Sr. told Stolfe; he would see what he could do about getting that payment amount lowered for him.

As a couple of weeks went by, threatening phone calls started coming in to Connie's. The demand for money was no joke, the man on the phone told Stolfe. Pay up or get hurt, he said. But before long, Calabrese had returned with news. He had knocked the payment amount down a bit. Now instead of $300,000, Stolfe could pay a third, or $100,000.

Stolfe decided he would pay.

"I didn't want anything to happen to my business or myself," he said. There could have been a fire or who knows what. So he came up with $50,000 as an initial payment, giving it to Frank Sr., of course.

Was Frank Sr. in the courtroom, he was asked? Yes, he was, and Frank Sr., watching intently in a gray jacket over a black shirt, sat straight up in his chair, stuck up a hand, and gave a wave hello.

Stolfe said that thereafter he paid Frank Sr. $1,000 a month in street tax. Year after year. He told almost no one, he said. The police couldn't help him, and he didn't want his wife knowing either. The one person he trusted with the information was his longtime associate, Donald "Captain D" DiFazio, who would later come to deliver the Connie's cash to the mob.

Frank Sr. and Stolfe developed a cover story for the extortion payment, should anyone find out or ask about the monthly envelope. They would say that Frank Sr. had work with Connie's as a spotter, someone who would be out on the streets keeping track of trucks and making sure that the drivers weren't speeding. And someone eventually did ask—Stolfe went so far as to tell a grand jury in 1990 that Frank Sr., the ghost on the pay roll, was doing an actual job.

He still thought he might get hurt, Stolfe said, so he lied when asked about the arrangement. After he testified back then, Frank Sr. appeared unannounced, he said, coming over to his house to find out what kind of questions were being asked about him. Stolfe was surprised to learn that Frank Sr. had any idea there was a grand jury investigation, but he told him what he had said about the supposed spotter job.

"He thanked me and gave me a hug," Stolfe testified.

Frank Sr. even horned in on his family vacations, Stolfe told the court. And when Frank Sr. asked him to go to dinner or play handball, he went. The mobster had a pretty intimidating demeanor, and Stolfe wasn't about to start telling him no.

With that, a fairly animated Frank Sr. shifted in his chair at the defense table and could be seen gesturing with his hand and whispering intently to Lopez, who just nodded.

Eventually the payments went down, Stolfe said, cut in half when Frank Sr. went to prison in the 1990s. And they stopped altogether in 2002 when the Family Secrets investigation started to become public. Then in 2004, Stolfe was back before a grand jury, this time testifying about paying the mob some $270,000 over a span of twenty years.

Joseph Lopez went to the podium having traded in his favorite pink socks for red, to match a crisp red tie. He wanted to know whether it wasn't true that Frank Sr. and Stolfe were actually friends. Stolfe's brother-in-law had been Larry Stubich, after all, Lopez said. Stubich was Frank Sr.'s original loan-sharking partner before he was killed in a fight at a nightclub. And then Frank Sr. had helped support the kids of Stubich's widow, Stolfe's sister, so wasn't the Stolfe family grateful for that?

When Stolfe stopped paying the $1,000 a month in 2002, nobody set a Connie's Pizza restaurant on fire, Lopez said. Wasn't that right? No one forced Stolfe to hang out with Frank Sr.

"Did anyone put a gun to your head and say you had to go play handball with him?" Lopez asked.

"I felt very intimidated," Stolfe answered.

Hadn't he invited Frank Sr. to go with his family to Colorado on trips?

"He asked me if he could come," Stolfe told the lawyer.

And what about these two guys who showed up that day at Connie's, Lopez wanted to know, asking Stolfe whether he ever found out who they were. No, Stolfe said, but it didn't matter because he knew he was being extorted.

"Nobody had a baseball bat," Lopez pointed out. And wasn't it true that Frank Sr. gave Stolfe $30,000 as an investment when his pizza chain was going to open a place in Naperville in the western suburbs?

Yes, Stolfe said, that was true. But he had given it back when the proposal didn't come together right away.

"He never asked you for interest," Lopez said. And when Frank Sr. was in prison, no one had been sent to threaten Stolfe, Lopez asked, right? That was true, Stolfe said.

And this "Captain D," didn't he run a bookmaking operation out of the back of the restaurant? Had Stolfe ever complained to Frank Sr. about how he was being treated, or what his business supposedly was being asked for?

"I have eaten there, just so you know," Lopez added.

"That's good," Stolfe answered.

Donald "Captain D" DiFazio was in court that day to testify, even though he was supposed to be at the Taste of Chicago summer food festival in Grant Park as the director of special events for Connie's Pizza. He looked polished and sharp as he sat in his chair and straightened his suit jacket.

Mitch Mars asked whether he was familiar with Frank Sr.

Sure he was, DiFazio said. He'd been introduced to him by James Stolfe twenty-five years earlier. Plus he'd grown up in the South Side neighborhood, Bridgeport, on Twenty-Fifth Place. Frank Sr. had a reputation.

"Tough guy," DiFazio said.

And DiFazio testified about how he eventually had been the one to turn in the envelope that the Calabrese crew expected. Stolfe, rising in stature as his business did well, didn't want anyone to see him doing it. DiFazio would cash checks that Stolfe had made out to himself to get the cash, and pay Frank Sr. that way, he said.

Did Frank Sr. work for Connie's as a spotter, Mars asked, or as anything else for that matter? DiFazio said he did not, as far as he knew. And when he was physically handing over the envelope, was he giving it to Frank Sr.?

No, DiFazio answered. He would only give it to one of Frank Sr.'s sons, Kurt or Frank Jr. Though at one point he did hand it off to Ronnie Jarrett, he said.

"Another tough guy."

Was DiFazio familiar with something called the Italian American Club? Yes, he said, he had been its president for ten years. So was he familiar with Angelo LaPietra? Yes, DiFazio said, LaPietra was one of the club's founders.

"He was another tough hombre," he said.

There was a time that he had been approached at the Italian American Club, in the parking lot, by Joseph "Shorty" LaMantia, DiFazio told the jury. Connie's was going to be expanding to a new location in the suburban town of Lyons, which had its own Outfit history. LaMantia appeared and said it was time to take a ride, DiFazio said, so they did. They drove to Archer and Normal avenues, across from Connie's second location.

Standing there was Tony Chiaramonti. "He had a nickname, 'The Hatchet,'" DiFazio said. "The name speaks for itself."

The mobster pointed his finger and had a message for DiFazio. The Lyons project was never going to be built. Workers had just hung a sign on a fence at the spot that said the pizzeria was coming soon, but that was no matter. It would never open, Chiaramonti told him. Lyons apparently was the territory of someone who didn't want Connie's encroaching on their turf.

"Somebody's gonna get hurt if it does," DiFazio remembered Chiaramonti saying. And the deal for the new restaurant was scrapped.

By 2000, Frank Jr. was out of federal prison and was still cooperating with the FBI. Part of his work for the government was wearing a wire as he made some of his pickups, including taking the envelope from DiFazio. Jurors listened to recordings made as Frank Jr. met up with DiFazio to make the collections.

In March 2000, Frank Jr. told DiFazio that he had talked to Frank Sr. and would be making the pickup, asking if it would be all right if they met every other month. That would be fine, DiFazio said on the tape.

In October that year, they were meeting again. There was some confusion about what months were being covered with the payments and what Ronnie Jarrett had gotten on behalf of Frank Sr. Don't worry about all the questions, DiFazio told Frank Jr.; he didn't feel put out by the grilling.

"I don't own this company," DiFazio said on the tape. "This is the deal that was made between two guys a long time ago, and it's been goin' on. It doesn't make no difference to me, you know. I'm just the guy who, who just brings the stuff, that's all," he said.

Lopez approached DiFazio with his normal series of quick questions. He asked whether the whole neighborhood wasn't filled with tough guys, including DiFazio. Hadn't he paid street tax to Frank Sr. as a bookmaker?

No, DiFazio answered.

And the attorney spent a lot of time asking about which Outfit members DiFazio did know and whether he had been surprised to learn that he had been taped by Frank Jr. The taping and Frank Jr.'s cooperation were not a surprise, DiFazio answered.

When the payments stopped in 2002, Lopez asked, nothing happened to you?

"I'm here," DiFazio said.

Lopez was also interested in DiFazio's expensive-looking suit and asked him about his stylish eyeglasses. DiFazio had a reputation as a nice dresser, the lawyer told him.

"Mr. Lopez, it's been a long day," Judge Zagel interrupted.

Frank Sr.'s eyes went to the back of the room as a man with a cane came through the door, and then followed as the man limped down the aisle toward the witness box.

It had been some time since he had seen his son, Frank Calabrese Jr.

The forty-seven-year-old, stricken with multiple sclerosis, sat down and looked straight ahead, avoiding the stare of his scowling father a few yards away. He wore glasses and a short-sleeve, white golf shirt with thin, horizontal stripes. He was balding, and what hair he had left was buzzed close to his scalp.

Frank Sr. turned his chair to get a direct look, but his son did not return the gaze.

With his voice shaking slightly, Frank Jr. said he'd had one year of junior college and that he had lettered in football at Holy Cross High School, near Elmwood Park. Even that seemingly trivial point had Frank Sr. leaning over to whisper in Lopez's ear.

He wasn't married, Frank Jr. said; he had been divorced. And for the past five years, he had been living in Arizona and managing a carryout restaurant in a Scottsdale strip mall anchored by a grocery, he said. It was a small mom-and-pop pizzeria.

"Chicago style," Frank Jr. said.

Before the pizza place, where he said his ex-wife still worked, he had been a representative on the West Coast for a skin care company. He'd left the Phoenix area a few weeks before the trial, moving into temporary housing provided by the federal government.

As Frank Jr. answered questions put to him by John Scully, he leaned forward to speak into the microphone. He'd stop to sip from a water bottle but was careful to keep his eyes fixed on Scully, who was at the podium just in front of him. Off to his left, Frank Sr. kept his eyes on his son, with his chin stuck out and a slight curl to his lip.

Frank Jr. had worked at a pizza restaurant near his home in high school, had dabbled in Outfit activity as a teen, and then had worked on a Chicago city sewer crew. After a brief time working at a car dealership, he helped start an Italian restaurant at Lake Street and Ogden Avenue in the Grand Avenue area. It was called La Luce and sat just south of the Lake Street "L" train tracks. He had gotten into that project with $200,000.

"I stole it from my father," he told Scully.

He actually had taken as much as $800,000 in cash in the early 1990s, Frank Jr. said, before the Calabreses pleaded guilty in the loan-sharking case. Frank Jr. knew of a hiding place where his father kept large bundles of cash, and, being a drug addict, he blew much of it on cocaine and vacations.

"I just would spend it all wildly," he said, as his father whispered almost continuously to Lopez. Word eventually spread on the street that Frank Jr. was flush with cash, and his theft was discovered. Frank Sr. confronted his son outside Frank Jr.'s home in the northern suburbs.

His father bore responsibility for the cash to mob higher-ups, Frank Jr. said, and he was not happy. The father had grabbed his son by the arm.

"He told me if I tried to run, he had a gun in his truck," Frank Jr. said. "I started crying."

He denied taking the money, he told the jury, but his father was having none of it. He slapped Frank Jr. hard in the head and told him he would be getting the money back. Frank Sr. went to the restaurant to demand what had been invested, even as his wife tried to cover for their son.

But that only made Frank Sr. angrier, his son said, remembering when his father finally took him to a garage in Elmwood Park where a collection of Outfit work cars were kept. The loan shark was furious.

"My father cracked me and started yelling at me," Frank Jr. said. "He said I'm making my mother lie for me to him. He pulled out a gun and stuck it in my face and said, 'I'd rather have you dead than you disobey me,'" he remembered as jurors looked on. "I started crying. I started hugging and kissing him. I said, 'Help me. Help me do the right thing.'"

He had seen his father angry like this before.

In the early 1980s, his father had brought him along to take care of a little business. They arrived at a closed restaurant on Belmont Avenue to meet with two men, one of them a man nicknamed "Peachy" and connected to the Chinatown crew. Peachy had been spending the mob's gambling money, and Frank Sr. wanted his son to witness what he would do about it.

Peachy came in, and Frank Sr. walked right up to him, Frank Jr. recalled. He belted the man in the face, knocking the man down.

"He got on top of him and said, 'You better stop doing what you're doing,'" Frank Jr. said.

Afterward, he had explained. Peachy had been on the street telling people that it was his money when he actually was working for Frank Sr., who had gotten permission from Angelo LaPietra to give the man a painful message about how to act.

It wasn't his first exposure to life in organized crime in Chicago. He had worked as a teen with his uncle Nick, collecting quarters from adult bookstores. One was in a building near Walton and State Street, and another about where the Harold Washington Library is now, farther south on State.

"We'd go once a week and empty the video booths and bring the quarters to another location to count them," Frank Jr. said. The money would eventually go back to his father.

Other times he would sit with Nick and Frank Sr. and help them do the organization's paperwork, he said, assisting with juice loan, gambling, and street tax records by 1990. The Calabreses used nicknames scrawled on cards to record cash moving around their network of loan agents and bookies, which included "N.F.," shorthand for Angelo LaPietra's nephew, Michael Talarico.

Exactly who owed what would be logged mostly on Saturdays, and money would be set aside to pass up the Outfit's chain of command. Balance sheets would be kept to show which bookies were up or down, which customers were on time with their loan payments, what was being collected from whom, and who was meeting their obligations. Not everyone was.

Frank Jr. once found himself out with his father to send a message to an associate who was letting things slide. The elder Calabrese had rigged up a homemade device to start a garage fire: a plastic container of gas and kerosene placed in a cardboard box that was stuffed with newspaper. The idea was to light the box with a flare, which would soon heat and melt the plastic, spilling the flammable liquid and producing a burst of flame.

"I was to put the box up against the door, put the flare in, and get back in the car," Frank Jr. told the jury. That's what he did, and his father warned him not to go back to the scene of the crime for a look at how it had worked.

"It was successful," he said.

Frank Jr. described for the jury how he and his father spoke in the kind of code they would hear on the undercover recordings he had made in the prison at Milan. His father would change the genders of people as he spoke about them and use multiple nicknames in a single conversation to make it seem he could be talking about several people.

And his father schooled him in the rules of the Chicago Outfit, things that were acceptable and things that were forbidden. Committing crimes without bosses' approval or stealing could mean a member would find himself on the outs. Drugs also were off limits, and anyone tangled up in using them could be frozen out of the organization.

A member was a member for life, and there was no saying no to any direction given from syndicate leadership. Even "retired" members who had stepped back from active roles and been placed on the shelf would have to act if called upon.

Absolute loyalty was expected. The Outfit became the top priority for those who were a part of it—no exceptions. Its members were expected to live for the organization, and there was no turning back.

"Your family, the Outfit family, came before your blood family," Frank Jr. said his father told him. "It also came before God."

It was after the Calabrese organization was taken down in the mid-1990s, Frank Jr. said, that he decided to write his letter to the FBI. Before he was imprisoned, he had violated his bond by failing a drug test. He was still struggling with cocaine addiction.

He met with his attorney at the lawyer's office, and his father decided to attend without telling him, Frank Jr. testified. Frank Sr. had had it with his son's failures and demanded that he "be a good person." His father made him promise to quit using forever.

The son would go clean but asked his father to end his own criminal ways. He wanted his father to at least semiretire from his Outfit life as he tried to deal with his own struggles.

"He said he would," Frank Jr. told the jury.

But once the men were at Milan, it became clear to the son that his father was what he was. The pledge to give up his ways was only smoke. His father was not going to change. The bitter and dejected son would write Tom Bourgeois, promising to help keep "this sick man locked up forever."

So for the next few days, Frank Jr. walked the jury through all of the recordings he had made, explaining his father's code and deciphering what he was talking about. With his father glaring nearby, he led them through his father's statements and admissions about killings. Albergo, Cagnoni, Ortiz and Morawski, and the Daubers.

Jurors listened as Frank Sr. explained how "Doves" Aiuppa wanted Anthony Spilotro "knocked down."

Among Spilotro's many sins was a rumored affair with the wife of mob associate Frank "Lefty" Rosenthal, a former bookie the Chicago mob had sent to Las Vegas to help run the casino skimming. Robert De Niro's character in *Casino* was based on him.

After the affair started to become known, Rosenthal survived an unsanctioned car bombing. Outfit leaders suspected Spilotro and felt he was recklessly bringing attention to the Outfit's western branch.

"That's a friend and that's a commandment," Frank Sr. said of the affair on one tape. "He, right then . . . nail went in the coffin; right then, that was one nail."

Frank Jr. had led his father through it all, and now a jury was sitting in the jury box, watching and listening intently.

It was the Outfit way to exploit an advantage, to get an angle and put someone away, to use a relationship to deliver a knockout blow. Frank Jr. was just doing it in slow motion. He had learned well, and his father could do nothing but sneer in his suit and whisper in frustration to Lopez.

The jury heard as Frank Sr. talked about his beloved Outfit, his suspicions about Nick and DiForti and their possible cooperation, and his statement that he would give his blessing if something had to happen to Nick. They heard Frank Sr. talk about the gloves. They heard him unknowingly giving up inside information on how things worked when you were a made member, and even how you became one. Frank Sr. described the secret making ceremony to the son who had given him so much trouble but whom he had believed he was growing closer to behind bars.

"I lived the life I practiced," Frank Calabrese Sr. told his son on one of the early recordings played for the jury. "I preached, I lived it."

Others knew only what they'd read about, he said. But Frank Sr. knew what really happened when the mob "made a new uniform," he told Frank Jr., using a coded phrase.

"I thought that was just in the movies," the son answered.

Well, Frank Sr. said on the recording, the making ceremony depicted in *The Godfather* was pretty close to the real thing.

"So whoever wrote that book, either their father, or their grandfather, or somebody was in the organization," he said.

He had done it, Frank Sr. said, as had Nick. The fingers of those being made were cut, to draw blood. And pictures were set on fire and placed in their hands.

"Pictures of . . ." Frank Jr. said.

"Holy pictures," his father answered. "And they look at you and to see if you'd budge . . . while the pictures are burning. And they, and they wait till they're getting down to the skin."

One at a time, those pledging their loyalty were tested, as the Outfit's capos gathered around. "They're watching you," Frank Sr. said, watching for any show of fear as the cards burned, the kind of prayer cards with saints on them, the kind that might be passed out at a funeral.

"You know what I regret more than anything," he told his son. "Burning the holy pictures in my hand. It bothers me."

But what about the other things he had to do? Frank Jr. asked. An order came, and his father had been required to act, and to kill. And sometimes he hadn't fully known the reasons why, his son reminded him on the tape. Didn't that bother him?

"The real model here was not to hurt innocent people," his father answered. "That was the real model from back when it started. There were people who were trying to hurt our people or people who are stool pigeons. Very few people ever got hurt—for money."

Frank Jr. had spent days on the witness stand walking the jury through the tapes he had made before Joseph Lopez had the chance to cross-examine him.

The attorney had a few goals in mind as he stepped to the podium to question his client's son. He couldn't do anything to change what had been recorded, but he could press Frank Jr. on his motivation, question his manhood, and try to get him aggravated.

Lopez would ask questions in his rapid-fire style, trying to get Frank Jr. flustered and trying to make the jury think about what kind of a person would betray his own father this way. What kind of a son would do this kind of work to keep his dad "locked up forever," as Frank Jr. had written?

Lopez asked whether Frank Jr. had used deceit to spin Frank Sr. into saying the things the jury heard.

"You were pushing the button and pulling the levers, weren't you?" Lopez asked.

No, Frank Jr. answered. There was only so much he could do to steer the conversation toward certain topics. There was no way to force his father to say anything.

With Frank Sr. smiling and chuckling through much of the questioning, Lopez asked whether hate was involved. No, Frank Jr. would say again. He didn't hate his father at all; he just decided that he needed to stay behind prison walls. And he believed his father still loved him, too.

"I know he loves me, just not some of my ways," Frank Jr. testified. "And I love him, just not some of his ways."

That seemed a little contradictory to Lopez. Frank Jr. had his own mob history. He had done mob work and had pleaded guilty in the loan-sharking case. And as Lopez had already told the jury, Frank Jr. certainly hadn't rejected his father's reputation when he was making the rounds at nightclubs as a younger man. So if he was so opposed to Outfit life, why not walk away a long time ago?

"I tried to get away before, but I was told I couldn't get far enough [away]," Frank Jr. answered. "I detested the Outfit. I didn't like what I seen."

Frank Jr. said it was after he went to prison with his father in the 1990s that he realized his father was never going to keep a promise to retire from his Outfit life, as he had pledged to do. His father hadn't really worked any legitimate job since the 1960s. Any side businesses he had, including a remodeling company, were run with mob cash.

"He was not going to change his ways," Frank Jr. said, so he made his fateful choice to contact the FBI.

As Lopez asked about particular conversations on the tapes, the younger Calabrese told the jury his father was teaching him some of the Chicago mob's rules and principles. Part of the way Frank Jr. got his father speaking about his crimes was to act as if he was interested in a deeper part in Frank Sr.'s organization.

"I'm telling him I want to be involved," Frank Jr. told Lopez.

Lopez challenged Frank Jr. over and over again, pressing him with the idea that he had betrayed his father and his family. And it seemed to happen regularly, Lopez pointed out. Judge Zagel had prohibited Lopez from explicitly arguing that Nick and Frank Jr. were working together in a conspiracy because there was no evidence to support that idea. Lopez would have to try to get a witness to say it. But the younger Calabrese did admit that he had taken hundreds of thousands of dollars from his dad. And those thefts came at a time when his father was showing genuine concern for him over his drug use, Frank Jr. acknowledged. He remembered his father confronting him over his addiction and his theft.

"People will cut your hands off for doing things like that," he remembered his father said.

Frank Jr. had turned his back on his dad, Lopez suggested. In fact, he continued, he favored his uncle Nick over Frank Sr. It was part of Lopez's strategy to imply for the jury that in some ways the two had worked together to steal from Frank Sr. and then conspired to keep him in prison.

Frank Jr. at least agreed that there were things he spoke about with Nick that he did not tell his father. "I confided in all my uncles like older brothers," he said.

Lopez also attempted to portray Frank Jr. as a liar, to inject doubt about him into the minds of jurors. Combating what was on tape was its own problem, but Lopez could demonstrate that Frank Jr. had a propensity for being untruthful when it suited him.

As the case against the Calabreses was under investigation in the 1990s, Frank Jr. had been questioned by the FBI. He had lied then, he admitted to Lopez, but it was Frank Sr. who was telling him what to do and say.

"I did that for my father, for the crew, for myself," he testified.

Damon Cheronis would cross-examine Frank Jr. for Doyle, trying to home in on exactly what the former cop's role was or wasn't in the organization.

The attorney began with a letter that Scully had asked Frank Jr. about. It was the kind of message that Frank Sr. was often trying to get out of the prison at Milan to his operatives in the field, but this one was an attempt to contact Nick at another prison through Doyle. Cheronis wanted to make it clear that the letter hadn't been sent at all.

"So, when your father told you he was thinking about sending a letter to Anthony Doyle, he was basically just thinking out loud, correct?" Cheronis asked.

Frank Jr. eventually agreed that was true.

"He decided there was no way of getting a message to my uncle," he said.

Frank Jr. acknowledged that of the crimes he had talked about committing with his father and others, Doyle had never been present. When he had picked up coins from adult theaters or collected on juice loans, the officer wasn't around. Doyle wasn't indicted with the Calabrese crew in 1995, and Frank Sr. had only ever said that Doyle was a friend. Frank Jr. agreed.

Frank Jr. had been able to point out Doyle only in a photo for the jury. He couldn't identify the now-older Doyle seated at the defense table in court.

"So as you sit here today, so the jury is clear, you've never had a conversation with Anthony Doyle once in your life, correct?" Cheronis asked.

"That is correct," Frank Jr. said.

Cheronis tried to show as best he could that it was Michael Ricci, the other allegedly corrupt officer, who was much more of an agent for Frank Sr. than Doyle was. Frank Jr. agreed that he knew Ricci routinely passed information to his father and that it was Ricci who had alerted his father to the FBI investigation of the Fecarotta homicide in the first place. Ricci would run license plates for Frank Sr., and the men were part owners of a hot-dog stand together. Frank Jr. said he believed Ricci knew of the Fecarotta probe after seeing the actual report on the killing once the investigation was reopened.

Frank Jr. also agreed that Ricci seemed to have far deeper sources inside the Chicago Police Department than little Anthony Doyle, sitting at his computer in the basement evidence locker under the criminal courthouse. Ricci was getting information from a sergeant who supervised the police detective who was the chief investigator of the Fecarotta murder, Frank Jr. said.

Monday, July 16, opened with another full gallery at the trial, with the typical contingent of media representatives and supervisors from the FBI and the U.S. Attorney's Office stopping in to watch, along with Kurt Calabrese, who would come and go at times during the trial. On this day he sat in a back corner of the courtroom, taking in the whole scene.

There were dozens of the curious, too, including a man wearing a T-shirt that read YOU DON'T KNOW ME and featured a federal witness protection seal on the back.

He was wearing it as a joke, but U.S. marshals made him turn it inside out.

Among the first witnesses was Lorri Lewis, the supervisor whose name Doyle had seen on the records of the physical evidence from the Fecarotta murder. She wasn't on the stand for long, merely testifying that she was a supervisor in the Chicago Police Department evidence evaluation unit. Forensic evidence in the case had in fact gone from her facility to the FBI, and no, she stated, that kind of information was not typically given to the public or especially a convicted felon.

Michael Talarico, who appeared as N.F. on many of the Calabrese records the jury saw, took the stand. The fifty-five-year-old from
Bridgeport with swept-back, salt-and-pepper hair said he had been a
bar owner for twenty-five years.

He had once been married to a Nora Schweihs, he said.

"And was your father-in-law Frank Schweihs?" asked prosecutor
Markus Funk.

"Yes, he was," Talarico answered.

Talarico said he had been, and actually still was, a bookie. He
was dealing with twenty or twenty-five customers, he testified. He'd
been involved in bookmaking since the 1970s, he said, running his
operation out of different Bridgeport apartments and taking action
on football, baseball, and basketball. His uncle, Angelo LaPietra, had
given his blessing.

"Basically I was a gambler before I was a bookmaker and just
went from one end of the business to the other," he told the jury. He
handed out juice, too, but kept it as a separate part of his business, not
giving loans to those gambling with him.

Once a month a portion of the profits went to LaPietra, an
arrangement that lasted into the early 1980s, when LaPietra directed
him to begin working with others—Nick and Frank Calabrese Sr. But
Talarico was careful to testify that he dealt only with Nick.

At the height of the operation, he would meet with Nick weekly
around Grand Avenue, he said, passing on a part of the profits he
earned from some two hundred gambling customers and thirty juice
loans at an interest rate of 260 percent per year. The number of people
Talarico was dealing with eventually required too much paper—slips
that kept records of who owed or was paying what. It became in incon-
venience, so Talarico said he just switched to paying a straight street
tax.

"I paid to Nick Calabrese—I think [it was] $650 a week that I was
paying back then," he said.

Funk walked Talarico through a number of slips projected onto the
overhead screen for the jury, small pieces of paper that had been recovered by authorities from Ronnie Jarrett's mother-in-law's garage. They

included names of individual juice loan customers, their addresses and phone numbers and, in many cases, their occupations.

Track teller, truck mechanic, Connie's driver, pizza maker, sewer worker, shoe salesman, bar owner, city worker, sheriff's department, plumber. With such figures as $400, $500, $1,000, $2,000, and so on. Some just listed nicknames like "Smiley" or "Irish," with a note showing what was paid.

Nick had asked him to make lists showing how money was moving.

Talarico had other Outfit tasks in the 1980s, he testified, including running surveillance for the crew. He bought a yellow Plymouth under the name "Anthony Mendell," and would park and watch people when asked. Once, he said, Angelo LaPietra asked him to keep tabs on a man who was in the fireworks business. He was given a car description and a license plate and was told to do nothing but wait at a location and report back if the vehicle ever appeared. Another time he sat in the parking lot of the Sportsman's Park racetrack at Thirty-First and Laramie, watching the car of a teller there. Sometimes he would be given a radio to communicate with others who were part of such efforts.

"I never knew who was on the other end," he said.

There was a surveillance on a police officer and one on a man named Cacciatore at the Chicago Yacht Club. Another time, LaPietra asked him to throw a dead rat in the doorway of an office on Thirty-First Street near the Dan Ryan Expressway. Did he know why? Funk asked.

"No, he never gave me a reason," Talarico said.

But he did it anyway, tying a noose around its neck.

"Did you get the rats from a pet store?" Funk wanted to know.

"Yeah, I believe so."

By 1997, Nick was headed to prison, and Talarico said he was told things were folding up in the Calabrese operation. It was after the brothers and Frank Sr.'s sons had pleaded guilty in the federal case. The men met in a restaurant to discuss the immediate future.

"He just told me I didn't have to pay anymore," Talarico said of Nick. "He was leaving and I was done."

Talarico cleared his sheets, he testified, closing out the money he had on the street. He thought he was clear of Outfit commitments, but not everyone felt the same way.

He was approached, he said, by Ronnie Jarrett. The mob tough guy said that Talarico should start planning to come in to him, meaning pay him the street tax he had been giving Nick. The men went back and forth, and Talarico said he told Jarrett that Nick already had cleared him.

Jarrett seemed to take no for an answer, until he appeared one evening in May that year at Talarico's door. They took a walk, with Jarrett again asking about the street tax. They got about half a block from Talarico's house.

"I was walking down the street talkin' with him, and I got hit from behind," Talarico testified. "I went down on the ground and got kicked, punched, and that was it."

Was Jarrett involved in the beating?

"I believe so. I covered my face and my head and never seen who was hitting me," he answered.

The next day Jarrett approached him again at his bar, Talarico said. He refused again but said he did eventually decide to pay.

"It just, businesswise, it was easier just to do it and get it over with."

Lopez stood up to cross-examine Talarico, deciding he definitely needed to draw some lines around his client and try to show who was directing things. Frank Sr. had never threatened him or told him to do anything, Talarico testified, and he didn't pay Frank Sr. anything.

"Never did," he said.

After being asked by Lopez, Talarico agreed that he was close to his uncle, LaPietra.

"And your uncle used to refer to Nicky as his right-hand man, is that right?" the lawyer asked.

"Yes, he did," Talarico answered. It was Nick who had provided the funds that Talarico put on the street in the form of juice loans, he said. And he had once driven LaPietra to Nick's wedding.

In addition to the incident with the rat, hadn't Nick sent messages with animals, too?

"You also remember another time when Nick cut off a puppy's head and threw it on someone's hood of a vehicle?"

"Yes," said Talarico.

Nick and the hit man Frank "the German" Schweihs, Talarico's former father-in-law—weren't they friends? Yes, Talarico told Lopez.

And when Talarico went to see Nick in prison in 1997, did he complain about Jarrett demanding the street tax? Yes, he did, Talarico replied, answering that Nick had told him not to pay or give in to Jarrett's demand.

"And eventually, also during your visits with Nicky, he told you to watch out because something was going to happen, is that right?" Lopez asked.

"He said there was a possibility," Talarico answered.

Jarrett would be on the street for another two years before unknown assailants gunned him down outside his Bridgeport house.

By 3:00 P.M. that day, Richard "Richie the Rat" Mara was on the stand. He had worked for the Teamsters at McCormick Place and had been an agent getting horse races for jockeys. Also on his resume was some time as a prolific thief and Outfit hanger-on, committing burglaries, home invasions, and armed robberies for the Calabrese organization.

But he was having memory problems, and said he couldn't identify Frank Calabrese Sr. in court because it had been some twenty-five years since he'd seen him last. He also said he didn't know Joey Lombardo, Anthony Doyle, Paul Schiro, or James Marcello.

He did admit to having been involved in all sorts of crimes, hundreds in fact, until he "retired" and began cooperating with the FBI in 1980. The nickname didn't come from that, though, said Mara, a balding man with a mustache and glasses. It dated to the time he was thirteen, growing up in Bridgeport.

When he came clean, Mara told agents about burglaries, armed robberies, and fixing races. Oh, yeah, and he tried to kill a guy in the 1970s, a man named Ronnie Brown who was "associated with us." Mara thought Brown was snitching on him, so he found him and pulled a gun, shooting him five times, he told the jury.

"Three in the face and two in the chest," Mara said, but Brown pulled through.

Afterward, he'd been confronted by his Outfit connection, James "Turk" Torello, who had scolded him for doing a shooting without getting the OK first.

Mara's time running in those circles included doing burglaries with Ronnie Jarrett, he said, a list of crimes that included a large theft of Dunlop golf balls. And he'd given out and picked up juice, too, and once tried to devise a plan to impose a $5-a-head street tax on horses at local stables. The boss of the men he ran with was "Frankie Calabrese," he said, and his boss was Angelo LaPietra. He had known Jarrett since he was a teenager, he said, and told the jury he also used to live across from Frank "the German" Schweihs.

"Frankie showed us how to peel a safe," he said.

Mara had definitely seen Frank Sr.'s ugly side, telling the jurors he had once watched the loan shark and Jarrett "beat the shit outta Shorty" LaMantia, who had been making juice loans without getting permission.

"They beat him with their fists, and Ronnie hit him a couple of times in the back with a bat," he said.

On his list of jobs with "the Dunlop score" was the theft of a couple of tractor-trailers filled with Maxwell House coffee from a warehouse, he said. Some of the coffee had been sold to Lombardo, he testified, despite being unable to pick him out from among the group of defendants.

Despite all of his various entanglements, and his decision to rat out his former friends, Mara said he escaped being victimized. He took a juice loan from William "Butch" Petrocelli in 1979, he said, $10,000 at 5 percent a week. That was $500 he needed to come up with regularly, and soon realized he would be getting behind.

So he did what any smart customer would do. He fled to Alabama. It was nine months in the South until he could make another score and get some money.

"Butchie was gonna break my leg," he said.

It had been a full day, but just before 5:00 P.M., Zagel would allow the government to get one more witness started.

9

NICK

"Mr. Calabrese," Judge Zagel said after Nick had walked into the courtroom and past the empty jury box. "I've just entered an order which immunizes you. The scope of immunity is such that anything you say in the witness stand cannot be used against you in this or any other court, but there's at least one circumstance in which it can be used against you, and that is if you commit perjury. If you lie while you're on the witness stand, you are not immunized from prosecution for perjury."

Zagel asked whether Nick understood what he had just been told.

"Yes, Your Honor," was the answer, and Nick sat waiting for the jury to emerge.

For a moment he was nearly completely still in the witness box, at floor level, his eyes fixed on a dark computer screen in front of him. With his mouth clenched shut, his head never turned an inch toward his brother, who sat at his table watching him. If the brothers had gotten up and taken just three or four steps toward each other, they would have been able to shake hands.

Nick had on a light gray sweatshirt and sweatpants, wore eyeglasses, and had his white hair neatly parted. In another context he could have been a senior citizen making a Saturday afternoon run to the hardware store, sitting on a park bench, walking at the mall, or meeting a pal for lunch. He was a bit doughy. And he was anything but threatening, at least at first glance.

But something wasn't quite right. It would have been one thing to sit and purposefully look in another direction than at Frank Sr., allowing the eyes to stare away at something else. Nick, though, was completely frozen and unflinching. He had the look of a wild animal suddenly caged and too wary to move. The government indeed had snared a rare creature from the shadows, and now it was caught, stuck in the light with everyone looking at it for the first time.

Nick was sixty-four and married, he told Mitch Mars after being sworn in, his long-awaited questioning finally under way. He had been in custody since October 1997, or most of the prior decade. Yes, he said, he was familiar with an organization known as the Chicago Outfit.

"Were you a member of that organization?" Mars asked.

"Yes, I was," Nick answered, speaking deliberately and matter-of-factly with a bit of a nasally Chicago accent. He looked directly at Mars.

"And were you, in fact, what is known as a made member of that organization?"

"Yes," he said.

And, yes, he had committed murders for that organization, too. He had committed murders with James Marcello, with a man in Phoenix known as "the Indian," and with his brother, Frank Calabrese Sr. At the mention of his name, Frank Sr. leaned forward and straightened his glasses with a quick move of his hand to his face, but still Nick wasn't going to take a look in that direction.

Did he know what the charges against him and in the case in general had involved?

"The charge involves illicit gotten gains from juice loans, from gambling, conspiracy, and also commit murder on behalf of the mob to protect—protect if somebody would talk or to set an example," Nick said. "To show people."

He had pleaded guilty, Nick agreed. And he had an obligation.

"I have to take the stand and tell the truth," he said as his brother leaned over to say something to Lopez, even stopping at one point to chuckle with a hand over his mouth.

As part of the arrangement, Mars went on, the government had collected letters from the state's attorneys of three counties. They were promises that, knowing what Nick was about to describe, they wouldn't charge him with murder in state court in Cook, DuPage, or Will counties. The federal prosecution team would recommend that Nick receive something less than life in prison for the fourteen murders he had admitted to, but it would be up to Zagel to decide his ultimate punishment.

Nick was currently incarcerated outside of Illinois, he said, making visits from his family difficult while he was being protected. One had been arranged for him more than three years earlier. His wife, son, and youngest daughter had come to see him, he said. And when he had been in Chicago in 2005, his wife and her parents were allowed ninety minutes with him.

Other than that, Nick said, the government was giving him about $300 a month, which he was using in his commissary account in prison and "for a few magazine subscriptions." His wife's home had been outfitted with a security system.

Now, with that out of the way, Mr. Calabrese, Mars began again, could he tell the jury when he had begun an association with the Chicago Outfit?

"I started on October 1969," Nick said, pausing to take a sip from a Styrofoam cup.

That association had continued until 2002, when he was confronted with evidence linking him to the murder of hit man John Fecarotta. That included DNA evidence, Nick agreed, left on a pair of bloody gloves.

"Did you, in fact, murder John Fecarotta?" Mars asked.

"Yes, I did," Nick answered.

Jimmy LaPietra was the capo of the Twenty-Sixth Street, or Chinatown, crew at the time. He had given the order, and Nick told the jury he had carried it out with the help of his brother and Johnny "Apes" Monteleone.

He was familiar with street crews and with how the mob made money.

"What is a crew?" Mars said. "Let's start with that."

"A crew is anywhere from three, four, five guys," Nick answered. "You work together with gambling, juice loans, extortion. And usually with the crews, you usually do work. *Work* meaning if you got an order to go kill somebody, you'd have to do it."

Led by Mars, Nick told the jury about the Outfit's crews and who he knew to be their leaders. Elmwood Park, Rush Street, the Wild Bunch, Chicago Heights, Melrose Park, Grand Avenue.

Who was the capo of the Grand Avenue crew?

"Joey Lombardo," Nick answered.

He also knew Louie "the Mooch" Eboli but could only guess at whether he was a capo.

"He didn't really answer to anybody except, I had heard, right to "the Old Man," which was Joey Aiuppa," Nick said.

In the jury box to his right, the jury was seemingly trying to write down everything Nick said. They took notes furiously, stopping just for a moment here or there to have a look at the hit man in their midst. Overall he presented himself as a fairly introverted and soft-spoken person, with the kind of Chicago accent that could sometimes turn "th" into "d" at the beginning of words like "these" and "them."

There were positions of authority above the capos, he said. There was a boss, Aiuppa, and an underboss, Jackie Cerone. They were known as Number One and Number Two, but his brother called Aiuppa a different name, Nick said. "Two-two, because he was from Twenty-Second Street."

So Mars showed Nick the government's first exhibit, the "Last Supper" photo of the mob's aging leaders around the table in the nameless restaurant. Nick identified them one by one. Accardo and the leaders of various crews. And there was Lombardo standing behind the table with Cerone.

So if one crew's business bumped up against another crew's business, how would that be resolved? Mars asked. The Outfit had a mechanism. If things didn't get ironed out quickly on their own, Nick said, there would be what was known as a sit-down. There might be an instance where two crews couldn't decide who was going to take a certain juice customer, when neither side was willing to buy the other out of the arrangement.

His brother had two sit-downs over disputes with William "Butch" Petrocelli that required the presence of Angelo LaPietra for Chinatown and Joe Ferriola from the Wild Bunch. There was no resolution, so Aiuppa himself was at the third meeting, Nick said.

The jury had heard tapes of Frank Sr. describing such meetings. His strategy always had been to let the other side talk first, so he could react and come up with an argument that would cancel out what the first party had offered. But in Nick's example that apparently hadn't worked.

Things had gone in circles, with Aiuppa finally having his fill.

"If you guys can't straighten it out, I'll straighten it out," Aiuppa finally said. And what did that mean?

"It meant that if they couldn't straighten it out, by him straightening it out, they probably both get killed," Nick said, with no hint of exaggeration in his voice. His tone was that this was a simple statement of reality, as if he was telling Mars what he ate for breakfast that morning.

He and his brother were in the same crew, Nick testified, though his brother "was around them first."

Frank Sr. had been giving out juice on his own, without Outfit involvement, so LaPietra ordered him to partner with a man named Steve Annerino, Nick said. But that relationship quickly soured.

"My brother couldn't get along with him, so he went and told Angelo that if you don't—if he can't get away from this guy, he's going to hurt him," Nick said, drawing again a chuckle from the nearby Frank Sr., who was beginning to look more entertained than angry.

Frank Sr. was later partners with Larry Stubich, Nick said, the man his brother handed out juice with until Stubich was killed. It was a memory that could still upset Frank Sr.

It was late in 1969 that a subpoena had arrived for the loan shark from the commission investigating the juice loan business. The Calabrese brothers went to Arizona for a while so Frank Sr. could be out of the area, Nick said. They stayed for about a month, after which, Nick said, he returned and his brother told him to go and see someone for him. It was Frank "Cheech" Furio.

Furio had an envelope to pass, Nick said, which he took to his brother's building in Elmwood Park, the suburb the brothers had moved to after leaving the old neighborhood. Nick didn't know what was inside, though he assumed it was cash. He just put it where his brother had said it should go. It would be Nick's first small foray into mob activity.

But when his brother returned, Nick just went back to work with the Teamsters, he said, living life as he always had until his brother called him in the spring of 1970. There was a place called Slicker Sam's where they could meet, Nick said his brother had told him.

Unlike versions of the meeting the jury already had heard from Frank Jr., where Nick had asked to be a part of the crew, Nick's testimony was that his brother flatly told him that they would be working together.

"You're going to be with me now," Nick quoted his brother as saying. "I asked Angelo, and Angelo says it was OK."

Nick started small, he said, collecting on a couple of juice customers. Frank helped him along, and he picked it up quickly. Five percent would be due per week. Lend out $100 and $5 is owed. And that's just the interest. Paying the $5 doesn't knock the $100 down.

Nick met some of his brother's juice collectors, he said, including Ronnie Jarrett. And there were others, including a man he knew as "Twan."

At Anthony Doyle's defense table, Ralph Meczyk objected, asking the judge for a foundation. Where and when was it? That was the information that was coming next, Zagel answered.

"It was down in the old neighborhood around Grand and Racine," Nick said. "I met him—I met my brother there, Frank."

A group including his brother, Jarrett, and Twan were discussing who would be making pickups while some of the men were in Las Vegas. Nick said he later learned about Anthony "Twan" Doyle.

"Well, at one time he was an agent [for] collecting and giving out juice loans, and he says that he wanted to stop 'cause he wanted to get on the police force and [Frank Sr.] got upset about that," Nick said. It was 1971, and Frank Sr. was upset about losing someone he thought was a good man.

Next Nick talked about how he had moved into gambling with the crew. First there were parlay cards, which give odds for players to bet on multiple games in groups, then more traditional betting on football. Nick or Ronnie Jarrett or someone else would sit in an office taking bets. Frank Sr. wasn't really that involved with the particulars, occasionally making collections from higher-stakes agents such as Frank DiCostanza, who inexplicably went by the nickname "51."

"Just a number to give him to use," Nick would explain.

There were tiers of agents, Nick said. Some were 50-50 agents, who would split profits down the middle with the crew. Others were "25 percenters," Nick said, who would turn in three-quarters of their winnings. Still others, such as 51 and Michael Talarico, paid a street tax to operate that wasn't calculated by winnings. The brothers called Talarico "Neff," for *Nephew*, Nick said, because LaPietra was his uncle.

Some were required to settle up weekly, while others might have what amounted to a tab that went up and down as they won and lost, reconciling at the end of the year. If they finished in the minus column, they got nothing, and if they won, Nick would pick up the crew's cut.

This went on for around six years, Nick said, telling the jury that he did the paperwork. The "business" was hugely profitable, he said, even after half of what the Calabreses made went up the Outfit chain of command.

"Over that time frame, besides what my brother turned in at the end of the football season to Angelo LaPietra, I figured my brother made between $500,000 and $750,000," Nick said.

Half of everything went to LaPietra, he added, whether it was the proceeds from gambling or juice loans.

"He's our guy," Nick explained. "That's where it goes. In turn, he probably had to turn in half of what we gave him."

They'd never dared to forget to pay LaPietra, he said. The mobster the Calabreses called "the Bull" would have come calling. Others called him "the Hook" because it was rumored that he had a habit of hanging his enemies on them. There was always a chance of violence, Nick said. There really was no choice but to turn in. That was the system. Every decision would be cleared with Outfit members the next rung up the ladder.

"In other words, say you were to open a hot-dog stand," Nick offered. "You had to go and tell him, 'I'm going to open a hot-dog stand; is that OK?'

"And when things start going good, I'll start doing something that I'm supposed to."

Once the place started to turn a profit, funds would go to the Outfit for permission to run, Nick said. That was what you were supposed to do.

And his brother wasn't always completely on the square, he told the court. Nick said his brother didn't give LaPietra a good count, and Nick knew this because he did the books. He feared there could be a time when a short would be discovered and it would be his neck on the line. Frank Sr. had told him the things to say if Angelo or Jimmy LaPietra called for that kind of meeting, but still Nick feared he and his brother could both be killed.

Nearby at the defense table, Frank Sr. was again smiling, his shoulders slightly bouncing as he laughed.

Nick said some bookmakers and crew agents were paying street tax well into the 1990s, until not long before the federal case came down on the organization. Nick picked up from the likes of Neff and 51, with Frank Sr. deciding what the tax amount would be.

"I would meet them either early in the morning or when it was dark once a week," Nick said. With Neff, it was often Wednesday evening.

"He would turn in a list to me—he also gave out money for juice loans. And then when he would turn in the sheet with his name on it and what these guys paid, he would give me the tax money along with it," Nick said.

Nick would attempt to meet with as many of his pickups as he could in a single evening and then turn in the money to Frank Sr. It would come with two lists that Nick had made, one showing who was paying what and the other a list of "lates." Nick was his brother's employee, he agreed with the prosecutor, working inside the China-town street crew.

As testimony ended for the day, the jury was dismissed. Everyone in court stood as they exited, including Nick, who turned his back on Frank Sr. and kept it there. After the jury was gone, Nick stayed in his position, facing away from the defense tables and toward the jury box, which was once again empty. He stayed there, unmoving, until court security stepped forward and led him from the room.

Frank Sr. was standing, too, and still chuckling and shaking his head like he couldn't get over what he was seeing and hearing.

He shook hands with Lopez and "Twan" Doyle for the night and smiled all the way out of the room.

The next day Mars started by having Nick identify men in a series of photos, Outfit leaders he said he knew. There was Sam "Wings" Carlisi, who succeeded Aiuppa as boss. And when Carlisi took over, leaving his post as capo of the Melrose Park crew, James Marcello became capo there. There was Johnny "Apes" Monteleone, who rose out of the Twenty-Sixth Street crew to follow Carlisi as the mob's "Number One."

Mars asked Nick if he could look around the room and see Marcello.

"He's the fellow with the dark sports jacket on," Nick said, "next to the attorney with the blue suit, in the back row."

Nick said his brother's gambling operation had a wing in Rock-ford, which had been established through Frank "Gumba" Saladino, the crew's six-foot-three enforcer. There were two men working for the Calabreses there, Frank Geraci, who Nick believed was a fireman, and the other a cousin of Gumba, a man named Joe Saladino. The men were 50-50 agents, and Nick or Frank Jr. would drive well into the suburbs to collect from them.

But it was an arrangement that wouldn't last, Nick said. All three eventually broke away from the Calabrese ring, in fear for their lives; even Gumba eventually disappeared. The flight of the men resulted in a Rockford sit-down to decide on their futures, Nick said, with Angelo LaPietra, James Marcello, and Sam Carlisi taking part. The brothers would have taken the Rockford men back, but things didn't wind up going Chinatown's way.

"They sat down and we no longer had these guys as agents," Nick remembered his brother telling him. "They were going to stay out there in Rockford, and that's where they belonged."

And by the way, Mars finally asked, did Nick see his brother in court that day?

Yes, Nick said, glancing at last in the direction of his brother's table. He leaned away from the microphone and pointed with his left hand. Frank was sitting there in a beige shirt and gray sport coat, Nick said.

Now it was Frank Sr. who seemed to be looking ahead and not right at Nick, then tilting over to say something to Lopez once Nick identified him.

Mars asked whether the Calabrese brothers had any assistance from law enforcement as they ran their gambling business. Nick said they did, sometime in the late 1970s or early 1980s. Mike Ricci, one of his brother's police officer friends who came to visit him at Milan, knew someone on the Chicago vice unit at the time.

For $500 a week provided to the corrupt cops, Nick could call each Friday to get a list of phone numbers for locations that officers would be raiding over the weekend. Nick would take the numbers and see if any matched his list of phones for the crew's agents.

"One week we did have one guy," Nick told the jury. "His name was Beezy, and he was from Bridgeport. I got hold of my brother; my brother says get a hold of Beezy and tell him not to go to where he's taking action for the weekend."

In addition to the bookmaking, the crew would sometimes run card games. Frank Furio had one on Cumberland, Nick said, a game that would run three or four nights before getting cut. A portion of the pot at the end of that period was due to be paid to Frank Sr., and in addition to that take, the games were used as a venue for giving out juice. Saladino put thousands on the street at a card game run by Joey Lombardo, an arrangement that lasted for a couple of years until Saladino left the area. His replacement was Furio, who eventually was told to stay out. "Lumpy" would give out juice himself, Nick said.

The testimony mentioning him apparently wasn't that interesting to Lombardo, who sat at his defense table with his head leaning back against his chair and his eyes closed.

There was little the brothers could do about having gotten the boot, Nick said. They weren't even made at the time, and Lombardo was a capo. They went to LaPietra to see about it, but he just told them to stay out of Lombardo's business.

So the Calabreses continued their own work, with Nick staying involved by picking up juice payments from agents and his brother's customers. The interest was so high, at 5 percent a week, that payments on loans of just a few hundred dollars could go on for years. In many cases, Nick said, the principal was never fully forgiven.

Every juice customer went into the crew's book. What they paid and what they owed were constantly being recorded. Agents would mark slips with notes on who was paying and who was late, and they would be turned in to Frank Sr. It was a system that worked for more than twenty years, Nick said, running until around 1993.

Disputes with other crews weren't rare. Sometimes one juice customer would be on with more than one crew. When the money got low, there might only be enough for the customer to pay one or the other. He remembered an Elmhurst car wash owner who was paying his brother and Rocky Infelice, a conflict that ended when Infelice bought the brothers off by paying what the customer still owed. It was known as buying a guy out, in this case for something like $20,000, which Nick turned over to Frank Sr.

Sometimes Nick would meet directly with customers, as a way to check up on agents. It was good oversight, he said, because it wasn't unheard of for agents to funnel money away to themselves. Some would run up their own debts while claiming that so-and-so on the street owed what they were pocketing themselves.

There were plenty of options when debts went unpaid, Nick said.

"There's a possibility that he might get a slap, or maybe if it was really bad enough he might get his car burned," Nick said. "Or maybe if he had a house with a garage, maybe the garage would get burned, sending him a message. He don't know where it's coming from, really, but he's got to surmise it came from us."

Sometimes all it took to get a customer scared and compliant was to bring Gumba along to check on the debt. Nick would tell the three-hundred-pound man not to say anything, just stand there and give the guy "one of those looks." It was threatening enough just to have him looking over Nick's shoulder, giving a little extra punch to the speech Nick would have to give about paying up.

"I would talk to [the customer] and say, 'Listen, you gotta take care of this. This is not going to go away; you have to pay this,'" Nick remembered. "I says, 'Next time, I'm not gonna come; he's going to come.'"

Nick recalled one stubborn customer named Pat Kirby, who owed the crew money and wound up being hard to find. He could stay out of sight, but there were other ways to get the message across. The result was the incident where Frank Jr. had been pressed into service to light the garage on fire with Frank Sr.'s incendiary invention.

Frank Sr. had bankrolled the whole operation, Nick said, acting as what was known as the juice "B.R." The business gained momentum over time, until his brother might have several hundred thousand dollars to give out in juice at any one time.

This claim of his supposed riches actually sent Frank Sr. rocking back in his chair he was chuckling so hard. He again held his hand to his mouth, keeping any sounds of laughter from escaping. Nick continued to look straight ahead, and if he caught a glimpse of his brother out of the corner of his eye, it certainly didn't throw him off. He pressed ahead as if there had been no reaction. His brother had about $170,000 out on the street at the beginning, he said, a figure that grew and appeared as about $400,000 on the ledgers at the end of some months. The books were his brother's own creation, Nick testified, complicated sheets that showed figures for each customer going up and down as they made payments.

Nick and others making pickups originally met with agents once a week. But that had eventually become twice a week for fear that the crew's money would be too tempting to spend if they were asked to hold on to it for more than just a few days. Especially after Gumba took off on them, Frank Sr. didn't want his money roaming around for too long before being gathered up. Each agent would give Nick a slip tracking what was being collected, as well as their cash.

"It was always done at night, and the locations would change every two or three weeks, and I would always park two or three blocks away and walk to the first guy," Nick said. "Sometimes I had it set up to where I would meet the first guy and get in his car with him after we were through discussing the business he had, and then he would drive me and drop me off a block away from the second guy I would meet."

Each agent was given two pay phone numbers, he said, just in case there was a meeting that for some reason didn't happen. The agent was to wait by the first pay phone at a prearranged time the next day and wait for a call. If that phone happened to be out of order, the second would be used as a backup.

There were no pagers in those days. So if an agent had to be called on an off day, a call to his home would include a coded message telling him which of the two pay phones to wait near.

"I'd get into a conversation, say, 'How you doing, I heard you're not feeling well,'" Nick told the jury. "'Gee it's a shame; you gotta take care of yourself. My friend is sick, and they got this new medication you take twice a day.'"

The reference to "twice" would be enough to let the agent know it was pay phone number two that the call would go to.

Once Nick collected all of the slips and cash, he would make a separate master list, his own, showing what he was collecting and who was late. That would go to his brother in Elmwood Park.

As for his own take, Nick wouldn't be paid straight out of those funds, or dip into them at all. His brother would pay him—an amount as little as $100 a week at the beginning. His brother would say that things weren't going that well and it was all that could be afforded. In 1973, Frank Sr. got his brother another job with a hotel union as an organizer and told him that was part of his pay. There would later be a time when Nick did make a monthly salary with the Chinatown crew, he said. It was $500 a month, and it would go up over time.

No one took anything from the gambling and juice loan profits until money had been set aside for the higher-ups. At one point, LaPietra told the brothers to take $300 off the top and give it to Johnny "Apes" Monteleone, a crew member rising in stature and influence.

Half went to LaPietra, with one or both of the brothers taking thousands to the mobster's garage near Thirty-First and Laramie, stuffing it into a barbecue glove hanging on the wall. There were plenty of good years, when anywhere from $18,000 to $21,000 would go to Angelo or Jimmy LaPietra at a time. There were some hiccups. One was in 1983, Nick said, when Phil Tolomeo was found to have a "bad book."

Tolomeo was claiming loans he wasn't making, keeping thousands at a time, and making the juice payments himself: $125,000 wound going up in smoke.

"He got to be where he got so backed up that he couldn't do it any longer," Nick said. "So he finally told my brother that most of his book was bad."

A second time a few years later, the same problem was discovered. But his time the blown amount was $150,000. Tolomeo didn't stick around to see how the brothers would handle the information a second time around, choosing instead to flee Chicago.

But it had been mostly good news. Nick was responsible for tracking the safe-deposit boxes used to store the money being held by the Calabrese ring. There were at least six around the area, all rented under phony names. One was near McCormick Place, Chicago's lakefront convention center, where Nick would work with union machine removers. There were two on North Avenue in the city and others in the western suburbs. At one point there was $1.6 million in cash being kept in them.

As at earlier times when Nick would mention actual dollar amounts, Frank Sr. had an incredulous look on his face. And as before, Nick had no reaction at all.

There were times when his brother didn't even realize how much money he had in the boxes, Nick said. He remembered getting a call in the middle of the night sometime in 1990. He went to meet his brother for coffee at about 2:00 A.M.

"I knew something was wrong because he had this look on his face," Nick said. "He goes, 'You know, there's a lot of money missing.' I says, 'What's that got to do with me?'"

Nick had the keys, Frank Sr. had said, accusingly. Frank Sr. had gone and emptied the boxes but had forgotten the two on North Avenue, creating what he thought was a short. The brothers went to the bank on North Avenue and took the cash out. His brother had lost track of more than $400,000, Nick told the jury. Frank Jr. took the money out of the bank, stuffing a large coat with it and walking out.

Another time, the brothers actually buried cash in an effort to store it safely. They put between $200,000 and $250,000 in a steel box and hid it underground near a home they had in Williams Bay, Wisconsin.

"I went to check on it, I don't know, maybe six, eight months, maybe a year later," Nick testified. "I went—I dug up the spot where the box was; I . . . got all the dirt out, and when I opened it, all the money was wet and stinky."

If you bury money in canvas, that supposedly doesn't happen, Nick said, but he didn't know that at the time.

Nick began carefully peeling the money apart and trying to dry it. Once a week the brothers would take $20,000 or so to someone they knew at a bank and exchange it. The rest of it was recycled out into the juice pipeline, he said.

"It smelled of mildew," he said. "You could never get that smell out. We tried to use cologne and made the smell worse."

Occasionally the brothers would invest some of their proceeds. Frank Sr., Mike Ricci, and Johnny "Bananas" DiFronzo had a hot-dog stand together, Nick said. At the end of one football season, Nick and Ronnie Jarrett were owed $11,000 from the year's winnings, but Frank Sr. asked them whether they would like to invest their share in the fast-food place. Nick agreed, he said, an arrangement that eventually saw his brother give him $100,000 in the early 1990s.

As for Frank Sr., Nick testified, he bought jewelry and antique cars, starting a collection of sorts. He had a 1936 Ford, a Thunderbird from the '50s, and a limited edition Buick Grand National.

Mars walked Nick through some of the same documents he had shown Michael "Neff" Talarico, gambling slips and lists of winnings. One was when Talarico was on street tax, he said; it showed the bookie as being up nearly $38,000 for the year and having won more than $7,000 just that week. Besides a street tax, Nick testified, Talarico would turn in 10 percent of his winnings at the end of the year. An agent nicknamed "Curly" appeared on other documents, with amounts showing as the tax he paid the crew to take bets on football and the World Series, which was taking place around the same time.

Slowly Nick walked Mars through the records, showing who was collecting on gambling winnings and who was making money on juice loans. "John Comp," "Jim Van," "Joe Urgo," and "PK."

"PK is Jimmy DiForti," Nick said. "That's Poker; we called him Poker."

"And Pat Manning, he had $18,000, and once a month he would come in with $1,100, and he would leave it by Nick Nitti's travel bureau or be there and I would see him to get it."

There was an owner of a wood pallet company, but he got shot and killed, so the agent owed the crew for his tab.

"How about number fifty?" Mars asked.

"Number fifty is Chucky Romano," he answered.

"Shelly" was a furniture store owner his brother collected from, and "Pete" was Phil Fiore. Some of the notations on what was owed were in red and the interest payments in black—a flurry of numbers that all made perfect sense to Nick, even if it left some spectators' heads spinning.

Soon the defense attorneys had had enough.

"Judge, I'm going to object," Joseph Lopez piped up. "This is really cumulative of Junior, and we're going over and over the same thing. It's not part of the indictment, [nor] has he been convicted of it."

That rambling objection set off Mars.

"I object to that last comment, Your Honor; that's totally irrelevant," Mars said. And the judge agreed.

"It is, and maybe the next time you can just say, 'objection, cumulative,'" Zagel told Lopez. "Save us a little time."

But the judge did urge Mars to move along. The prosecutor said he would but immediately had another handwritten record up on the big screen. Nick said it was a record for a man named Jimmy, who owed several people.

"Judge, I'm going to object," Lopez interrupted again. "I don't know if it was a question. I don't know if it was in response to what the prosecutor asked him. It's not in response to his question."

"That was shorter. You got down the nonresponsive," the judge said, sending laughter through the gallery.

"I'm getting there, Judge," Lopez said.

So Nick continued, going through records of more men who owed the crew and agents who owed more than one mobster. And there were more nicknames. "Carl Lift" was a friend of Jarrett's who fixed forklifts. There was "FIV," which for some reason stood for a man named Terry Scalise. "TP" was Phil Tolomeo. "Baker" was a name for Louie Bombasino. "Gus" was a nickname for Nick himself.

A number of the records carried the note "OK me" on them, which Nick said meant that Frank Sr. had reviewed them. Some had Michael Talarico's notes on juice loans.

"Your Honor, I'm going to try another one of those cumulative objections," Tom Breen interjected. This time the judge was more inclined to agree, and he urged Mars to wrap it up.

Mars said he would, lastly showing Nick a record for a safe-deposit box. There was a line at the bottom that appeared to show what was being kept in it.

"970 K."

One of the few known official photographs of Nicholas Calabrese. (Courtesy *Chicago Sun-Times*)

Frank Calabrese Jr.

Undated photo of James Marcello. (Courtesy *Chicago Tribune* Archives)

Anthony "Twan" Doyle (center) arrives at the Everett M. Dirksen U.S. Courthouse with lawyers Ralph Meczyk (left) and Darryl Goldberg.

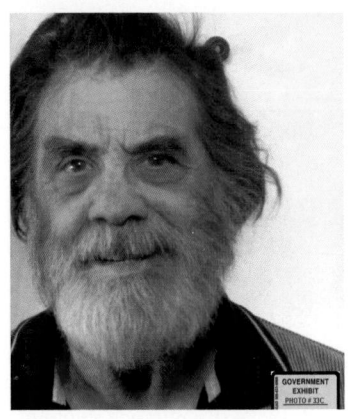

Joey "the Clown" Lombardo at the time of his capture.

An undated photo of John Fecarotta.

Government Exhibit 1, known as the "Last Supper" photo. Taken in 1976 at a Harlem Avenue restaurant, the shot captured a gathering of key mob leaders. Seated in the front row from left to right are Tony "Big Tuna" Accardo, Joe Amato, Joseph "Little Caesar" DiVarco, and James "Turk" Torello. Seated in the back row from left to right are Joey "Doves" Aiuppa, Dominick DiBella, Vincent Solano, and Al Pilotto. Standing in the back are Jackie Cerone (left) and Joey "the Clown" Lombardo.

Jimmy DiForti

Angelo LaPietra, known as "the Hook" and "the Bull."

A 1980s surveillance photo of Paul "the Indian" Schiro in Arizona.

Ronnie Jarrett

Johnny "Apes" Monteleone

Tony "Big Tuna" Accardo

Michael "Hambone" Albergo

Daniel Seifert

John Mendell

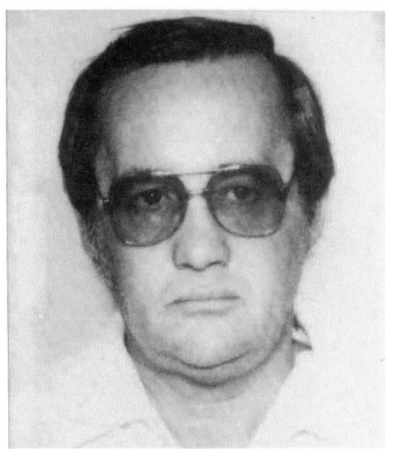

William Dauber

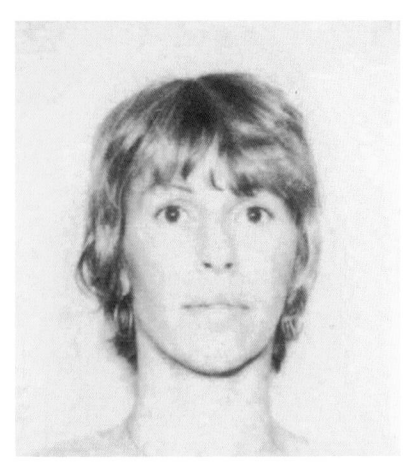

Charlotte Dauber

Anthony Spilotro

Michael Spilotro

Michael Cagnoni

Emil Vaci

Surveillance photos shown to the grand jury that investigated the Seifert killing.

The abandoned Ford LTD that fled the scene of the Seifert ambush.

The flip-down license plate holder on the Ford, used to quickly switch plates while the car was being used for Outfit "business."

Blood left at the scene of the Seifert ambush.

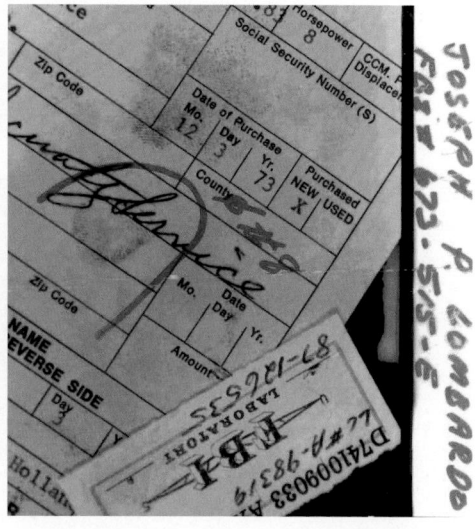

Joey Lombardo's fingerprint, left on a registration form for the Ford used in the killing.

An aerial view of the destruction caused by the bomb in Cagnoni's Mercedes-Benz. The trigger car that carried the transmitter that activated the bomb can be seen parked in the left of the photo (marked with an arrow).

The remains of Cagnoni's car on a tollway ramp.

The Mercury in which Richard Ortiz and Arthur Morawski were shot, parked outside Ortiz's Cicero bar.

Artist's rendition of Nick
Calabrese testifying at trial,
and all five defendants
(clockwise from top left):
Anthony Doyle, Paul Schiro,
Joey Lombardo, James
Marcello, and Frank Calabrese
Sr. (Courtesy of Carol Renaud)

Assistant U.S. Attorney
Mitchell Mars questions
Nick Calabrese as his brother,
Frank Calabrese Sr., looks on.
(Courtesy of Carol Renaud)

Frank Calabrese Sr. makes
a point before the jury.
(Courtesy of Carol Renaud)

Rick Halprin leaving the Dirksen U.S. Courthouse. (Courtesy *Chicago Tribune* Archives)

Joseph Lopez meets the Chicago press. (Courtesy *Chicago Tribune* Archives)

Prosecutors and agents address the media after the verdict. From left: John Scully, Robert Grant, and Michael Maseth of the FBI, Alvin Patton of the IRS (center rear), Mitchell Mars (at microphones), U.S. Attorney Patrick Fitzgerald, Markus Funk, and Gary Shapiro, Fitzgerald's first assistant. (Courtesy *Chicago Tribune* Archives)

10

A KILLER TELLS HIS TALE

Were there times when Nick was involved in arsons on behalf of his street crew, Mars asked, times when explosive messages had to be delivered to those who wouldn't follow orders or give the Outfit its due?

"Yes," Nick answered.

There were occasions when pornographic bookstores were bombed as the Outfit was trying to "arm them," or extort street tax. The mob was taking a cut from a man who was from the old neighborhood and who owned some of the shops downtown. Nick would pick the money up, at times with his nephew, Frank Jr., and they would count the change that customers paid for peep shows—the take that Frank Jr. and Alva Johnson Rodgers had described as being in quarters.

"He had these porno bookstores, and inside the bookstores he had these dirty movies that you would pay a quarter for every minute or whatever," Nick said.

And there was arson at a suit store where Nick, Frank Sr., Ronnie Jarrett, and a man named Frank Santucci were to set a business on fire. Santucci showed up for the job but didn't get to participate.

"Well, he came, but he had liquor on his breath and my brother yelled at him and told him don't ever do that again," Nick said. "You don't drink when you got something to do, and he shagged him, told him to go about his business."

Nick had helped his brother put together some of his special fire-bombs with the plastic milk jugs filled with gasoline and kerosene. The store was torched, and Nick got $3,000 for participating, he said.

How about restaurants, Mars asked, Tom's Steakhouse on North Avenue in Melrose Park, in particular, and another called Horwath's?

Nick remembered them both. The Outfit targeted them in the early 1980s. Angelo LaPietra had given the command, and Nick and Frank Sr. had made the bombs with dynamite they stored in a little refrigerator in Jarrett's mother-in-law's garage, the street crew's workshop. The businesses were to be bombed, though nobody told Nick exactly why.

The Calabreses and John Fecarotta would take Tom's Steakhouse, and LaPietra would take the other with Jimmy "Poker" DiForti and a man named Fred Barbara, who later became a wealthy trucking executive with links to Chicago mayor Richard Daley. Both places were to be attacked simultaneously. To get coordinated and discuss their plans, the six men met first at Fecarotta's hot-dog stand on Grand Avenue.

Fecarotta, the noted mob wheelman, drove to Tom's, Nick said.

"And when we got there, I lit the fuse; it was in a bag," Nick said. "I got out of the car, jumped on a Dumpster, and maybe ten, fifteen feet from the edge of the roof was an air-conditioning unit."

Nick said he flipped the lit bomb over his head, and then the men waited to see whether it would detonate.

"Did it?" the prosecutor asked.

"Yes."

Another time the target was Marina Cartage, owned by another man with Daley ties, Michael Tadin. This one didn't go as smoothly. DiForti had placed the lit device at the business, but as the men waited in the area to hear it go off, they realized there was a problem. For some reason it was a dud.

DiForti had to fetch it, and the team went back to the Jarrett garage to replace the fuse and blasting cap.

"We taped it up again, went back, and Jimmy DiForti put the bomb back and put the bomb on the side by Marina Trucking, and this one went off."

Once again, Nick had just done what he was told. Even when he went with Frank Sr. to Angelo LaPietra's home to tell the crime boss that his orders had been carried out, Nick remained in the dark as to why the business had been blasted. It didn't matter. Those weren't the kinds of questions that got asked when a capo gave a direction.

In the 1980s a theater was about to open in west suburban Oakbrook Terrace, and it too was noticed by the Outfit. Nick, Frank Sr., Fecarotta, and DiForti found themselves driving to it one evening with a bomb the Calabrese brothers had made. Nick lit the fuse and found a place to put it at the base of a cinderblock wall.

When it went off, it blasted a hole in the back of the building, exploding so loudly even the mob crew talked about it later.

"Were you ever advised as to why this bombing had to take place?" Mars asked.

"No."

Nick was also never given a reason for the dynamiting of a convenience store around 1986 or 1987, but he did come to learn why the home of the mother of a man named Mario Rainone was bombed. James Marcello and others suspected that Rainone had flipped and decided to help the feds. A message had to be sent, and an explosive was placed at the woman's home.

Mars asked whether it had worked.

"I believe so, because then he decided not to cooperate with the government," Nick said.

Sometime thereafter, Nick was summoned to Jimmy LaPietra's house. So he picked him up in his alley, and they drove to a restaurant called Mother's Day on Roosevelt Road, a regular meeting place for some members of the Outfit. Jimmy Marcello was there and needed Nick to do something.

In the wake of his "decision" not to help the government, Rainone had asked the syndicate for financial help for his family. And with him no longer a threat, Marcello was willing to oblige. He gave Nick cash to hold for Rainone's father, which Nick remembered was something in the neighborhood of $15,000 or $25,000.

"If Mario's father come to me and says, listen, I talked to Mario—his family needs some money for the rent, for the phone or food—I was to give him the money," Nick said. John Rainone, the father, had given out juice loans for the Calabreses.

But it was decided the Rainone family wouldn't get all the cash at once. When the father would come and ask for help with a bill, Nick would tell him he would see what he could do and then would produce some of the money Marcello had given him a couple of days later.

In addition to the gambling, juice loans, and street taxes, the Outfit had other ways of bringing in cash. One was the outright extortion of legitimate businesspeople. It was what Frank Sr. eventually would do to James Stolfe, the Connie's Pizza founder. Frank Sr. told his brother that he "got Jimmy Stolfe for $100,000," and they had resolved to make the tactic a regular source of income. The right threat here or a dead chicken hanging from a door there could bring a big payday with little work. One such target was the successful real estate developer and Chicago lawyer Victor Cacciatore, a city power broker.

The model was to scare the target and have him bring the threat back to a third party he felt more comfortable with but who was really in on the shakedown. Frank Sr. had played the friendly in the Stolfe scheme.

Angelo LaPietra was calling the shots on the Cacciatore effort.

"Ronnie got a dog, a little dog from the pound, and cut his head off, and he threw that on Cacciatore's lawn in River Forest, where he lived," Nick told the jury, maintaining his matter-of-fact delivery. It was another attempt at making $100,000.

"He wanted Cacciatore to run back to him, meaning Angelo; that's basically what you want to happen, and he particularly didn't like this Cacciatore."

But the dog head didn't prove to be effective in the case of the stubborn Cacciatore, so Nick delivered another animal-related message.

"There was a time when I went to a pet store and got some mice and put little nooses around their necks and put them on the windshield of his car," Nick testified.

But as threatening as a collection of hanged mice might be, Cacciatore still failed to bend.

So what happened next? Mars asked.

"After the mice?"

"Right."

"It was decided that we would blow his back windows on his car with a shotgun," Nick said as if he were telling the prosecutor that they were deciding where to eat.

Jarrett had stolen a car, a Ford, and the crew would wait until Cacciatore had parked in a spot near his business but far enough off Halsted that they could get away before help arrived. They watched night after night, until finally the car seemed to be in a good place. Frank Sr. decided it was a go, and radioed his brother. They would surprise and scare Cacciatore, not kill him.

"We had to time it to where he'd walk, and then as soon as he opened his car door, I was to shoot the back—the back window off, not on the side but the back window, on an angle, because we didn't want to hurt him with any of the pellets," Nick explained.

Cacciatore got to his car as the crew approached. Nick readied himself as Cacciatore opened the door to his car and got in; as he was leaning to close the door, Nick pulled the trigger.

"Did you hit him at all?" Mars asked

"I don't think I did, no," Nick answered.

The shotgun blast did the trick, with Frank Sr. going to pick up the $100,000 in a sack not long after. But in both the Cacciatore and Stolfe extortions, Nick said, his brother was upset that he'd been required to pass the whole amount to LaPietra. There had been nothing for the Calabreses.

So the brothers made an unsuccessful run at a Bridgeport tavern. And Frank Sr. even talked about extorting Frank Giudice, Nick's friend whom the Marcellos called "the Drywall Guy" on their prison tapes. Nick protested, and the subject was dropped.

For much of the 1980s, if anyone asked, Nick was working at McCormick Place with a forklift company. In reality, he didn't do much at all that wasn't Outfit business. The owner of the company with the rights to have its forklifts at McCormick Place would give Nick a paycheck, which Nick would cash and give the money back to the owner. In exchange, Nick stayed on as a ghost-payroller, he told the jury, so that in a pinch he could prove on paper that he had a legitimate job.

Slowly Mitch Mars built toward the murders at the heart of the case as he questioned Nick. Starting with gambling and collections, Mars had moved through arsons and bombings and extortion. But there were a few more incidents for the jury to hear about.

In the 1980s, Nick said, three crews had been involved in the surveillance of a suburban man who owned a chain of discount movie theaters. Nick wasn't sure but said DiForti had told him the effort probably had something to do with a dispute with a movie operators union.

"I believe he was going to get killed," Nick said.

The large murder team stayed on the surveillances for a time, lurking near the man's home in the DuPage County suburb of Downers Grove. Eventually the operation ended, Nick said. The crew members were called off for a reason Nick never was told.

Next Mars asked whether Nick ever had been involved in any physical confrontations. He had, he said, remembering an incident involving a man who sold fireworks. Jimmy LaPietra had told Nick to find the man and give him a slap.

"So I went there early one morning with my nephew," Nick recalled. "My nephew just stood in back. And this guy Angelo—they call him the Monkey—he come up to me, because I had met him and he knew who I was. So when he got up to me, he started to say hello, and then I slapped him and I said, 'That's from Jimmy.'"

Frank Sr. had told Nick to bring his nephew, Nick said. But Frank Jr. hadn't gotten involved.

It was the late 1980s. Nick by then already had risen to trusted status in the Chinatown crew. He was a veteran of all manner of Outfit activities, including more than a dozen killings.

In 1970 he told the jury, he had been involved in the murder of a man he would come to know as Hambone, a juice agent for the crew.

His brother had told him they needed to put someone in a hole, Nick said, remembering how he was thinking it was all a joke.

He recounted the search for the right spot to leave someone, the finding of the construction site near Old Comiskey Park on a Friday. Frank Sr. had told him why.

"He said this guy made a statement that he says he wouldn't be going—if he had to go to jail, he wasn't going to go by himself."

Jarrett was to pick up Hambone in the stolen Chevy, and they would surprise him in the dark.

"My brother says he would get in the back first and I would get behind this guy," Nick said. "And he said to make sure before we got in the car to put the glove on my hand. . . . so I wouldn't leave any fingerprints, and once I was in the car, to just hold my hands down and put my gloves on."

Frank Sr. stared intently at his brother as Nick described the brief struggle in the car, and how he had held one of Michael Albergo's arms as his brother pulled the rope around the man's neck. He kept his eyes fixed on Nick, once breaking his gaze to tell Lopez something.

"Did he kill him?" Mars asked.

And for the first time, there was a pause.

Instead of simply answering in his flat tone, as though what he was describing was just business as usual, Nick seemed to be working to stay on top of his emotions. At least one callous layer of Nick Calabrese peeled away for an instant at the memory of his brother killing someone right in his face, close enough that he would certainly have heard every sound Albergo made as he fought for air. He would have heard his brother straining against the rope.

"Yes," he answered.

Some jurors were taking notes, but others had stopped to just watch what was happening. A courtroom filled with spectators was nearly completely quiet.

Nick told the jury he helped remove Albergo from the car, placing him near the pile of dirt the brothers had made as they dug their hole. His brother told him to take Albergo's pants.

"I don't remember him having a wallet," Nick said, "but that was what the purpose was."

He told the jury how he had come back only to be ordered by his brother to throw the pants farther away, and how he returned the second time to find his brother with the knife. His brother had cut Albergo's throat, and they had buried him.

Again Nick paused. He was clearly bothered by his first murder. His voice was more urgent and louder as he described wetting himself in fear.

"I never said nothing," he said. "And it would have been hard to talk because it was real dark and I had a lot of dust and dirt on my pants, so you couldn't really see."

By this point in Nick's account, Frank Sr. had leaned forward so far at his table he was resting his chin in one hand. And as his brother talked about the moment of weakness, Frank Sr. smirked.

Nick could have seen his brother's expression only out of the corner of his eye, since he continued answering questions from Mars while looking directly at the prosecutor at the podium in front of him. Mars had Nick explain how he had later learned the name of the man he had helped kill but had still referred to him as "It."

"Mr. Calabrese, I'm going to ask you to direct your attention to an individual named Paul Haggerty," Mars said.

Nick described the stalking, the halfway house, and the kidnapping. The emotion he showed as he spoke about Albergo was fading again. A harder glaze was re-forming as he talked about running surveillance and having a police scanner and a walkie-talkie to do the job. He had watched as his brother and Gumba had to punch Haggerty and stuff him into their car.

After Haggerty was questioned in the garage about the jewelry store, Nick described being left alone with the victim. The courtroom was silent again as observers imagined Nick sitting there in the garage, with Haggerty nearby, his mouth taped and hands cuffed.

"I don't know if it was at this time or a little later that he had to pee, so I helped him pee, and I gave him some water because he was thirsty," he said.

Nick was back to his straight-and-steady delivery, offering no further explanation for the small mercy he had offered a man who had been as good as dead.

As with Albergo before him, Haggerty was strangled with a rope, Nick said. He had watched his brother cut the man's throat to ensure he was dead.

"He was put in the trunk, and then he was searched," Nick said. "And in his pockets I found a hypodermic needle and some drugs, so I left them on his body."

In 1977, Nick said, he had been involved in surveillance on a man named Henry Cosentino. He was from the Calabreses' old Grand Avenue neighborhood and was a low-level mob associate. But he had made a big mistake.

Cosentino and Frank "Gumba" Saladino had been in an argument, and Gumba had wound up getting shot in the leg. Pulling a gun on an enforcer for the Chinatown crew without anyone's permission was a pretty good way to drastically shorten your life expectancy, and the Calabreses were soon following him around. Frank Sr. had done things the proper way, Nick said, going to Angelo LaPietra for the approval to kill Cosentino for his infraction.

Nick remembered stalking Cosentino with Ronnie Jarrett, again in a car with a police scanner and a walkie-talkie so he could communicate with the rest of the hit squad. He had tried to follow Cosentino, who hadn't shown up where the crew thought he would. There was one night in particular, Nick said, where he waited for hours on a North Side street for Cosentino to come by, but he never did.

Finally the crew caught up to him on a Friday night when Nick had left early. Frank Sr. told him the next day that Cosentino had finally gotten what he had coming.

Nick recalled his brother telling him, "It happened last night—we hog-tied him," and then making a slashing motion across his neck. In the world of the Outfit, Nick's failure to have been present when Cosentino died could have put his own life in jeopardy, but his brother promised to tell no one that he hadn't taken part. Cosentino's body would be found weeks later, decaying in the trunk of a car that turned up at a city auto pound.

Nick would not repeat the mistake when, about a year later, the crew worked to take out burglar John Mendell as payback for the Accardo burglary.

He was there in the garage waiting for Jarrett to bring Mendell to his death. "Ronnie stole with him," Nick told the jury. "Ronnie knew him; that's how he was going to bring him."

Nick had waited with his brother and Gumba for Mendell to walk in first, with Jarrett following close behind.

"We grabbed him," Nick remembered. "Gumba grabbed him, and my brother grabbed him and had him leaning against the car, and they were punching him in the stomach."

He had helped Gumba hold Mendell down as his brother strangled the burglar with a rope. Frank Sr. had killed him, Nick said, as his brother sat at the defense table with a hand over his mouth, shaking his head as if in disbelief.

"The clothes were taken off, and he was put into the trunk and a black, a big black plastic bag was put over his head," Nick said, remembering how his brother had then held the knife out for him to make sure the job was truly finished, to cut Mendell's throat.

"And did you do that?" Mars asked.

"Yeah," Nick said. "Yes, I did."

And he was well aware of the motive, too, he said.

"To set an example," Nick testified. "This is what happens to you if you—if you screw up and you rob the wrong house."

Renno and Moretti died for the same reason, he said, although Renno just happened to be with the older thief when the mob exacted its revenge on him in the restaurant. He recalled his phone conversation with Jarrett and the "party" they would be going to.

What did that mean?

"That somebody was going to get killed."

Fecarotta had brought them to their death, Nick remembered, he had watched through the door to see the men arrive.

"When they walked in, there was a space between where they walked in and the kitchen was maybe between ten or fifteen feet away, and that's where they walked towards," Nick said. "They were walking towards that way, and they went—everybody just jumped in."

Nick had wound up on Moretti, helping his brother strangle him.

"I was pulling one end of the rope and I had my foot against the side of his head, and then I noticed Gumba got on and started jumping on him. He jumped on him, three or four times on his chest."

Once they were dead, the pair were taken out to a car.

"And I seen Tony Borse come back, went to the sink. They had a rack, and he took out a butcher knife about that big with a wide blade," he said, showing the jury with his hands.

"He walked back out to the car and I summarized, but I knew he was going to cut their throats, because he come back not long after that [and] washed the blood off, because there was blood on the knife."

William Dauber was looking at going back to prison, facing a new gun case, when he decided he'd had enough and that he would cooperate with Alcohol, Tobacco, and Firearms (ATF) agents.

Dauber had plenty to say, having been a collector of street tax for the Outfit in the south suburbs, controlling chop shops, and even serving as a prolific hit man for the mob. Plenty of people had a reason to want him silenced, including bosses in the Chicago Heights crew, such as Albert Tocco, who had asked Dauber to do another murder not long before Dauber decided he was done with organized crime.

Dauber had information not only on Tocco but also on Al Pilotto and Frank "the German" Schweihs. Federal agents were meeting with him at least twice a week, and the debriefings were fruitful. A search warrant had even been served on Tocco's house in late 1979.

On July 2, 1980, Dauber was at the Will County Courthouse with his wife, Charlotte, for a status hearing in a state case. His ATF handler, Dennis Laughrey, was there, too, watching in casual clothes, fully aware that there was a price on Dauber's head. Dauber too was fearful. He had begun starting his car by remote control and sleeping under a bulletproof blanket.

So the agent approached him about an escort home. It might be wise for someone to follow the couple to make sure they got home safely, he told them.

But Dauber declined the offer, deciding he and his wife would be going home alone.

The night before, Nick was in his basement apartment in his brother's Elmwood Park building when Frank Sr. came by with a message, Nick recalled. He needed to get one of their vehicles ready, a Mustang the brothers had nicknamed "little Casey" because it was used in casing jobs. Nick should make sure it had gas and oil and was ready to go, his brother had said.

"Then he says something to the effect that Ange says that this is another one of the Wild Bunch and they've been dogging it and that something had—they were going to do some work," Nick remembered. "They were going to do some work, so my brother sort of like lit a fire under their rear ends."

The Wild Bunch wasn't carrying out the orders to eliminate Dauber quickly enough. "They were taking a long time trying to kill these people," Nick explained.

Near Diversey Avenue and Richmond Street on the North Side, the brothers kept a garage for two vehicles near the Kennedy Expressway. Nick parked a couple of blocks away and walked to fetch the Mustang. He needed to approach carefully, on foot, because the crew kept a true work car in the garage as well.

"The difference is the Mustang that he was going to drive was a legit car under a phony name," Nick said. "The work car was strictly used . . . for work, 'work' meaning if you were on the street and you were going to use guns or whatever, you would use this car."

Nick took the Mustang and filled it up and checked the tires, leaving it for his brother on a one-way street a few blocks away.

The next day, in the afternoon, Nick said his brother told him what had happened.

"The Little Guy," Ronnie Jarrett, had been driving a van that would be used in the killings. Gerald Scarpelli and William "Butch" Petrocelli had been inside, Scarpelli with a shotgun and Petrocelli with a carbine.

Frank Sr. in the Mustang had been the blocking vehicle, moving around the Daubers as they drove home from court. He had moved in front of them and slowed, keeping them in place.

"To get the van enough time to get alongside of them and open up on them," Nick said.

The bullets fired from the men in the van tore into the Daubers as they made their way from the courthouse in downtown Joliet to their home in the outer suburb of Crete. Their car left Manhattan-Monee Road, and was found by authorities up against an apple tree six hundred feet off the pavement. The couple had been hit with multiple rounds from the rifles, and shells were found inside their car, indicating someone had shot them at close range to finish them off.

"And he says once they did it, the car went off," Nick recalled Frank Sr. telling him. "And then Ronnie, the Little Guy, was driving, and he drove the van off to near where the car was, because it hit a tree. And that Scarpelli got out and leaned in and fired some more of his shotgun shells."

Frank Sr. and Petrocelli both had done their jobs, but their history of bad blood would boil over just a few months later.

It was around New Year's Eve in 1980 when Outfit leaders reached their limit in dealing with the outspoken mobster. His profile was rising, and he wasn't doing much to stay below the radar as those in charge wished. He'd thrown a lavish Christmas party that year at a Chicago hotel with booze and hookers, not the kind of thing the bosses approved of.

And there had been a juice agent Frank Sr. worked with, a man named Tommy McCarthy, Nick told the jury. He had been introduced to the Chinatown crew by a guy named "Blind Louie."

"He was actually blind," Nick said.

Blind Louie and McCarthy would give out juice, and Frank Sr. had agreed. Nick would meet McCarthy on Saturdays, sometimes at a bar he owned near the old neighborhood. One Saturday Nick couldn't find McCarthy, and he turned up shot at O'Hare International Airport a week later. Petrocelli was being blamed for it.

"In Italian there's a word; it's called *spaccone*," Nick said. "Which means flamboyant and stuff. [Petrocelli] was—people were afraid of him in the neighborhood he come from, and he was doing things he wasn't supposed to be doing, saying things he wasn't supposed to be saying, things like that."

McCarthy's hit wasn't authorized, but Petrocelli's would be. Angelo LaPietra himself would become involved in seeing "Butchie" taken out.

The men would meet at a club on Fourteenth Street in Cicero, and LaPietra would come up with a reason to send Petrocelli a few doors down to an alley office. Waiting inside would be a hit squad that included Frank Sr., Nick, Jimmy LaPietra, and a man named Frank Santucci. Outside, communicating with the killing team by walkie-talkie, would be Johnny "Apes" Monteleone and Frank Furio, watching for Petrocelli. Monteleone was driving Nick's wife's car, Nick said, after they had pulled the license plates off it and put a license-applied-for sticker in the window.

The first time Petrocelli had arrived to see Angelo at the social club, where men would relax and play cards, he had brought someone else. This had thrown a wrench in the plan, because the hit team didn't want the person who was with him to become suspicious when Petrocelli didn't come back from his errand.

The killing was called off, with Nick and the others waiting in the nearby office, a small space with a desk and a chair. Nick's job was to allow Petrocelli to get into the room and then make sure the door was shut and locked behind him.

It was just a day later when the crew decided they would try again. It was the same plan, with Angelo LaPietra again seeing Petrocelli at the social club. This time, though, he sent Butch down to the office on some kind of business.

"I don't recall how long we waited," Nick told Mars. "It might have been a half-hour, forty-five minutes, I'm not sure. And we could see—there was a front window—we could see down by the sidewalk, and I forgot if it was myself or somebody else said, 'Here he comes.'"

Petrocelli came walking up, Nick remembered, and through the door, which was quickly closed behind him.

"It happened so fast," Nick said. "He was on the ground. I don't remember if we taped his legs or what, but I remember holding him down and my brother choking him."

A few moments later Petrocelli was dead. His body lay on the floor of the office "for a while," Nick said, while his brother went to look for the mobster's car.

Frank Sr. brought the red 1977 Ford LTD into the alley, which was mostly out of the way and out of sight. The group had to wait only for a moment, to allow a woman and a small boy to walk past, before they could move Butchie out. The body had been wrapped up and was placed in the backseat with the head on the passenger's side, Nick said.

Frank Sr. got in the car with the body, Nick said, he believed to follow the normal procedure and cut Petrocelli's throat.

"But I don't know if he did anything else, 'cause he didn't particularly like Petrocelli," Nick said. "There was friction between them."

The men had feuded over juice customers and Frank Sr. hadn't forgiven Petrocelli for getting Tony Borsellino killed not long after Renno and Moretti had been murdered in the restaurant.

Frank Sr. and Furio parked Petrocelli's car with the body inside on a side street, and they returned to the office. But as it turned out, Petrocelli had again come to the club with someone else. It was Gerald Scarpelli, a fellow member of the Wild Bunch.

Scarpelli had stayed with Angelo LaPietra while Petrocelli walked down the street for his errand. Once his friend was gone, LaPietra had told him that Butch would not be returning, Nick said.

"We have to go back," Nick remembered his brother saying when he returned from parking Petrocelli's car. Scarpelli wanted to go to the vehicle to make sure he hadn't left anything in it. The capo had said that was OK but had a message for Frank Sr. behind Scarpelli's back.

"Angelo LaPietra told him, if he balks, flatten 'em," Nick remembered. LaPietra gave Frank Sr. instant permission to kill Scarpelli if there was any funny business at the car.

"It meant to leave him right there, kill him and leave him there."

So the Calabrese brothers and Scarpelli drove in Nick's wife's car to where Petrocelli had been left. Nick sat as Scarpelli was allowed to look in the vehicle for a few minutes under the watchful eye of Frank Sr.

When he was done, they returned again to the social club. Frank Sr. and Scarpelli got out, and Nick again waited in the car. But his night wasn't over.

"I don't know how long it was, my brother come back and he says, 'Ange wants us to burn the car,'" Nick recalled.

So the brothers would have to return to Petrocelli's car yet again, but not before stopping at a local convenience store for two large cans of Zippo lighter fluid.

They pulled up, and Frank Sr. parked at the end of the street, watching to see if anyone would drive into the area. He ordered his brother to the parked car, telling him it was still open.

Nick said he emptied one can of lighter fluid in the front and one in the back, and then threw a lighted book of matches inside.

"I heard like a 'phewww,'" Nick remembered. "So I got out of the car, and I walked back where my brother was parked, and he yelled at me, he says, 'You were supposed to leave the window open, the fire went out.'"

The attempt to burn the car had merely blackened the windows, but the brothers wouldn't be hanging around to try again. They drove back to the club for Frank Sr. to talk to LaPietra. There would be some concern that the car hadn't been fully engulfed in flames. Even weeks later, Nick said, the capo had some concern that maybe Petrocelli had actually survived the hit.

Nick went by on a main street that he could see the car from, just to check on it.

"Could you see in the windows?" Mars asked.

"No, because it was too far away; plus there was snow on the car," Nick said.

But there was no doubt Petrocelli was out of their hair.

On March 14, 1981, two Chicago patrol officers were flagged down on South Kostner and told that a body had been found in the backseat of a car. Its windows were darkened, and there was a dead man inside, wrapped in a blue comforter. His face appeared to have been burned, except around his mouth, where a piece of duct tape had been placed. With no knowledge of Nick's failed attempt to burn the car, they were left to speculate that maybe he had even been tortured with a blowtorch.

As they did with the other murders they committed together, the brothers had a code for the Petrocelli murder, in case they needed to say something about it in the presence of someone else. They would pinch their left cheek, Nick said.

"That's a gesture in Italian that means like a *spaccone*, a big shot, or something."

11

EXPLOSION ON THE TOLLWAY

Michael Cagnoni was in his midthirties in 1980, but he was already a very successful businessman.

He had come up with a model for a shipping organization that moved dried fruit and produce between California growers and their customers with more than twelve hundred trailers on rails and trucks. Cooperative Shippers used contracted carriers to get the fruits and vegetables where they needed to go.

Cagnoni was living with his family in Hinsdale, a tony suburb west of Chicago, and driving a shiny new Mercedes. He would drive it most workdays from his home, heading up Vine Street to Ogden Avenue. He would head less than a mile east to the Tri-State Tollway, taking a southbound ramp to merge with the morning traffic. On the tollway he would make his way down to the Stevenson Expressway, taking that east into the city and exiting at Damen Avenue, where his business offices were located.

Cagnoni was the brain coordinating the shipping lines for peak efficiency, and as the chief executive, he did what he could to ward off any problems that might slow down the business. Those problems included headaches with some of the Teamsters who labored for the company, doing jobs such as running trucks and working the docks.

One of the contracted companies making deliveries around Chicago for Cagnoni was Flash Trucking of Cicero, described by prosecutors as a longtime mob operation in the suburb. The company was run by organized crime figures Michael and Paul Spano, who were reputed to be connected to mob leadership in the town made famous as a base for Al Capone. Cagnoni's head of security would drive him there for meetings. The Spanos would see Cagnoni, and sometimes so would John "Pudge" Matassa, a chubby mobster who had roots with the Outfit's North Side crews and became the driver for James Marcello. Matassa was among those with his hands on unions that could trip up Cagnoni's system.

Flash would be paid by check, but that wasn't all Cagnoni was bringing on his visits to Cicero. He would carry a briefcase stuffed with so much cash he sometimes had to bring extra brown paper bags to tote the overflow. The mob wanted its tribute paid by the truck, which added up to several thousands of dollars every couple of weeks. His efforts to pay off Matassa and others above him saw the businessman create forty or fifty fake names to generate what was being demanded. He would give the checks to his security chief, Fred Pavlich, who would cash them at a currency exchange.

The meetings and the passing of cash went on and on, with Pavlich sometimes shuttling Cagnoni to hotel meetings in the northwest suburb of Rosemont, near O'Hare. There he saw Cagnoni meet Paul Spano as well as Rocky Infelice, another Cicero mobster, and Dominic Senese, the secretary-treasurer for union produce drivers who would survive a hit later in the 1980s. Tony "Big Tuna" Accardo even made an appearance.

Cagnoni and his lucrative business were known to the highest echelon of the Chicago Outfit.

But eventually Cagnoni grew weary of paying. He felt like he was undercutting his own efforts by spending more time making up ghosts for his payroll than he was coming up with the next innovative idea in his industry, and he was complaining and trying to cut off the mob.

Enter the Calabrese brothers.

In October 1980, Nick drove Frank Sr. to a restaurant after he was summoned by Angelo and Jimmy LaPietra. Nick waited in the car for thirty minutes or so until Frank Sr. reemerged with two addresses and a name. It was another instance in which the Wild Bunch was dragging out a killing, so the mob's real enforcement arm was being pressed back into service. Frank Sr. and his crew had some work to do.

"What did you understand that to mean?" Mars asked during Nick's second morning on the witness stand.

"Well, we were going to start checking on this guy and see if we could find a pattern," Nick told the jury in a near monotone. "See what he does, if he does something the same time every week or goes to the same place every so often, to try to nail him down to a spot."

"For what purpose?" Mars asked quickly.

"To kill him."

There were two addresses on Frank Sr.'s slip, one on Damen Avenue and one on Vine Street in Hinsdale. The brothers would use the code word *wine* for the home of Michael Cagnoni.

Nick took trips to both to have a look.

"The business was on Damen, south of Blue Island, because he had a big, big piece of property where there was a lot of tractor-trailers, a lot of empty trailers, and there was an office building about maybe 150 yards off Damen," Nick said. You could see Nick picturing it as he spoke, remembering how he coldly studied it.

"There was one way in and out."

Cagnoni's house was just a few blocks south of Ogden on the west side of the street in a nice neighborhood. But it wouldn't be the easiest to scout. There was no street parking, making it hard to sit outside for long periods and see who came and went and what time Cagnoni typically left for work.

Were there two crews targeting Cagnoni at the time?

"The other crew stopped," Nick said of the Wild Bunch. "We were the ones that were going to do it."

And perhaps of all the killings that Nick would describe, the Cagnoni murder was the one that took the most determination. It would be an attack on a civilian completely outside the normal circle. There would be little chance of luring Cagnoni anywhere, and the crew's opportunity to observe him would be limited. It would somehow have to be done in public, and it would have to take some cruel ingenuity.

Without the ability to sit outside of "wine" to watch Cagnoni leave in the morning, the crew tried to watch the office on Damen, a very busy arterial. If they could figure out when he was leaving, they would be able to follow him. But there was no parking on Damen, either, just a small area off the roadway where a car could sit for only an hour or so before the hit squad feared a vehicle would start drawing attention.

"So we took turns," Nick explained. "One guy would stay parked for an hour, an hour and a half, and then leave. Then another guy would do the same so it wouldn't be the same car there all the time."

But even with all of their precautions, the crew would not go unnoticed. An FBI agent in a special operations group following John Fecarotta trailed him from his Riverside home on March 11, 1981. He had watched Fecarotta have breakfast and then meet up with Frank Sr. The men had driven a white Oldsmobile to an industrial area at 2520 S. Damen, in the area of the Cagnoni office. They could be seen talking briefly to Frank Santucci, who was behind the wheel of a somewhat conspicuous AMC Hornet. Agents weren't clear what the men were doing, watching as the group eventually headed north to the area of North Riverside Park Mall.

Unable to sit long enough on the street at either location, the hit team began to "spot-check" the locations, Nick said, sending different cars by in fifteen- to twenty-minute intervals in the hope of getting lucky and catching Cagnoni leaving.

Once, around the time the FBI followed Fecarotta to the area, Nick did manage to see Cagnoni leaving his house. So he followed him, again hoping to establish something about his movements. But that's where his good fortune ended. He followed Cagnoni all the way to Rockford, where apparently he happened to be going to a funeral. The trail was worthless, and the crew was back to zero.

There would be no chance for a Haggerty-style kidnapping or even the kind of orchestrated vehicle hit employed against the Daubers. A decision was made to change tactics.

"And what sort of plan was developed as to how to effect the murder?" Mars asked.

"To use a bomb," Nick said. It was either Fecarotta or his brother who had come up with the plan, or possibly both of them, he said.

"It appeared that there was no way that we'd be able to set up on Mr. Cagnoni to shoot him or to grab him because there was no place that he went that we could catch him at that we could do this."

Over at his defense table Frank Sr. was again leaning toward his brother. His hearing was a little suspect, so he had a hand cupped to his ear to make sure he didn't miss anything.

A remote starter would be the way to go, Nick said his brother had decided, so it was determined that Frank Sr. would go to see Michael Spilotro about getting some. Spilotro eventually came through, giving Frank Sr. ten of them.

They were taken to one of the crew's work garages, where Frank Sr., Fecarotta, and Jimmy "Poker" DiForti, who by then also was in on the project, began their experiments. By this time the hit was taking longer than expected, Nick said, so there came a time in 1981 when Angelo LaPietra had to be updated.

"Just that we were working on it and it was difficult," he said.

The killing substance would be a challenge, too. Frank Sr. thought dynamite would be too unstable, Nick told the jury, because the bomb idea had evolved into getting to Cagnoni's car and planting a device under his seat. Eventually the brothers wound up waiting on Twenty-Sixth Street for Johnny "Apes" Monteleone. He brought the brothers a bag that would help them. It contained a package, and inside the package was a powerful plastic explosive wrapped in duct tape, Nick said. It was a small brick around eight inches long and five inches wide.

If the plan was successful, the crew could one day extort business-men by showing up with a garage door opener, as one of their associates would one day joke.

Meanwhile the experiments with the remote starters continued. Frank Sr., Fecarotta, and DiForti used them over and over and marked the distances from which they were effective. It was a crude laboratory set up with the goal of killing one man.

"First they found out how the unit worked and how it went together and how you'd have to rig up the detonator cap to the receiving unit of this remote starter," Nick told Mars as the jurors scribbled their notes. "One time they hooked up the detonator cap to it and put it in an empty five-gallon plastic container to see how far away they could go before it wouldn't work with the remote."

The crew thought it would work, but now they needed access to the car. Still sitting on Cagnoni from time to time, they eventually followed him to a Michigan Avenue parking garage, and while he was gone, Poker went at it with a slim jim.

But there would be another hurdle. DiForti couldn't get it open. He tried until the squad felt it had overstayed its welcome.

"So what he did was, he knew somebody that had a similar Mercedes and borrowed it and brought it to his shop," Nick said. "He had a mechanics shop on Cicero and Twenty-Second. He took the door apart and found out there was a piece of steel that went crossways on the door so you couldn't use a slim jim to open it."

With a little practice, DiForti found he could manage to get in. And with all their difficulties seemingly behind them, the crew set to planting the device. But there would be more trouble. On the way to Cagnoni's home, a blasting cap exploded in Frank Sr.'s hand—the incident he would describe to his son on the tape in prison more than twenty years later. Frank Sr. had blamed it on some unknown transmitter in the area, but Nick said he believed someone in the car keyed a walkie-talkie without knowing it was on the same frequency as the remote starter.

The explosion sent shrapnel into Frank Sr.'s hand, Nick said, so the kill was once again scrapped. The medical treatment would be given by a neighborhood doctor in Bridgeport.

Yet another attempt on Cagnoni was made sometime later, after Frank Sr. had healed. The team actually had gotten the bomb into the car while it was parked at the Hinsdale house. Cagnoni had gotten all the way to work and been there for the day, before Fecarotta saw him leave the Damen office. He followed Cagnoni back toward the Stevenson Expressway as the target made his way home, but as he repeatedly pressed the remote, nothing happened.

The signal wasn't strong enough. So the team went back that night and had to retrieve the bomb from the Mercedes.

More testing ensued, Nick told the jury. The crew tried a series of different antennas to boost the strength of the remote, eventually deciding on a six-foot CB antenna known as a K-40. Nick bought it at a Berwyn store. To the receiver the crew hooked up a tester that would light up when the receiver was getting the signal. It was decided that the remote now was strong enough, and they were close to accomplishing their ghoulish task.

Not long thereafter the crew was able to follow Cagnoni to a restaurant where he was having lunch. They pulled up next to his car in a van, and DiForti went to work. Using the technique he had developed in his garage, he used a heavy screwdriver, with a rag under it so as not to scratch the paint, to pry out a corner of the door of the Mercedes. He got it open, and placed the explosive and the receiver under Cagnoni's seat, a unit powered by a small motorcycle battery, Nick said.

Cagnoni would have lunch that day with a woman named Rita Daly, who worked on setting shipping rates. As they got out of the car, she would distinctly remember Cagnoni hitting his auto-lock button. But when they returned from eating, she reached for the door handle and found it was unlocked. That was odd, she thought, but Cagnoni hadn't seemed to think so.

"Just get in the car, Rita," he had said.

Cagnoni would finish working and drive his Mercedes home for the night. And there the bomb would sit, waiting for him to head back to the office in the morning.

To fire the explosive, the crew would take another step to avoid being caught. They had stolen a car that fall, leaving it in an Outfit garage to use as a work car in the future. Often vehicles would sit, Nick would explain, waiting until the time Chicago police would take them off their current rolls of stolen cars. License plates would be stolen for them, often from cars of the same make, model, year, and color found on the street. In this case it was a black Buick that would be pressed into service.

"Well, my brother and John Fecarotta had figured out that the best way to do this would be to . . ." And again Nick paused. He was clearly having difficulty recalling this murder, too. He exhaled deeply and tapped his fingers on the stand as he controlled his emotions and continued.

"To park the car near the ramp that Cagnoni used to get on the tollway."

The crew would park the stolen car at an Ogden Avenue restaurant with a parking lot that backed up to the ramp. They would leave the remote starter, boosted by the K-40 antenna, locked in the on position. As Cagnoni went to work along his usual route, all he would have to do was drive into range.

Nick would park the Buick in position, and Frank Sr. would drive by and pick Nick up as he left the lot on foot. Nick left the remote on the floor of the car, and the antenna had been placed in the center of the car's roof.

Fecarotta would be in the area of the Cagnoni house as spotter and would watch as the crew got its final surprise of the effort.

Cagnoni's wife and son were the first to get into the Mercedes that morning, June 24, 1981, as Mrs. Cagnoni drove the child to school before her husband went to work. She had left the house as Fecarotta watched, but she'd turned the opposite direction from where the remote starter had been planted in the stolen Buick. She made her quick school run, never getting near the tollway.

The jury would later hear from Margaret Wenger, Cagnoni's wife, who told them her husband had been acting strangely in the weeks leading up to that day, the day after her birthday, but he wouldn't tell her what was bothering him. She didn't think he had any enemies.

When Wenger returned with the car, her husband was ready to leave for work. "He hugged me and kissed me goodbye and said, 'Remember, I love you very much,'" Wenger would say in a soft voice. She didn't know it as her husband walked from the house, but she was pregnant that morning.

Cagnoni got into his Mercedes as he usually did, apparently still not noticing the device hidden under the seat. He headed up Vine Street, turned right onto Ogden, and then went east.

James Mammina was on his way to work, too. He was driving his bronze-colored Club Wagon van from his condominium in Downers

Grove to a container business in Summit and allowed a car to turn in front of him on the ramp to the southbound Tri-State.

He followed it down the ramp—a Mercedes—trailing it by about twenty-five feet and accelerating to merge with traffic.

It was then that the Chicago Outfit's persistence finally paid off. There was a white flash and a thunderous explosion, catapulting much of the car into the sky and sending a wave of heat over the van. The air suddenly smelled of gunpowder, and a pockmarked crater appeared on the seared concrete where the bomb had detonated under Cagnoni. Mammina realized the roadway in front of him had suddenly become slick, and he hit the brakes, sliding on something.

He turned on his windshield wipers, pushing splattered liquid to the side. The roadway in front of him was a horror, littered with debris and body parts.

Michael Kown was on the Ogden overpass above the tollway, headed to pick up a girlfriend, when there was the shock of an explosion to his left. His reflexes made him look in time to see the airborne pieces of the car. Much of the chassis of the Mercedes continued forward for about fifty yards, drifting left before coming to rest against a guardrail.

Kown had worked as a firefighter and thought maybe he could be of some help. He turned and drove down the ramp, parking about a football field from where the sedan had come to rest. First he ran up to the van, checking to see that its shaken driver was all right, and then he continued walking toward what was left of the Mercedes.

It had stopped where the guardrail separated the southbound ramp from a curved northbound ramp going back toward Ogden. Kown stepped over onto the other ramp to make an approach on the driver's side of the Mercedes. There was no fire as he approached, and he remembered no sound.

As he walked up, it quickly became clear that there would be no one to aid.

From just five yards away, he could see the driver still in his seat; the driver's door and the roof above his head were gone. His skin was ashen gray, and his lungs were exposed.

The bottom half of his body had been completely blown away.

From somewhere nearby, Frank Sr. was calling Fecarotta to find out what had happened. The brothers would meet him at a nearby plaza, where he had parked in a service drive.

"And John says it went off," Nick remembered. "And then he said that his wife had taken the car that morning. . . . Mr. Cagnoni's wife had taken the car with the kid in it, with her stepson . . . and drove him to school," Nick said, his voice growing a little louder and then trailing off. He was again having trouble keeping his emotions in check.

"When I heard that, I just . . ." Nick said with a quiver in his voice. "I don't know what I felt. I just . . . all I kept thinking was this poor woman got in this car, and if she'd come the opposite way, the bomb would have went off, because the remote was set. If she had come east instead of going west, that bomb would have went off."

It had upset him at the time, too, Nick told Mars. He had said something to his brother about their plan nearly killing a woman and a child.

"After John Fecarotta left, I got into an argument with my brother about this happening, and with that he hit me on the left side of the face."

It was only later that he learned the blow actually had broken a bone in his face, he testified.

"He hit me hard enough that at the end of the year, 1981, I had to go to a doctor because when the weather started changing, my face hurt a lot," Nick said, and he'd had an operation. Over at the defense table, Frank Sr. was smirking again.

It was during the course of the Cagnoni surveillance that Nick said he'd heard about the killing years earlier of federal witness Daniel Seifert. There was a conversation at a Melrose Park restaurant among Nick, Fecarotta, and his brother, Nick told the jury. Fecarotta, one of the Outfit's top wheelmen, told the brothers he had been involved in the 1974 killing.

"He was driving one of the work cars," Nick testified.

And what did he say about the event?

"Well, he started talking, [and] he says the German screwed up because he didn't cuff this guy right and the guy got away," Nick said. It had been Frank Schweihs who had left the cuffs at the Bensenville business for investigators to find.

A mob soldier named Joey Hansen had been the one to shoot Seifert in the head. Also there were Schweihs, Jimmy LaPietra, Anthony Spilotro, and Joey Lombardo himself.

"Did Fecarotta tell you why this murder was committed?" Mars asked.

"Because the guy was supposed to testify at a trial against Lombardo," Nick answered.

Mars proceeded to show Nick photos of the work car left at the Pontiac dealership as the killers fled the shooting. Did anyone in his crew know how to modify cars for Outfit business?

Yes, Nick answered. Jimmy DiForti was an expert in such work. DiForti had been the one to figure out how to get into Cagnoni's Mercedes.

"Well, what was done was switches were put inside the car so at any time you can use these switches to turn either the brake lights, the headlights, the taillights, the parking lights on and off," Nick said. "In case you were being chased, you could change the appearance of a car from a distance. You wouldn't see any lights in the back of the car or in the front if you use these switches to turn them off."

Nick looked at photos of the brown Ford LTD. The quick change plate on its rear bumper was a typical mob modification, he said. It would allow the crew to slide stolen plates in front of the plates actually registered to the car to do a job and then quickly pull the stolen plates away without a screwdriver as they left.

Probably in the same conversation about Seifert, Nick also recalled Fecarotta telling him that Lombardo was a made member who had "done some work" with Anthony Spilotro.

"And when you say he had done some work, what does that mean?" Mars asked.

"Means killing."

And Nick recalled efforts to take out a man named Sam Annerino, a south suburban enforcer that government witness Alva Johnson Rodgers had once placed on Lombardo's "hit parade." It was 1977, and the Wild Bunch and the Chinatown crew again were both placed on the same job. Nick said he had heard that Annerino had become an informant and that he was to be quieted for good.

The plan was to lure Annerino to the site of an old hot-dog stand and another building on Twenty-Sixth Street that was being remodeled and turned into the Italian American Club. "Shorty" LaMantia would bring Annerino around to show him the site of the new club, and the hit squad would be waiting for him in the empty building. As in prior murders, it was Nick, Frank Sr., Gumba Saladino, and Ronnie Jarrett lying in wait.

For a couple of weeks they waited in the evenings, but Annerino never appeared. LaMantia wasn't able to get him there but did appear once at the site with Angelo LaPietra. Nick remembered Shorty walking in and seeing the Calabreses and their henchmen.

"And when Angelo walked in and [Shorty] seen us standing there, he got scared; he turned white because he thought that he was going to be killed," Nick recalled.

Eventually the crew had enough of the waiting and decided to hang out at Jarrett's mother-in-law's to wait for word on whether Annerino would be making it to the club. As they waited, the phone rang and Frank Sr. would get the message. The Wild Bunch had come through, and Chinatown wouldn't have to trouble itself with Annerino.

Just a few months after Cagnoni was killed, Nick said he participated in his first murder without his brother. He went to a meeting with Frank Sr. and Angelo, where he got his assignment.

"Angelo said that I was to wait home from now on for a call," Nick said. Stay there all day, LaPietra had said. If there was no call by late afternoon, Nick could go about his business. For two or three weeks, he stayed at home waiting, and no call came.

Finally LaPietra summoned him, and Nick had done as he was told. He was there to take the call. LaPietra would meet Nick without

Frank Sr. They met on the Southwest Side, and LaPietra picked Nick up, driving around for a time to make sure he was "clean."

"That's a term you used to make sure you don't have anybody following you."

Nick wasn't really paying attention to where they wound up, but LaPietra drove to a location where a van was waiting. In the van were Sam "Wings" Carlisi, and James Marcello of the Melrose Park crew, Nick told the jury. He knew who they were but had never worked with them before.

The men drove to a Chicago Heights restaurant, stopped briefly as the leaders took a look, and then drove right back to where LaPietra was parked. And that was it. Nick was told to go home and wait again for another phone call.

Wasn't there any talk about what this was all about? Mars asked.

No, Nick said, especially not in a car, and not when they returned either.

"You're not supposed to ask," Nick said. "When you're told, you're told. You just don't say, 'What do you want me for? What am I supposed to do?'"

But Nick wouldn't have to wait nearly as long this time around. He got the call and picked up Fecarotta the following Sunday, he said, using another "little Casey" the crew was employing. Fecarotta took Nick south again, this time following orders to be at a highway oasis at a certain time.

Fecarotta dropped him there, and Nick got into a green Cadillac with Carlisi and LaPietra that was driven by Marcello, Nick told Mars.

They drove back to Chicago Heights, meeting two old men Nick had never seen before at a fast-food place. They were standing near what looked like an unmarked squad car from the 1960s, a Ford. They were dressed in black, he remembered, and were wearing black gloves. Nick would be in prison with Marcello almost two decades later before he would learn that one of the men was the father of Melrose Park crew member Tony Zizzo. The old Ford pulled away and the Cadillac followed.

Nick found himself at a building that looked like a warehouse, with an overhead garage door and a service door on the side. Inside were aisles and rows of shelves. Nick stood inside with the three men who had ridden there in the Cadillac. The older men who had shown them the building were now out of sight, he said, and Fecarotta and Tony "the Hatch" Chiaramonti were waiting outside to make sure the scene was clear.

Even standing in the warehouse, Nick still had no idea what exactly he was doing there. He would wait for Carlisi to reveal what was going on as the boss handed Nick a baseball bat.

"He says, 'Somebody is going to bring a guy,'" Nick explained. Of the two guys that walked into the building, Nick was to let the shorter one have it with the bat, Carlisi had said. Hit the shorter guy in the shoulder and knock him down. The four men then hid in the aisle, Nick gripping the bat with gloved hands.

The plan seemed simple enough, but there were always curve balls.

The door opened and closed, and the taller man and the shorter man walked in. But they had come in only about thirty feet when the taller man—the guy Nick *wasn't* supposed to hit with the bat—took off, complicating the picture.

"He just ran," Nick explained; the element of surprise was gone. "And the other guy caught the play; he figured there was something wrong. Why would the guy run? There's only one reason why he would run."

So Nick decided there was no time like the present, and he moved from his hiding place with the bat. The shorter man was moving toward a wall with a pair of doors, looking for a way out. Nick swung the bat, striking the man in the shoulder.

"The bat just bounced off like I was hitting rubber," Nick remembered. "Shorter" definitely didn't mean weaker, since the man he was attacking was built like a fireplug. "I dropped the bat, and I jumped on his back, and this guy was super, super strong."

It was easy to believe looking at a man in the courtroom gallery that day. Bob D'Andrea, the son of the man Nick was describing, was glaring around the room at Nick and Marcello, the latter seated at his defense table with a passive expression. Wearing a tight T-shirt,

D'Andrea was an obvious weightlifter, with huge arms and a wide back. He wore his hair short and had a goatee. His mouth was drawn tightly as he stared at Nick. If he had decided to make a break for the witness stand to exact revenge, it might have taken ten U.S. marshals to keep him on the ground.

"I had my arms around his neck and I finally worked my way and he fell on top of me," Nick said, describing how Nicholas D'Andrea was wrestled to the ground. Marcello, Carlisi, and LaPietra joined in, getting D'Andrea cuffed as he struggled.

Someone had tried to shoot Chicago Heights gangster Al Pilotto not long before, angering some of his fellow capos. Now Carlisi was looking for information, believing that D'Andrea, a mob associate, at least knew something about it. He started his attempt at extracting that information with a .45, Nick said, whacking D'Andrea with the butt end of it over and over, at least a few times while Nick's hand was in the way. Finally, they had cuffs on him and his ankles taped.

Marcello backed the Cadillac in through the overhead door, and D'Andrea was placed in the back on the floor in front of the backseat, Nick remembered. The men got in and headed for a house, he said, but Carlisi wasn't through pummeling D'Andrea.

"On the way there, Carlisi was—the guy was moaning and Carlisi was hitting him with the back end of a shotgun," Nick said, telling Mars that Carlisi was cursing their victim and telling him to shut up.

When they got to the house, they pulled into a garage and left D'Andrea in the car for a time, Nick said, and when someone went back out to check on him, it was discovered that he was dead.

"That's when it was mentioned that they wanted to talk to him," Nick said.

Too late for that. So the men began deciding what to do with the body. First they took off some of their bloody clothes from the fight with D'Andrea, and then someone went to go through D'Andrea's pockets.

"And we were in, like, this den; there was a pool table there, and I don't remember who said it, but there was some money in the guy's pocket," Nick told the jury. "Somebody said, 'Give it to the guys that are not made.' Which was me, Chiaramonti, and Marcello."

They each got about $200, he said. Nick left and made his way to a hotel closer to home, where he had some coffee and called it a night. He would have nothing to do with the disposal of the body, which would turn up in the trunk of a burning car in the suburbs.

When he got home, he took a walk with Frank Sr., and told him everything that had happened, even though he wasn't supposed to. Frank Sr. had been puzzled by why Nick was chosen for the job, and he urged him not to screw it up, "because I'm not really that sharp," Nick said.

Nick also never saw the taller guy again, either, the one who brought D'Andrea to the warehouse that day. Prosecutors said that was Sam Guzzino, another mobster who ran in south suburban circles. Jimmy LaPietra had filled Nick in about a week after the warehouse incident by showing him a newspaper article. Apparently Outfit leaders were unhappy to learn how Guzzino had fled and nearly botched the D'Andrea killing.

LaPietra pointed to the paper and said that was the guy, Nick recalled.

"I said, 'What guy?' And he says, 'That was the guy that run,' and he had been found dead."

"If I give up my brothers"

On Sunday, October 9, 1983, most of Chicago spent the day watching Walter Payton and the Bears lose at Soldier Field to the Minnesota Vikings. But not Nick and Frank Calabrese Sr.

Jimmy LaPietra drove the brothers to a closed restaurant on Roosevelt Road, west of Mannheim Road, in western Cook County, not far from Mt. Carmel and Queen of Heaven cemeteries, where mobsters such as Al Capone and Sam Giancana were buried. Frank Sr. had gotten a car with dealer plates from a mob-connected car lot, just in case someone might try to follow them. The place they were headed—and who was there—would require the extra step to keep things secure.

After they parked, Frank Sr. and Nick walked into the kitchen and looked around, finding an Outfit waiting room of sorts. Sitting here and there were Jimmy Marcello, Tony Zizzo, Rocky Infelice, Johnny "Pudge" Matassa, Albert Tocco, and others. Several of the Chicago Outfit's crews had sent men to the restaurant, men who were ready to make the ultimate commitment to their brothers in Chicago's powerful crime family.

One at a time, the men would be called into the dining area, escorted by Al "the Pizza Man" Tornabene, a member of the Outfit's Chicago Heights crew. The rest would be left waiting for their turn to be brought before the mob's "Number One."

Nick waited for a time, and then it was his turn. Along with the other men waiting in the kitchen, he was to be made that day.

Nick walked through the dining room and up to a table where Chicago's boss, Joey "Doves" Aiuppa, was seated with his court. Most

219

of the capos from the Outfit of the day were seated around him. Dominic "Toots" Palermo from the Chicago Heights crew had brought Tocco and another man, Sam Carlisi of the Melrose Park crew had brought Marcello and Zizzo, Vince Solano from Rush Street had brought Matassa and a man Nick knew as Frank Belmonte. John "No Nose" DiFronzo was there for Elmwood Park but had brought no one, while Angelo LaPietra had brought the Calabrese brothers for the mob's Chinatown crew. And there was no Grand Avenue representative; Joey "the Clown" Lombardo was in prison at the time, Nick would later remember.

Nick stood before a long table facing Aiuppa, with all of the capos looking at him. He was alone, looking back at the lords of Chicago's underworld.

He looked down, and before him on the table were a gun, a knife, and a candle.

Later he could barely recall what Aiuppa and the others had said to him, remembering at one point he was asked a question and responded that he hadn't been brought up that way.

Aiuppa rose from his seat and walked around to where Nick was standing, holding a Catholic holy card with a picture of a saint on it. He lit it, and dropped the burning card into Nick's waiting open hand.

Nick held the burning card, trying not to show any distress. The point was to ignore the small fire on his palm, to show that he had divorced himself from all fear. Aiuppa told him the time to take his oath had come.

Say it three times, the boss said.

"If I give up my brothers," Nick repeated, "may I burn in hell like this holy picture."

The card was removed, and Aiuppa took a pin and stuck the end of Nick's finger. A drop of blood appeared on his skin.

With that final reminder that his blood was no longer his own, the ceremony ended. Aiuppa and the capos congratulated him on his formal induction into the organization. LaPietra shook his hand.

The brothers had been at Angelo's home in Bridgeport just two days earlier, the Friday before the ceremony, having been summoned without knowing what their capo needed. They had sat at a table in his basement when he gave them the news that he had recommended them to be made, and they could have it if they wanted it. The brothers had said yes, with Nick wondering what saying no would have meant.

Only trusted soldiers who had been tested by committing one or more murders on the Outfit's behalf could be made, and even then it admitted only those who were full-blooded Italian and loyal to their capo. A man like Ronnie Jarrett wasn't a candidate. He was half Irish, and his crew had given him the slang nickname "Menz," meaning half.

Typically the honor meant there was a little more money to be brought in, but being made was a lifelong commitment. The only way out now was "feet first," as Nick would put it, meaning only death could separate a made member from his obligations.

The title brought a measure of respect in the syndicate, and made members were expected to carry themselves a certain way. But it wasn't something that was worn on the sleeve. It was a membership in a shadowy society.

One made member would never introduce himself as being made. Another made member would have to make the introduction. To introduce someone who was not made, the expression was "this is a friend of mine," but in introducing one made man to another, it was *amico nostro*, "this is a friend of ours."

It would be another five years before the Outfit would hold another making ceremony. Jimmy "Poker" DiForti would be among those brought into the fold, as would Tony "the Hatch" Chiaramonti and Gerald Scarpelli. It was also on a Sunday, Father's Day 1988. The Calabrese brothers hadn't been aware of it before it was already over. They were at a party Jimmy LaPietra was throwing for one of his daughters when he quietly told the brothers that their friend Poker had been made that day.

After the ceremony at the restaurant on Roosevelt Road, the brothers were in Angelo LaPietra's presence again. Jimmy and Angelo took Nick and Frank Sr. out to eat for a small celebration of sorts. The men discussed what had happened, with Angelo telling Nick that along with everything else that came with it, the event had provided at least a little more protection.

"We're brothers now," LaPietra told him, "and you've got some insurance. Not much, but you've got some insurance now."

12

FROM CICERO TO LAS VEGAS

Nick could recall at least two other times the Outfit attempted to use a remotely activated bomb in a murder.

One was in 1982, when the Outfit wanted to take out a restaurant owner involved in gambling. Jimmy Marcello had been involved in planning the hit, he said, along with Angelo and Jimmy LaPietra, Sam Carlisi, John Fecarotta, and Joe Amato, leader of gambling rackets in the north suburbs. The target was named Nicholas Sarillo Sr.

"There was some conversation about how this guy was doing the bookmaking without belonging to somebody and he wouldn't—I guess they tried to call him in to talk to him and he wouldn't show up," Nick said. Amato wanted to charge Sarillo street tax, but he wasn't cooperating.

Fecarotta and Frank Sr. went to additional meetings on the killing, Nick said, but he didn't go, because it was determined there were enough men involved already. His brother just asked him to get one of those remote starters like the one the crew had used to blast Michael Cagnoni's Mercedes. It was just a few days later that Nick learned Frank Sr. and Fecarotta had followed Sarillo and set off a device.

Sarillo had been driving down a rural road near Wauconda, and as in the Cagnoni bombing, the effects of the device were devastating. The explosion peeled the blue Ford Econoline open like a tin can, shooting shards and chunks of it all over the road. The main section, still on its wheels, rolled to the left off the asphalt and came to rest in an area of grass a couple of dozen yards from an above-ground swimming pool behind a house.

But unlike in the Cagnoni bombing, the driver survived. The bomb had been planted in an empty storage bin underneath the front passenger's seat, the crew probably figuring the device was so powerful it wouldn't matter that it wasn't right under Sarillo. And the size of the mostly empty van probably provided more space to absorb the blast, investigators believed, sparing him.

Still, former ATF agent John Malooly would later tell the jury that when he rolled up to the debris, he "would have bet his paycheck" that anyone in the van had been killed.

Malooly had investigated the Cagnoni crime scene, finding pieces of the device in the Mercedes wreckage and the equipment in the trigger car still transmitting when authorities located it. At the Sarillo site he found bits of a circuit board that matched the one used when Cagnoni was killed.

Federal agents tried to talk to Sarillo about who might have been looking to eliminate him, but he wasn't interested in giving them any help. That was good enough for the Outfit, since there was no further attempt to kill him.

"They figured he survived that one [and] he kept his mouth shut, so they just let it be," Nick told the jury.

Another bombing around the same time had targeted a motorcycle gang member, Nick said. He had given a remote starter to DiForti to use after a member of the Outlaws was overheard in a bar saying that the gang was going to kill Joey Aiuppa and take over the mob's territory. Not long thereafter a van had been spotted seemingly casing Aiuppa's home, so the mob decided it was better to be safe than sorry. DiForti eventually followed the biker from the bar as the biker drove his Chevy Blazer, and he blew it up, Nick testified.

Nick had been on the sidelines for two straight jobs, but he would participate directly in the crew's next killing. It was July 1983, the summer before the making ceremony, when the Chinatown crew marked Richard Ortiz for death. Ortiz was a popular Cicero bar owner with a lot of friends who knew him as "Chico," but he was on the bad side of Johnny "Apes" Monteleone. Ortiz had been an agent for the burgeoning crime boss but had suddenly stopped turning in the Outfit's take from his juice loans. He wasn't responding to any of Monteleone's messages and was suspected of selling drugs. In addition, Nick said he had learned at a crew meeting that Ortiz was suspected of having a connection to an unauthorized murder of a pizzeria owner.

Any one of those infractions might have brought Monteleone's wrath.

Nick was growing more comfortable on the witness stand as he spoke, sometimes even leaning back in his chair in the black sweatshirt he was wearing that day and crossing his legs as Mitch Mars asked him questions. But he still didn't appear to look in his brother's direction. When the jury would leave on breaks, he would sit at an angle away from the defense tables, resuming his nearly frozen posture.

The crew spent weeks following Ortiz around, Nick said.

"What was going to take place was we were gonna—we knew where his place of business was; he had a bar on Twenty-Second," Nick said. It was the main street cutting east to west across Cicero.

"Jimmy DiForti knew Oritz and knew about the bar. So what we started to do was we were gonna set up and try to follow him, see what kind of pattern he had, and then try to set up at one of the places he went to if he went there often enough."

For this hit the crew actually set up a base in an apartment atop a local catering business and restaurant, where capo Angelo LaPietra would sit near a tall antenna and communicate with crew members. Frank Sr., Nick, Fecarotta, DiForti, and Monteleone would be out in teams with police scanners and CB radios to help get themselves coordinated.

As they moved and watched, they would speak in layered code. Sometimes the code was so thick even LaPietra was clueless about what his men were doing.

"For instance, we would use—talk about like we were driving trucks and that we were backing trucks and spotting them," Nick told Mars. "So we would use a term like, 'Yeah, where you at? I'm by the yard. You got any trucks coming in? No he didn't come in yet,' or something along those lines, so it wouldn't sound like we were talking about doing anything other than working for a trucking company, or driving, or whatever."

LaPietra decided it would be Nick and DiForti who would do the shooting. Frank Sr. would drive the work car.

For much of that summer the crew worked on Ortiz, checking up on him at his bar or at one of the horseracing tracks in the area.

They were having a hard time keeping up with him. Eventually it was decided to make a try at Ortiz's house, Nick said. The three-man hit team would sit in the work car near Twenty-Second and Central Avenue, with Fecarotta on a radio acting as a spotter. If Ortiz was headed their direction from the bar, he would let them know.

One night, Nick said, Fecarotta radioed and Ortiz was coming their way. They had previously decided to approach him from an alley through a gangway. Frank Sr. pulled around, and the plan went into action. He stopped behind the house, and DiForti and Nick made their move.

"We got out of the car. We didn't slam the doors; we just closed them a little bit so we didn't make any noise," Nick told the jury, his voice low and flat.

"Did you have any weapons?" Mars asked.

"We had shotguns and wore ski masks."

The men moved quietly through a gate and through the gangway. They waited in the dark near a porch, trying to get in position to make a strike.

Suddenly Nick realized it wasn't going to work.

"I sort of froze," he explained. "There was no way that we could have gotten from the spot we were at and walked the length of the house and get close to where he parked his car. And it was called off, and I went back to the car."

Mars wanted clarification. Who called it off?

"I did."

Nick and DiForti went back to the car where his brother was waiting, in the alley. They couldn't get to the guy, Nick told him. Frank Sr. was angered, and they drove away. They went back to the garage to ditch the work car and go see their capo.

It was after 1:00 A.M., but LaPietra wanted a meeting anyway. It was outside in a parking lot, Nick remembered, with members of the kill team present. It didn't last long.

"The Old Man," meaning Aiuppa, wanted Ortiz killed, and that was that. If they couldn't do it, LaPietra said, he would do it himself. The stakes were raised, and Nick and his brother spoke afterward.

"I told him, I says, 'The reason it didn't happen was Jimmy, Poker, grabbed my arm,'" Nick said. He had put the blame on DiForti, hoping to spare himself from his brother's anger. LaPietra had been disappointed.

"I didn't want him to start yelling and screaming, so I lied and said it was Jimmy DiForti, Poker," Nick explained.

Well, Mars asked, how did Frank Sr. react to that?

"He said, 'Next time, flatten him.'"

"Meaning what?"

"Kill him."

It was a cold order that Nick wouldn't soon forget, a warning about what could happen to him once the wheels were in motion for a murder to take place. It stayed in his mind, even as the crew pressed to eliminate Ortiz. They would try again within days, taking him out either back at his house or at the Ortiz bar, named His & Mine.

Before long they had their chance. Fecarotta in a spotter car found Ortiz at the horse track, Sportsman's Park, on Laramie Avenue.

Frank Sr. was driving the work car with DiForti in the front and Nick in the back. As before, they had masks at the ready and were armed with shotguns. And this time there would be no screwups. Frank Sr. was armed with a carbine.

In a third car, Nick said, were Monteleone and Jimmy LaPietra. They would act as a crash vehicle in case anyone got too near the shooters in the work car. It was a Ford with a pale top that the Calabrese brothers had dubbed "Blondie."

Fecarotta was following Ortiz as the hit squad, parked on a one-way street near Twenty-Second Street, waited to hear where "Chico" would go. Angelo was back at the apartment, listening on the CB radio. Fecarotta noticed that there were two men in the car. Ortiz had gone to the track that day with a buddy, Arthur Morawski.

Someone radioed LaPietra in the apartment. It wasn't just Ortiz; there were two people in the car, a light gray Mercury Grand Marquis with spokes. What should they do?

LaPietra's voice came across the radio.

"Go ahead," Nick remembered him saying. "Both of them."

Fecarotta followed the Mercury as it came up from the racetrack, heading north on Laramie and then east on Twenty-Second. Ortiz had won a trifecta that day and was heading back to his bar. The tail car slowed to create some space, leaving enough room for the shooters to turn from their side street and get behind the target.

Ortiz slowed and parked in front of His & Mine. There were parking spaces on Twenty-Second, but they were angled and not parallel. "Blondie" was pulled up behind the Mercury, coming to a stop. Frank Sr. left it so that Ortiz couldn't back up and the crew members could make a quick escape.

"And my brother says, 'Go,'" Nick told Mars.

DiForti and Nick stepped out, wearing their masks. They raised their shotguns. Poker was at the driver's window at an angle, and Nick was closer to the Mercury's back window. Nick pulled the trigger, and nothing happened.

Frank Sr. had his mask on, too, and had the carbine.

"And in my mind, I knew I had to do this, because if I didn't, my brother would've flattened me right there," Nick said. "I would've been left there, and more than likely Poker would have been left there, too."

Nick's gun was a pump-action shotgun, so he ejected a shell to get the weapon going. He pumped it again, he said, firing through the window into the car. DiForti was shooting, too, Nick said, holding up his hands like he was shooting a rifle and recalling that he fired until the gun was empty.

In seconds they were back in the car. Frank Sr. turned right at the first block, Nick said, and then left toward Cicero Avenue. The crew had a garage that wasn't far away. Nick remembered getting out of the car to let his brother back "Blondie" inside. The guns and masks were left in the car for a few days, Nick said, until the brothers could make it back to Bridgeport and Ronnie Jarrett's mother-in-law's garage. They disassembled the guns there, eventually taking them to a canal.

As they had in the past, the brothers came up with a nickname for the murder. They would call it "the Bean," apparently a derisive reference to Ortiz.

"Blondie" would be used off and on and kept in the garage near the Ortiz and Morawski site for another decade. Finally, Nick said, the brothers just left it on the street somewhere in the summer of 1993. It had been stolen by the crew two decades earlier.

"Let them tow it," Nick said.

In February 1986, Nick was running an errand with Fecarotta, accompanying him to a car dealership to have a look at a certain model Ford. Fecarotta wanted to eyeball the car's interior, especially the space underneath the front seat.

Afterward, Nick said, they stopped at a pay phone and he watched Fecarotta make a call to DiForti.

"I seen him dial 702, the area code; I knew 702 was Las Vegas," Nick told the jury. Plans were afoot, and Nick soon would be drawn in. His first assignment was to take a train to Phoenix and meet Fecarotta there. Nick would be bringing something special in his luggage that had come from James Marcello, he said—a pair of explosive devices.

"They were shaped like a pear, and they were orange," he testified.

Fecarotta handed him the bombs in a bag, Nick remembered, and gave him a train ticket.

"So, when was the train leaving?" Mars asked.

"That evening," Nick answered.

Fecarotta got Nick a sleeper car so he could be alone, with the explosives locked in a suitcase. Frank Sr. was in Florida at the time, Nick said, and his trip to Arizona had been so sudden he hadn't even had time to let his brother know he was leaving. Nick would leave his room on the train only to eat, and he made it to Arizona with his deadly cargo. Waiting for him were Fecarotta and an Outfit soldier he'd often heard about but never worked with, Frank "the German" Schweihs. Fecarotta and the feared hit man then introduced him to another partner in their plotting, a man named Fred Pordyla, known to Nick as "Porky."

Nick would soon learn that he was no simple courier who would quickly head back to Chicago. He was part of a top secret hit crew, he said, that was being coordinated by Schweihs and Fecarotta and staging in Arizona. The targets were several hours away in Las Vegas.

"They were going to kill a couple of guys," Nick told Mars. "The Spilotro brothers. Michael and Tony."

The plan still was being formulated, with the explosives Nick had brought being one option the men wanted to consider. The hit squad, which also would include DiForti, was getting itself organized. Vehicles were being acquired, Nick remembered, including a gray Ford Thunderbird, a cargo van, a red-and-white Bronco, and a Chevy pickup with a camper bed. The team left on a Monday morning to drive the three hundred or so miles to Las Vegas, with Nick and Fecarotta in the Thunderbird, which had been bought with a phony name. Anthony Spilotro's sins were catching up with him.

They found a hotel off the strip where Nick, Fecarotta, and DiForti would stay, Nick told the jury. Schweihs and Porky would stay elsewhere but close by. Nick still didn't know exactly why the Spilotros were to be killed, he said, but as it had many times before, the crew began to look for an angle.

They knew Anthony Spilotro was facing a racketeering case at the Las Vegas federal courthouse, so they began tracking his movements. His home was on a cul-de-sac, Nick remembered, with one way in and out.

"I took a ride with Frankie Schweihs, and he showed me where his lawyer, Tony's lawyer's office was," Nick said. It would be hard to kill Anthony Spilotro there, though, because he always parked at ground level, where there were too many people around. He would leave his car right in front of the lawyer's building. But Schweihs had another thought.

"He said what he'd like to do—he drove through the alley and there was a gate that had a key," Nick explained. Someone might approach from there and get the drop on the mob's man in Las Vegas.

"He says, 'Me and you go,'" Nick recalled Schweihs saying. "He had an Uzi with a silencer on it; he says we can use that."

The high-powered weapon was being stored in Las Vegas, Nick said, in an apartment the crew had rented for a few months. DiForti had been staying there as the plan was coming together.

Once as the men were staking out Anthony Spilotro's house, a light brown van passed in front of them to make a turn. Nick said he noticed Illinois dealer plates on it, which were traced to Celozzi-Ettleson Chevrolet, a dealership the Outfit had been collecting street tax from. At the wheel was Michael Spilotro, so the crew decided to move out and follow him. Schweihs, Fecarotta, and Nick watched where the van went, Nick said, but were led right back to the lawyer's office.

With no other real leads, the crew took turns staking out the federal courthouse, where in April a mistrial would be declared amid fears someone had tried to bribe a juror on the case. Every ninety minutes or so, the members of the hit team would switch off watching to see if Anthony Spilotro would leave and go anywhere they weren't aware of.

In short, they were reaching a dead end.

"Over a period of time there was no way we could pick up any pattern," Nick told Mars. "Another [Spilotro] brother had a hot-dog stand out there in a small shopping center. We laid on that for two or three different nights."

Another time, Nick said, he wound up following the lawyer to an apartment complex, only to trip over Porky.

"I spotted him in the truck, and he had a mustache on."

"When you say that, was it his own, or was it a disguise?"

"It was a disguise."

So with all attempts to figure out a way to wipe out the Spilotros proving futile, the crew headed back to Phoenix.

The attempt would be put off for the time being, but Nick at least was part of a conversation that gave him a few more details about why Anthony Spilotro was being targeted in the first place. Schweihs and Fecarotta filled him in while the crew had some downtime. Spilotro had been running the town like it was his own little fiefdom.

"They were saying that ever since Tony Spilotro come out to Vegas, he brought a lot of heat," Nick said, resuming his matter-of-fact tone. "He was messing around with Lefty Rosenthal's wife, and he supposedly is the one that had something to do with planting a bomb in Lefty Rosenthal's car, and that they were supposed to be dealing with a motorcycle guy, a motorcycle gang dealing with drugs."

Chicago wanted Spilotro's reign ended, but the bosses could wait a little longer. It was there with the crew back in Arizona that Schweihs informed them of an executive decision. They would abandon the Spilotro effort for the time being because there was something else to do right there in Phoenix, Schweihs told the men. There was another guy to work on.

Emil Vaci's mob problems had their origin back in Glitter Gulch more than a decade earlier, when the mob's plans for the Stardust Hotel-Casino were coming to fruition and the Outfit was worming deep into the rising desert playground.

The Central States Pension Fund of the Teamsters had made a loan of more than $140 million to a front man named Allen Glick, who had used the funds to take over the Stardust. Tony "Big Tuna" Accardo had sent Anthony Spilotro to be the caretaker of the mob's Las Vegas interests a few years earlier; Joey "the Clown" Lombardo was the mob's Teamsters liaison and Spilotro's overseer; Frank "Lefty" Rosenthal, a Chicago bookie and ex-con, had been brought in as casino boss at the Stardust; and in turn, a man named George Jay Vandermark, whose forte was boosting coins, was installed to run the Stardust's slot machines. It wouldn't take Sherlock Holmes to figure out that there was a monumental scam under way.

"It was sort of like putting the fox in charge of the chicken coop" is how Dennis Gomes, a former investigator for the Nevada Gaming Control Board, would later describe Vandermark's hiring for the jury. Casino regulators came to believe that funds were being siphoned out of the casinos somewhere during the accounting process, but they weren't exactly sure how it was being done. Cash literally was being stolen before it hit the books.

Then on May 18, 1976, Gomes decided to see for himself, conducting a raid on the Stardust at night with just one other person from his office. He kept many out of the loop, he would say, believing that leaks from within the ranks of his investigators could be tipping casino owners off to when they were to be paid a visit.

Informants had let it be known that operators at the Stardust had an auxiliary change vault, where a coin cushion of sorts would be kept for the slot booths. When the casino was short of cash, coins could be taken out of it to trade, and vice versa. The issue was that the vault wasn't listed on any official paperwork the casino was required to keep.

After first being told the vault didn't exist, Gomes was informed that only Vandermark could open it. The investigator asked for Vandermark but was told he was out of luck; the slot man was going on a Mexican vacation, and it just happened to start that night.

Upon further investigation, Gomes was able to figure out the sleight of hand involved in the mob's skim. None of the casinos would count each quarter; instead they would weigh large containers to determine the value of thousands of coins at once. Only the Stardust and other casinos the Outfit controlled were using scales with switches, investigators learned. One setting gave an accurate weight, and another setting gave an undercounted reading.

With the scales set to undercount, there would be coins, and therefore cash, available from the auxiliary vault for the mob to just walk out the door. Vandermark could tie Rosenthal to similar skims going on at other casinos, such as the Hacienda and the Marina, investigators believed.

Vandermark was on the run not just from the government but from the Outfit, too. Investigators would estimate that in the year prior to the discovery of the undercount, some $7 million had been skimmed from the Stardust. It was a surprising amount even to the Outfit, which was under the impression the skim was more like $4 million. Vandermark apparently was missing with as much as $3 million in mob cash.

Gomes would try to track Vandermark to Mexico through his son, who promptly had his head smashed in not long after investigators made contact with him. Vandermark himself was never seen again. His trail would go cold at a hotel and nightclub in Phoenix called the Arizona Manor. He had spent a final night there under an assumed name.

Emil Vaci was the general manager there and a onetime pit boss at the Stardust. The Arizona Manor was popular with certain people from Chicago, and Vaci counted Paul "the Indian" Schiro—the Outfit's man in Phoenix—among his friends. He was an insider suspected of having more than a passing knowledge of Vandermark's whereabouts and the Stardust skim, for which Aiuppa, Lombardo, and others were about to go down.

In the middle of the 1980s, a Las Vegas strike force of state and federal authorities was organized to investigate organized crime activity in the city, and a grand jury was convened to look into the disappearance of Vandermark.

Among those called to testify in September 1985 was Vaci, who would invoke his Fifth Amendment right against self-incrimination when he appeared. But investigators wouldn't quit. They sought and obtained immunity for Vaci, forcing him to answer questions or face being jailed, and he was called again. Vaci had begrudgingly started to answer a few questions. Word of Vaci's talking got out, and it wasn't something the Outfit was going to take a chance on.

As Mars continued to question him, Nick told the jury he knew that Vaci could hurt Jimmy LaPietra in the grand jury. Vaci knew that LaPietra was involved in killing someone Vaci had known from the Stardust counting room, Nick said, though Nick didn't use Vandermark's name or even seem to know it. Nick talked to LaPietra about it in the spring of 1986.

"He said that this guy [Vaci] can cause me a lot of trouble because he knows about the guy that we had in the motel out there at one time," Nick said. "He knew this guy from the counting room in the Stardust, and they had grabbed the guy in Phoenix, and they had him in a motel room, and they took him out in a wheelchair. They had killed him and took him out in a wheelchair and put him in a van and went and buried him in the desert."

So fresh out of the Spilotro surveillances, Nick and the rest of the hit squad went right back at it, having learned where Vaci lived and where he worked, as a maître d' at a five-star restaurant called Ernesto's Back Street, with tableside cooking and waiters in tuxedos.

Employees parked away from the building that housed Ernesto's, so the crew came up with a plan. They might be able to get their van alongside Vaci's brown Pontiac, and then they could slide the door open and shoot Vaci as he got into his car.

Joining the team back in Phoenix was a member of Schweihs's crew, Nick said, Joey Hansen, one of the men he had heard was involved in the killing of Daniel Seifert in 1974. He was living in California at the time.

"And in addition to Joey Hansen, was there anybody from the Phoenix area involved in assisting with the alternate plans to kill Mr. Vaci?" Mars asked.

"A guy they call the Indian," Nick answered. Nick had never met Paul Schiro, who was a childhood friend of Anthony Spilotro, but Hansen had quickly vouched for him, he remembered. Mars asked Nick to point him out in court, and Nick pointed to Schiro, who sat in a light-colored jacket and still had a placid look on his face.

Schiro had been present when Vaci actually was killed but hadn't been part of planning some of the particulars, Nick said. Schiro and Vaci had known each other for some time, so the crew didn't want Vaci to recognize him during a surveillance. At one point Schweihs decided the crew should dig a hole in the desert ahead of time, so they could just drop Vaci into it if they kidnapped and killed him. They drove around and found a deserted spot, where Nick and DiForti would prepare a makeshift grave.

With the plan advancing, Schweihs stole a new car from a Phoenix dealership, Nick said. The crew would wait for Vaci to arrive for work and then park the stolen car as a placeholder to occupy the spot next to Vaci's Pontiac. When the time for the hit drew near, they would move the stolen car out and park the van in position for their strike.

The stolen car was put in place on a Friday, Nick said, and then the van, but the murder didn't come off. When Vaci walked out of the restaurant toward his car, there were other people walking nearby, so the shooting was scratched. Little did the crew know it would be their last attempt on Vaci for a while.

Back at their hotel they got a surprise, Nick said. A friend of Fecarotta's who Nick knew as John Rita appeared at their hotel and said he had a message. Everyone was to return to Chicago as soon as possible. Fecarotta and Nick made their way to Tucson and then back to the city.

Nick met his brother as soon as he could to fill him in on what had been going on. "We better go see Brother Jimmy," Frank Sr. had said, so the brothers went to his home. They knocked on the door, and LaPietra was surprised to see Nick standing there.

"He said, 'What are you doing back?'" Nick recalled. He told him the crew had gotten the message but a signal had gotten crossed. Only Schweihs was supposed to return, not the entire killing team. So a few weeks later, it was Nick, DiForti, Fecarotta, and Schweihs meeting in a Rush Street restaurant off Grand Avenue. They were all going back out west, all except Schweihs, that is.

"We had a drink, and [Schweihs] says, 'I'm not going back, but good luck,'" Nick remembered. And that was the end of the conversation.

By the middle of April 1986, Fecarotta and Nick had driven the Thunderbird they got in Phoenix back to Arizona to finish what they had started as it related to Vaci. They retrieved DiForti from the airport, Schiro had reappeared, and Joey Hansen was back from California. They put the same plan back into play, the surveillance, the van, and the stolen car holding a place next to Vaci's car. Jimmy Marcello was the financier, Nick said, sending the crew cash in FedEx boxes when they needed it.

But once again, things were less than smooth. Someone had cut the tires on the crew's stolen work car, and when they went to check the hole Nick had prepared weeks earlier, they found it had been disturbed. Nick had slid a wooden covering over it that someone had moved. So it was abandoned, with Nick and DiForti digging a second hole.

"But we had to abandon that one, too," Nick said, without really showing much frustration at the memory on the stand. There was more machinelike determination in his voice as he said that the second hole also had been disturbed, so he had simply dug a third.

And there were more problems. For several days the crew couldn't even find Vaci. He wasn't at home or work, and his car was missing. Fecarotta returned to Chicago to find out what they should do next, only to learn that Vaci was there, too, visiting relatives.

Fecarotta returned to Phoenix to wait it out with the crew but invited Nick to take a side trip to Tucson to see a son he had living there. It was just for a few days, but on the last day something happened that raised Nick's eyebrows. Fecarotta's sister-in-law appeared with her children, and it would soon become clear that Fecarotta was seeing her—not long after his brother had passed away. It was a violation of an unwritten rule to be in such a relationship so soon after his brother had died, and it was an even more questionable move to have such a distraction when the crew was supposed to be on a job.

A rift already was growing between the two men, with Nick becoming more distrustful, he said. He thought there was a possibility Fecarotta could try to hurt him, he told the jury, so he had brought a .38 with him to Phoenix when he had returned from Chicago.

In another odd episode Fecarotta and Nick stopped at a casino in Bullhead City, Arizona, on a run to Las Vegas to retrieve the Uzi from the apartment there, Nick said. Fecarotta was playing a slot machine when he happened to win $2,000. A tax form had to be filled out to claim it, and not wanting to leave a paper trail that he was there, Fecarotta had Nick sign the forms and present his identification. Frank Sr. would later get upset and tell Nick that Fecarotta had made a sucker out of him, Nick recalled.

"Why didn't you refuse?" Mars asked

"I don't know."

The jury would be shown Nick's 1986 tax records, listing his address in the 7100 block of West Cortland in Chicago. His wife Noreen's name is listed, and one dependent, his daughter Michele. He claimed a little more than $15,000 in income that year and had expenses in his job as an "inspector." And on a line where he had written in "gambling income" was a notation for $2,000.

"And by the way, did you gamble at this casino?" Mars asked.

"No, I'm not a gambler."

Eventually, the crew turned its attention back to the murder of Emil Vaci, Nick said. One of the options considered was to catch up to Vaci at a dress store his wife owned at a shopping center. On some days Vaci would be there in the morning preparing the store.

The plan was to have Schiro head in the front as if he had randomly stopped by and then have Nick make a coordinated knock on the back service door. Nick had bought a blue shirt, shorts, and a hat, to make it look as if he could be making a delivery. When Vaci went to the back and opened the door, he would be shot in the head.

The crew went to try it once, Nick said, but as he and Hansen brought the van around to the back of the shopping center, they noticed a worker on a telephone pole and again had to call it off.

Members of the team were growing more jumpy by the day. Another attempt at the delivery ruse was scratched when Schiro said he didn't want to do it that way for fear of getting caught. Then Hansen vanished.

Nick said he and Fecarotta arrived at the hotel where he had been staying to find a note in the van. Hansen thought he had seen Fecarotta and Schiro following him and felt like he was in jeopardy of becoming a target himself. Hansen went all the way back to Chicago for assurances that he wasn't in some kind of trouble and then returned to Phoenix yet again.

Hansen would be on hand as the squad made another move against Vaci, but Fecarotta ultimately wouldn't be. Fecarotta had suddenly decided he shouldn't be there because he could be in trouble if he stayed, so he was going back to Chicago. He complained to Nick that because of his union ties, he had been called to Washington, D.C., to testify before a commission on organized crime. Authorities could be watching him. Nick was shocked but told Fecarotta that if he wanted to go, then he should go.

It would be another strike against the hit man that Frank Sr. ultimately would use to get permission from Outfit leaders to kill Fecarotta.

There were four men left to kill Vaci, Nick said—himself, DiForti, Hansen, and Schiro, and the group pressed ahead. They went back to the original plan of using the van next to Vaci's parked car and waited for him to walk to his Pontiac the night of June 6, 1986. Hansen and Nick would take the van, with Schiro and DiForti on backup duty watching for police.

Hansen pulled the van up, Nick said. It was a cargo vehicle with no backseats. Nick was waiting in the back, with a tarp spread out on the floor. They knew Vaci would be leaving work at 10:00 or 11:00 P.M., so they watched and waited, with Nick leaving the van's sliding door open a crack so he could make a quick move when Vaci was near.

"Joey spotted him walking," Nick said. "He had his sports jacket over his arm, walking towards us."

From his position just behind the van's door, Nick could hear Vaci's shoes on the pavement. He said he let his ears decide when the seventy-three-year-old man was close enough, standing between his own car and the blue van parked next to it.

"So I swung it open, and I jump out, and I grabbed him; and I had a hard time with him," Nick said, recalling that Hansen had to leave the van to help shove Vaci in. Once inside, Nick said, Vaci's first thought was that he was being robbed. He pleaded with Nick to take his wallet.

Then, in an instant, the realization of what this was really about.

"Then he says, 'Oh no'; he says, 'I promise I'm not going to say nothing,'" Nick said, remembering that he gave no reply.

Instead he raised a .22-caliber pistol at Vaci's face. He went to pull the trigger, and the gun jammed. That type of gun would often lock up because a bullet would pop up and stick the slide. So with Vaci still sitting there, Nick said he hit the top of the gun and adjusted the clip.

"What did you do then?" Mars asked.

"I, uh . . ." Nick stammered to a pause, tripping over what he was trying to say. "I shot him in the head."

Nick thought he was dead, but Hansen, who was by now driving the van away from the lot, thought more shots would be a good idea.

Nick was scared, he said, deciding he didn't want to drive all the way to the desolate spot where the men had dug the third hole. He wanted the body out of the vehicle as quickly as possible.

Much closer was a dry canal where they could stop and get rid of the body. He and Hansen pulled the body out in the tarp, Nick said, and were able to slide Vaci's body down the slanted wall of the canal.

Nick would ditch the .22, and the crew would sell the vehicles; the two odd, pear-shaped explosives had much earlier been disposed of. He would keep the Uzi for his brother, but Nick soon discovered he had lost the .38 he had brought for protection. Investigators at the scene where Vaci's body had been found would find the mysterious handgun that had been stolen in Chicago rolled up in the tarp. It had fallen from Nick's waistband in his rush to get the body ready to be dumped.

Nick and Hansen would try to drive straight through to Las Vegas that night, pushing to get out of town and out of sight. Nick wouldn't see Schiro again for more than twenty years, until he walked into court to testify in the Family Secrets trial.

Nick and Hansen cut over into California briefly as they made their way up to Las Vegas. It was early in the morning but enough time for Nick to call Frank Sr., he remembered. He was able to get him on the phone and relayed what had happened in code.

"I says, 'You know, I haven't been feeling too well. But last night, I had some soup.'"

13

ONE AND TWO

The story of Anthony "the Ant" Spilotro is hardly unknown. Like Joey Lombardo, Spilotro rose to become a crime boss from humble beginnings in the old West Side neighborhood, one of six children born to his immigrant parents. He dropped out of Chicago's Steinmetz High School and turned to crime early on, taking up with local theft rings and getting noticed by the neighborhood's Outfit leaders. He would be placed in charge of a significant bookmaking operation and work in Irwin Weiner's bail bonding business. His reputation for brutality dated to the early 1960s, when he would be connected to what became known as the "M&M murders," so named for victims Billy McCarthy and Jimmy Miraglia, two members of a burglary crew believed to have taken part in an unauthorized murder. When McCarthy was too slow in providing information about the killing and who was involved, Spilotro resorted to putting his head in a vise until one of his eyes popped out.

Spilotro would go on to become a trusted associate of Joey Aiuppa and Lombardo, sent to Las Vegas in the early 1970s to be the guy on the ground who ensured that the Chicago mob's will was done there. Once he was installed, local authorities famously noticed a spike in gangland killings, and Spilotro started his own burglary ring, known as the "Hole in the Wall Gang" for its favorite tactic to avoid alarm systems while stealing jewelry. He was accused but never convicted of employing a team of thieves that included the likes of Sal Romano, Frank Cullotta, and feared hit man "Crazy Larry" Neumann.

Some members of Spilotro's family still say that his reputation is overblown and that he wasn't the criminal he has been made out to be, but his Las Vegas exploits were immortalized in the 1995 film *Casino*, where Joe Pesci played a character named Nicky Santoro, who was based on Spilotro.

By the middle of the 1980s, Spilotro had done a good job of avoiding prison. After being indicted along with Lombardo in the Teamsters pension fraud case involving Daniel Seifert, the case had come apart in 1974 with Seifert's murder. He was indicted in the M&M murders in 1983 but had dodged responsibility in a bench trial conducted by Cook County Judge Thomas J. Maloney, who was later convicted himself of taking bribes to fix murder cases. And three years later the racketeering case against Spilotro that was the result of his burglary ring being busted had ended in the mistrial with a possible jury bribe. Prosecutors in Las Vegas were preparing to take him to trial again in the summer of 1986 when Chicago called and summoned Spilotro home. The Las Vegas operation was coming apart, with Aiuppa, Lombardo, Jackie Cerone, and Angelo LaPietra already having been convicted in the Stardust skim as a result of the "Pendorf" and "Strawman" investigations. Spilotro, whose own trial in the Stardust case had been delayed for health reasons, was being blamed for getting too big for his britches, bringing too much federal heat at almost every turn.

The bill was coming due for all of the problems he was causing.

Michael Spilotro also was charged in the Hole in the Wall case, but a judge had dismissed the allegations against him for lack of evidence. He was a Chicago restaurant owner and also a part-time actor who landed some minor television roles, including playing an FBI agent on the show *Magnum P.I.* But like his brother, his legal troubles weren't over in the summer of 1986. He was facing trial in Chicago on extortion charges out of the federal "Operation Safebet," which targeted organized crime and suburban prostitution.

Both brothers were at Michael Spilotro's Oak Park home in early June, Anthony having told a judge in Nevada that he was traveling to have dental work performed by his brother.

Nick said it was John Fecarotta who first talked about a ruse to get the Spilotro brothers back to Chicago and comfortable. The crew had given up on finding an acceptable way to do the job in Las Vegas. The brothers would be told that Michael had been recommended to become a made man, Outfit leaders decided, and Anthony would be promised an elevation to capo.

Nick had returned from Phoenix on a Sunday, and by the following Friday, he said, the plan against the Spilotros already was in motion. Fecarotta paged him, and the men spoke on the street. Nick was to meet Fecarotta and others the next day at a shopping center on Twenty-Second Street west of Illinois Route 83 near Oak Brook in the western suburbs.

"Did he tell you what the purpose of that meeting was going to be?" prosecutor Mitch Mars asked.

"It was about the Spilotros."

Nick said he immediately went to meet with his brother to tell him what was happening. He was supposed to head to the rendezvous point early that Saturday afternoon, he told Frank Sr., and it was for the Spilotro brothers. His brother had become irritated at learning that wheels were in motion without him, Nick said.

"He got upset because, he says, 'Why didn't they ask me? I want to be there,'" Nick told the jury. His brother wouldn't be part of it but asked Nick to let him know when it was finished.

The FBI wasn't completely unaware that something was afoot. Agents had been listening to Outfit telephone calls going between James Marcello, Rocky Infelice, and Joe Ferriola, and were aware of a meeting on June 13, 1986, at a suburban McDonald's. No fewer than five agents were dispatched to cover it and were at various points watching Marcello, Ferriola, and another man meet Sam Carlisi at 12:18 P.M. Whatever the men had to discuss was quickly taken care of. Not even twenty minutes later, all of them had left.

The next day was Saturday, June 14, 1986. As a result of the Victor Cacciatore extortion, Angelo LaPietra had picked up some new equipment for the crew, so Nick drove a new blue van west to the shopping center where Fecarotta had told him to be. He said he parked it at the far end of the lot and walked up to the store to find Fecarotta and Jimmy LaPietra waiting for him. The plan was for the three to wait for a fourth person to arrive to drive them to where they would be going.

That driver was James Marcello, Nick said, adding that when he had first begun his debriefings with the FBI, he had lied to them.

"And what was the lie?" Mars asked.

"That I said that Johnny Fecarotta was the one that drove us to the house," Nick replied. He had intentionally left Marcello out of his initial admissions to agents.

"I was trying to protect him."

The house, Nick said, was due north up Route 83 in a suburb called Bensenville adjacent to O'Hare International Airport, a town known for warehouses and having its neighborhoods of modest homes in the way of airport expansion. Marcello drove the men in his "fancy" conversion van to within about a mile or so of O'Hare's runways, turning near Irving Park Road into a subdivision that, like so many developments in the area, had a set of small brick walls marking the entrance. He and Fecarotta were in the backseat, Nick remembered, and LaPietra was in front.

In Oak Park, Michael Spilotro had been getting ready for what supposedly was his making day, but there were signs that the brothers weren't simply blindly heading for their doom. With the recent troubles they were certainly suspicious, but not answering such a request for their appearances was not an option. Michael was worried enough to give his daughter his jewelry in a plastic sandwich bag and ask her to bring it to a graduation party they were to attend that night. He had told his wife he would meet her after his business was finished, but if he wasn't there by 9:00, she should assume that something was very wrong.

Marcello parked the van, and the men walked into the open garage. Turning left into the house, they were met by a collection of Outfit heavyweights, including some of the men who had been present for Nick's own making ceremony. John DiFronzo was there, he said, a man he knew as "Johnny Bananas." Carlisi was in the house, too, Nick said to Mars, as was Wild Bunch leader Ferriola. And what did Nick do then?

"Shook their hands, said hello, and then when I got to Sam, he made some kind of comment about my tan," Nick said, because he was still showing the sun he had gotten in Arizona. And Carlisi made a wisecrack about money, too, he said, an unnerving remark because Fecarotta had blown a good deal of cash in Phoenix for things that didn't have to do with the work there. The comment scared Nick a little, but it seriously rattled Fecarotta.

He and Fecarotta walked down to the house's basement, Nick said, and Fecarotta went straight for the bathroom.

"He was in the bathroom quite a while, and I kept thinking something's wrong," Nick recalled. "When he came out, he was pale. I figure, he thinks this is for him."

It wasn't. But it would be only a few months until Nick and Fecarotta were driving up an alley together, with Nick reaching into a bag for a pistol.

On Nick's left in the basement were mobsters Louis Marino and Louie "the Mooch" Eboli, he said, along with three men he didn't recognize. He remembered that one of the men he didn't know was wearing glasses and that everyone was wearing gloves.

Thirty minutes or more passed as the men waited in the basement, listening and watching again for Marcello to appear, a sign that what they had come to do was about to happen. Then there was a voice. Someone had seen Marcello and said, "Here he comes."

On edge in the basement, Nick heard the door and then the sound of voices greeting each other. The Spilotros were being welcomed to the death house with smiles and handshakes.

Mars asked whether Nick could recognize the voices drifting down to the men in the basement. No was his answer.

"I wasn't—at this time I'm wound up," Nick remembered. "I'm tense, and I'm not really—I'm focusing on what I'm going to do."

Moments later, Michael Spilotro was coming down the stairs. Nick approached him first, he said, because he knew him.

"I said, 'How you doing, Mike?'"

Spilotro walked toward Marino and Eboli next. And then it began. The men moved on Michael, just as his brother was reaching the bottom of the stairs behind him.

Realizing what was happening, Anthony made a final request. Nick said he heard it as he was grabbing Michael's legs and the struggle was beginning.

"All I heard was that when he come down he said, 'Can I say a prayer?'"

"And then what happened?" Mars asked in the silent courtroom. Everyone in the gallery was straining to listen so they didn't miss anything Nick might say next.

"I didn't hear anymore."

Nick was holding Michael as Eboli put a rope around his neck and strangled him, Nick told Mars. Somewhere nearby in the basement, Anthony was being killed, too.

Once it was over, Michael's pants were searched for his car keys. Michael's suspicion had led him to bring a pocket-size .22-caliber pistol, which apparently he couldn't reach in any final, panicked bid to save himself. DiFronzo was holding it and trying to unload it.

And there was a small spot of blood where Anthony had been killed, Nick said. So he went to the bathroom where Fecarotta had been and got a tissue to try to wipe it up.

And that would be the extent of Nick's help in getting rid of the bodies, he told Mars. The brothers would turn up a little more than a week later buried in Enos, Indiana, more than one hundred miles from the subdivision, near land Aiuppa had used for hunting. A farmer had noticed a disturbance in the neat rows of corn he had planted that spring and, thinking maybe someone had buried a deer on his property, made the gruesome discovery. Michael and Anthony were found about five feet down, buried one atop the other. Fecarotta has long been suspected of botching the burial, and it reportedly contributed to the decision of Outfit leaders that he should be killed. But Nick, who would wind up shooting him, made no mention of the supposed Fecarotta mistake in his testimony. Fecarotta did move Michael Spilotro's Lincoln, Nick said, leaving it at a nearby hotel.

Nick said Fecarotta was with him and Jimmy LaPietra as Marcello drove them back to the shopping center where they had met him earlier. The three from the Chinatown crew were dropped off and left in the van Nick had parked there in the lot.

They wound up having coffee, and Nick recalled Ferriola joining them. The Wild Bunch leader had a little advice about gloves as the men made small talk, Nick said.

"He says, 'Yeah, what you gotta do is, when you're done with a pair of gloves, just cut them up and throw them a piece at a time because they can take fingerprints off the inside of the gloves," Nick said. It sounded like a good idea, and he would destroy his own gloves in just that way later in the evening.

He would of course not get the chance to destroy the gloves from his next murder. If he had, he might never have been in court testifying that day.

Nick recalled that after another job well done, Jimmy LaPietra had demanded to know how much Frank Sr. was paying him. It was only $3,000 a month, Nick said, so Jimmy, who had by then taken over for his brother Angelo while he was in prison, told Nick that he should tell his brother to up his pay to $5,000 a month instead. Nick would pass along that message as he talked with Frank Sr. about what had happened. And as they had always done before, the brothers would come to use a code name for the murders of Anthony and Michael Spilotro.

"One and Two."

When Nick told his brother about how Fecarotta had been so careless on the Phoenix trip, Frank Sr. had decided not to do anything about it right away. The Calabreses would keep the information between them, with Frank Sr. deciding he would hold on to the damning details as a trump card to use if he needed it in the future.

Nick had filled his brother in on Fecarotta bringing his brother's wife to Arizona and about making Nick sign for his gambling winnings. There was Fecarotta's spending of the cash that was supposed to be used by the crew, which had led to Nick earning only $3,000 for all of his work, and then to top it off, Fecarotta hadn't even stayed until Emil Vaci was killed, having his bizarre breakdown in the hotel and then leaving.

In the end it was only three months after the Spilotros were killed that Frank Sr. had finally had it with the crew's former trusted confidant. A man named Richie Urso owed Frank Sr. money, Nick told the jury, from a juice loan that the father of Urso's partner had taken out in the 1960s. Fecarotta had stepped in the middle of things, Nick said, by demanding that Urso make his house payment. Nothing was left over for Frank Sr., who had a meeting with Urso where he held a knife to his crotch and demanded that he be paid over Fecarotta.

"Well, my brother and Johnny Fecarotta had a confrontation; there was, like, an argument," Nick explained. "And that sort of put the nail in the coffin. [Frank Sr.] said, 'We're going to go talk to Brother Jimmy.'"

And the Calabreses did meet with LaPietra, Nick said, with Frank Sr. telling him to spill to the capo all of the miscues Fecarotta had made out west. The brothers essentially were asking for permission to kill him.

"So I went ahead and told Jimmy about signing for the money that [Fecarotta] won in the casino, and about his sister-in-law being in Tucson and Las Vegas, and about the money that was—that he had received and that I only received $3,000 of that money for all that time we were out there, and also that we got into an argument and that he says he shouldn't be there," Nick said. "And I says, 'I told [Fecarotta], "You want to leave, leave," and he left. He went to Las Vegas.'"

Fecarotta had repeatedly had money problems, LaPietra had answered. Fecarotta had bought a Mercedes from John DiFronzo and hadn't paid for it and had borrowed from the LaPietras and John "Johnny Apes" Monteleone. But leaving the Vaci murder was a serious infraction, and LaPietra said he would get back to the brothers. The capo would have to speak about the situation with those above him.

"So sometime after that—I don't know how long it was, a week, ten days, two weeks—we get a call," Nick said. LaPietra was summoning them back for another talk. "I don't know if my brother came also, but I know I was there, went to Jimmy's house, and he says, 'Go ahead.'"

The brothers had been cleared to take Fecarotta out. They began planning it with Monteleone, Nick told the jury. At his defense table Frank Sr. continued to look on, sometimes shaking his head and leaning over to talk to Joe Lopez.

"They was trying to figure out how to do it because my—both my brother and Johnny Apes had said Johnny Fecarotta will not get in a car with them," Nick explained. "Johnny's demeanor had changed."

"He knew he might get hurt."

So the plan was devised for Nick to be the shooter. Jimmy LaPietra would give the order for the men to carry out a "bombing" at a union dentist's office, and it would put Nick in a position to finish off his friend. The Calabrese brothers would make the dummy device, taping road flares together to look like a bundle of dynamite with a fuse and blasting cap. The car to be used was a blue Buick the crew had stolen and parked in Ronnie Jarrett's mother-in-law's garage to have as a work car.

As for the guns, Nick would be armed with a pair of .38s and would file down the firing pin on one left in the glove compartment. Fecarotta, who would be driving, would no doubt check for one as he and Nick started the job. Frank Sr. and Monteleone would be on the street, acting as if they were watching for police as they normally might.

Nick described for the jury how he saw Fecarotta get dropped off at their meeting point and how he had waited a few moments to roll up to him in order to let the ruse unfold at a relaxed pace.

"I don't want to just come right up on him; he might think that I was watching him," Nick said, which, of course, Nick was.

They drove by their target, Nick said, having to circle back once because of a man in a garage. But on the second pass, the plan began to unfold. They parked where they had planned to, and Nick reached into his bag.

"I reached down and pretended I was going to light the bomb, and what I did was, I come out with a gun," Nick said. "I was supposed to shoot him in the side first, but he caught the play and I believe I shot myself when I shot him. And then I start struggling with him."

Nick remembered wrestling with Fecarotta for the gun, and the bullets falling out of it when its cylinder came open. He had pulled the second pistol from his waistband, and Fecarotta had jumped from the car. The job had to be finished.

"My mind—my adrenaline is going and he's running, and the only thing I could think of was what happens," Nick remembered, visibly becoming tense in his chair. "If I don't do this, if he gets away, I'm dead."

For more than fifteen years Nick had been taking lives for the Outfit, and he knew the rules. There was only one punishment for botching a hit. With Fecarotta running from him, it was kill or be killed.

Nick reached Fecarotta at the door of the bingo hall, he said.

"I shot him in the head, in the back," he said.

The plan had been for his brother to pick him up as he walked along Austin Boulevard, but as Nick left the scene of the shooting, his brother wasn't there. He described for the jury how he walked and kept watch, hoping Frank Sr. would appear and drive him away.

But he didn't. And a disoriented Nick, shot through the forearm, had decided to head for his own car. He had started taking off his tight, black gloves in an alley after leaving Fecarotta.

"I started pulling my gloves off because it's September and I've got black gloves on—it didn't look right," Nick said. "So I took them off. And I thought I had stuck them in my pocket. I didn't know at the time that I had dropped them."

Mars had something to show Nick: Government Exhibit Fecarotta 12. It was one of many dozens of images the jury would see, but it was the one that had been the key to unlocking all that came after.

"Mr. Calabrese, can you describe what is depicted in that photograph, Fecarotta 12?" Mars asked.

"Looks like a pair of gloves laying on the sidewalk," Nick answered.

From there he described how he had made it home and how his brother arrived not long after to whisk him away to a Cicero apartment. Nick would stay there for a week, nursing his wound. The crew arranged for a doctor to see him, a man who had removed the splintered bone protruding from his arm and wrapped the arm. If anyone asked, Nick would say he had fallen on some stairs and broken his arm, but the injury was kept a secret from most people. With the shooting in the news, no one needed to know that Nick had recently suffered a mysterious gunshot wound. It was even kept from Jimmy DiForti, Nick said, because he and Fecarotta were so close. DiForti had been left out of the murder planning altogether for fear he would tell Fecarotta that his life was in danger. After the fact, Frank Sr. had asked Jimmy LaPietra not to mention to DiForti that "Gus" had been shot.

It was the nickname the LaPietras had used most often for their trusted soldier and hit man, though he had a few others. Some called Nick "Slim," he said, and at least one person called him "the Karate Kid."

Before Nicholas D'Andrea had been killed in Chicago Heights, Angelo LaPietra had asked Nick whether he knew any martial arts.

"I says, 'Well, when I was in the navy there was a guy that lived in Japan and showed me a few things,'" Nick said. "And then I found out later that it was Sam Carlisi that called me the Karate Kid."

In the final stages of his questioning by Mars, the prosecutor led Nick through the period when he had been imprisoned after the Calabrese racketeering case. He had been sent to Pekin, where James Marcello also happened to be housed. The men had spoken nearly every day for more than a year, talking about Outfit business and what they would be doing when they were released. Nick said Marcello told him he planned to straighten out a few things when he regained his freedom. People had been doing things without asking permission, Nick said, and Marcello had told him he knew some younger capable guys on the street.

And what did capable mean?

"That perform murders and killings," Nick said.

He and Marcello actually spoke of one murder in particular, Nick said. It was the D'Andrea killing, where Nick had been told to use the baseball bat when the victim walked in.

"We talked about how strong he was and how hard it was to get him cuffed and stuff," Nick said. "Just that he was exceptionally strong."

There were constant reminders of Nick's criminal life at Pekin, including the fact that he had had noted mob hit man and Wild Bunch member Harry Aleman for a cellmate at one point. Nick and Marcello talked about the history of organized crime, Nick said, with Marcello knowing more than his fair share of stories. When the men got out, Nick said Marcello had told him he could join up with his crew, leaving his difficulties with his brother behind.

The topic of Frank Sr. came up often, Nick said. He blamed his brother for not doing enough to keep his sons, Frank Jr. and Kurt, from having to go to prison on their case. And he explained to Marcello how he felt like his brother was shoving him aside and not doing anything to take care of his family financially while the Calabreses were in prison. Marcello was responsive, Nick said, and quickly made arrangements for Nick's wife, Noreen, to receive $4,000 a month. The payments started in December 1997 and lasted until the time period when word of the Family Secrets investigation was beginning to leak out. Nick's friend Frank Giudice would get the cash from Marcello's brother, Mickey, and bring it to Nick's family.

And what exactly was the $4,000 for? Mars asked.

"If I could set this up a little bit, like if somebody went in front of the grand jury and he refused to speak and he belonged to a certain crew, if he had to sit in jail, they would take care of his family to make sure this guy don't feel that he's being neglected," Nick explained. "And I felt it was not only to help me financially, but to make sure that I wouldn't get the same kind of idea about flipping and turning out to be a rat, like I am."

Marcello must have heard something in his voice, Nick started to say, when Breen cut him off with an objection.

Whatever Marcello's goals were with the payments, the money did buy Nick's silence. He told jurors that when his debriefings began with the FBI in January 2002, he left Marcello out of his version of the Spilotro murders. When he talked about that Saturday in 1986, he told agents it was Fecarotta who had driven to the Bensenville house where the brothers were killed. It would take ten months for Nick to acknowledge he had been untruthful.

"I was trying to protect him because he helped my family, and I was stupid," Nick said. "But I was trying to protect him."

Nick recounted for the jury his journeys to Chicago, where he had tried to lead agents to some of the murder sites he had described. The Michael Albergo burial site was a parking lot near U.S. Cellular Field, and he couldn't recall exactly which house in the Bensenville subdivision had been used to kill the Spilotros.

"There's hundreds of houses in there," Nick said.

Mars also needed to ask Nick whether he could identify the two men in court that he hadn't already pointed out during his testimony—Doyle and Lombardo. Joey was in the back, Nick said, a gray-haired man in a blue suit.

"No objection," Halprin piped up, "with the exception of the gray hair."

And Mars asked Nick about the gun that he had used to shoot Fecarotta. He had thrown it down a sewer but had asked his nephew to retrieve it. When Frank Jr. did, Nick said he had taken as many of the markings off it as he could, including drilling into the barrel to destroy the signature the weapon would have made on the bullets that hit Fecarotta. Then he threw it into another sewer.

"Thank you, Judge," Mars said. "I have no further questions."

Nick had been on the stand for the better part of a week, covering a quarter-century of Outfit business, violence, and murder. The defense lawyers couldn't challenge every detail he had laid out in his historic testimony, but they were eager to try to punch holes in what had been a convincing account of an organized crime insider and determined Outfit killer.

Rick Halprin stepped to the podium first, speaking loudly into the microphone and amplifying his already booming voice.

"Let me see if I've got this straight," he began. "You killed thirteen people for $3,000 a month. Then you were involved in a double homicide, and you got a raise to $5,000? Is that your testimony?"

"Yes," Nick answered flatly.

Halprin moved quickly to Nick's accusation that Fecarotta had told him Lombardo, Frank Schweihs, and others were part of the hit team that had shot Seifert. That was a shooting that Nick hadn't seen with his own eyes, and Halprin wasn't so sure about the second-hand account either.

"I can't call Mr. Fecarotta to the stand to refute your testimony because you killed him in 1986, isn't that right?"

"Yes," Nick answered robotically.

Halprin pointed out that in 1981, when Fecarotta supposedly said he was a wheelman in the Seifert killing, he would have been telling the Calabreses about the killing when the brothers weren't even made yet. And the conversation had allegedly been in a restaurant of all places.

"Did he order pie and coffee when he told you about the murder?" Halprin asked mockingly, leaving Nick shrugging his shoulders at the treatment.

To put a fine point on it, Nick had no direct evidence that linked Lombardo to anything, Halprin said, and his name had come up only in connection with a Grand Avenue card game. Joey Lombardo's name hadn't come up in anything Nick had personal knowledge about, the lawyer told Nick.

"No," Nick said, agreeing that what Halprin had said was essentially true, as Frank Sr. leaned over at the defense table for a better look at his brother's grilling.

Halprin wanted to know whether Nick was saying that to his direct knowledge, Joey had nothing to do with anything, especially killings. It was a sidewinder of a question that Nick seemed to be trying to take apart in his head.

"I can't answer that with a yes or no," Nick finally replied. Halprin backed away, having kept his questioning brief in an attempt to make a quick point and end the cross-examination.

Ralph Meczyk stepped up next, trying to take the same tough approach. He immediately asked whether Nick was a confessed serial killer.

"I'm a killer but not a serial killer," Nick answered, seemingly put off a bit.

And he was an extortionist?

"Yes."

And an arsonist?

"Yes," Nick said again, slipping back into robot mode.

Meczyk tried to pick at what he called inconsistencies in Nick's testimony, but he was stopped by the judge after accusing Nick of having an "amnesia problem." How could the jury believe anything Calabrese said when he had been involved in so much deceit?

"When you live the life I was living, you lie a lot," Calabrese conceded.

"You only want to help yourself on the backs of others, don't you?" Meczyk said.

It wasn't the last time Nick would have that thrown in his face. In fact, Joseph Lopez was already getting up from Frank Sr.'s table. For the occasion, he had left his pink socks, and ties, shirts, and handkerchiefs at home. He walked to the podium wearing black on black on black.

"Good afternoon, Mr. Calabrese," Lopez said with a layer of contempt.

The lawyer wanted to understand why Nick was doing what he was doing. Was it to avoid the death penalty?

"Yes," Nick answered.

And that's why he was on the witness stand, Lopez pointed out, "rather than sitting over at that table next to your brother."

Wasn't it true that Nick didn't like his brother?

"No, I don't," Nick answered solidly.

"You haven't liked him for a number of years," Lopez said.

"That's correct."

Lopez found it interesting that when he was testifying for the government, Nick characterized himself as a rat.

"I characterize myself as a coward and a rat," Nick said.

Did Frank Sr. ever call him a coward? Lopez wanted to know.

"There's not many names he didn't call me," Nick answered.

At the defense table, Frank Sr. seemed to be enjoying himself for once, smiling and chuckling at some of the questions and answers. His head went back and forth between Lopez and his brother as if he was watching them play Ping-Pong.

Lopez jabbed at Nick to get him ruffled, asking about when he was told his DNA matched blood left on the gloves found near the Fecarotta scene.

"When you learned that, you really wet your pants, didn't you?" Lopez said.

Nick had little reaction to being made fun of in front of a full courtroom, agreeing only that he had been "concerned."

Nick had to know he couldn't beat DNA evidence, Lopez pressed on, as he sat in a cell night after night. He had cooperated because he didn't want to get "fried."

"Yes," Nick agreed.

So he had contemplated how to get out of it, Lopez said. He had violated his oath to his criminal organization, and then he had lied to the FBI about Marcello. He had lied repeatedly, Lopez continued, including to his friend John Fecarotta. When he lied to get Fecarotta into the car that day, did he do it with a straight face?

"If I had a straight face, yes," Nick replied.

Well what about loyalty?

"I was loyal because I was afraid," Nick said, barely raising his voice. "I was a chicken and a coward because I didn't walk away from it."

Nick and Lopez were virtually arguing now, with Frank Sr.'s grin becoming a sneer off and on. At times something would catch him especially funny, and he would jerk back in his chair in quiet laughter.

The lawyer mentioned the Calabreses' father. He was a union worker. Now Nick was sitting there a coward and a chicken and a mass murderer.

"I killed a lot of people, yes," Nick said. "I did it because I didn't want it to happen to me."

Nick had never said no, Lopez pressed. He had pulled the trigger on men such as Emil Vaci. Nick had lived the life of a Chicago mobster.

"I lived the life, yes," Nick said.

And did he like it?

"No, I didn't like the fact that people would look at me and respect me for that," Nick answered. "And it was only a very few people that knew."

And what about the ceremony? Didn't that change his life?

"It made my life harder," Nick said, agreeing that he would never forget it. "There's a lot of things I'll never forget."

Lopez and Nick were firing back and forth at each other. How about Nick's pledge with the burning holy card?

"You're gonna burn in hell anyway for killing those people, aren't you?" Lopez asked, drawing an objection from prosecutors.

Nick just stared back through his glasses, his lips drawn tightly across his face.

Had he always wanted to be a gangster? Did he ever watch *The Untouchables* television series from the early 1960s?

"I can't remember if I liked it or not," Nick answered.

And it wasn't correct that Frank Sr. had never helped him, Lopez said. He had gotten Nick jobs, including as an ironworker on the John Hancock Center construction project on North Michigan Avenue in the late 1960s. Nick agreed he had gone to Slicker Sam's to talk to Frank on his own and that he had expected to make money working with him collecting on loans. Nick had managed other jobs, too, such as working with the Teamsters and with the Cook County Sheriff's Office at the Maybrook Courthouse after taking an eight-week course.

Lopez asked how often he'd seen socially any of the men he'd spoken about. Nick said he saw the LaPietras, DiForti, and Jarrett very little outside of the Outfit world. He wanted to get away from them and his brother, he said.

"But you didn't leave Chicago, did you?"

"No," Nick said.

And how about Frank Sr.'s sons? Had Frank Sr. put a gun to Frank Jr.'s head to get him involved in the family business?

"No, but he put a fist to his face," Nick answered. "Those kids went through hell with their father."

As for himself, Nick said he couldn't say that Frank Sr. disliked him, but his brother had certainly turned him into his "stooge." To have run away from his situation would have taken money, Nick said, plus he had a family.

Well, if things were so bad, Lopez said, he could have cooperated in 1995, when the FBI took down the loan operation.

"I thought about it," Nick said.

"I'm sure you did," Lopez shot back.

And all in all, the lawyer said, didn't Nick know what he was doing all those years? He had been a criminal, and he had been a killer. After the Spilotros died, Nick had gone out for coffee, and he didn't have any problem drinking it.

"Yes, I did," Nick said, his voice trembling.

"You drank it anyway, didn't you?" Lopez said, pushing him.

"I didn't drink it all."

Well, if it was so hard and Nick had let himself get involved, why not make the ultimate escape? Lopez asked. Nick could have hanged himself, the lawyer pointed out, staring at the witness stand for a reaction. Nick stared back as Mars objected and the judge cut the question off.

Nick's final day on the witness stand was Monday, July 23, 2007, beginning with Lopez wrapping up his cross-examination. Nick took his standard position as he waited for the questioning to start. His face was fixed in a frown as he sat turned away from his brother.

Lopez wanted to know if Nick recalled getting a box of Cuban cigars with $20,000 in it. It was for his birthday two years before he went to prison, Lopez said.

"No, I don't," Nick answered, actually causing his brother Frank to give an audible laugh and lean well back in his chair.

And Lopez mentioned a list of minor disputes and complaints Nick had made to Frank Sr. over the years, and he accused Nick of blaming his brother for everything. Nick said he blamed himself too for many of his actions but claimed he knew his brother would have killed him if he had not followed orders.

"Your brother never killed you, did he?" Lopez asked.

"No," Nick said. "I'm still here."

The lawyer and the witness argued about who had really done what during some of the murders, most specifically the Cagnoni bombing. Didn't Nick sit inside a cardboard box in the back of a Ford Bronco at one point during the Cagnoni surveillance? Nick had decided on using the K-40 antenna to boost the transmitter, and wasn't Nick in radio communications in the navy?

"Yes," Nick said.

Did Nick just hate Frank Sr.? Is that what the case was all about?

No, Nick answered. "Hate consumes you. I don't have that much time left, so I don't hate him anymore."

So, Nick thought he was going to die soon? Lopez asked.

"We all die," he said.

Representing Marcello, Tom Breen would question Nick next. He started by asking how Nick had been approached at Pekin by agents wanting to take his DNA, sarcastically calling it "kind of a big day."

Nick said he knew the DNA would match but still wasn't ready to cooperate the next time he was visited, by Agent Michael Hartnett and police detective Robert Moon in the summer of 1999. The men hadn't told him then what punishment he was facing, he said.

"I had it in my mind that it was a death penalty case," Nick said.

But from that meeting forward, it would be some thirty months until Nick finally sat down with Michael Maseth and other agents in January 2002, Breen pointed out.

"You had thirty months to think about what you were going to tell the FBI," Breen said, insinuating that Nick had concocted his tale to maximize his own position.

"I had a lot to tell them," Nick answered.

And what did it mean that he wasn't ready? Breen continued in his sarcastic tone. He wasn't emotionally ready? He wasn't financially ready? Nick said he had decided that he didn't want to rot in prison or face the death penalty.

"You didn't want to be executed for the crimes you had committed," Breen said, emphasizing the second "you."

The lawyer pointed out that Nick now had "a complete pass" from prosecution for murders in Cook, DuPage, and Will counties. So, maybe things were working out OK for him. Breen listed all the times Nick had sat with agents in 2002 and 2003, all with the understanding that he had "carte blanche" to "bare it all."

"I told them what I knew," Nick answered.

"And you had the opportunity to tell them things you didn't know," Breen said.

"I had the opportunity, but I didn't," Nick said.

In the early briefings, Nick hadn't mentioned Marcello, Breen pointed out. Did Nick know that the Spilotro murders had gained more attention than any others in the case? Nick said he did but didn't pay attention to it because he didn't want to think about the weight he was carrying.

"Is the weight off now?" Breen asked.

"No, it's still there, because I gotta live with it."

With that, Breen began to go through the slides the government had used when John Scully gave his opening statement in the case. They included lists of the men that Nick had said were at each killing. And one by one, Breen pointed out that most of the men Nick had blamed were now dead. Maybe Nick had picked on Marcello to give the feds a big fish—and one that was still alive.

"I didn't put him in this case," Nick said earnestly. "He was there."

Breen asked about the 1983 making ceremony, where Marcello allegedly had been among those welcomed. Nick had said candidates had to be 100 percent Italian and had to have committed at least one murder.

Well, had Nick ever met Marcello's "lovely mother, Mrs. Flynn?" Breen asked. "Mrs. Flynn is as Irish as Paddy's pig, isn't she?"

It was a revelation that seemed to catch Nick off guard. Maybe Marcello had lied to the bosses about his heritage, he said.

"Yeah, somebody's lying," Breen said.

"I didn't know he was half Irish," Nick said. The truth is the truth, he added.

"Everything I've said here and every name that I gave were at those murders," Nick said defensively, leading Breen to ask without missing a beat whether Nick had ever been in sales.

The lawyer was clearly under Nick's skin; he had stopped slouching in his chair and was now sitting up with his back straight.

Breen asked about the attempted murder of Nicholas Sarillo, whose van had been blown up in the north suburbs. Supposedly Marcello and Sarillo were friends, but that wouldn't matter in the Outfit, Breen said. In the mob you can kill a friend, just like Nick had killed Fecarotta.

Nick's mouth tightened up again.

"You weren't there," he said to Breen. "You're trying to make it look like I enjoyed this. I killed my friend."

But Breen continued. The Ortiz and Morawski murders. Everyone Nick said was there were dead, too. Paul Schiro and Schweihs were still alive to face the consequences of Nick naming them in the Vaci murders, Breen said, but Nick had added that Marcello funded the murder by sending cash through the mail.

Had Nick seen a newsletter naming Marcello the comptroller of the Outfit? Breen joked.

"Do you have a copy of the newsletter?" Nick said icily, his expression completely unchanged.

Well, it was clear that Nick had the smarts to come up with a story that could help himself, Breen suggested. Within the time frame of all the murders, from 1970 to late 1986, Nick had been arrested only once. That was on a relatively minor gun charge.

"You're not stupid," Breen said.

"Yes, I am," Nick answered.

But Nick had collected on street loans, had stolen, and had hidden money from the IRS.

"You don't give yourself enough credit, Mr. Calabrese," Breen said.

"I was stupid and dumb," Nick said. "It doesn't take much to become a coward and do that."

Breen would soon move to the Spilotro murders but not before getting in one more dig about Marcello's mother. He named everyone Nick had said was at the making ceremony. Was it a celebration? Was there food there?

"No corned beef for Mr. Marcello?" Breen wondered, drawing laughs from the full courtroom.

How about a parting gift, some little party favor? Breen asked mockingly.

"You're allowed to walk out with your life," Nick answered with little emotion.

On the Spilotro murders, Breen asked about Nick's contacts with their brother, Patrick Spilotro, the dentist who had given up Joey Lombardo. Nick had met him, too, and had visited him as a patient. The men had become friends, and Spilotro had even visited Nick when he was being housed at Pekin in 2001.

Did Nick know that Spilotro had been wearing a wire during that meeting? Breen asked. Nick said that he had just found out that day in court.

Among the questions that had been recorded was Spilotro asking about his brothers, Breen said and then continued by asking Nick if he remembered his visitor asking what his brothers had done wrong.

Breen said Nick's response had been, "If I knew, I would tell you."

Maybe that actually was the truth, the lawyer said.

"You have told a story about the Spilotros being killed, and you, in fact, were not even there, were you?" Breen said loudly.

"Yes, I was," Nick answered.

But so much of the story was unbelievable, Breen suggested. Nick supposedly had met two other wiseguys in front of a store in broad daylight to drive to the killing site.

"I was told to be there, and that's where I was," Nick said, again in a flat tone.

At the house, most of the Outfit's big shots were there. Michael Spilotro had supposedly come in first, walking into a home where Nick had said everyone was wearing gloves. Didn't Michael look around and say, hey, "This looks like a hit?"

"No."

Breen said he didn't find it credible that Nick didn't know exactly who killed Anthony Spilotro. His testimony had been that he had his back to the area of the basement where he died.

But Nick had told Pat Spilotro that he didn't know anything about why the men were killed. "And for a brief moment, that was the truth, wasn't it?" Breen said, raising his voice again.

"No," Nick repeated.

Well there was at least one discrepancy in Nick's accounts, Breen suggested. In one of his debriefings, Nick had told FBI agents that he believed Rocky Infelice was in the house where the Spilotros died. In fact that couldn't be true, Breen said, because Infelice was under FBI surveillance at the time the brothers were killed. Nick answered that he had told agents he thought he might have seen the mobster out of the corner of his eye.

Paul Wagner's questioning of Nick, on behalf of Paul Schiro, was much shorter, with the lawyer concentrating on asking Nick about his state of mind and whether he saw himself as some kind of victim. Schiro had supposedly been close by watching for the police when Vaci was killed, but Nick hadn't even said Schiro had helped him dig a hole for the body, he pointed out.

Did Nick feel sorry for his own family?

"Yes, because of the shame I brought on them," he answered.

And how about the families of the victims?

"Doing what I'm doing now is the only thing I could do."

When Mars had the chance to question Nick again, he kept his questions limited. He had one major point to make.

Nick said he hadn't seen his nephew in ten years.

Well, before testifying in the Family Secrets case, had he seen any reports on what Frank Jr. had said? Had he heard any of the recordings his nephew had made of Frank Sr.? Had he heard the tapes of Frank Sr. talking about the details of killing Albergo, or the Daubers, or Ortiz and Morawski? Had he ever heard what his brother's version of events was, something that might have given him an opportunity to match what his brother had said?

"No," Nick said, not long before he was led from the stand.

He walked out of the room and away from his brother, and he didn't look back.

14

THE BEAK, THE OVEN, AND THE DENTIST

O ver the next few weeks, prosecutors would call a series of witnesses to bolster the account that Nick had given to the jury, those who had been part of the mob's dirty business and those victimized by it.

Victor Cacciatore was first, chairman of the successful Cacciatore real estate firm founded by his father. He'd lived in Bridgeport but moved to River Forest in 1955, about ten years before a man named Tony Accardo moved in next door. He used to see his neighbor cutting his lawn.

"It was heavily rumored he was head of the Outfit," the white-haired Cacciatore said.

He also had been familiar with the mob-connected family of Frank "Skids" Caruso, the onetime leader of the Twenty-Sixth Street crew, having had some members of the family as clients. One of his earliest clients was Fred Roti, he said, who went on to become a mob-connected alderman convicted of racketeering and identified by the federal government as a made member of the Outfit.

In the winter of 1980, Cacciatore said he was leaving his office near Halsted and Thirty-Third streets when two men walked up behind him with a message. They wanted money. But this was no street robbery. They wanted Cacciatore and his business to pay $5 million.

"They weren't kidding," Cacciatore said. "It was very threatening."

But not threatening enough to make Cacciatore give anybody a nickel. He went about his business but before long began to get threatening phone calls.

Then one day someone put the head of a dog on one of his son's cars, he said.

"We didn't know what the reason for it was," he said.

Another night, he had just gotten into his car when he heard a loud explosion, and his rear window blew out, he said, telling the jury he didn't know how. Later on he was told it was a shotgun blast, he said. Still, he decided not to put together any cash for the Outfit.

It wasn't until 1981 that he had a change of heart. There was a lot of publicity about a man in a Mercedes being blown up as he was getting on the Tri-State Tollway. Another call came in, Cacciatore said, with another ominous warning.

"Unless I pay up, the same thing's gonna happen to me," Cacciatore said.

He left $200,000 in cash on the floor of his car behind the driver's seat for someone to pick up, he told the jury.

"My life and my children's lives were in jeopardy," he explained.

The amount had been lowered, though Cacciatore was notably hazy about the name of the person he might have negotiated with. He had once told authorities he knew who was behind it but didn't want to identify them.

On the stand he did say he recalled visiting Roti, at least to discuss who might have been threatening him. "I may have gone to his house," Cacciatore said.

Sidney Epstein was a successful businessman, too. He was chairman of the board of A. Epstein & Sons, founded in 1921, an architectural firm that designed buildings. The company was known in Chicago for its additions to McCormick Place, and it had helped in the planning of the Dirksen courthouse, where Epstein was testifying.

In August 1970 the company was involved in something of a little smaller scale. It was a warehouse in the 3300 block of South Shields, not too far from the Old Comiskey Park.

Construction had involved digging through a layer of topsoil and then clay.

When Joe Lopez had a chance to question Epstein, he wanted a little detail on that tougher layer beneath the dirt. Would it be tough to dig through the clay with, say, a shovel?

"You could," Epstein said.

Had there been any complaints among workers there about holes appearing on the site?

No, Epstein said.

Testifying in an open blue shirt and jeans was Carl Galione, who said he'd been in the forklift business for more than thirty years. He knew Ronnie Jarrett, Galione said, and Nick, too. He would take out loans from Jarrett, he said—$20,000 one year to help his business and $40,000 another year to buy equipment for snow removal. He was hoping winter business would make it easy to pay back the loan and boost his profits.

One problem, Galione said.

"Did not snow."

Still, he said, he found a way to pay the interest he owed, which had been as high as $800 a week. Even when Jarrett went to prison in 1980, someone would come to collect from him. Some years that was Nick, he said.

Galione was paying something in the order of $10,000 a year during that period. So what would happen if he had quit?

"I didn't know, and I didn't want to find out," he said.

Lopez tried to paint the arrangement as more of a business deal, asking whether Frank Sr. was someone known to give loans to people who needed help financially. Galione agreed that he liked Ronnie Jarrett and that loans he took out helped his business grow. Jarrett had taken up a partnership in the business, Galione agreed.

It was two days before Christmas 1999 when Ronnie Jarrett's violent life caught up to him.

"He was shot in front of my mother's house," his son, Ronald Jarrett Jr., told the Family Secrets jury. The mob hit man who had worked closely with the Calabreses was shot as he left the family's home on South Lowe to attend a funeral.

Ronnie Jarrett had spent all of the 1980s and some of the '90s in federal prison. And when he got out, he had been involved in an illegal gambling operation with his son.

Ronald Jr., a thirty-five-year-old with short, dark hair, had been involved in a host of petty crimes, he told the jury, including burglaries and trying to steal an automated teller machine. He knew Frank Sr. and Nick, he said, as well as Anthony Doyle. And he knew Michael Talarico and Family Secrets defendant Nicholas Ferriola, the son of Wild Bunch boss Joe Ferriola.

Nicholas Ferriola was involved in the Jarretts' bookmaking operation, Ronald Jr. said. His father had introduced him to the younger Ferriola and had told him he would be having calls coming into the bookmaking office. The operation had four or five agents, and Ronnie Jarrett bankrolled it with a wad of cash he kept in the pocket of a coat stored in a closet in their home. The gambling ring would take bets on college and professional football, basketball, and baseball as well as hockey and major horse races.

As the business grew, it ran two offices, Ronald Jr. said, in a pair of South Side apartments. Betting slips would be kept up in the ceiling of one of the offices. Larger bets could run as high as $10,000 a game, he added, and while his father was alive and things were going well, some cash from the operation was delivered to Diane Calabrese, Frank Sr.'s wife.

"My father told me," he said.

As for who was responsible for his father's death, Ronald Jr. said he had asked Nicholas Ferriola to find out who wanted him dead, and the answer was John "Johnny Apes" Monteleone.

Lopez asked if that wasn't because Monteleone was trying to control his dad and the gambling operation. Maybe, Ronald Jr. said. Johnny Apes had taken over as capo of the Chinatown crew after the death of both LaPietra brothers, and Ronnie Jarrett was seemingly resisting paying any street taxes to the new leadership.

And as for Frank Sr., he had tried to steer the younger Jarrett away from gambling, Ronald Jr. agreed.

On one curious point, Ronald Jr. talked about the death of his grandmother, Ronnie Jarrett's mother-in-law, in 2001. Her garage had been the street crew's workshop and the site of at least two murders. Ronald Jr. said the family went through the garage once she died and found "a bag of guns" inside as well as a lone stick of dynamite hidden in a refrigerator.

"I tried to set it off at first," Ronald Jr. said. "But it was old. I ended up throwing it out."

After Ronald Jr. the government called a series of witnesses who talked of doing business with M&M Amusement, the video poker business owned by the Marcellos. Several bar owners, testifying with immunity, said they allowed customers they knew to play the machines for real, collecting winnings from cash reserves they kept behind their bars. Representatives of the company would appear regularly to settle up with them, the owners said, splitting the profits and directing them to throw out receipts.

Thomas Paine owned a bar on Ogden Avenue in Berwyn, he said, and had a pair of the machines.

"They're still in my bar," he testified. "Nobody ever picked them up."

Jurors also heard from Teri Nevis, the former wife of Nicholas D'Andrea, who had long, blond hair and who testified in a whispery voice that she had moved in with D'Andrea when she was fifteen. She lived with him in Chicago Heights, she said, and knew him to be in the Outfit. There were plenty of times when associates would appear at the home with envelopes.

Nevis remembered in particular one call D'Andrea took in 1981, when he learned that Al Pilotto had been shot and wounded at a golf course.

"He was visibly upset," Nevis said, and then he had become wary.

"Nicky had gotten paranoid. He would watch out the windows for vehicles in front of the house."

On the day he disappeared in September 1981, it was Sam Guzzino who had called for him, Nevis said. D'Andrea had gotten dressed, put a gun in his belt, and left the house.

It was testimony that appeared to further corroborate Nick's account of why D'Andrea had been killed and the government's information about Guzzino being the taller guy walking into the garage as Nick hid with his bat. But Nevis wouldn't leave the stand without giving prosecutors a problem.

Breen asked her if the man in a photograph he showed her was her former husband. "Absolutely not," she said, looking at the image the government had stated, in Scully's opening statement, was of D'Andrea.

But while it showed a mistake had been made in organizing the photos, it still didn't cast much doubt on Nick. When Nick had viewed the same image during his testimony, he hadn't been able to identify the man in the photograph, either.

Still trying to bolster Nick's account of the D'Andrea murder, prosecutors next called Karen Brill, who worked at Murphy Cab in Chicago Heights in the 1980s. It was owned by Richard Guzzino, Sam's brother.

She said Sam would stop in regularly at the cab company's office. It was in a building on Emerald in the town—a structure with a garage, a bar called the Vagabond Lounge, and an upstairs "whorehouse" and gambling hall.

Taking a look at a photo of a dilapidated garage, Brill said that it was the one the cab company used to run out of, and it was the same photo Nick had told jurors looked like the garage he was talking about when he described the attack on D'Andrea.

Career thief Robert "Bobby the Beak" Siegel had only a fifth- or sixth-grade education, but he was smart enough to know what was happening when some of his friends began disappearing in early 1978.

John Mendell was first, Siegel told the jury, seated on the witness stand in a light-colored T-shirt with eyeglasses stuffed in his front pocket, another visitor to the trial from witness protection. He was a tall and talkative seventy-one-year-old, had a prominent nose that was the source of his nickname, and looked relaxed with his gray hair swept back on top of his head. He'd been in prison in Minnesota with the burglar Mendell, he told prosecutor Markus Funk, and sure, they'd done some burglaries together, too.

"We had worked together on a few," he said in a deep voice.

There was a house where they had stolen antiques, and factories where they had taken safes. Mendell would usually be the one to get them inside the buildings in the first place, because he "knew a little bit about alarms," Siegel explained.

So it was nothing out of the ordinary when Mendell called on January 16, 1978. Siegel was at home recovering from an all-night drive from Texas, he said, so he turned down an offer to join Mendell at a meeting. His friend told him that "the Little Guy," meaning Ronnie Jarrett, had called and had something good for him, so he'd stop by and see Siegel later.

"I never seen him again," Siegel said.

Next came a call from Bernard "Buddy" Ryan, another burglar, who told Siegel that John DiFronzo had called about a score involving gold coins. "I'll get back to you after I've talked to him," Ryan had told his pal.

"Never heard from him no more, either," Siegel said of Ryan, who would turn up shot to death in a Chicago suburb.

Siegel's own call came through a man known as "Snuffy," he said. A mobster he knew by the nickname "the Dinger" wanted Siegel to be involved in a great job. And the take?

Some gold coins.

"That's when I knew I was on that list," Siegel said. "I didn't have to be too bright to figure out what that was."

Siegel had fallen into his life of crime on the West Side as a teenager when he and his friends would take "anything we could make a buck with," he said. "We started going on armed robberies when I was about sixteen."

He'd become aware of the Outfit guys in his neighborhood in the 1950s. They seemed to have a lot of power.

"They made all the money, and they didn't go to jail," Siegel said with a chuckle. "Most of the police were on the payroll at that time."

Siegel had been involved in burglarizing "maybe one hundred" stores during his lifetime; he'd robbed three or four banks and even killed three people, he said. He had eventually become an informant after others he worked with turned, and his cooperation had helped lead to charges against William Hanhardt, the Chicago police chief of detectives who had pleaded guilty to masterminding millions in jewelry thefts with the mob.

As Siegel was coming up as a criminal, he eventually fell in with the Outfit himself. He remembered being at a place called Parker's, a hangout where wiseguys would play cards. And, Siegel said, he wound up on the payroll of Frank "the Calico Kid" Teutonico, a mobster who earned his gunslinger nickname because he once sat down to play cards and fired a pistol into the ceiling. "This is to make sure the game's on the square," Teutonico had said, Siegel remembered, holding his hand up like a gun above his head.

Siegel made his way as a collector at first, telling the jury he would "go out and get a hold of" those who wouldn't pay what was owed to Teutonico, who lived in a hotel on Jackson Boulevard on the West Side. For this Siegel brought in $400 a week, but the men were close, he said.

"It got to be something like a father and son deal."

Teutonico schooled Siegel on who was who and what was what. There were rules about who earned respect, who shouldn't be crossed, like the enforcer "Willie Potatoes" Daddano, and other ways not to get hurt. He watched the Outfit evolve, too, he said, such as when the 1970 Racketeer Influenced and Corrupt Organizations, or RICO, Act went into effect. Back in the day before RICO, Outfit guys would give threats and orders with their names attached for emphasis.

"When that RICO came out, it was, 'Well whatever you do, don't mention my name,'" Siegel said.

Siegel came to work for Angelo Volpe, who, he said, was in charge of South Side numbers rackets and who knew of the Chinatown crew that was led by the LaPietras and included Frank Calabrese Sr. Money from men he worked for was going into that crew through Fiore "Fifi" Buccieri, he said.

James "Turk" Torello of the Chinatown crew even sent him to Las Vegas once to collect on a debt owed to Frank "Lefty" Rosenthal, Siegel said. It was 1968 or 1969, and someone owed Rosenthal $87,000. He met with the bookie, and "we straightened it out," he said, remembering the debtor was warned to pay up or face the consequences.

He was working for Volpe, he said, when he watched the mobster pay off the head of the vice unit of the Chicago Police Department.

"He gave him a package of money," Siegel said, and then the pair discussed the site of an upcoming police gambling raid. Volpe didn't have a problem with it.

"He told him that was OK; it wasn't one of ours."

It was through Volpe, Siegel said, that he was first exposed to Hanhardt. Volpe gave the corrupt police official Siegel's name and told Hanhardt that Siegel was an employee who shouldn't be bothered.

Hanhardt and his partner were getting $1,000 a month to look the other way, Siegel said, plus a new car every couple of years.

As for the offer on the gold coins, Siegel said he was so concerned that he had a polygraph test done to prove that he hadn't been involved in the burglary at Levinson's Jewelry, which eventually led to the burglary at the home of mob boss Tony Accardo. He passed the test and had the results delivered to the Outfit through a network of defense lawyers to Marshall Caifano.

It was later that Siegel asked another syndicate pal about why he had been targeted. And another thing he wanted to know was why Buddy Ryan would have been killed, since everyone knew Ryan wouldn't have had the heart for breaking into Accardo's place. Gerald Scarpelli, who had robbed an armored truck with Siegel, fielded the question.

The killing of the burglars—at least six in all—was meant as a broad message.

"They were trying to make it one guy of every nationality," Siegel recalled. "He said, 'You just happened to be the Jew.'"

It wasn't hard to see why Ernest Severino would be popular with members of the Chicago Outfit in the 1970s, seeing as how he owned both a crematory and a gun shop.

They called him Ernie "the Oven" or just "Digger," and they wanted the keys to Severino's furnace. They even offered money to use it. For what, anyone could guess.

Severino paid street taxes to Scarpelli, and one of the mobsters he knew was William "Butch" Petrocelli, he said.

"He would come to the funeral home and say, hey, do this or that," Severino said, remembering how Petrocelli would ask him to take a ride or hold an envelope every now and again. He paid what he was asked and did as he was told, Severino said, seemingly still nervous in 2007.

"I didn't want to have to put myself in harm's way, let's say," Severino told the jury, remembering one time he drove Scarpelli to a mob meeting held in the cafeteria of Oak Park Hospital.

On the gun shop side, Petrocelli always was requesting weapons or Scarpelli was appearing for them. Hunting rifles, .38s, MAC-10 submachine guns, .22s. The men took them and paid for nothing.

More than fifty guns were kept in a secret location for Petrocelli, Severino said, their serial numbers obliterated.

Then, at the beginning of 1981, Petrocelli disappeared. Scarpelli and another man came by to say that anything being hidden for Petrocelli should be put in Scarpelli's hands. Severino didn't want any problems, but he didn't want Butch reappearing and looking for all of his stuff either.

"I just told them, 'I'll see what I can do,'" he remembered.

Not long thereafter, Severino was called to a meeting where he learned Joe Ferriola was turning over some of the Wild Bunch leadership to Scarpelli and was told he should do what he was told. Now, Scarpelli wanted to know, where were Butch's guns and cash?

"Those fellows don't ask a question unless they know the answer," Severino said. And Butch apparently was no longer a problem.

"He says, 'He's never coming back,'" Severino recalled. "[Scarpelli] said he was at a meeting with the older guys, and they told him to take care of the garbage in the next room. And that was supposedly Butch."

*

Richard Cleary was indicted with the Spilotro brothers in the Hole in the Wall Gang case in Las Vegas; he had pleaded guilty and appeared at the Family Secrets trial as a sixty-eight-year-old gray-haired man.

Cleary had worked in bookmaking and had a long history of residential and commercial burglaries. He liked to steal jewelry. Tiffany lamps.

"Stuff like that, you know," he told John Scully.

He had worked as a bartender for Paul "the Indian" Schiro and had recalled seeing him at the Arizona Manor in the mid-1980s and later, when Schiro was afraid for his life. Schiro had told him that Anthony Spilotro had been his boss, and beyond him, Joey Lombardo. Schiro would sometimes complain about having to answer to the mob, Cleary said.

"He said, 'It doesn't matter if your mother's dying . . . if they call, you better go,'" Clearly recalled in a quiet voice.

And Schiro had told him something else, too, he told the jury. It was 2003, and Cleary was visiting his friend in prison. His wife had seen something in a news report about a guy named Nick Calabrese telling the feds "where all the bodies are buried." He wondered if Schiro knew him and whether the new informant could hurt him.

"He said, 'Yes, he could put me away forever.'"

On cross-examination, Halprin was most interested in the Lombardo claim, and Cleary acknowledged he had no firsthand information that Joey was a mob boss.

Sal Romano was another Hole in the Wall defendant, and he too pleaded guilty and then turned on his onetime cohorts. He went into witness security and said he was living under an assumed name elsewhere in the United States when he was called to the witness stand. He was brought into the Family Secrets trial in a wheelchair, a frail man with a blue coat, a yellow tie, and a tuft of gray hair.

Romano had received about $1,700 a month from the government, but he also remembered getting a lump sum of $40,000 in 1987.

"I guess it was a bonus," he said in a voice barely above a mumble.

Unlike some youngsters who slip into a life of crime while growing up in broken homes, Romano admitted his own childhood was "rather good." His father owned a bar and was involved in real estate, and his mother worked part-time at Oscar Mayer and was otherwise at home. He went to school before simply running into the right people, he said, or the wrong people, depending on your view.

Locks and alarms fascinated Romano. "I developed skills in those things," he said, explaining how he would buy locks just to take them apart, see how they worked, and come up with the right pick.

He was on the road all over the Chicago area by twenty-six or twenty-seven, he told the jury, traveling with a partner to steal over and over from coin machines. It was sometimes risky, but getting caught by the police wasn't necessarily a problem. If he got pinched, there was always a bribe to be paid to grease his way back to the street.

"You indirectly paid the lawyer they requested you get," Romano said, mainly officers in Area 5 and Area 6; he named lawyers including Dean Wolfson, who pleaded guilty in 1985 to bribing judges. William Hanhardt was another police contact, he said, who was regularly doing favors for those in Romano's line of work.

More dangerous than landing in jail was stepping on the wrong toes, a fact Romano would be reminded of in the mid-1970s. Stealing from the wrong place could be hazardous to your health. So, he wasn't pleased to get a call from Joe Ferriola, who wanted a meeting with him at a local Laundromat.

"Probably hit the wrong machine or something," Romano figured, but he showed up when someone like Ferriola said to appear. "He's not the kind of you guy you say, 'No, I don't want to talk to ya.'"

Ferriola had a hand in some laundry businesses and apparently was interested in how easy it would be for a thief like Romano to steal from him. He asked Romano to have a look at the machines where they were meeting to see whether he could break into them. Of course he could, Romano said. And that was basically the extent of it, but Romano told the crime boss he wanted to make sure he didn't knock over any machines connected to his organization.

"I said, 'Have them put a star on them or something.'"

It was a period when Romano was doing about one residential burglary per week and breaking into businesses regularly, too. But wanting to steer clear of anything with mob links, he said he avoided businesses in such towns such as Oak Park and Forest Park, never knowing whose business was controlled by which Outfit crew in an area he viewed as heavily connected. John Mendell, the shining example of the principle of not ripping off the wrong people, was a friend of his, Romano said.

By the late 1970s, Romano's career had brought him to Las Vegas, where he'd been recruited to join the Hole in the Wall Gang. Stealing artwork was becoming a problem because of the increasingly sophisticated alarm systems, so Romano's skill set was tapped for the job. Frank Cullotta was among the ring members, Romano said, a man he knew reported to Anthony Spilotro in Las Vegas. And he knew of Schiro, too, and his partner Richard Cleary. In fact, Romano said, he even had a conversation with Spilotro once where the Las Vegas boss had told him to listen to Schiro and do what Schiro said to do if they ever did a job together.

That sounded like an order, but even Romano had his limits.

Romano said that later he was involved in a job that Schiro set up. Schiro knew the owner of a home the crew was targeting and knew that when the owner was away for a family wedding, it would be a convenient time to take what was supposed to be $50,000 in a safe. Schiro's alibi was going to be that he would attend the wedding, but he was able to supply the burglary crew with a key before leaving. Romano took care of the alarm, and things were going well until a tiny dog appeared, "screaming, hollering, and barking," Romano remembered.

He broke off the job, hearing from Cleary a few minutes later on a walkie-talkie. Cleary wanted to know why Romano just hadn't taken care of the scrappy pooch and gone on with the plan.

"I said, 'I don't do dogs,'" Romano said.

As for Cullotta, Romano derisively referred to him as "Faraway Frank," because he tended to hang back from jobs. "If you were looking for him, you had to wait around awhile," he said.

But Cullotta wound up in a fistfight with the man who had helped bring Romano west, he said, Peter Basile. A Persian rug in a store had caught Basile's eye, but someone else had stolen it before Basile could get there, and he blamed Cullotta. After the scuffle, Romano said, Spilotro got involved in settling the dispute. The men got a dressing-down, Romano recalled, but Basile clearly got the worst of it. If he ever touched one of Spilotro's guys again, Spilotro promised to cut off Basile's hands.

When Anthony Spilotro arrived in the Chicago area in the summer of 1986, he spent a lot of his time at his brother Michael's home in Oak Park. He had told the judge in Las Vegas he was going home for dental treatment, and he did go see another of his five brothers, Patrick the dentist, on June 11.

And Anthony was back at the dental office the next day too, June 12, Patrick Spilotro told the jury when he got his chance to testify. His brother asked to use a private office phone, he recalled. It was no problem, and Anthony disappeared to make some phone calls.

Prosecutors couldn't say for sure who had made which calls that appeared on the office's phone records for that day, but they asked the dentist whether he would have had any reason to make one of the calls listed in the documents. That was the one that went to the home phone of James Marcello.

Prosecutors would argue the call was made as final arrangements were being made for a meeting between the brothers within days. Marcello had regularly called Michael Spilotro at home in the weeks and months leading up to that June, Michael's wife, Ann, remembered. She told the jury she knew Marcello's voice and that he had called many times.

Her husband told her he had to go to a meeting on Saturday, June 14. Michael had been confident in the weeks leading up to that summer that he and his brother were going to be moving up in the organization.

"He said that they were going to become Number One," Ann Spilotro remembered her husband telling her.

But at 2:00 A.M. the night before the meeting on the fourteenth, Michael was nervous. He had a specific warning, telling Ann that if he wasn't back by 9:00 P.M. that next day, she should know something was wrong.

"I didn't think as if he would lose his life," she said. "I just thought that it would be a problem."

Michael's family was mostly accustomed to his life by the mid-1980s. His daughter Michelle worked as a hostess at the family's restaurant and pub, a place called Hoagie's on North Avenue on the Chicago–Oak Park border. She testified that she had seen a number of her father's friends there. They would have meetings in a back room, and she could see through a fireplace that opened up to the front and back of the pub. She had met men such as Paul Schiro, Rocky Infelice, Joey Aiuppa, and Louie Eboli. And she had seen Joey Lombardo.

"Ninety times," she said when she testified.

That included in her home, where the men would sometimes whisper to one another or write notes back and forth on rice paper, which they would dissolve in a toilet when they were through. Other times they would write to one another on a child's toy known as a Magic Slate, which would allow them to write a message and lift a plastic sheet to erase it.

"You'd see them scribbling, and they'd lift it up," she said.

When she was a child, she had gone to Louie Eboli's warehouse, she said, remembering playing with all of the jukeboxes he had there.

But not every memory was without fear. She had met Frank "the German" Schweihs, too, recalling seeing him at her house two or three times in the early 1980s. Her father had given her "very emphatic instructions" about him.

"If I ever see him near my house I'm to lock the door and call the police," she said, remembering the instruction from her youth.

Testifying at the Family Secrets trial, she was a thirty-eight-year-old homemaker with long dark hair.

Throughout much of the early 1980s and up until Michael Spilotro's death, Michelle said she took at least a couple of calls a month from a man she knew as "Jim." Her father was often expecting him to ring the house, she said, telling her ahead of time to either get him right away or tell "Jim" that he wasn't there. The caller had a heavy Chicago accent that she always recognized.

"It definitely left an indelible impression in my brain," she told the jury.

She had even met him once, she remembered. A man had come into Hoagie's and asked for her dad, and she knew his voice immediately. Once the man left, she told her dad that was the man who called all the time. Michael told his daughter she was observant "and nosy," but he told her his name was Jim when she asked.

On Saturday, June 14, another of the calls came in like many before it, Michelle testified. Her father and her uncle Anthony had been getting ready that morning, getting showered and dressed. Michael was acting peculiar, Michelle told the jury. He had always told her that he loved her, she said, fighting back tears as she spoke.

"That day he said it at least ten times," she remembered.

And there was more weird behavior. Michael gave his daughter a bag with his driver's license in it as well as a medallion he always wore around his neck. "Tell your mother to bring this later when I see you guys," he said, telling her he would meet up with the family later at a graduation party.

And then he left.

Ann Spilotro said she knew all of her husband's associates, too. She would also see Lombardo and men such as "Turk" Torello. Her husband had been on a hunting trip to Mexico with Joey Aiuppa, she had been to Frank Calabrese Sr.'s house for dinner, and she knew Lombardo as "Lumbo." She knew Schiro, too, saying he was one of the men that Michael and Anthony had told her they trusted with their lives.

Ann had grown up in Chicago and the western suburbs. James Marcello was someone in the family's circle of friends during those teen years, she recalled. She wore a light-colored jacket on the stand, testifying calmly and confidently with her hands folded in front of her.

She remembered a lot of calls from Marcello between April and June of 1986, she said.

"Sometimes he'd have to leave," she said of her husband.

The Saturday of Michael's meeting, Ann said she left the Oak Park house between 10:00 and 11:00 A.M. for a Little League game and then went to the grocery for a few things for the next day—Father's Day. When she came home, she was alarmed by the bag of her husband's belongings that Michelle had been given. It wasn't like Michael not to have his things.

But she tried not to be too nervous, put the medallion and other items in her purse, and went to the party at about 6:30 or 7:00 P.M.

"I was there and kept looking at the clock," she remembered, her voice trembling.

Then, it was nine o'clock, the time Michael had mentioned. A woman arrived at her table and sat down next to her, Ann said. It was a woman whose husband had been killed by the Outfit.

"I started shaking," she said. "I couldn't stop shaking."

Not wanting to panic, she went home and paced most of the night. For hours she waited, she said, but her husband's car never reappeared. She started calling her five brothers-in-law first thing the next morning to see whether anyone had seen Michael and Anthony. "Nobody had," she said, wiping tears under her eyeglasses.

Patrick Spilotro said his first call came from his brother Victor, telling him that Michael and Anthony hadn't come home the night before. "He said he thinks something's terribly wrong," Patrick said. So he went to the Bridgeport neighborhood on the South Side, looking for the car, and went to the Howard Johnson's where Anthony had gotten a room, he said, taking what things were left there over to Michael's house in Oak Park.

The family would wait until that Monday, June 16, to report the brothers missing. And it would be a week later that their bodies would turn up in the cornfield.

Both Ann and Patrick would come to ask Lombardo whether he knew anything about how or why the brothers had been killed. Ann said she remembered asking him in an upholstery factory.

"He said that if he wasn't in prison, if he was out, then it wouldn't have happened," she told the jury.

Patrick had heard the same message over the years, too, years he spent quietly trying to work his connections to give the FBI information about what could have happened to them. He had asked people in the old neighborhood around Grand and Ogden, and had worn a wire when he asked Nick Calabrese about the murders in 2001. And the dentist would ask the question of Joey again once he was a fugitive in 2006. Lombardo's friend Dominic Calarco had called to set up the secret appointment to get "the Clown's" ailing tooth taken care of. Patrick remembered seeing Lombardo arrive with a heavy beard, a bandage over his nose, and a hood pulled over his head.

It was then that Lombardo had given the answer about following orders when they were given and Patrick had made the decision to turn the fugitive mobster in. Agents would be waiting when Lombardo returned for more dental work.

"They knew the exact time," the dentist said.

Two or three years after the murders, Michelle Spilotro said FBI agents brought her to a mall parking lot for a test. They wanted to know if she could pick out the voice of the man who had called her house on the day her father vanished. Agents had used a few test subjects to read a paragraph from a story in the *Sun-Times* that Marcello had been directed to read during an investigation of the killings. Michelle knew the voice immediately, she said, telling the agent to stop the tape. She had chosen Marcello's voice.

"That's it," she said she told the agent. "No doubt whatsoever."

When defense attorneys had their chances to cross-examine the Spilotro witnesses, they picked away at some of the details in the accounts. Michelle Spilotro acknowledged it had been three years between the last time she had heard the voice of the man she knew as Jim and the time the FBI had her listen to the voice lineup in 1989.

Tom Breen cross-examined Patrick Spilotro for Marcello and challenged him on why he had cleaned out Anthony's hotel room before the family had even reported the brothers missing.

"It's what I did at that time," the dentist answered. "I really didn't have my whole head on at that time."

But why empty the room so fast? Breen pressed. What if the brothers had returned and thought there was a burglary?

"That would've been a blessing for me, then," Patrick said, trying to keep his emotions in check.

He already knew there was trouble, he said. His sister-in-law had called and told him that Michael had said if he wasn't back by 9:00 P.M., something had happened. She was crying, he remembered.

"She told me where they went," the dentist added. "They went with Marcello."

Breen couldn't believe what he had just heard. He left the podium and walked around to stand in front of Patrick. His sister-in-law hadn't said her husband went with Marcello when she testified, Breen angrily told the dentist, and he accused him of taking an extra shot at the man he obviously blamed for killing his brothers.

"You were the first person to ever share that, Doctor," Breen said sarcastically. "Ever report that to the FBI?"

"The FBI was aware that Marcello had called there and [my brothers] went to meet him," a defiant Spilotro answered.

"Yeah, right," Breen shot back. "That's the problem when somebody does [their own] investigation."

When the bodies of Anthony and Michael Spilotro were found in the cornfield on June 22, 1986, Patrick would supply his brothers' dental X-rays, which forensic pathologists would use to positively identify the men.

Dr. John Pless was one of those pathologists performing autopsies on the bodies of the brothers after they were brought from the recovery site in Enos to the Indiana University Medical Center. The bodies were clad only in underwear and were still covered with dirt and sand. Pless and Dr. Dean Hawley worked together in an L-shaped room, with Pless doing Michael's autopsy and Hawley performing Anthony's at the same time.

The bodies were "moderately decomposed" from being in the ground for more than a week, Pless told the jury. They were swollen and discolored. The skin had begun to slip and peel away, but still there was much evidence to record about how the Spilotros had been killed.

Michael had suffered contusions and blunt force injuries "over the entire body," Pless said, speaking in a clinical monotone. There were bruises on the right side of his face and temple, on the back of his head, and on his lip. His nose was broken, and there was more extensive bruising on the right side of his neck. On the left side of his neck was a superficial abrasion. There was a fracture of the cartilage around Michael's larynx, a fracture of the left thyroid bone, and a fracture of the Adam's apple. Blood had gathered under the trachea. There was bruising to the right shoulder and upper arm, and Michael's right kidney was torn.

The cause of death, Pless said, was multiple blunt force trauma to the head and neck, and there was evidence of asphyxia. Almost the entire right lung was filled with blood.

Like his brother, Anthony also suffered blunt force to the head, with four heavy bruises to the face and left temple. He also had aspirated blood into his trachea, lungs, and nasal passages, Pless said methodically. There was hemorrhaging in the muscles of the larynx, and he had suffered heavy bruising injuries to the chest and the front of the upper arms. Anthony also had severe coronary disease, with the pathologists finding evidence that he'd had bypass surgery.

"All of these things compounding to produce death," Pless said.

Neither brother had any skin broken by a blow. But more at issue for both sides was something else that pathologists didn't find. Neither Anthony nor Michael had what are known as ligature marks around their necks, the kind of linear marks that are left when someone is strangled.

In the film *Casino* the characters based on the Spilotro brothers are shown being beaten with baseball bats in the cornfield, then buried alive in the movie's climactic scene. Pless immediately dispelled the idea that the men were clubbed. The fact that neither man's skin was broken suggested that no object with mass—such as a bat—was used to kill them. Fists, knees, and feet were most likely the murder weapons.

In addition, no sand or dirt was found in the airway of either man, Pless said. So, Mitch Mars asked, were the brothers buried alive?

"No, there was no evidence of that," Pless answered.

No indication they were alive at the time of burial, Mars repeated.

"That's correct."

But the pathologist wasn't part of the government's case to confirm the account of the deaths in a Hollywood film. Prosecutors hoped his findings confirmed the account of Nick Calabrese.

Mars asked whether the lack of ligature marks would preclude the use of a rope, as Nick had described in the killing of Michael. No, it wouldn't, Pless said, but it would indicate that the use of a rope wasn't what had killed the men.

Not surprisingly, the cause of death and the supposed use of a rope was the area of concentration for Tom Breen, who cross-examined Pless for Marcello. After jokingly asking whether Pless had done any government surveillance in 1986, he immediately asked about all of the blunt force injuries. There were punishing blows delivered with punches and kicks, injuries inflicted with knees and elbows.

None of those injuries were signs of strangulation, were they? Breen asked, trying to chip away at Nick's account.

"No," Pless said.

In layman's terms, Breen said, was it fair to say the brothers were "just beaten to death?"

"Yes," Pless answered.

When Pless had given an interview to the FBI on the cause of death, he had noted that no ligature or rope binding marks were present at all.

Mars got up to question Pless again, and he went back to the missing ligature marks. While there were no such marks, that wouldn't preclude the use of a rope, would it? Mars asked.

Pless agreed. Especially in Michael's case, he pointed out again, there were fractures in the neck that might suggest a rope could have been used. Nick had specifically testified to seeing Louis Eboli with a rope around Michael's neck and had said he didn't see exactly how Anthony had died.

It had been a rough round of evidence against Marcello, and it wouldn't improve when the slim woman in her fifties walked through the door to the courtroom and up an aisle. The man believed to be the Chicago mob's acting boss looked uncomfortable as he rose up slightly in his chair and resettled when she went to the witness stand. She had shoulder-length brown hair and spoke in a quiet voice.

Her name was Connie Marcello, but she was not his wife. She was his mistress—a woman who had felt so close to Marcello that she had changed her name to his. She'd had a relationship with him since the early 1980s, meeting him when she tended bar in Cook County strip clubs. There was Michael's Magic Touch in suburban Lyons as well as The Hollywood in Cicero, she said.

Connie was giving information about drug activity to the ATF when she met James, taking a liking to him as he brought liquor to the Cicero club a couple of times a week. They started dating, she said, and by the end of 1984 he was living with her part-time in a small town on the fringe of the metro area.

"He took care of the bills," she explained. Connie had a daughter and had adopted a son in 1988.

"We just changed the name to Marcello," she said, telling the jury that she and James and her children acted just like a normal family when they were together. James cared for them all. She said she thought her man worked for a trucking company, though she admitted she had never seen him drive a truck.

James would give her around $5,000 a month, which was brought for a time by his brother-in-law. But if anyone ever asked, Connie said, she was supposed to say the money was coming from her mother. In later years, Mickey Marcello would arrive with the money, she said, and after that, it was James's friend Nick Vangel. Often her cash came in the form of a wad of big bills stuffed into a coffee cup.

She would use it to buy food and go shopping for clothes, making the kind of purchases a single mother needs to make. Extra expenses were no problem, either, Connie said, like the month she ran up $15,000 in losses at a local casino boat. James made that go away without any trouble.

"Mickey gave me the extra money."

There was always an understanding that the arrangement was secret. Even if she were ever called in front of a grand jury, Connie should just take the Fifth Amendment, James had told her. If pressed, she was expected to just go to jail for a while, maybe until a trial was over, and then everything would eventually be OK.

In March 2005 she got a chance to prove her loyalty when she was called before a grand jury that was working what would become the Family Secrets case. She was asked about her relationship with James, but instead of sticking to the plan, she buckled and told the truth. When asked about getting money, she said she was being given cash every month without fail.

James was waiting to hear how her appearance had gone, so Connie drove as fast as she could to a pie restaurant to tell him about it. Her concerned boyfriend wanted to know what was asked of her. "I just said it was things about the '80s," Connie remembered telling him, making it sound as innocent as possible.

And James bought it. Satisfied that his secret was safe, he continued to give Connie her monthly allowance. In fact, she kept getting her $5,000 all the way up until June 2007, the same month the Family Secrets trial started. Only when prosecutors revealed to the defense the identities of their final witnesses did it become clear that Connie was playing her man for a fool.

15

JOEY

With prosecutors preparing to rest their case, jurors watched on the screens in front of them as James and Mickey Marcello met in the visiting room of the prison in Milan, Michigan, making gestures and speaking in code about the possibility that Nick Calabrese was cooperating.

They watched the hand signals, such as the touching of the nose to signify John DiFronzo and the touching of a knee to mean Angelo LaPietra. They listened to nine conversations as the men spoke back and forth, sometimes covering their mouths in an attempt to keep anyone from hearing them or reading their lips. And they heard the brothers agree that what the government was most interested in was the "Zhivago" deal—the murders of Anthony and Michael Spilotro.

The government didn't have a case, James told his brother. The $4,000 a month he was paying Nick was a fantastic investment. The FBI and prosecutors were on a fishing expedition, and he'd be walking out of prison soon to straighten things out on the street.

Marcello obviously never imagined he'd wind up sitting across from a jury listening to himself say those things, but he was keeping a good poker face as he watched the jury view the tapes. If he wasn't leaning over to say something to one of his attorneys, his expression stayed the same. He didn't appear rattled or disturbed at all, looking more like a man watching a boring play and wondering when it would ever end.

And the jury never would hear him speak in court or watch him bend under pressure from a prosecutor's questioning. Given the chance to testify on his own behalf, Marcello would pass, leaving the talking to his two attorneys and choosing to minimize any more damage he might do to himself by opening his mouth.

He would not be in the majority.

Despite Rick Halprin's hope that Joey Lombardo would set himself apart by being the only defendant brave enough to testify, it had become apparent that nothing was going to keep Frank Calabrese Sr. from getting up and telling his side of the story. He had been making faces and talking to Joseph Lopez almost constantly since the trial began, and he was eager to be able to talk to the jury and explain it all away. His brother was weak and a liar, and he wasn't backing down.

So with both Lombardo and Frank Sr. heading for the witness stand, it was clear that a trial that already had earned a place in Chicago history was going to peak again. It's a rarity to hear from even one made member of an organized crime family in any criminal trial, but the Family Secrets case would feature the testimony of three.

And as a bonus, Anthony Doyle too would roll the dice and give the jury his version of events. After being on the fence about having Doyle address the jurors, Ralph Meczyk had decided they needed to hear him say he had done nothing wrong.

Lombardo had to testify, Halprin told the court. There was no one else to properly explain to the jury how Lombardo was wrongfully thought to be wrapped up in a fifty-year conspiracy. And there was no one else to fully articulate that if the jury did believe he had been involved, he had withdrawn from activity upon his release from prison in 1992.

"I'm not putting on anyone to show he was a good boy," Halprin said.

He would have a handful of witnesses testify that Lombardo was at certain places at certain times, including working at Seifert's business. And he would call others to try to demonstrate that after 1992, Lombardo was doing nothing that looked like taking part in a conspiracy to prosper through extortion and murder.

But before any of that was the unfinished business of Halprin's delayed opening statement. He had taken the option at the start of trial of waiting until the defense case to address the jury. Now he walked right up to the jury box, standing just feet away from the panel as he started to explain Lombardo's view of the case.

"I'd like you to look over there at that screen," he told the jury, motioning toward the large screen above the floor of the courtroom on the dais. It was blank, but Halprin quickly explained himself.

"Keep an open mind."

Lombardo was entitled to completely separate consideration from all the codefendants, he said. The men were all being tried simultaneously, but it would be impossible to be fair without considering each independently.

Lombardo was going to take the stand and tell them his own story, Halprin promised.

"Joey Lombardo did not kill Danny Seifert," Halprin said, his deep trademark voice beginning to swell. "Joey Lombardo is not, was not, and never has been a capo or a made member of the Chicago Outfit."

Lombardo had only one real connection to the illicit Chicago economy, he told the jury with a smile.

"He did, in fact, run the oldest and most reliable craps game on Grand Avenue."

The jury should look at the seventy-eight-year-old Lombardo and imagine his life in stages. One of them was the early part of his life, when he was making his way in the West Side neighborhood. He was a scrapper and didn't wind up in and out of prison like other young men in the area. He was a "hustler, not a gangster."

At his table Lombardo adjusted his glasses and looked toward the jury and then out into the gallery. It was as if he was looking to see if he could catch anyone reacting to his lawyer's statements.

Lombardo knew men such as Joey Aiuppa and the Spilotro brothers, but he was a working man, Halprin continued. He had a trucking business and got into construction until rising interest rates drove him out. He was also an associate of Irwin Weiner, the bail bondsman, Halprin said, a man who seemed to know everyone. Weiner took an immediate liking to the young Lombardo and hired him to do odd jobs.

And then when Weiner helped to open International Fiberglass, he brought Joey on there, Halprin said. Lombardo worked at the business between 1972 and 1976.

As for the Seifert murder, there was evidence that Lombardo was twenty miles away when his former work associate was killed. And Lombardo actually did work there, too, Halprin said, beginning to wave his hands as he made his points. The jury would hear from some who remembered working with him and that when there was a fire there in 1973, it was Lombardo who organized plans to keep things going while repairs were made.

It was at the end of that time frame that Lombardo would come to meet Allen Dorfman, Halprin told the jury, and start an association that would be one of the defining relationships of his life.

Dorfman was an owner of Amalgamated Insurance Services and had an office above that of Roy Williams, who would become president of the Teamsters Union. Lombardo spent a lot of time in his friend's office, Halprin said, unfortunately right around the time the FBI was investigating loans out of the Central States Pension Fund that were being used to build casinos. Dorfman's offices were wired, and some 22,000 hours of recordings later, Lombardo found himself indicted for trying to bribe a U.S. senator. If Howard Cannon would help delay and defeat a bill intended to deregulate the trucking industry, he would be given the inside track to purchase Teamsters-owned land near his Las Vegas home that the senator did not want developed.

Lombardo had been captured in some of the recordings giving Dorfman advice on complex financial transactions and discussing articles in the *Wall Street Journal*. Williams and Dorfman had been pulling the strings on the Cannon effort, Halprin said, with Lombardo taking a much lesser role. It was Lombardo's friendships that were getting him noticed by law enforcement.

Lombardo would get ten years in prison, but his troubles weren't over yet. He would be in prison in 1986 when he got word that he had been indicted in "the biggest mob union case in the entire world," Halprin said. It was the Stardust skimming case involving mob leaders from Chicago and figures from Milwaukee and Kansas City.

Joey was tried again and convicted again.

"Joey Lombardo never received a dime of skimmed money," Halprin said. "Joey Lombardo never had an interest in any casino."

His major deal with Dorfman involved a Florida golf course that was put in the name of Lombardo family members.

But it was too late for those kinds of arguments, Halprin told the jury. Lombardo received more prison time and realized that he was forever going to be guilty by his associations.

The lawyer was asking the jury to swallow a pretty tall tale, but at least he was doing it with conviction.

"We're not bitching about it," he said.

"He knew for the rest of his life, in the public perception [it would be]: reputed mobster, reputed gang boss," Halprin told the jury. Lombardo decided to be much more careful about those he associated with, bending over backward to eliminate even the appearance of being a part of the wrong organization. He was placed on probation and had ten years of supervised release.

"He knows if he has any more problems, he is going back to prison," Halprin said, adding a slight dramatic pause.

"He decides to withdraw from his life."

He worked in an upholstery factory and in a job sharpening saw blades. He published his notice in the *Chicago Tribune* announcing he had never been made. And since that time in 1992, he had remained clean. No witness would come in and testify that Lombardo had done anything for the mob or anything illegal, period, in the prior fifteen years.

No one would come in and identify the new Lombardo as anything other than "older, smarter, wiser, and a decent citizen."

Halprin started by calling Eli Jacobs, a sixty-nine-year-old who used to work as a director of parts for NuArc, a provider of graphic arts, printing, and photo darkroom equipment. One of the vendors the company had dealt with decades earlier was International Fiberglass, with which NuArc had contracted to produce fiberglass sinks for use in smaller darkrooms.

Daniel Seifert would stop by NuArc to make courtesy calls from time to time, as would a man Jacobs would come to know as Joseph Cuneo.

But there was a time Jacobs would learn Cuneo wasn't the only name that man used. When newspapers and television news began reporting that Seifert had been killed, he saw Cuneo mentioned as a suspect. It was Joey Lombardo.

That was, of course, no surprise to Halprin, who had called Jacobs to ask about times he had shown up at International Fiberglass to drop off blueprints or pay a visit to the vendor. Had he seen the man he knew as Cuneo there? He had, Jacobs said.

"Him and Mr. Seifert were using this air gun," Jacobs said.

And Jacobs remembered the fire at International Fiberglass. It was in 1973, and it jolted Jacobs because the company was NuArc's only supplier of the sinks they needed. It was Joey who took up the task of setting up a temporary facility and reassuring him, Jacobs told the jury. Lombardo had promised production would restart in two or three weeks after the original location burned.

On cross-examination, Markus Funk made it clear that Jacobs knew Seifert to be the foreman at International Fiberglass. Cuneo, or Lombardo, seemed to handle administrative issues and certainly wasn't at the business around the clock.

Two former International Fiberglass employees also took the stand for Lombardo.

Bonnie Venturini was a girlfriend of Lombardo's when she worked at the company. Venturini, who had testified for Lombardo in the casino skimming case, remembered him working to chop and sand fiberglass for the sinks, wax molds, and box-up products.

"Plus, he looked for new customers after Danny left," she said.

And Venturini tried to turn the tables on Ronald Seifert, Daniel's brother, who had testified earlier in the trial that Lombardo did no work there. She said she never remembered seeing Ronald there, and she laughed at part of his testimony. Ronald had said a photo of Lombardo wearing short sleeves in the business proved he never worked handling air-blown fiberglass. But Venturini said it was just the opposite. The process was known to coat clothing with particles that would build up and eventually cause sleeves to lock up and become unbendable.

Ralph DiCapua remembered seeing Lombardo working at International Fiberglass while he was an employee there. He had also testified for Lombardo in the skimming trial, and during his cross-examination, Funk concentrated on one thing in particular he had said there.

He had mentioned Lombardo's neighborhood ties and called him "the godfather of the community."

He meant godfather as "a person that would help you," DiCapua tried to explain. "It's a religious statement."

But Funk wasn't going to let it go.

"Sir, are you the godfather of your community?" he asked, as people in the courtroom gallery started to laugh.

"No," DiCapua said.

Halprin called former FBI agent Peter Wacks next, trying to clean up Emma Seifert's claim that she had told Wacks several weeks after her husband was killed that she thought Lombardo was present at the murder. She had testified that she had told the agent her belief while sitting in her office.

"She did not," Wacks said when the question was put to him.

Under questioning by Mars, Wacks said that Emma was under a tremendous amount of stress after the murder; she was worried about herself and her children. And whether Emma suspected Lombardo or not, the FBI certainly did.

"Mr. Lombardo's name was at the forefront in all of our discussions."

And finally, Halprin called Chicago boxer Johnny Lira to the stand, a man who walked into court nodding at people he knew and shaking hands with reporters such as John "Bulldog" Drummond, who was covering the trial for the Chicago CBS affiliate. Drummond was a legend who had covered organized crime for decades, and he had been on the scene at many of the murder locations in the case when the killings were breaking news. He knew Chicago athletics almost as well as he knew his Outfit history. He certainly remembered the fighter's glory days as a city Golden Gloves champ and a light-weight title contender.

Lira, fifty-six, walked to the stand a little slowly and apologized for having to read lips to get the questions that would be asked of him. He told Halprin he was nine years old when he met Lombardo at a Union League Boys and Girls Club in the Grand Avenue neighborhood. In his teenage years he would see Lombardo playing handball at the YMCA or at the "firemen's and policemen's gym."

Lira's career took him away from Chicago, and Lombardo landed in prison, so the men didn't see each other until sometime after "the Clown" was sprung in 1992. It was a chance meeting, he said. Lira was walking down Racine Avenue on the West Side when he noticed Lombardo in the yard of a warehouse working with a grinder.

The former boxer started visiting regularly as they struck up their friendship again. Lombardo would be getting machines ready for the next day of work at the business.

"We'd play a lot of chess."

Funk took a turn questioning Lira and asked for more detail about Lombardo's job.

"He was a grease monkey," Lira said, "which is the guy that worked on the equipment."

He had seen Lombardo at the factory even as the FBI was looking for him, Lira said.

Did he know Lombardo was a fugitive at that time? Funk asked.

"He didn't act like a fugitive," Lira said. "He came there every day."

And the fighter stepped from the stand, shaking more hands on his way out.

Joey Lombardo was looking dapper in a silver tie as he moved toward the witness stand with the help of his cane. Slowly he took his seat but couldn't resist flirting with the blond court reporter first. He got a smile before turning his attention to his lawyer.

"OK," Halprin started. "Do the people who know you, as opposed to those who write about you, know you as Joey Lombardo?"

"It's the same as Joseph, Joey," Lombardo answered, in a raspy, gravelly voice. He took off his glasses and leaned toward the microphone.

"I'm going to call you Joey; is that OK?" Halprin asked.

"It's OK with me, sir."

Fine. Halprin cut right to the chase. Had Lombardo killed Daniel Seifert in 1974?

"Positively no."

Had he ever been a capo or even a made member of the mob?

"Positively no," Lombardo said again in a singsongy tone. His voice went up through the word "positively" and back down again with "no."

Halprin and Lombardo had rehearsed the testimony from time to time over the prior year. It was supposed to track like Halprin's opening statement, with Lombardo himself explaining his past connections. To help him prepare, Lombardo had been given a copy of a transcript of a deposition he had given in 1989, before he was released from prison. He had been called to testify under oath in New York in a civil case related to mob influence over the Teamsters. He had denied killing Seifert then, too, and had denied killing Dorfman, who was gunned down in 1983 before Lombardo had begun serving a prison sentence.

Halprin asked Lombardo if he had taken a look at the document to help him prepare for his questioning in the Family Secrets case.

"I read it five times," he said.

Halprin decided to go back to the beginning, having Lombardo tell the jury that he was born in Chicago to Michael and Carmella Lombardo on New Year's Day, 1929. Along with five brothers and five sisters, he lived in the 500 block of North Elizabeth Street, in the heart of the neighborhood around Grand and Ogden on the West Side. He had lived in the neighborhood his whole life, later with his wife, Marion, on West Ohio.

"I would say about seventy-eight years," he said of his lifetime in "the Patch." His wife owned the Ohio house before they were married, Lombardo explained. They'd had two children there, Joseph Jr. and Joanne.

"Her grandmother built the house in 1928, and when she died, she left each one of her daughters and sons an apartment," he said. "My wife bought her aunt out, and then she sold it to her father."

So far so good for Halprin, who was doing his best to keep Lombardo on track. But the lawyer suspected it probably wouldn't last.

Halprin asked Lombardo about his athletic prowess, and he started to wander.

"I wrestled for high school. I played basketball for high school," he answered. "I took fencing for a year at high school; I took swimming in high school. I could do other sports, too. I could ice skate, roller skate, Rollerblade, ride a bicycle, and bowl."

He knew the Spilotro family's restaurant in the neighborhood and said he used to shine shoes.

"On Saturdays and Sundays I would go to Racine Avenue police station," Lombardo said. "I used to shine policemen's shoes."

The cops had paid him a nickel, he recalled.

"Very cheap people."

That brought a laugh, not exactly what Halprin was going for. "Let's not press our luck," he told his client.

"You told me to tell the truth," Lombardo said, raising his voice in mock protest as laughter in the gallery grew.

At Frank Sr.'s table, Lopez let out a loud guffaw.

It was all a little too much for Judge Zagel, who stopped everything to issue a stern warning.

"One thing about this case, there's absolutely nothing humorous about it," he began. "And I expect that I will not hear audible laughter again, and I particularly expect not to hear it from counsel."

With the first land mine having been firmly stepped on, Halprin pushed Lombardo back to his hardscrabble early jobs. He had worked at Union Station and had worked a dumbwaiter at the Blackstone Hotel, remembering he would send food up to parties in the Balinese Room.

Next, Halprin wanted to go over the dice game.

"Well, I started to tell you, I was a shoe shine boy," Lombardo began again, only to have Halprin dive in.

"I said, Joey, tell us about the dice game."

"Well, I'm going to lead you to the dice game, sir," Joey said, remembering a dice game at Ohio and Elizabeth when he was young.

"I used to go to the dice game and shine guys' shoes," he said. "When a guy would win, he would give me a dollar for a shine. When a guy was losing, he would give a quarter for his shine."

In high school Lombardo said he ran a dice game at lunch and started one in the neighborhood in 1976. Prison was no obstacle; he recalled running a dice game behind bars when he was sentenced for the attempted bribery of Senator Cannon.

The neighborhood game was known as a "floating" game, Lombardo explained, because the location would change. He had a partner, Lombardo said, and he took 25 percent of what was collected.

"At the end of the year, I filed taxes under 'miscellaneous,'" he said.

Joey got 25 percent because a partner had made the connection to get permission to have the game. But the permission didn't come from an Outfit capo, he said.

"There's fifty bosses in Chicago, and the fifty bosses are the fifty aldermen," Joey explained. "In each ward there's an alderman. You cannot get anything done unless you go through the alderman."

It was just like zoning, and it ran Friday, Saturday, and sometimes Sunday.

"If you want to get a card game going, you have to see the alderman. He gets you the OK."

But his string of legitimate jobs had continued through young adulthood, Lombardo said. In around 1949 he started in the trucking business, he told Halprin, buying two trucks that were hauling for a South Side company before he was even twenty-one.

"I think I got $150 or $175 a truck, for a truck and for the driver," he explained, sometimes looking up toward the ceiling as he thought about a detail. "At that time, the union driver was getting $2 an hour, and gas was eleven gallons—let's see, thirteen gallons for a dollar at that time was gas."

For most of ten years, Lombardo said he worked in trucks, moving next into construction. He and a partner built places on the West Side, including a pair of six-flats in the 5900 block of West Huron, he said. They built more than thirty homes on Laramie, and Halprin tried to show Lombardo a photo of the development.

Those were them, Lombardo agreed, staring at the photo. But he wanted to explain how he had bought the property from the county assessor, as Halprin tried to keep him focused.

Mars objected, asking the judge to instruct the witness to just be responsive to the question that was pending.

"I have no objection to the objection," Halprin said. So he showed Lombardo a series of the photos, just trying to get him to acknowledge that the buildings in the pictures were, in fact, the ones he had built.

But Lombardo wasn't through with his story.

"Could I ask you a question?" he said as Halprin turned away from the witness stand. "Or could I ask the judge a question? Whoever can answer it. There's more to the story to this here project of thirty-one things."

The judge stopped things again. Everybody would like to tell long tales from the witness stand, but that wasn't for the best, Zagel said. It would be best to follow Halprin's judgment on what needed to be told to the jury.

"So, let him be your lawyer," Zagel said, peering over the edge of the dais at Lombardo below.

"Sounds like a good idea," Halprin piped up again.

Now, back to the employment record. Halprin wanted to know about another business, Salvage Circus, where Lombardo had worked in the 1960s. Irwin Weiner had gotten him that job.

Weiner was a man Lombardo had met as a teenager, he said. Because Weiner was a bail bondsman, a lot of the kids in the neighborhood came to know him. It's where Lombardo said he went to get friends out of jail.

Salvage Circus was a storefront that kids from the neighborhood had helped clean, Lombardo said. Shelves were built and stocked with leftover materials from dilapidated buildings in the city. "Milwaukee Phil" Alderisio was a partner, Lombardo recalled.

With a mobster's name on the table, Halprin asked whether Salvage Circus was legit, and Lombardo said it was. He had never given "a red penny" to Alderisio, though he said he was friendly with him.

"Did you ever commit any crimes with Phil Alderisio?" Halprin asked.

"Positively no," Lombardo said, slipping back to his singsongy answer.

Regardless, Salvage Circus eventually closed, Lombardo said, and his next job was at International Fiberglass.

He went for a ride with Weiner in around 1969 to the suburb of Elk Grove Village, where International Fiberglass was getting off the ground. Weiner had incorporated the business, Lombardo recalled, with a group of others. Weiner had a quarter, Seifert had a quarter, a man named Mitchell Kaplan had a quarter, and Alderisio's son, Dominic, was given a quarter.

Seifert, who was the main person on the floor, had more work than he could get out the door, Lombardo remembered. The business was having a hard time getting workers out to the area. One major order was for aerators for the Sanitary District, Lombardo remembered, so he volunteered to help.

"I says, I got a lot of kids in the neighborhood that ain't working, I'll scoop 'em up and bring them out there and try to see if we can get fourteen, sixteen aerators out for the Sanitary District," he said, remembering that he brought two carloads of workers out for the job.

"Is this the short story, that you began to work at International Fiberglass for a period of years?" a slightly exasperated Halprin said.

Yes, Lombardo said, he worked there.

He began to learn from Daniel Seifert, Lombardo said, taking his glasses on and off as he testified and sometimes leaning on his cane as he spoke, and he knew that the business was in the red. Lombardo told the jury he began to pay the company's bills out of cash in his pocket.

When the company made money, Seifert would cut him a check, Lombardo said.

During this time, Weiner had other businesses, too, Lombardo testified. One of those was what Halprin called a "team of ambulance chasers," meaning lawyers and tow trucks, but International Fiberglass was completely legitimate.

It was so legitimate, in fact, that Lombardo didn't use his own name dealing with purchasing agents such as Eli Jacobs from NuArc. He used "Joe Cuneo."

A man with a similar name, Joseph Lombardi, was always in the papers for criminal reasons, he said, as was his own name. The judge wouldn't allow Halprin to bring up the time when the two men had been mixed up, allowing Lombardo to walk from a case involving the beating of a debtor.

So Halprin moved on to who was doing what at International Fiberglass and then the fire in 1973. It was the same year Lombardo and Weiner were indicted in the pension fraud case involving Dorfman and the loan for the pails. Anthony Spilotro was indicted, too, along with trustees of the Central States Pension Fund. Lombardo said he met Dorfman only through Weiner and claimed they weren't even that close at the time of the indictment. Lombardo said he had no control over money coming out of the fund or any way to direct it.

He learned of money allegedly going to Spilotro only from reading the indictment, he told the jury. Also included was the allegation that more than $5,000 had been diverted to Lombardo. He had received money from International Fiberglass but not for a bogus reason, he said.

"That check was for my cash receipts that I paid out to the vendors," he said.

Another check had been labeled "back pay" Halprin noted, and both were signed by Seifert.

Lombardo said he gradually got to know Dorfman better, visiting him in the offices of his insurance company. On the next floor were offices of the Central States Pension Fund of the Teamsters. He said he would head to see Dorfman many afternoons if it was warm, because the men would leave to play golf.

"Did you understand the Central States Pension Fund to have amounts of money in the hundreds of millions of dollars?" Halprin asked.

"Well, I didn't know that," Lombardo answered. "I know they had a lot of money, but I don't know how much."

It was during this time he also continued to run errands for Weiner, Lombardo said. Among those errands was picking up things at a business called C.B. Center of America, for a towing business called AT&S, Lombardo said. Halprin had Lombardo look at some of the receipts for CB radios and scanners that government witnesses had reviewed weeks earlier. Lombardo said he recognized them and said he had signed the name "J. Savard."

He had picked them up only at Weiner's instruction, Lombardo told the jury.

"I had no use for them."

Savard was the maiden name of the wife of Frank Schweihs, Lombardo said. But that didn't mean he had ever done anything illegal with Schweihs, he said, telling Halprin that he had never given Schweihs a penny as a result of a crime, and vice versa.

"If you pick up a bill and he's a cook, and you pay for meat and potatoes, that's not giving him money," Lombardo said.

Maybe Lombardo was missing the point.

"Have you ever given him any money as a result of criminal activity," Halprin repeated. "Got that so far?"

"Yes," Lombardo said. "No such thing."

So why use the name Savard?

"Mr. Weiner told me to sign it Savard," Lombardo explained. "He was thinking of them hockey players, Canadian hockey players, the Savard brothers," he continued, apparently talking about Blackhawks great Denis Savard and his brothers.

Did it matter what name you signed?

"I didn't care," Lombardo said. "It's bilingual material."

Among Weiner's other features at his business, American Bonding, was a notary public service, which Halprin led Lombardo to next.

Lombardo was often at the offices in the 1000 block of South State Street.

He used to make deliveries to NuArc in the city, he said, and after he was done moving a truck around, he would stop at American Bonding to see if Weiner needed anything.

There was a desk near the front door, Lombardo said as Halprin showed the jury a rough sketch of the building. Anyone who came in could sit there for a minute, he said. It was a desk that belonged to Millie, the office's notary.

The headquarters of the Chicago Police Department were across the street at the time, Lombardo agreed, and he said he often saw officers and others in the offices of American Bonding to have Millie notarize license applications and other vehicle documents.

And with that, Halprin showed Lombardo the title application for the Ford LTD that had fled the Seifert shooting, the one for "Acme Security Service" with Lombardo's fingerprint on it. How did his fingerprint get on that document? Halprin asked.

"Was this document in Irv Weiner's office?" Lombardo asked in return.

"Might have been," Halprin said.

From there the lawyer moved Lombardo back to Dorfman and the FBI intercepts on his phones in the late 1970s. Lombardo said he always expected the place was "bugged" but said no one ever tried to figure out if that was true.

Lombardo said he of course recalled being indicted with Dorfman, Roy Williams, and other Teamsters officials in the case involving Senator Cannon, but he tried to minimize his role. He told the jury he'd never met the senator and had never spoken to him. Cannon and some of his Las Vegas neighbors were interested in buying ten acres of land across the street from their homes in order to keep it from being commercially developed. Lombardo recalled Cannon calling Dorfman about the property, which was owned by the Teamsters. Cannon at the time was chairman of the Senate Commerce Committee and was in a position to make things difficult for the trucking deregulation bill the Teamsters opposed. The property Cannon was interested in was being controlled for the union by a management company, so the senator and his neighbors were told they needed to bid on the land. Attempts were made by some of the indicted men to have competing bids withdrawn, and Lombardo had been recorded discussing ways to make sure Cannon got the land.

In one conversation that Halprin highlighted, Lombardo had said, "It ain't no problem" when he learned that the high bid for the site was submitted by casino developer Allen Glick. Halprin asked if that conversation had been played at Lombardo's trial.

"They must have played it; I was convicted," Lombardo answered, adding he had no control over Teamsters loans and no personal interest in the trucking bill.

"And so, essentially, you got nothing—what did you get out of this whole plan?" Halprin asked.

"Fifteen years and five years probation," Lombardo said.

But there were at least a couple of times Lombardo did well because of his relationship with Dorfman, he admitted, or at least he acknowledged his family did. In one deal in particular, Dorfman's links to a golf community called the California Club in Florida allowed Lombardo to leverage a deal to borrow $1 million from club members and purchase it. Lombardo held the property in a trust in the names of his wife, son, and daughter.

Lombardo's second day on the witness stand started with him waiting while his other attorney, Susan Shatz, read a stipulation to the jury.

The sides had agreed on some of the details surrounding the purchase of the Ford LTD used in the Seifert homicide; it was bought at a dealership in the suburb of South Holland on November 30, 1973.

A man who introduced himself as David Kemp was the purchaser, telling a salesperson the car was for a security business his son was starting. He wanted a large engine, would be paying cash, and preferred to make arrangements to get license plates himself.

Kemp was told he could sign tax forms and the title application and then return the next day to pick up the documents.

The month after Seifert was killed, the FBI was doing its best to trace the purchase of the car, and agents interviewed the salesman. He was shown photos of a number of men the bureau suspected in the Seifert shooting, but he was unable to identify any of them as David Kemp.

Lombardo sat leaning on the witness stand and looking at Halprin as the lawyer restarted his questioning. They had already covered Lombardo's use of various names, but how about "David Kemp?"

"No," Lombardo said.

Halprin had Lombardo explain in more detail his role at International Fiberglass, including the work he did and how he had cleaned up the bills. Lombardo said he had figured out what was owed and how to do the work, and he continued the business after Seifert decided to leave it and go his own way. What was their relationship like when Seifert quit in 1972?

"Very, very friendly," Lombardo answered.

He had never threatened his former partner, he said, and was owed nothing by Seifert after he left. He had visited Seifert's new place of business in Bensenville, he said, but he denied Emma Seifert's allegation that he had driven by the Seifert home.

As for the Ford LTD, Lombardo again denied buying it or signing any papers for it.

So Halprin went back to the scenario where Lombardo could have touched paperwork for the car at American Bonding. One of the documents had been notarized by Millie, Irwin Weiner's secretary. Lombardo said again that he would sometimes sit at her desk when he was hanging around.

"If she wasn't sittin' there, I'd be sittin' there reading a newspaper," Lombardo said. Maybe he had inadvertently touched something.

Prosecutors would argue it was an almost unbelievable coincidence that Lombardo had accidentally touched a document used to buy the car that just happened to be used in the shooting of Lombardo's former friend and business partner, but it was the best Halprin could do under the circumstances. Next he and Lombardo tried to cover for the time of the murder itself, though Halprin had been limited by the judge in how deeply he could get into Lombardo's supposed alibi.

On September 27, 1974, Lombardo said he woke up at 6:00 A.M., more than two hours before Seifert had been killed, and drove to buy a new garage door opener at a store near California Avenue. He got there at around 7:00, he told Halprin, but the place was closed.

"Well, I figure I'd kill some time and then wait till they open," Lombardo explained, leaving some in the gallery giving each other looks over his choice of words. He wound up at a pancake house, he said.

"I went there to have breakfast to kill time until the place opened," he said again.

He ate in thirty to forty-five minutes, he said, and then walked back to a four-door Dodge he had driven to the area. But when he walked up to his car, Lombardo told the jury, he saw that its glove compartment was open. He looked inside and noticed his wallet was missing.

"How did you pay for breakfast if your wallet was in the car?" Halprin asked.

"I keep my money in my pocket."

So Lombardo said he returned to the restaurant, where he noticed two police officers in the middle of breakfast. He said he told them what had happened, and one officer told him to follow him back to a police station to make out a report. He was at the station for at least an hour, he said, and then went to a secretary of state's office for a new driver's license. It was 2:00 P.M. by the time he was finished, he said.

"I heard the news about Danny Seifert when I left there," Lombardo said.

Lombardo was careful with the details of what investigators believed was a clever, carefully constructed attempt to officially be someplace else when Seifert was killed. At minimum, a report had been generated at the Shakespeare police district, though the jury wouldn't see it. The jury also wouldn't be told that the commander of the district at the time was none other than William Hanhardt, the corrupt cop who would later be linked to the mob-sanctioned ring of jewelry thieves that involved Paul "the Indian" Schiro.

From there Halprin moved to Lombardo's second conviction in the 1980s, in the Stardust skimming case.

He was indicted along with mob higher-ups such as Jackie Cerone, who Lombardo said he knew from the old neighborhood through relatives and because he had caddied for him on the golf course. Aiuppa was part of the case, too; he was an Outfit leader Lombardo said he knew because Aiuppa would stop by Cerone's summer home on a lake to golf and ride a speedboat. Aiuppa was the boss of Cicero, according to Lombardo, but he was just a pal, not someone who directed Lombardo to do his bidding.

Well, what about the meeting FBI agent Art Pfizenmayer said he saw in Chicago, the one where Aiuppa seemed to be barking orders at Dorfman in a restaurant?

Lombardo said he had been at Dorfman's office when he told Dorfman he was going to see his pal, Aiuppa. Dorfman said he hadn't seen Aiuppa in a long time and asked Lombardo to set up a lunch that day. Lombardo said he did just that, and the men met.

"It was just cordial," Lombardo told the jury, some of whom seemed to be fading in and out of paying close attention during the testimony. "How are you, how you feel, and this and that. That's all it was. How's your family, how's your family."

As for the casino skimming itself, Lombardo said he learned during the trial that Lefty Rosenthal was running it at the casinos Allen Glick owned. Large amounts of money were being funneled out to mob families, including those in Chicago.

So, did Lombardo make any money?

"Well, I have to tell the truth," Lombardo said with a straight face. "I'm under oath. Not a red penny."

With the first part of his questioning beginning to wind down, Rick Halprin had Lombardo make a series of denials.

He denied extorting street tax from William "Red" Wemette and his porn shop, he denied passing envelopes to Michael Spilotro, he denied saying within earshot of Alva Johnson Rodgers after Daniel Seifert was killed that Seifert wouldn't be testifying against anyone now. He denied telling Ann Spilotro that if he hadn't been in prison, her husband and his brother wouldn't have been killed.

He was just trying to make points with Dorfman when he told Morris Shenker he would never reach seventy-three, dismissing it as tough talk for a friend and nothing he really meant. He knew Louie Eboli as a businessman, and when they had been recorded talking about massage parlors, Lombardo said he didn't have anything to do with them. When he had used the word "we" in the conversation, he said he didn't mean himself and Eboli. It might have been that someone from his craps game was interested in buying a place or something.

He denied knowing any of the men he was on trial with. He didn't know Frank Sr., James Marcello, or Anthony Doyle, he said, and told the jury he met Paul Schiro only once, at the grand opening of Hoagie's, the pub the Spilotros owned on North Avenue.

And there was the matter of the photo, the one known as the "Last Supper," with the mob's hierarchy seated around a table. There was Lombardo, standing in his suit with Jackie Cerone. How was he going to explain that away?

"I couldn't begin to count the number of times that's been shown in this trial," Halprin started.

He asked Lombardo to identify the men at the table, and Joey did, pointing them out one by one.

"The fat guy there? That's Turk," he said when he got to Torello. He easily recognized Tony Accardo and Aiuppa.

Seated next to Aiuppa was a frail-looking elderly man in a light blue shirt and white suspenders. It was Dominick DiBella, who would die the year the photo was taken, 1976. Lombardo identified the man as "Dominick."

"He was dying," Lombardo said. "He had three months to live, three to six months to live."

"When he met me, he said they're giving him a farewell party because the man's dying of cancer."

OK, Halprin said. But what was Lombardo doing at an Elmwood Park restaurant with all of these men?

"I got dressed to go to a wake," Lombardo said. "So I went to the wake; after I was there for a while, I met a friend of mine there named Albert Milleri, and I said I was hungry. And he lives up west around there, around Elmwood Park somewhere."

"And I says, 'I can go for a nice beef sandwich,'" he continued. "He says he's got just the place."

So Lombardo contended he had essentially randomly happened upon the meeting of the Chicago mob's leadership. He had been invited over to the table by men he knew.

Men such as Accardo and Aiuppa were his friends, and aside from the conduct in his convictions, he had never done anything illegal with any of them, Lombardo said.

"What does the term *Chicago Outfit* mean to you?" Halprin asked.

"A group of people that get together and conspire," Lombardo said. "They do illegal things and legitimate things. They go partners."

And of all the men in the picture, Halprin asked a few moments later, was Lombardo the last man alive?

"That is correct."

16

CROSS-EXAMINATION

L ombardo sat with a hand on his cane, his head tilted back slightly, watching through his glasses and down his nose as Mitch Mars prepared to question him.

In many ways, it could be argued that much of the prosecutor's career had been aimed at this moment. He had spent his professional life making the cases that had led to this one, and now he had the elusive Lombardo not only on trial but also pinned down on the witness stand in front of him. The accused mob boss was staring at him, and Mars was staring right back.

The prosecutor began by asking Lombardo about his convictions, the attempted bribery of the senator and the casino skim. He listed all of the men found guilty in the cases.

"So, you have two federal convictions for crimes that you did not commit, is that what you're saying?"

"I was convicted of them, but I did not commit no crime," Lombardo answered.

Mars tracked back through Lombardo's jobs, from the shoe shining to the trucking and construction to the salvage business. Even at International Fiberglass, Lombardo said, he was making about $200 a week. And after that closed in 1976, Lombardo said his main job was the dice game.

"And at the time, I think you said, you had no credit, right?"

"I didn't hear you."

"You didn't have any credit at the time?"

"Any what?"

"Credit."

Yes, Lombardo finally agreed, he had no credit.

Yet he found himself in the office of Allen Dorfman, a man running a multimillion dollar company, Mars pointed out. Dorfman dropped investment opportunities in Lombardo's lap, he said, including a real estate development in Las Vegas known as "Liberty 200," which had been extremely profitable. Anthony Spilotro was in on it, too, though neither man had put up a dime.

Then there was the California Club, the Florida golf course and hotel. Lessees of the club worked a deal through Lombardo that saw them loan him $1 million. Lombardo only had to bring $100,000 to the table to close it.

"You didn't have a job then?" Mars asked.

"No, I had a dice game," Lombardo answered.

"Worth $1.1 million?"

"No."

It was a sweetheart deal, Mars pointed out, especially for a man with no credit. And in the arrangement with leaseholders, Lombardo actually got more than half of his $100,000 back instantly, followed by $40,000 a year on the investment.

Well to be particular, Lombardo said, a trust set up for his wife and children earned the $40,000 a year. Eventually the property sold, and the trust took in an additional $1.4 million.

"So, that the government couldn't touch your money, isn't that true, Mr. Lombardo?" Mars asked.

"That is not true, sir."

The point was, Mars said, it was someone giving a "unique" deal to a friend.

"I'll take them all day," Lombardo said of the arrangement.

"I'm sure you would."

"Absolutely," Lombardo said with a wide smile.

Access to such deals came from Lombardo's position in organized crime, wasn't that true? Mars asked. It was Lombardo's duty to watch over Dorfman for the Outfit and watch over the Teamsters Union, right?

"That is positively no, sir," Lombardo said, lapsing into the up-and-down tone in this scratchy voice.

Lombardo repeatedly denied being part of organized crime. He had never been a member or a boss, he told Mars. He had never been the capo of the Grand Avenue street crew.

"I never took an oath," he said. "Never pierced my fingers, never put a Catholic card in my hand. I never took an oath to any secret organization in the world."

It took only moments for Mars to go back to the "Last Supper" photo, pointing out the grinning Lombardo in his three-piece suit.

Weren't the guys at the table members of organized crime?

"They never told me they were."

But hadn't Lombardo just said that day that Aiuppa was the "boss of Cicero"? And didn't that mean the boss of the mob in Cicero?

"The Cicero crew?" Mars asked.

"That is true," Lombardo said. "The jury heard me."

"No," Mars answered back. "I don't think they heard you say the Cicero crew."

"Well, ask them," Lombardo said, growing more irritated.

By now Mars was leaning over the podium toward Lombardo, firing off his questions. Lombardo was leaning forward, too, not backing down.

Mars named some of the men in the photo. Vince Solano wasn't the boss of the Rush Street crew, Lombardo said; he was a union guy. Al Pilotto? Same thing. Union guy, not the capo of the Chicago Heights crew.

He didn't know if Jackie Cerone was the Outfit's underboss, Lombardo said. And he thought Caesar D'Varco probably owned a nightclub. He wasn't a former Rush Street leader whom Lombardo had feuded with over Wemette's street taxes.

And what about Accardo, the boss of bosses?

"No, I read in the paper they say he is, but as far as me knowing, no, I don't," Lombardo said.

"You were getting something to eat and you walk into a restaurant with a dozen Outfit bosses by chance?" Mars asked.

He went, Lombardo said, and saw the group eating.

"That was by chance," he said firmly. "I went to get a sandwich."

And what about the man Lombardo supposedly was with. He wasn't in the picture. Lombardo said he was in the other room, and Mars made it clear he had his doubts.

"I say he's in the other room, and you say, 'If he's there at all,'" Lombardo responded flatly.

Lombardo acknowledged again that he had the craps game but denied anyone was there giving out juice loans to the losers. That included Frank "Gumba" Saladino, a man Lombardo said he wouldn't know if someone showed him a picture.

Mars moved next to street taxes, which Lombardo admitted came in two forms, "muscle tax" and "investment tax." Muscle tax was the one that was extortionate. So, Mars asked, which was charged to Wemette?

"I never charged Wemette a penny," Lombardo said.

Didn't he charge Wemette $250 a week?

"Well, the ladies and gentlemen of the jury heard the evidence," Lombardo said in a tone that almost suggested he was growing bored. "I never received a penny from Mr. Wemette, sir."

Marshall Caifano had never collected for him, Lombardo said. And Alva Johnson Rodgers had never worked for him. Rodgers was "positively a liar."

Mars reminded the jury of the story with Rodgers and Lombardo driving as they listened to their police tail on a scanner. Lombardo liked scanners even then, Mars suggested, before an Outfit work car equipped with a similar scanner was recovered after the Danny Seifert murder.

"I just got through saying I never had a scanner in my car," Lombardo said. "I could tell a liar when I hear it."

And how about Frank Schweihs, the man who emerged during the trial as the most feared hit man in Chicago. Wasn't he a friend?

The jury had heard the undercover tapes from Wemette's apartment, the ones where "the German" said he was there on Lombardo's behalf. The jury had seen the grainy video. Did Lombardo see it?

"I sure did, and he's a liar," Lombardo said. Anyone could go and pull the recordings of phone calls Lombardo made to Schweihs or anyone else for that matter, Lombardo said. There was nothing illegal being discussed.

How about Louie Eboli? Wasn't Lombardo in a criminal organization with Louie Eboli?

"That's positively no. Where's the evidence?" Lombardo said. "Where's the picture? Where's the conversation?"

"How about where's the tape?" Mars answered.

There was the recorded phone conversation with Eboli where he and Lombardo had talked about who was controlling which massage parlors. One was open too close to one of Joe Ferriola's and would have to close or "we'll flatten the joint," Lombardo had said. It was 1979, and Lombardo had been on the phone with Eboli from Dorfman's office while agents were tapping the lines there.

Mars played the tape for the jury again and immediately concentrated on something Lombardo had told Halprin. Lombardo had said that "we" didn't really mean "we," as in "we don't have nothing to do with" a massage parlor.

Mars asked if it was correct that "we" didn't mean "we." What followed was an exchange that Abbott and Costello might have come up with.

"Your testimony is 'we' means what?" Mars asked.

"Him," Lombardo said.

"'We' means 'him'"?

"He don't have nothing to do with it."

"Who, who doesn't have nothing to do with it?"

"Louie don't have nothing to do with it."

"But Louie Eboli doesn't say, 'no, I don't,' does he?"

"What's he say?"

"He says, 'we don't,' right?"

"He puts me right back in," Lombardo relented.

Joey chalked up the confusion to not knowing the conversation was being recorded. Maybe he would have chosen his words more carefully if he'd known for sure the men weren't alone on the phone line.

Think of the president, Lombardo interjected. Even the president would say he didn't choose his words carefully at times.

"Well, the president didn't have a crew like you did, Mr. Lombardo," Mars said.

"He's got a bigger crew; you know where I'm at?" Lombardo answered, smiling again.

There were several more go-rounds about the real meaning of "we," with Lombardo insisting he really didn't have anything to do with any muscling of street tax. And there was a dispute about what it meant when Lombardo told Eboli, "You better take them out," meaning take his jukeboxes out of the massage parlor before the place got flattened.

Mars tried to pull Lombardo back to the idea that the reason the business would get flattened in the first place was because no street tax was being paid. The men looked at a transcript. Can't you read it? Lombardo asked Mars.

"Sir, sir, sir, sir, let's read it together," Lombardo said.

And the men sparred about what Lombardo meant went he talked to Eboli about "putting the arm" on the place. Didn't that mean to extort them?

He didn't know what he meant, Lombardo said. But Mars wasn't going to let that go either. Didn't it mean that the place would be shut down if it didn't pay up? No idea, Lombardo said again.

There were more tapes from Dorfman's office, of course, including the tape of Lombardo apparently threatening Morris Shenker over his unpaid debt. Halprin had made it sound as if Lombardo was just playacting, Mars said. He was playing the role of a gangster as a favor to Dorfman to get the money collected.

Mars asked if that was a good role for Lombardo.

"Yeah, like James Cagney," Lombardo replied. "Edward G. Robinson."

A couple of Hollywood tough guys. How about Joe Lombardo, boss of the Grand Avenue crew?

"That's not true, sir," Lombardo answered.

Well, didn't the jury hear him threaten a man's life on the tape?

"I threatened my wife, too," Lombardo said. "I would strangle her more times and never did, sir."

Mars played the Shenker tape for the jury again. Lombardo could be heard talking about who was behind Dorfman, how he belonged to Chicago, and how those people wanted what they were owed. They were not meek and harmless.

"It didn't really need to be said that you were there for the Chicago Outfit, did it?" Mars asked.

"That's what I made him think it was."

Lombardo said over and over that he was misrepresenting who he was. The goal was to make it look like the mob wanted Dorfman to be paid, just so Shenker would stop ignoring his debt.

Didn't Lombardo know that making such threats was illegal? You can't tell a seventy-two-year-old he won't reach seventy-three if he doesn't do what you say. If Shenker had reported it, Lombardo could have gone to prison. Lombardo had told Shenker that he could send one man to jail but only one man; he couldn't fight "the system."

"Because you knew the Outfit would back you up if Morris Shenker beefed on you, right?"

"No, that's not true," Lombardo said. "I'm lying to the guy, sir. I'm lying to the guy. I'm playing a script with him."

Well, when he told Shenker that the people behind Dorfman were not meek and harmless, didn't Shenker take that as a threat? What Lombardo had said was threatening; he had told the debtor he was in his final year of life if he didn't pay up.

"I did it in a way like it was a threat, yeah," Lombardo said. "If he didn't pay and the people behind Allen would be mad and he'd never reach his seventy-third birthday, but that's me writing a script, sir."

Lombardo insisted that Dorfman actually was owed a debt and he was just trying to sell Shenker on the idea that the mob wanted the money, too. It wasn't an actual threat, telling him he wouldn't reach seventy-three.

"And how do you interpret that for a man that's seventy-two?" Mars asked incredulously.

"No, no, no, he didn't pay, sir; and he lived to be seventy-three, seventy-four, seventy-five."

The afternoon was waning, but Mars had a bit more territory to cover. He tried to get back at Lombardo's role as a mob intermediary between Aiuppa and the Outfit and Dorfman and the Teamsters. There was the meeting, Mars pointed out, the restaurant meeting that Lombardo drove Aiuppa to.

The FBI had been listening as it was set up, and Agent Pfizenmayer had made it to the meeting as Lombardo and Aiuppa arrived. He had seen Aiuppa dress down Dorfman from his seat at the bar.

Pfizenmayer had said Aiuppa seemed upset and was doing all of the talking. Wasn't it true that Dorfman was there to get his orders from the Outfit? Mars asked. No, Lombardo said, the agent was not telling the truth.

"Special Agent Pfizenmayer was lying?" Mars asked.

"I don't care if he's super special—he's lyin'," Lombardo answered.

Mars went after the details of the attempted bribery of Senator Cannon. Allen Glick had submitted a higher bid for the property near the senator's house, but it was Lombardo who had figured out a way to see the deal through. The idea was for a couple of Teamsters officials to go and remind Glick that he had borrowed tens of millions of dollars, Lombardo acknowledged, so maybe something could be worked out.

But Lombardo refused to agree that he had sent them, again growing irritated with the questions from Mars.

"Sir, are you having trouble understanding me?" he asked the prosecutor.

"At times I am, Mr. Lombardo; I have to admit," Mars said.

"Well, we all have that problem," Lombardo responded, telling Mars again that he had no authority to send union officials anywhere.

But Lombardo had the power through Dorfman, whose insurance company was contracted through the fund. He was a special consultant with great authority over the hundreds of millions of dollars in the fund's coffers.

And that, Mars said, is why Daniel Seifert had to be eliminated.

The fraud case involving Seifert and International Fiberglass could have derailed everything. Some $1.4 million had been loaned from the pension fund to a New Mexico company called Gaylur Products in a bogus deal, with some of the money being laundered through Seifert's company in a contract for work pails. Phony bills had been created and money had gone to Lombardo. Seifert could have testified about that. He could have talked about Lombardo and the company's links to men like "Milwaukee Phil" Alderisio.

Seifert could have destroyed the pipeline to the Teamsters fortune—slain the golden goose, as Mars liked to say.

"Mr. Seifert at any time did not jeopardize one penny of my assets or Mr. Dorfman's assets," Lombardo said.

But Mars would press Lombardo rather than ease off. Seifert was going to say that Lombardo had asked him to make a phony invoice. Lombardo had gotten the money.

"No, I did not know that, sir" Lombardo said.

Anthony Spilotro. He got money, too. The Outfit was able to get at the deep reserves of the pension fund.

"And you were concerned that Danny Seifert was going to upset the whole applecart, weren't you?" Mars asked.

"I had no idea that Mr. Seifert was going to testify against us until he got killed," Lombardo answered. It wasn't true, he said, "We didn't know that he was testifying against us."

But the anger in Mars was welling up. His voice was growing louder.

The questions and answers were piling on top of one another. The prosecutor bore down on the old man with the cane, the funny man with the dark secrets. Joseph Seifert, a confused four-year-old the day the men shot his dad, sat in the gallery watching.

"It was Danny Seifert that wrote those phony checks to you, didn't he?"

"Danny Seifert did not write no phony checks to me, sir."

"And so you knew Danny Seifert had to go, didn't you, Mr. Lombardo," Mars said, his voice quaking with emotion.

"Mr. Mars, that is not true, sir," Lombardo answered, thumping his cane.

"You and your crew killed Danny Seifert, didn't you, Mr. Lombardo."

"That is not true, sir," Lombardo said. "I do not have a crew."

Hadn't Lombardo been at the business just a week before the murder? No, that was a coincidence, Joey said.

Didn't Lombardo buy the work car, the Ford LTD that was used to flee Bensenville? No, Lombardo replied, the salesman would testify he couldn't recognize "David Kemp."

But Lombardo had used lots of fake names. Joe Cuneo. Savard.

It was time for Lombardo to see his fingerprint again on the document for the Ford. Nice and big for everyone to get a good look while Lombardo sat there, unable to run. No basements to hide in.

"This is the application for title for the car that was used to murder Danny Seifert—you understand that?" Mars asked.

"I understand that."

There was an address for the security firm on the document, but it was the address of a plumbing company. A plumbing company in Lombardo's own neighborhood and a company owned by a friend of his.

And the Dodge that outran the cops that day, Mars continued. That was from a Dodge dealership owned by a man named Larry Mack. Lombardo had shopped there before. Larry Mack was a friend of his, too.

And the police scanner left behind in the Ford, it was from C.B. Center of America. Lombardo had been there many times—even admitted it. He had gone for AT&S, a nonexistent towing company. Store employees had pointed to Lombardo's picture after Seifert was gunned down.

George Rusu had sold the actual scanner that was recovered, and had selected two photos of Lombardo when asked to pick out the man who bought it.

"He's wrong," Lombardo said. "The guy made a mistake, sir."

Didn't Lombardo go to the store with Frank Schweihs?

"Never," Lombardo answered. "Never. Never. Never. That's a lie."

He had gone with John Fecarotta, and he had gone with Jimmy LaPietra. Not true and not true, Lombardo said.

And he had signed his name as "Savard," after a hockey player?

That was right, Lombardo said, but he was only following Weiner's directions. It had nothing to do with the fact that it was the maiden name of the wife of Frank Schweihs.

"And so we have a coincidence that he's married to a woman whose maiden name is Savard, and Irwin Weiner just happened to like hockey players named Savard?" Mars asked.

"That's what Irwin Weiner told me to write."

Wasn't the plan for Schweihs to handcuff Seifert and take him away?

"I don't know anything about the murder."

Now, about the alleged alibi. Mars wanted to make it clear that Lombardo had reported a wallet stolen, first telling a couple of officers at the pancake house and then following them to a police station.

But on the day of the murder, FBI agents had visited Lombardo at his house, the one on Ohio in the old neighborhood. There was a story about the killing in an evening edition of the *Chicago Daily News*, and the agents had found Lombardo reading it.

His name was mentioned, and Lombardo had told the agents that the article was "full of crap." Wasn't that right? Mars asked.

"Well, I might have said that," Lombardo answered. "Go ahead."

The point was that Lombardo had said nothing about the supposed alibi. He hadn't told the agents about the garage door opener, the wallet, the pancake house, or the police. In fact, he hadn't spoken to the FBI at all after commenting on the article, wasn't that right?

Mars demanded a yes or no.

"Just a yes or no?"

"Yeah."

"I don't speak to the FBI when I have a problem."

Lombardo started to talk about hiring Anthony Pellicano to help with his alibi, the same Pellicano who had gone on to work in Hollywood. Mars left it alone and instead asked about his contacts with Dr. Patrick Spilotro, the dentist.

He had seen him a number of times as a patient, including just before his arrest in the Family Secrets case. Lombardo denied telling

Spilotro that if he hadn't been in prison in 1986, his brothers would not have been killed. He denied telling Spilotro that once you were given an order you had to follow it, "or you go, too."

And Mars asked whether he trusted Spilotro. It seemed that while he was on the lam, he had trusted the dentist with his freedom.

"No, I did not," Lombardo said gruffly. "I knew he was going to beef on me. I knew he was a beefer."

Mars had questions about Lombardo's life on the run. Didn't he know he was required to come to court after being indicted? Lombardo said he figured someone would come looking for him.

He claimed that when he got indicted, he was driving a car and quickly called a friend, asking for shelter. He had stayed in a basement in Oak Park and out of sight. He had written the court, asking for bond and a separate trial. He felt alone, he said, like he had three hundred million people against him.

He knew the FBI wanted him, and he had read the papers.

But he denied trying to disguise himself.

"No, I just let my beard grow, sir," Lombardo said, trying to keep his raspy voice up.

"That's not how you normally appear to people, is it?" Mars asked.

"Well, maybe I wanted to change my ways."

So Mars showed Lombardo a government exhibit. It was 33C, the photo after his arrest where he appeared with long, thick hair and a bushy beard framing his face.

That didn't look like the Lombardo who was seated in front of the jury now, did it?

"No, there's a little difference," Lombardo said with a smirk. He was looking at the image and trying not to laugh.

"Yeah, that's pretty funny, isn't it, Mr. Lombardo?" Mars wanted to know.

And of course, Lombardo had an answer. He always did.

"Well, a little joke once in a while ain't gonna hurt."

17

FRANK SR.

J oe Lopez's first witness was an unusual one. It was the gray-haired and somewhat disheveled Terry Pretto, who said he was "petrified" to be testifying.

Pretto stood and faced the wrong direction as a court officer was trying to swear him in. Judge Zagel gave a look and asked him to go ahead and turn around to face the bench.

"Sorry, guy," Pretto said.

He lived above Richard Ortiz's bar at the time of the shooting on Cermak Road in 1983, one of those Lopez would rely on to cast doubt on the version of the shooting that Nick had provided. Of all the killings, it was the best one for Lopez to try to attack. Police reports and official accounts had provided the names of witnesses who could talk about what they thought they'd seen.

"I only knew him by 'Chico,'" Pretto said of Ortiz.

He told the jury his pregnant wife was upstairs when he left to get some beer on July 23 that year. He would see the shooting take place out front, he said, as Ortiz and another man sat in Ortiz's car. He saw one man with a gun—not two—standing near the Mercury, and the man wore a cap on his head, not a mask or gloves. He heard the shooter shout a curse and then open fire, Pretto testified, as Frank Sr. watched nearby with a hand on his chin.

"He blew them away."

Pretto stayed around the area for a moment but then continued on with his errand.

"I wanted a six-pack," he explained. "Sorry."

Pretto seemed a little scattered on the stand, leaving some of the lawyers wondering if he had gone on the same errand before coming to court. But Pretto said he was just nervous and told Lopez he thought the shooter of Ortiz was a Cicero police sergeant who had been trouble in the past.

"I've seen a lot of people turn up dead around that place," he said of the town. He estimated he had been about twenty feet from the gunman, and he didn't get any closer just to make a better identification. "It's not like you see someone shooting and run out there and say, 'Hi, how're you doing?'"

Mitch Mars would cross-examine Pretto, who had given no statement to any authorities the night Ortiz and Morawski were killed. Instead, Mars asked, wasn't it seventeen years later, in 2000, before he gave any information to anyone?

That was right, Pretto said, but he told Mars he had tried to talk to the police that night. He was told they had plenty to work with and didn't need him, he told Mars. Still, Pretto seemed to have trouble recalling the statement he eventually did give to those investigating the murder. In that version the shooter was wearing "nice pants," and approached Pretto afterward and told him not to tell anyone what he had seen. Pretto continued to blame his shakiness and inconsistency on being scared.

"You might come after me tonight," he told Mars.

"No," Mars answered. "I can guarantee you it won't be me."

Lopez's second witness was a little more lucid. John Marino, forty-eight, grew up with Frank Calabrese Jr. after the Calabrese family moved from the old neighborhood to Elmwood Park. He remembered playing baseball with his friend and seeing him at school and said he was also around Frank Sr. at sports games and the neighborhood in general.

And how did he treat his sons? Lopez asked.

"Like a dad," Marino answered.

Marino knew Frank Jr. was in the restaurant business and had seen his friend as recently as that spring. Marino had been a bartender at La Luce, he said, one of the restaurants Frank Jr. had invested in after taking his father's stashed money. Marino said he had seen Frank Sr. treat his kids fairly well, taking them to dinner and not abusing them.

It was a hard job to paint Frank Sr. as the ideal father, but at least Lopez had found one person willing to testify under oath that his client wasn't a psychopath.

The next witness for Frank Sr. was an inmate himself. John O'Connell appeared in court in a yellow jumpsuit, having been brought from an Illinois state prison where he was serving a sentence for murder. On the day of the Ortiz and Morawski shooting, he said he heard a "loud explosion" from the direction of the His & Mine bar from his home a few doors away.

"It sounded like a shotgun or something like that," he said, hunched over on the stand, telling Lopez that shootings at the bar were fairly common. He remembered leaning over the railing of his porch to get a better look and said he too saw a single gunman.

"I seen a man standing by the car, and he was shooting," O'Connell said. He couldn't see the man's face because it was too dark but remembered he wore a three-quarter length coat. The man walked around to the driver's side of a car parked in front of the bar and pulled away, O'Connell said. "All I seen was just a driver."

On cross-examination, O'Connell told Mars he didn't really have a view of the bar from his porch but ran toward the scene afterward. Mars asked if he remembered telling police that he saw a handgun when he spoke to them, not a shotgun.

"I don't recall off the top of my head."

Frank Calabrese Sr. left his seat to testify and walked straight toward the jury box, greeting the panel with a wide smile and a slight bow of the head.

"Good afternoon, ladies and gentlemen of the jury," he said with enthusiasm and a nasally Chicago accent. Frank Sr. spoke like a man convinced he could explain his way out of anything—all they had to do was give him a chance to talk. To be sure, he had waited the entire trial to do what he was about to do. Two months into the trial, he had grown a trimmed, white beard, and he sat down in his chair looking like a chubby grandfather in a sport coat. He turned his seat so he could mostly face the jury, which happened to leave his one good ear aimed at Lopez, standing behind the podium.

Frank Sr. told jurors his name and that he was born in 1937.

"On the seventeenth of March," he said with a flourish.

He grew up near Grand Avenue, and like Lombardo, he tried to convey the idea that he had pulled himself up by his bootstraps. Communicating a bit of his old Chicago upbringing might humanize him somewhat, but the delivery was probably a little too eager.

"I worked on State and Grand selling newspapers," he said, a hint of a nervous quiver developing in his voice.

"I attended a few grade schools. I wasn't learning, and I felt like everybody was picking on me," he said. It had taken him many years to figure out he had dyslexia, Frank Sr. told Lopez, though it came out something like "dyslexius."

How was his relationship with his family as a youngster? Lopez wanted to know. The lawyer was doing his best to keep his client steady, and he'd chosen a fluorescent yellow tie for the occasion.

"When we were growing up, we were very close. We were a close family," Frank Sr. said earnestly, sometimes leaning on the witness stand. "We ate oatmeal many nights because there was no money to buy food."

His father was a saint in heaven, he told the jury.

"If that's where he is."

He was animated on the stand, clearly aiming to follow in Lombardo's footsteps and turn on some charm. But it didn't quite come off, and prosecutors would soon have enough of Frank Sr.'s efforts to spin a folksy life history for the jury. He seemed ready to settle in on the stand for the long haul, talking about how he was a troubled youth sent away to a military institute as a teen. He was in the army when the Korean War ended, he said, drawing a first objection from John Scully, who asked Zagel to put the brakes on the personal history.

But Frank Sr. went right back to it. The army wasn't going to ship him out, which made him angry, he tried to explain, so he went AWOL.

"I rebelled against that," he said, telling the jury that he was sent to the stockade. But he escaped twice, he said, finally stealing a car from the airport in St. Louis. That earned the young Frank Sr. a juvenile sentence that left him locked up until he was twenty-one.

The testimony was rambling on, and prosecutors objected again as Frank Sr. started to tell the jury about his limited hearing. Judge Zagel finally stepped in and told Lopez to cut back on the detail, which frustrated Frank Sr.

He had clearly taken the stand with a mental list of things he wanted the jury to know.

"How are these people supposed to know what I'm doing?" he said, twisting around to look up at the judge.

Lopez reeled him back in and asked again about his schooling. Did he like to fight?

No, said Frank Sr., the man accused of beating, stomping, and strangling his victims before cutting their throats. He had been picked on as a child, and he fought only to defend himself. He wasn't the kind of guy to be the instigator and go after others.

"I hated bullies, and I still hate them today," he said.

By the way, Lopez asked, had he ever testified anywhere before?

"No," Frank Sr. said almost gently. "This is my first time."

He continued on with his personal tale of growing up on the West Side, how he had gotten a job at Jefferson Ice and had met his wife, Dolores Hanley. They were married in 1961, when Frank Sr. was going on twenty-two, he said, and he was driving a truck for a dairy.

When he was fired, he had no trouble finding work. His wife's family had heavy union connections, Frank Sr. said, telling Lopez he got a job with Local 150, a union of heavy-equipment operators. Frank Sr.'s brother-in-law was Edward Hanley, who was elected president of the Hotel Employees and Restaurant Employees International Union in the 1970s, allegedly with a boost from Joey Aiuppa. Hanley had even offered Frank Sr. a post as head of that union in Las Vegas, which he had declined because of his lack of education. He didn't start getting a better handle on the basics of reading and spelling until he took some classes at the prison at Milan.

Lopez moved Frank Sr. along, touching next on how he met Angelo LaPietra.

Well, Frank Sr. started to say, that was at a favorite nightclub, a spot where they would have fashion shows on Saturdays and Sundays.

Scully started to object again, but the judge was way ahead of him. Zagel kept his calm demeanor, but he was becoming aggravated with Frank Sr.'s long narrative answers. At this rate the jury might be pressed into service until Halloween. The judge wanted the where, how, and when, not Frank Sr.'s opinion of fashion shows at a nightclub forty years earlier. Some jurors were starting to look disinterested, with one in particular obviously doodling in his notepad.

"I do not want the why," Zagel told Lopez, who was nodding at the podium. "His life history is not at issue."

Frank Sr. sat on the witness stand with a grumpy look on his face, starting to shake his head slightly.

The witness was charged with terrible crimes, Zagel said; the jury didn't need to hear him spend fifteen minutes talking about "how wonderful his mother is."

Well, that was Frank Sr.'s Italian ethnicity, Lopez tried to explain. "He loves to talk."

Good, but no one needed tremendous amounts of detail on Frank Sr. "abandoning his incipient military career," Zagel told him. The number of open questions Lopez would be allowed was dwindling rapidly.

"Can I have some extra ones maybe?" Lopez said hopefully.

"Let's see how it goes" came the flat response.

All right, Lopez continued, turning his attention back to the frowning Frank Sr. What year did he meet Angelo LaPietra?

"1964," Frank Sr. said, leaning back in his chair.

It was at the nightclub around Lawrence and Harlem. He was called over to a table.

Frank Sr. was a noted thief and burglar, but it was when he began putting money on the street in the form of juice loans that the Outfit really noticed him. He had started at around age twenty-two, and he had about $14,000 out when LaPietra had called for him.

"He said I shouldn't be doing that, he says, because it's not right," Frank Sr. told the jury, explaining how LaPietra had told him he needed to start following some rules. "Him and I had a nice conversation."

Frank Sr. described it in court as a business lunch establishing a partnership, not as a capo enlisting a soldier. Frank Sr. said the mob boss wound up giving him $60,000 one time and $80,000 another to get his "business" going stronger.

"I told him if I had more money, I knew I could put it on the street."

His first street partner was Steve Annerino, he said, a snotty man he didn't like and asked to be rid of. So he soon found himself working alongside Larry Stubich, and the business took off. Frank Sr. described it as a system where men who couldn't get loans from a bank could go to get some working capital to do something like improve a business. It all sounded close to being on the up-and-up, and Frank Sr. tried to paint it as a virtual community bank.

"I would get guys to sign notes for them loans."

There was no violence, he said, no threats and no physical harm to the customers. Frank Sr. seemed appalled at the very thought, shaking his head.

"There was never a time that anybody that I ever had got a beating from me over money," Frank Sr. explained. He just wouldn't do that. "I would sit and talk to them and ask, 'What's the least you can pay? What's the most you can pay?'"

His theory was to take the money, he told the jury. If the guy can come up with only $10, then you should stick it in your pocket.

By the middle of the 1960s, Frank Sr. said he had $350,000 out on the street, with something like thirty borrowers on the books. Things were going well. Frank Sr. and Stubich were a good team, and then Stubich was shot and killed outside the Bistro a Go-Go on Higgins Road in September 1966. Frank Sr. was clearly bitter about it more than forty years later, snarling that he "definitely" thought he knew who had done it.

Lopez asked about some of the other men Frank Sr. had met along the way, including John "Johnny Apes" Monteleone. What would happen when people didn't get along? Did he participate in "alternative dispute resolution meetings," commonly called sit-downs?

Why, yes, Frank Sr. said. He was familiar with such conflict-management gatherings.

He'd had sit-downs with the Wild Bunch, he said, naming such men as Harry Aleman and Butch Petrocelli. And, after a pause, oh, yes, there was James "Jimmy I" Inendino.

Scully objected.

"Counsel just pointed to his eye," he complained about Lopez. Scully believed the defense attorney was leading his client.

Zagel, who was making a face as if he'd had better days than this one, allowed things to progress, and Lopez was again asking about the sit-downs. They were civilized affairs, Frank Sr. said. There wasn't even any swearing.

"It was all done diplomatically," he said in a tone that suggested he was giving the final word on the matter. The boss would have one group sitting on one side, and the other sitting on another. Someone like Joey Aiuppa would listen to the conversation in the room, hear both sides out, and then make some kind of decision.

"He would side with the truth," Frank Sr. explained.

Frank Sr. had grown up in the neighborhood that produced Lombardo and Spilotro, but he had been connected to organized crime figures through LaPietra. That meant he was plugged in further south in Bridgeport, he said. He knew the Caruso family and Fred Roti.

Larry Stubich had men like Michael "Hambone" Albergo working the neighborhood pool halls and bringing in customers for loans.

Did you like him? Lopez said of Albergo.

"Yes, I did."

Did you kill him?

"I definitely did not."

But his brother had told the story about the hole. There was the supposed killing in 1970 with Nick and Ronnie Jarrett. Frank Sr. had been accused of reaching over the front seat with a rope.

"It's not true," Frank Sr. said, still mostly facing the jury. "Why would I want to kill him?"

Frank Sr. said he did know he had been subpoenaed to appear before the commission that was planning a book on juice rackets. Ed Hanley had found out and had told him about it, he said. That's when Frank Sr. had decided to "take a sneak" and duck the paperwork, taking the trip to Arizona with Nick.

Frank Sr.'s union connections had gotten Nick work, too, he said. He had gotten his brother a job with the ironworkers union, and Nick had worked on the John Hancock Center as it was being constructed on Michigan Avenue in the late 1960s. Frank Sr. had gotten his brother his job with the Teamsters at McCormick Place, as well.

"Every job he had I got him," Frank Sr. said.

Finally, Nick had hinted about working in Frank Sr.'s real business, his loan operation, leading to their meeting at Slicker Sam's. Nick had then started on the street, making collections.

"It was a lot of street driving," Frank Sr. explained. "Sixteen, seventeen hours a day."

It was when the brothers returned from Arizona that Frank Sr. said he learned that Albergo, one of his freelancing agents, had disappeared. He was holding several thousand dollars, Frank Sr. told the jury, so he'd figured Albergo had just left with the money. He had called his house looking for him, he said, but eventually he and Angelo had just decided to chalk up the money Albergo had as a loss and move on.

He definitely didn't kill him, he promised again, his sharp Chicago accent becoming more noticeable as he got excited.

"What did I do that he could testify [about]?" he asked, raising his voice. "There was no way that them loans meant that much."

Lopez seemed to have control again, and he asked about Ronnie Jarrett. Frank Sr. said he knew him, calling him a "nice fellow" who was friends with Nick. There was no hint of the Jarrett whom Nick had called a killer, though Frank Sr. said that he thought Jarrett was "a good breaker into safes."

He learned bookmaking only through his brother and Ronnie, Frank Sr. said. They started taking bets on horses and major sports. Frank Sr. said it wasn't really his thing, so he continued to concentrate on juice loans. He didn't know odds, but Ronnie and his brother were forcing the issue on the crew to get into sports betting, especially on football.

How about John Fecarotta, Lopez asked; was he familiar with him? Did he help anyone kill him?

"No way," Frank Sr. said—an answer he would start to repeat over and over again in an earnest voice. "I loved that guy."

Fecarotta was six foot three and about 250 pounds, Frank Sr. told the jury, his size earning him the nickname "Big Stoop." He and Monteleone had been partners of sorts, working and stealing together.

Was he good with his hands?

"That's what I heard."

Fecarotta had a hot-dog stand near Grand and Harlem, Frank Sr. said, repeating how much he loved the guy.

But don't get the wrong idea or anything.

"We were good friends, Joe," he told his lawyer. "It doesn't mean that I held his hand and he held mine. He had a wife and two girlfriends."

Frank Sr. acknowledged Angelo LaPietra was a boss, but he told the jury the mobster never controlled him. He continued to describe it more as a business partnership. Angelo was just a well-respected man, especially in the neighborhood, where he had helped establish the Italian-American Club.

It had been Angelo and "a bunch of us" that got it off the ground, Frank Sr. said, gearing up for another in-depth story and bringing another objection from Scully. Zagel cut off the testimony again, leaving Frank Sr. shaking his head much more noticeably as jurors looked on.

Anyway, Jimmy Stolfe was a member, Frank Sr. said. They were friends. Stolfe, the Connie's Pizza founder, was never someone he would extort. They would play handball and hang out.

Would Stolfe have any reason to be afraid of him?

"I loved the man, Joe."

"When he was sitting here, he was scared even to look at me," Frank Sr. said, tapping his fingers anxiously on the stand. "This man was my friend."

Lopez asked how it made Frank Sr. feel to find out his pal was getting the arm put on him. "Like a piece of shit," Frank Sr. answered. It wasn't fair. Stolfe would sometimes bring truckloads of pizzas to the club and charge nothing.

Frank Sr. said he was told to go talk to Stolfe after the payment was reduced. Nothing was taken by force.

"That ain't my M.O., Joe," Frank Sr. told his lawyer, claiming he eventually gave Johnny Apes $50,000 to leave his friend alone.

So was any of this related to organized crime? What about the Chicago Outfit?

Not him, Frank Sr. said; he was no mobster.

"Joe, Mr. Lopez, I'm sorry," he told his lawyer. "When they said, 'Outfit,' they're talking about guys like Angelo and Jimmy and Johnny Apes and John Fecarotta. Them are Outfit guys."

And it was his brother Nick who was closer to Angelo, Frank Sr. said. The capo called Nick "Gus" or "Joy" and treated him like his right-hand man. In the 1970s his brother had started to get more and more involved in Outfit activity, he said. Nick was doing more and more things for Angelo that Frank Sr. said he just didn't want to get involved with.

"I even told him he wasn't a man to do that," he said. "Stay away from that stuff."

Gone was the cunning Frank Sr. the jury had seen on the prison tapes, a man who had sounded menacing even when talking in code. It was the supposedly softer Frank Sr. before them now, a humble and friendly old man who might sit down next to them at a baseball game or something. But for the most part it just wasn't coming off. Jurors didn't seem to be buying it, and Frank Sr.'s temper was clearly flashing each time the judge cut off his lawyer. He would shake his head and contort his face into an angry scowl.

How about Paul Haggerty? Lopez asked. Did you kill him?

"No way," Frank Sr. answered again, telling Lopez he didn't remember much about his death.

"I read it in the papers," he said.

And he didn't really remember Henry Cosentino.

"I murdered Henry Cosentino?" Frank Sr. said loudly. "For what?"

John Mendell, the burglar, how about him? He was a friend of Ronnie's whom Frank Sr. said he had met only once or twice. But he didn't wait for him in a garage and kill him.

"No way," Frank Sr. said, with a sort of grimace on his face.

Vincent Moretti and Donald Renno, Lopez continued, working his way through the list of people whose lives allegedly had been ended by his client. Frank Sr. said he had met Renno in Elmwood Park, but he didn't remember ever meeting Moretti. Renno was the younger of the two, a victim Nick had said unwittingly walked into the restaurant death chamber while "Strangers in the Night" played on the jukebox.

"A real nice young man, believe me," Frank Sr. said.

Lopez suggested that Nick could have learned about details of the murders from the job he had been working at the Maybrook Courthouse in the western suburbs for the Cook County Sheriff's Office. He'd most likely have access to collections of documents related to some of the murders and could have gleaned details that he was using to accuse his brother now.

Nick also had "every gangster book ever written," Frank Sr. insisted, and there had been plenty of publicity about most of the murders anyway.

Take the killings of the Daubers.

"Joe, it was in the paper," Frank Sr. said, remembering various bulletins and news accounts of the double homicide. "John Drummond did a nice story."

Several reporters gave Drummond, who was seated in the gallery, a look, and he returned a little smile.

Frank Sr. said, "No way" to the notion that he had killed the Will County couple, "No way" to the idea that he could have killed Petrocelli, and he denied as well pointing a rifle at his brother and Jimmy "Poker" DiForti when Ortiz and Morawski were shot in front of the Cicero bar. He was actually too busy to kill anyone, he said. The Chicago Outfit had people who were moneymakers and people who did "heavy work" like killing. Frank Sr. said he was the former.

"Joe, my earning spoke for itself. I made millions," he said. "So, how would I have time to do this?"

And Lopez and Frank Sr. went over other details that, they argued, didn't line up in the government's case—such as the detonator cap that had supposedly gone off in Frank Sr.'s hand while the crew was trying to kill Cagnoni. He had said those things only because he was bragging to his son, he told the jury. Nick had told Frank Jr. all kinds of stories and swayed his affections, so in order to impress his boy, Frank Sr. said, he had done his best to give his own romanticized account of being in organized crime.

Authorities had executed a search warrant for X-rays of Frank Sr.'s hands, which Lopez said had failed to find any tiny metal shards or particles from an old injury. Government witnesses had suggested someone could lose a finger if they were holding a cap when it went off. Frank Sr. had all ten of his.

"Anything wrong with them?" Lopez said.

"Not a thing," Frank Sr. answered, holding his hands above his head for the jury to see and wiggling his digits. "There's no way I would even know about a thing like that."

He also hadn't been involved in the attempted killing of Nick Sarillo, the van driver who had survived a bomb blast. That wasn't his M.O., Frank Sr. said again.

"What was?" Lopez asked.

"Earning money."

Frank Sr. said he was very ill for part of the 1980s with a tumor on his pituitary gland. He'd had to step back and turn over the business to Nick, who promptly "screwed it all up." Lots of money had disappeared. Nick would tell him he gave out loans, Frank Sr. told the jury, but no one seemed to be paying on them. It was part of Lopez's attempt to show that money—and lots of it—had been stolen by Calabrese family members who were now conspiring to keep Frank Sr. locked up.

But prosecutors were doing a good job of keeping some of those allegations bottled up after Zagel had ruled to limit them. When Frank talked about his "second business," the purchase and restoration of antique cars, he wasn't allowed to allege that his son had taken any of the vehicles. He had owned a 1957 Thunderbird, a 1968 Chrysler Imperial Crown, and other vehicles worth a total of approximately $800,000. His family was doing very well in the 1990s, living in the wealthy suburb of Oak Brook.

But nearly any time he tried to suggest that certain things had been stolen, Scully would object. Frank Sr. got angrier each time he was interrupted, smirking at the prosecutor.

"How am I supposed to prove something to this jury if I keep getting objected?" he asked angrily in front of the jury.

And again, when Frank Sr. talked about having a number of driver's licenses in preparation for a run from the law in the middle of the 1990s, he wasn't allowed to bring up the money he was going to take and where it might have gone. Frank Sr. was in a lather as he was stopped again. He leaned forward in his seat and was almost shouting.

"They stole $2 million from me!"

Scully was objecting just as loudly, but Frank Sr. kept right on talking. "How am I supposed to explain myself?" he said angrily. The sneer was destroying the attempt to portray himself as a harmless senior citizen.

With that, Zagel stopped the proceedings and had the jury leave. It was clear to the judge that Frank Sr. was doing his best to have the jury hear what he wanted, no matter the court's ruling. Frank Sr. sat stewing on the witness stand, continuing to shake his head.

Zagel looked down to where Frank Sr. was sitting and told him directly that this kind of fighting in front of the jury was not going to continue. When Scully raised an objection, Zagel warned Frank Sr., he was to be quiet.

"If you violate this ruling I have just given you, or if you complain to the jury about my ruling, then I will find you in contempt of court," Zagel said calmly but sternly. The accusations of theft and a conspiracy to keep him imprisoned could not be proved.

"We are not going to battle out questions of law in this courtroom."

But Frank Sr. was still protesting.

"That's what bothers me," he said. He couldn't put forward a version of events that some jury member might hear and believe. "There will be somebody looking in other directions at things."

Well, it wasn't going to happen, Zagel said, warning Lopez again to control his client. The lawyer said he would. "I was going right and he turned left, so to speak," Lopez answered.

After about ten minutes the jury returned, and Lopez went to a topic that was at least in the neighborhood of what he and Frank Sr. wanted the jury to learn. When Frank Jr. was on the stand, he had testified that he took cash from his father that he invested in restaurants and blew having a good time. That was fair game.

Lopez asked Frank Sr. if he remembered the theft.

"I seen him spending money like crazy," Frank Sr. remembered, having settled back down. "He kept telling me he's going to Vegas and winning money in Vegas."

Frank Jr. had invited everyone to Disney World and had rented a suite, raising his father's suspicions to the tipping point. The cash had been kept in two bags in a family garage, he said, and he had to confront the restaurant owners and his son to get to the bottom of things.

"I was very upset," he said. "I never figured my son would do something like that."

Frank Jr. had finally admitted taking $1 million, Frank Sr. told the jury. Frank Sr. said he was furious his son would steal from him, and that he was "putting that stuff up his nose."

But he denied striking him. He also said he had never threatened his son with a gun.

"No way would I have stuck a gun in my son's mouth," he told Lopez.

Eventually some of the money started coming back from the restaurants in scattered payments. So did he forgive Frank Jr.? Lopez asked.

Frank Sr. paused for a second or two and then answered.

"I forgave him, but I didn't forget."

As for his brother, Frank Sr. said again it was Nick who involved the Calabrese operation in bookmaking and street taxes. Nick was collecting extortion payments from five or six businesses, he said.

Among the challenges for Lopez and Frank Sr. was trying to address Frank Sr.'s guilty plea in his earlier loan-sharking case. It meant he had previously admitted to being part of the kind of activity he was accused of again in the Family Secrets case. And the jury had seen videotape and read his notes from inside federal prison that certainly made it appear that he was still running his operation after being incarcerated. Frank Sr. acknowledged that he eventually was indicted along with members of his organization following the cooperation of one of his customers, Matthew Russo. On the stand in the Family Secrets case, Frank Sr. said that Russo was earning his money and that none of the Calabreses was involved in extortion. The Calabreses had pleaded guilty, he agreed, but he said, "I didn't want to." He had pleaded guilty only in an attempt to create better deals for his sons, who were sent to prison anyway.

And Lopez tried to create a sense of double jeopardy in the case, even though he had been barred from arguing that directly, too. He had made a separate failed attempt to convince the U.S. Court of Appeals for the Seventh Circuit that prosecutors were using the same conduct in Family Secrets that Frank Sr. had already been convicted of. Lopez kept picking at it, asking Frank whether the earlier case involved his loan business in the 1960s through the early 1990s.

"The same stuff we're bringing up here again?" he asked.

Frank Sr. said he had told Frank Jr. not to get involved in bookmaking but he hadn't listened. His uncle Nick had also urged him to stay out of it.

"He had a head like a bull," Frank Sr. said. "His mother would even vouch for that."

Father and son had been housed just a few rooms apart at Milan, Frank Sr. recalled, and he believed their relationship was on the mend at the time. Frank Jr. would even do some cooking for his dad with a microwave, and they had plenty of time to talk about the past. Frank Jr. was getting divorced while he was in prison, and they had spoken about it often as they walked the yard or ate together in the mess hall. Frank Sr. told the jury he remembered his son being depressed and sad about his life.

Their family, including Nick, had been close until the 1990s, Frank Sr. said.

"[Nick] broke away from me; I didn't break away from him."

He remembered the last time he had seen his brother before Nick walked into court to testify against him more than a month earlier. It was Christmas dinner 1996, before Frank Sr. had surrendered to Milan. He called it the last decent conversation he'd had with his brother.

"I remember it like it was yesterday," he told Lopez. "I opened up a bottle of Napoleon brandy for him."

They'd spent time together that evening, and Nick had even kissed his brother goodbye, Frank Sr. remembered. It was a gesture that had stuck in his head and was made more memorable when his brother disappeared from his life thereafter.

By the next year Frank Sr. was in prison, seeing his son nearly every day. He remembered it being about January 1999 when there was a period that it seemed as if his son was avoiding him. But then in February they began talking once more. Frank Jr. would tape his first talk with his father on February 14 that year.

Lopez began walking Frank Sr. through the tapes, asking him what he was talking about and what his motivation had been for saying certain things to a son he was trying to keep from abandoning him. They had spoken about someone taking a sample off a glove, Lopez said. What was the story behind that?

Frank Sr. told the jury that John Monteleone had gotten hold of him in 1986 and told him to meet him behind a Cicero restaurant, and that he had then been taken upstairs to an apartment. He went inside, he said, and there was Nick.

"I noticed he had a bandage on his arm," Frank Sr. told the jury. He was told Nick had shot himself, and supposedly it was during the killing of Fecarotta, he said. It was his brother who seemed to be hiding from the police, Frank Sr. told Lopez, and he had no firsthand information about any gloves or how the murder had taken place.

Frank Sr. said he was at home when the killing took place and had only seen it on the news, he said.

How about the idea that Johnny Apes was involved, too?

"They were buddies," Frank Sr. said of Fecarotta and Monteleone. "Real good buddies."

There was a lot in Frank Jr.'s tapes about getting messages to people, including Nick, which Frank Sr. chalked up to the prison grapevine. He wanted to get word to Nick only to see if he needed help or a lawyer. When he spoke about getting a message to Jimmy Marcello through Jimmy's brother, Michael, it was only to check on Nick.

When Frank Jr. had taped his father talking about the making ceremony, it was basically a joke, Frank Sr. contended, giving a little laugh on the witness stand. There was no gathering with candles, he said. "I seen that in a book." He remembered there being descriptions of mob inductions in *The Godfather* and *The Valachi Papers*, a book about how another mob traitor, Joseph Valachi, turned on the Genovese family.

He recalled telling his son he regretted the burning of a holy picture in his hand.

"I was trying to let him know that I couldn't do that."

What was Frank Sr.'s understanding of what it meant to be a made man? Lopez wanted to know.

"You're supposed to report to a group of people the rest of your life," he answered. In theory, a made member might be helped with legal fees, and there might be some support for his family when he went away. Well, no one helped him when he was headed to prison, Frank Sr. told the jury.

"Not one person," he said, echoing the complaint that Nick had made himself. Frank Sr. turned toward the jury again, shaking his head. "Nobody ever took care of me."

There were lots of conversations about bookmaking and, of course, murder. But it was all bluster, Frank Sr. promised.

"I never killed one person."

Not even his son appeared to believe him as they spoke in prison, Frank Sr. told the jury.

"Did he laugh?" Lopez asked.

"Yes."

Frank Sr.'s side of the story had two prongs: He said that Frank Jr. had been showing too much interest in being a gangster, so he was trying to talk him out of it with scary crime stories. And he knew that Nick had told Frank Jr. his own made-up adventures, so Frank Sr. said he decided to do the same to keep his son's attention and win back his affection. Some of the things he said were an attempt to instill fear in his son, Frank Sr. told the jury; and others were designed to boost Frank Sr.'s importance in his son's mind or make him look down on his uncle.

Even so, Frank Sr., said, anyone listening to the tape could hear that he told his son he wasn't directly involved in the killing of the Daubers. His son would ask him the same questions over and over, he said, hoping to get different answers. Frank Sr. said he finally told his son that he was in a lookout car just to make it seem like he was there.

In another conversation Frank Sr. seemed to be telling his son he had killed Michael Albergo, telling him that he knew construction workers had "dug deep" when they put a parking lot over the site where the agent of the Calabrese organization was buried.

"I don't remember if I said that, Joe," he said. "I could have said it. I'm not denying it."

In March 1999, Frank Sr. had been taped talking to his police friend Michael Ricci and asking about the gloves in the Fecarotta case. Yes, he did ask, Frank Sr. said, but not because he was concerned about the ramifications for himself. He looked toward the jury yet again.

"Because I'm concerned that my brother's in trouble," he said.

That concern began to fade as Frank Sr. began to suspect that Nick was cooperating. He said it was a conversation with his mother that made him think his brother was losing it. She had spoken to Nick, who was growing more upset.

"My mother told me he was crying like a little baby," Frank Sr. said, drawing yet another objection from Scully.

But that little baby in many ways was having the last laugh. Nick, seemingly the quiet guy standing in the corner waiting to be told what to do, had come in to court and put years of violence and murder into his brother's lap. To Frank Sr. it was the ultimate betrayal. Nick hadn't even looked at him during his testimony, and Frank Sr. told the jury that he realized his brother must hate him.

"It made me realize that kiss he gave me for Christmas was a Judas kiss."

John Scully went to the podium to cross-examine Frank Sr. and got right to the point. One of the predicate acts the racketeering conspiracy in the case was built on was extortion and the giving out of juice loans. Throughout his testimony Frank Sr. was seemingly admitting that he was doing just that, though he disagreed that he was doing it for the Outfit.

Could he possibly not know that those were illegal?

"I suppose they were," Frank Sr. answered.

In many cases the loans required interest payments of 5 percent per week, Scully told Frank Sr. That was 260 percent a year, right?

"I don't know," Frank Sr. said. "I never figured that out."

Scully took an aggressive tack with Frank Sr., questioning him with a tone that suggested his testimony had been completely ridiculous. Who could run a juice loan business without an element of physical threats to collect payments when debtors hadn't fulfilled their obligations?

Frank Sr. was supposedly proud of treating people like adults, but, Scully pointed out, he had hit his own adult children and his brother.

But that wasn't true, Frank Sr. said, his neck straining against the top button of his dark shirt.

"So your son's lying?" Scully asked.

"Like you would not believe."

Frank Sr. continued to contend that he had basically gotten out of the business in the 1980s, turning the reins over to Nick and keeping tabs on things from a bit of a distance.

Well, Scully said, Frank Sr. was in charge in 1992. He was directing men such as Frank Furio and Phil Tolomeo. It was right in his plea agreement in the loan-sharking case. He had already admitted to it, and signed the agreement, and presented it to a judge.

"Yes, but I never read it, because I didn't know how," Frank Sr. told the jury, leaning back in his chair away from Scully.

It was clear that Scully had Frank Sr. pinned. Frank would be trying to explain away something that he had told a judge he had understood. Scully reminded Calabrese that he had stood in that very building before a U.S. district court judge, James Holderman, and had told him under oath that he comprehended what was going on and that pleading guilty was his decision. Frank Sr. said that was only true "up to a certain point," because someone had to read it to him.

The prosecutor took time to read it again. It said right there that Frank Sr. was admitting he'd conducted the affairs of an enterprise known as the Calabrese street crew. The document said there was a pattern of racketeering in the collection of unlawful debt.

"That was never explained to me," Frank Sr. repeated. He had never read the plea agreement word for word.

"I probably would've looked cross-eyed at myself."

Scully pressed on, staying in Frank Sr.'s face like few men probably had ever done. The advantage was with Scully and his court document. Frank Sr. had agreed he'd operated an illegal business and that threats were involved. Wasn't it all done on behalf of the Chicago Outfit?

"It was mine," Frank Sr. said, growing a little more defiant.

He had signed the paper for his sons, he said. They were never in the business, and he wanted to protect them. He had told the government his boys were innocent, Frank Sr. said, his temper welling up as Scully's questions kept coming.

Well, the prosecutor said, was Frank Jr. lying when he came into court and told the jury about collecting on juice loans?

"He's been lying to you people real good," Frank Sr. said, raising his voice again and then slipping into the theme of his defense. For stealing a million dollars, his son had gotten a pretty light sentence.

Like Mars, this was a career moment for Scully. He had spent his professional life making cases against wiseguys. He would dig and dig and turn witnesses and find evidence until the target was taken down. Now Scully had a made member of the Outfit before him with no place to go. The pace of his questions was quick and steady, with Frank Sr. less and less in control as Scully pressed him. Frank Sr. had acknowledged that crew members had threatened debtors. He had acknowledged doing what he had to do to collect, and he had told a judge it was all true.

Frank Sr. began thumping his fingers on the witness stand as he answered, getting more agitated.

"If I signed it, it was against me knowing it," he growled. No one was threatened with physical violence. He would never have signed that paper had he known that was stated on it.

Hadn't he known that Angelo and Jimmy LaPietra, two men who infused the Calabrese operation with cash, were members of the Chicago Outfit?

"What their background was I did not know," Frank Sr. said. He wouldn't discuss such things.

But Angelo LaPietra was a capo.

"He was my partner, not my boss," Frank Sr. said, denying again that he himself was part of the mob.

"I was not affiliated other than being part of lending money."

But Joey Aiuppa was the boss of the entire Outfit, and Frank Sr. had admitted in his earlier questioning that Aiuppa was a part of meetings he attended. When there were disputes, Aiuppa would handle them with a sit-down, Scully had pointed out.

Now Frank Sr. tried to backtrack, telling the jury Aiuppa had nothing to do with any of their meetings, that he had nothing to say about what they were doing.

But hadn't Frank Sr. just said that Aiuppa would always side with the truth?

"If I did, it was an accident," Frank Sr. said. "He was only there once."

Frank Sr. might have thought Scully was done tying him up with the plea agreement, but not quite. He had admitted to defrauding the dealership, Celozzi-Ettleson, along with his son. And he had agreed he'd conspired with Nick, Frank Jr., and Kurt. He had admitted to laundering money and to trying to get the informant, Matt Russo, to lie to a grand jury.

Frank Sr. denied again that he was running a gambling operation, and he said he wasn't a collector of street tax. The coins the Calabreses collected from peep show booths had a purpose, Frank Sr. told Scully.

"That went to the politicians who were in charge of the First Ward then to help keep these places going," he said.

What about the extortionate payments by Stolfe? Frank Sr. had come into Stolfe's office after not seeing him for years, and suddenly two thugs had appeared demanding money, Scully said. Then Frank Sr. had magically acted as a friend to get the payment lowered. Wasn't that a classic ploy? Wasn't that a textbook good cop–bad cop routine?

"I don't know how you mean," Frank Sr. answered.

The money went to Angelo anyway, he said, and it was coming out of the company and not Stolfe's pocket. Frank Sr. told the jury again that it had been he who had come up with $50,000 finally to pay off the Outfit in order to rescue a man he called his friend.

For hours the prosecutor and Frank Sr. sparred, arguing and talking past each other as Frank Sr. repeatedly denied he was a leader or member of any crew. Scully asked about Nick. Was he lying then when he told the jury all about the recent history of the Chinatown crew and all of the murders? Was he lying when he said he, Frank Sr., and others had stalked Michael Cagnoni to kill him?

"Lying like a pig," Frank Sr. said with a sneer.

As Lopez had done before him, Scully went back to the tapes of Frank Sr. talking to his son in prison. He started to ask Frank Sr. about the murders he seemed to be discussing, and Frank Sr. made repeated denials that he had killed anyone. If he'd wanted to kill someone, he would have gone after the person who had killed Larry Stubich. The talk on the tapes was just that—talk—and all meant to impress his son.

What about having James Marcello watch Nick? The jury had heard Frank Sr. seemingly grow suspicious and order helpers to get a message to the imprisoned mobster to keep an eye on his brother?

"My brother was a very weak person, as you know," Frank Sr. told Scully. He didn't want any problem with his brother. "I was looking for him to have somebody to talk to," he said.

Right, Scully said; he didn't want a problem with his brother, so he needed him taken care of. His brother's word would be hard to combat in court.

Frank Sr. held the side of the witness stand with his right hand and leaned forward toward the prosecutor with his lip curled. It was the angry Frank Sr. who gave off a frightening energy to those watching him in court.

"I sure the hell didn't mean killing anybody," he said angrily.

His knowledge of the making ceremony came from books, he said again, and what he told his son about the murders in the case was spun from newspaper accounts so he could make it sound like he was a part of the Outfit. If he could impress his son, maybe he could win back his loyalty, he said. Frank Jr. sure seemed to look up to his uncle, when it was Nick who was the mobster. He said he had prayed for Cagnoni's widow when she testified, and he wasn't in any crew.

But it sure did seem as if Frank Sr. had inside information, Scully pointed out through use of the tapes. He had spoken about Joey Lombardo getting promoted and about Al "the Pizza Man" Tornabene being a "sleeper" in the Outfit whom no one knew about. Frank Sr. talked about the murders of burglars in response to the Accardo break-in and about the Cicero shooting.

He had never killed anyone, Frank Sr. told Scully again, raising his voice.

"How come I don't get paid?" Frank Sr. said back to Scully. "How come I don't get things like that, you know that?"

His frustrations were finally boiling over. His sons were never in the business, and he had pleaded guilty only to try to help them, he said again. He wasn't a violent man. It was ridiculous to think he was a made member of the Outfit.

"I would never wanna be affiliated with the mob," he said, suddenly noticing Kurt Calabrese seated a few rows back in the gallery. Frank Sr. sat up and pointed over Scully's shoulder while shouting.

"There's my son!" he blurted out. "Ask him; he'd be glad to tell you."

But Kurt wouldn't be telling anyone anything. He left his seat and quickly moved toward the door, waving his hand back over his head as he went through. Many in the gallery turned to watch him go.

Another member of Frank Sr.'s family had turned his back and walked away.

18

TWAN

Unlike some of the men who had appeared on the witness stand before him, Anthony "Twan" Doyle didn't look out of place as a defendant in a high-profile mob trial.

Doyle was thickly built and wore fitted suits. He had dyed hair, a square jaw, and the kind of accent you might expect from a guy who first made his way on street corners and then as a cop, nabbing muggers and pickpockets on "L" trains. And when he told his lawyer, Ralph Meczyk, where he had grown up, the word came out of his mouth as if you were supposed to know what it meant.

"Chinatown."

For Meczyk, having Doyle on the stand was a risk he believed they had to take. The jury was going to hear from his client one way or the other, as prosecutors played their secretly made tapes of Doyle and Mike Ricci meeting with Frank Sr. in prison. Meczyk thought Doyle could handle what he expected would be a withering cross-examination, and the jury needed to hear him explain his actions. Doyle's defense team wanted to suggest that it was Ricci who was really responsible for getting Frank Sr. the inside information. The only way for jurors to understand what Doyle thought he was doing and to get inside his head would be for him to tell them. "Doyle was the case," he would say later.

Those who testified on Doyle's behalf were essentially character witnesses who answered questions about what kind of guy he was. They were former cops who had worked with him on the transit detail and a one-time partner in his evidence section at the courthouse who liked him and trusted him enough to loan him money. Many of them hugged Doyle in the hallway outside of court and slapped his back in support. Meczyk thought the witnesses were key for Doyle, a way to separate his client from the group of alleged mobsters he was on trial with.

One substantive witness was Michael Baka, who had worked alongside Doyle in the evidence section. Baka told the jury that the counter where he and Doyle worked served both police officers and the public, which Doyle's defense hoped would aid them in communicating to the jury that the information Doyle was accused of passing was essentially available to anyone who might have wandered into the courts complex to ask. Entering an inventory number into the computer would cause its location to appear on the screen, not provide detailed statements about what it was, who had it, or why. He was among those who said they had loaned money to Doyle, and Meczyk asked whether Baka had been paid back.

"Absolutely."

As Doyle sat down to testify, the lawyer began by reminding Doyle that he was accused of using his position to obstruct a homicide investigation. Meczyk spoke slowly and deliberately, marking each word.

"Did you commit that offense?" he asked.

"No, sir."

And had he ever collected juice loans, as prosecutors contended, "on behalf of what is commonly known as the Chicago Outfit?"

"No, sir."

Doyle seemed relaxed on the stand, like a police detective in a tie who'd been in court hundreds of times. His air suggested he still believed law enforcement and the court system were his friends.

Doyle had left Chicago some eight years earlier, moving permanently to the desert town of Wickenburg, Arizona, about sixty miles from the center of Phoenix. He was married with two daughters and had volunteered with the Maricopa County Sheriff's Office on a search-and-rescue team to stay somewhat in touch with the career he had retired from back home. At sixty-two, he had settled into a comfortable life in the sun.

His father had been born in the city's First Ward and had worked as a book binder, but he died when Doyle was just fifteen months old. Young Doyle had grown up with the name Passafiume in their South Side enclave of Italian immigrants, and he wound his way through a series of reform schools. It was the kind of neighborhood where everybody knew everybody else but you didn't ask another kid what his father did for a living.

"Some worked for the city; some were bookmakers or might have been this or that," he said.

When he was just three, he had a little playmate next door, a pint-size Ronnie Jarrett.

Doyle answered questions quickly and directly, in a deep and strong voice. He seemed relaxed and confident as he described how he didn't really click with what was going on at school. He bounced from one high school to the next, telling jurors he would occasionally show up until "I was requested not to return."

When he finally ran out of school options, he hung out, he said. His mother supported him, and he used her car and visited guys in the neighborhood. One of those days on a street corner he met Frank Sr., he told the jury. It was at Twenty-Fourth and Princeton; Frank Sr. and Doyle's cousin Anthony pulled over in a car. He recalled that the young Frank Sr. was ten years older and "very muscular," with a bull's chest and big arms. But even with the age difference, the pair would work out and play handball, Doyle said, remembering he was "very comfortable" around Frank Sr.

They had taken a trip to Miami Beach, he told Meczyk, to attend a Teamsters convention where Jimmy Hoffa was elected president of the union. Sometime after that, Frank Sr. offered Doyle a job, inviting him to come see him and Larry Stubich. But Doyle said he believed the men wanted him to collect on juice loans, so he turned it down.

He just wasn't into that, he said.

"I was interested in going and hanging around on the corner."

Doyle said he did eventually let Frank Sr. help him get work. It was with the Teamsters at the convention center. Doyle was brought in to load and unload trailers for shows. Frank Sr. had grown concerned for Doyle and his girlfriend.

"He said, 'You're twenty years old, you have a child coming—how're you gonna support your family?'"

From there Doyle said he turned to the ward organization for a job. He walked neighborhoods, handing out pamphlets for the precinct captain, the kind of machine election work that can often lead to city employment. Doyle said he worked for the water department for a few years and then took his streets and sanitation job, pushing the kind of refuse cart that Meczyk had shown off in his opening statement.

As Meczyk had mentioned so many weeks earlier, Doyle still had his eye on the police department. And by 1971 he was working as a civilian handling the maintenance of police vehicles. The pay was good, he said, but he was constantly being encouraged to apply as a sworn officer. He changed his name from Passafiume to Doyle in 1975 when he started preparing for the police exam, finally passing it, going to the academy, and graduating as an officer in September 1981.

He started in the Twelfth District, he said, and then took a city-wide assignment working mass transit. Often that meant spending time riding trains and buses in plain clothes, Doyle said, performing undercover "lay-downs" on a night shift. Officers would literally lie down in train seats and try to look drunk or passed out, waiting to be mugged. He did it for eight years, making hundreds of arrests, Doyle told the jury. From there he worked in gang crimes on the North Side, concentrating on members of the Latin Kings and La Raza street gangs. Doyle was clearly still enthusiastic about his life as an officer. As he spoke about the work, he became excited, with some of his reserved persona peeling away. He grew a bit more animated, speaking with his hands and talking faster until some of his words ran together.

During his years with the department, Doyle said he lost track of men like Ronnie Jarrett and Frank Sr., recalling seeing his old friend only a few times at weddings and things. He had met Mike Ricci in the 1960s, he said, and then knew he was a Chicago police homicide detective.

Doyle wasn't new to visiting federal prisons when he went to see Frank Sr. One of his oldest friends was Aldo Piscitelli Jr., a convicted loan shark and stepson of Joseph "Shorty" LaMantia of the Twenty-Sixth Street crew. Piscitelli was being housed in a federal facility in Terre Haute, Indiana, and Doyle said he truthfully disclosed his job as a police officer when he filled out forms to visit him. He learned through the grapevine on that visit that his old friend Frank Sr. was at Milan, and would love a visit, too.

Doyle said he'd heard stories about Frank Sr.'s sons turning against him and decided to agree to a visit to support him.

"I thought maybe he was in need of a friend," Doyle told the jury. "When you're not in trouble, you don't need anybody."

Doyle said he went to see Frank Sr. more than once, but the most important visit was on February 19, 1999, the first conversation between the men to be recorded by agents. It was just days after Frank Calabrese Jr. had begun to have success getting his father to talk on tape about his past. Federal agents were listening in the prison visiting room as Ricci and Doyle met with Frank Sr.

Ricci, another of Frank Sr.'s friends, had called him at work the prior month, Doyle said, and had given him an inventory number to look up. Doyle had a computer at the counter of the evidence lockup under the criminal courthouse that could show whether evidence was there for court proceedings or being stored in a larger police warehouse. Ricci had called and made a "routine" request that he took to be police business, Doyle told Meczyk. Ricci asked Doyle to punch the inventory number into the computer. He did, and Doyle said he could see the inventory date of the item and that it had been checked out. It was the extracts from the gloves Nick wore when he shot Fecarotta, but Doyle said he had no idea what homicide investigation the evidence was tied to.

It was "everyday" information about the location of evidence, Doyle said, and he wasn't at all uncomfortable giving it to another police officer. An investigator named Lorri Lewis appeared to have requested records division item 401028.

"Did you have any notion that Lorri Lewis had turned over the extracts to the FBI?" Meczyk asked.

"No," Doyle answered.

The men flew to Michigan together to make the February 1999 visit to Frank Sr., and Doyle said he thought to ask Ricci during the flight, "What's with this inventory number?"

It was only then that Ricci told him it was for Frank Sr., Doyle told the jury.

"He said, 'You know this guy, he asks you for a million things, a million favors. He asked me about this inventory number.'"

During Doyle's visits Frank Sr. would speak to him in "mind-boggling code" and "gibberish" for hours, Doyle told the jury. He claimed to understand little or none of it, and said he felt like he was being paroled when he finally got to leave. He wanted to be a good friend but found that having a lengthy conversation with Frank Sr. was like "reading hieroglyphics," he testified.

It was more of the same during the first conversation that agents taped, Doyle said. Frank Sr. started using strange words he didn't understand, such as "Rotie" or "Rota," meaning Jimmy DiForti.

Did Doyle have any idea what "*Scarpe Grande*" meant, for example?

"Not the slightest," he told Meczyk. It was Frank Sr.'s coded term for the FBI, but Doyle shrugged and said he was again clueless. "Big shoes—I was totally lost."

Doyle said there was a reason jurors didn't hear him interrupt Frank Sr. to ask what in the world he was saying. He was trying to be a good friend and a good listener.

"Basically out of respect, I didn't wanna come out and say, 'Speak to me. What are you talking about? English.'"

He didn't know that Frank Sr. was talking about the Fecarotta evidence, the gloves, when he used the word "purse" instead, Doyle said. Frank Sr. was apparently looking for the date when the gloves were removed from evidence storage to see if they lined up with Jimmy DiForti making bond in his murder case. Frank Sr. was suspicious that DiForti could be an informant, but Doyle said he was in the dark about all of that. He knew DiForti and Ronnie Jarrett had been in an argument, he told the jury, and thought that's what Frank Sr. was interested in.

He also didn't know what Frank Sr. meant when he started talking about "sisters," which was code for DiForti and Frank's own brother Nick.

"I gathered he's talking about somebody else other than myself," Doyle said.

All he wanted to do was end the conversation. "Get it over with."

Meczyk took Doyle through the transcript, stopping on anything that might be incriminating or might suggest that Doyle knew he was helping Frank Sr. get to the bottom of the ongoing investigation.

Doyle certainly seemed to be following along in many places in the recording. He tossed around nicknames himself, calling Ronnie Jarrett by the name "Pancho," which Frank Sr. used. Doyle could be heard to say he had visited Pancho at a restaurant for a discussion about the ongoing situation.

"I'll bet you once it comes to light, I said, I'll bet you it's that fuckin' Mitch Mars; that's what I think I said," Doyle told Frank Sr. on the recording.

Nearby at the prosecutors' table, Mars appeared unfazed, looking down at papers on the table, removing his glasses briefly to wipe his eyes, and putting them right back on.

Meczyk asked Doyle about the quote.

"I'm quoting Ronnie Jarrett," Doyle tried to explain.

Did he know who Mars was at the time?

"No, sir," Doyle told his lawyer.

At points in the transcript where Doyle was seemingly answering "right" and following what Frank Sr. was saying, Doyle claimed he was simply agreeing to be polite and look like he was keeping up. In reality, Doyle testified, to his ears it was all "mumbo jumbo." He didn't know that when Frank Sr. talked about "the Doctor," he meant "Skids" Caruso's son Frank "Toots" Caruso, a man authorities believed had taken up a leading role in the Twenty-Sixth Street crew. Nick had told the FBI that Caruso knew a pharmacist and had supplied Frank Sr. with prescription drugs, perhaps accounting for the nickname.

And Meczyk stopped on the point in the transcript that was the most favorable for Doyle. There was a point in the transcript where Frank Sr. stepped away from Ricci and Doyle for a moment, leaving the two visitors alone in their row of chairs.

"I have to ask you a few things when we get out of this place as to who is who that he's talking about," Doyle could be heard to ask Ricci.

Meczyk had Doyle explain that comment for the jury, believing it showed for sure that Doyle really was playing along the whole time. He definitely didn't know that any of the conversation pertained to Frank Sr.'s brother Nick.

"I didn't know who he was talking about," Doyle said. He had planned to ask Ricci to sort it all out for him on the plane ride home, he claimed.

He was still in a fog, he said, when Frank Sr. had told the men to bring "Pancho" and "the Doctor" up to speed on their suspicions about possible cooperators and possible pressure being put on "the Sister." Frank Sr. wanted Mickey Marcello to be told to get a message to his own brother, James, who was in prison with Nick in Pekin. Ricci and Doyle should deliver the messages, Frank Sr. said.

"We'll take care of that right away," Doyle said on the tape.

Meczyk stopped again, wanting his client to explain that to the jurors. What had he meant by saying that to Frank Sr.?

"Absolutely nothing."

"Why would you say something so stupid?" Meczyk asked.

"Maybe it was a stupid answer," Doyle said. "I had no intention of telling anyone anything." He was no messenger boy, he said, stiffening his back. "I wasn't there to deliver messages to this one or that one."

Well, what about another recording a few months later? Meczyk next turned to May 17, 1999. Doyle and Ricci were back at Milan with Frank Sr., and Doyle seemed to have a message for Frank Sr.

"The 'Little Guy,' ah, said hello," Doyle said on the tape, leading Frank Sr. to correctly guess that Doyle was talking about Pancho, or Ronnie Jarrett. What was that about? Meczyk asked.

"You heard the term *lip service*, Mr. Meczyk? Or members of the jury?" Doyle answered. "Tell them what they want to hear."

Markus Funk would cross-examine Doyle, sure to press him on what seemed like an account of his conversations with Frank Sr. that would be pretty tough for the jury to swallow. Funk had an air of calm, well-schooled intelligence about him, an interesting matchup for the street-smart Doyle, a man who apparently knew the angles like an experienced street cop would.

Funk quickly moved to turn that factor in his favor, asking Doyle about his obvious knowledge of investigative techniques. He knew how police handled evidence, worked undercover, and developed informants. And he knew that criminal organizations, such as street gangs, would sometimes threaten possible cooperators or even develop inside information about them while deciding whether to kill them. Didn't street gangs sometimes use code to avoid detection?

"Occasionally," Doyle answered.

Insider information, Funk pointed out, could allow a criminal to destroy or hide evidence. If the criminal has some idea of what investigators are looking for, he or she could develop a better or more focused alibi. Would Doyle not agree that for such a criminal or criminal organization, the best source of that kind of information would be an insider in law enforcement?

Police information was supposed to be secure. There were regulations against disseminating information, Funk said. Weren't they in effect in the 1990s?

"You were allowed to tell where property was," Doyle answered, looking notably less confident than he had when Meczyk was at the podium.

But property that was known to be police evidence was supposed to be secure. In his job, Doyle had been responsible for hundreds of thousands of pieces of evidence, Funk said. Wasn't maintaining the integrity of the evidence important?

The men went back and forth over what Doyle would have seen on his computer, located at the counter of his evidence section in the basement of the courthouse. He couldn't have known the name of the victim in the case the evidence was tied to or even what the item of evidence was, Doyle said.

"I'd never heard of the bloody gloves," Doyle said. He wouldn't have typed in a victim's name, such as "Fecarotta."

Funk pushed the issue, but Doyle maintained that he never knew he was talking about gloves when he spoke to Frank Sr. Nowhere in the transcript would the prosecutor find a line where he had specifically mentioned what the item of evidence was, Doyle said. When he went to Milan, he gave Frank Sr. a date that something had been moved.

"You knew Frank Calabrese Sr. was an Outfit boss," Funk said accusingly.

"No, sir, I didn't," Doyle answered. "Not that he was an Outfit boss."

Well, you at least knew he was involved in bookmaking and juice loans.

"I was given permission by the federal bureau of corrections to visit Mr. Calabrese," Doyle answered. Doyle would make the argument that because he had filled out the proper forms to make a prison visit and included his employment, it constituted an allowance to see Frank Sr. Chicago police rules themselves prohibited officers from associating with known felons.

Funk acted thoroughly puzzled by that contention. Frank Sr. was Doyle's old Outfit boss, he would repeatedly say to Doyle, and he had been summoned. Did Doyle really believe the Federal Bureau of Prisons would go to every police department in the United States to check regulations and clear visits by officers to inmates?

"Of course not, Mr. Funk," Doyle said.

Under questioning by the prosecutor, Doyle again denied collecting juice loans for Frank Sr., and said he knew he was involved with a street crew only by reading it in the paper. But Funk pressed him on whether he hadn't worked with men such as Ronnie Jarrett. Nick had testified that when Doyle went to become a police officer, Frank Sr. had been upset to lose a good man. That was more like the truth, wasn't it? The idea that Frank Sr. was a "friend in need" was bogus, wasn't it? Funk asked.

"It's the truth, Mr. Funk."

The prosecutor was trying to draw a tighter and tighter circle around Doyle, who, like Joey Lombardo and Frank Sr. before him, was growing more agitated on the stand. Funk pressed again. Doyle, a police officer, had been ordered by an old Outfit boss to see him in prison and bring information he had access to about a murder that the boss had been involved in, Funk said again. That was the core of the matter.

"You knew the gloves contained physical evidence from a murder involving Frank Calabrese Sr.," Funk said again.

"The answer is no," Doyle said, with a more combative tone in his voice. He stared back at the prosecutor at the podium.

"You thought it was OK to give an Outfit boss information about a murder investigation?" Funk said, pointing toward Frank Sr. at his table.

"I had no idea it was a murder investigation."

Doyle continued to argue that the information he had given Ricci and Frank Sr. was common, and that he could have given it to any member of the public who had come into the courthouse or called his evidence unit.

Funk began to question Doyle about other things that Frank Sr. had said on tapes made by his son. Frank Sr. had said he had police contacts who were going to see him. "They're gonna tell me some more," Frank Sr. had claimed. If one of the contacts had had the chance, Frank Sr. said, he would have "glommed" the gloves, meaning snatched them.

"You said that?" Funk asked.

"Absolutely not."

Doyle blamed Ricci at least in part for calling and bringing him to see Frank Sr. Well, if that was true, and Doyle had learned what was really going on only when he got to Michigan, when was the first time Doyle had written an internal affairs report informing supervisors that Ricci had sought to pass information on a murder investigation to an Outfit member?

"For the tenth time, I didn't know it dealt with a homicide," said Doyle, getting more and more bent out of shape each time Funk found a new way to ask the same question.

Doyle continued to tell the jury that he was completely confused by Frank Sr.'s "gibberish."

So Funk pulled out each apparent code word to see what Doyle's understanding could be.

Doyle seemed to agree that "Pancho" was Ronnie Jarrett, but that's where the agreement ended.

"Sisters" meant brothers, right? Mickey Marcello and James Marcello, Funk said, and Nick was a sister, too. A "sickly sister" was an Outfit member who might cooperate, and "the Doctor" was "Toots" Caruso, who might have to write a prescription for a sickly sister. The "hospital" was prison, a "prostitute" was a cooperator, and the "purse" was the bloody gloves. When Nick was described as "fragile," it meant he could easily flip.

Doyle had grown irritated, and he was staying that way. He shrugged and said he thought Nick was dealing with back problems and depression. Funk was reading out of the "sixth page of the Calabrese-English dictionary," Doyle said, bristling.

Funk pointed to the page of the transcript where Frank Sr. had directed his visitors to tell "the Doctor" what was going on and to send a message that Nick should be closely watched. One of them should tell Marcello "what was missing," Frank Sr. had said. James Marcello should know a question was swirling: "why would somebody out of the clear blue sky, out of a hundred purses, take her purse?"

Doyle repeated that he was only paying lip service. He had no intention of delivering any messages but wanted to nod along and not come off like a goof in front of his old friend.

"I didn't want to look like a chumbalone," he said, using a Chinatown slang word, "an idiot."

Three of the five defendants had now testified, but the momentum would carry no further.

Paul Schiro continued to sit at his table, expressionless. Throughout the summerlong trial, he had been still as a glassy pool, watching things unfold before him without a hint of a reaction to anything. Only as he left court would he smile and shake a hand of his lawyer or a codefendant. He wouldn't testify, and he wouldn't call any witnesses. His defense was that Nick Calabrese was a killer and a liar, by nature unreliable, and that nothing had been said about him that should spell a conviction.

James Marcello had kept a poker face, as well, even when his mistress was on the stand telling the world how she had played the reputed mob boss for a fool, taking his money for her loyalty almost up until the moment she testified.

Marcello's defense would come in the form of stipulations—agreements between his lawyers and prosecutors that would be read to the jury. Both sides would agree on the facts and could argue them later if they wished. Marcello's first stipulation was an interesting one. It concerned his own birth certificate—a copy from December 13, 1943, that featured the names of his parents. His father, Samuel Marcello, was listed, as was his mother, Irene Flynn, the lady with roots on the "Emerald Isle." Nick had said that only full-blooded Italians could be made members of the mob. So, here it was for the jury in black and white.

Another stipulation was the details of an FBI interview in 1988. An agent had spoken to Michelle Spilotro, Michael's daughter, who testified at the trial about "Jim" calling her house and knowing who that was. She had said that one of the calls came the day her father disappeared. But when she was interviewed less than two years after his death, her story didn't exactly match up. After a second call from "Jim" the day before the disappearance, her father had told her he wouldn't be attending the party the next evening, and the agent interviewing Michelle had noted that she stated she didn't know who Jim was. On the day the Spilotros were murdered, her father seemed to be in a good mood, Michelle had apparently told the agents. He had taken phone calls, she said, but none had seemed important.

But the key evidence for Marcello would come in the final stipulation read by his lawyers. In one of Nick's debriefing sessions, on June 30, 2005, he had been speaking with FBI agents Michael Maseth and Luigi Mondini. The agents were asking about the Spilotro murders and exactly who was there in the house in the subdivision in 1986.

One of the names Nick mentioned was ranking mobster Rocky Infelice, the man Mitch Mars had prosecuted for conspiring to kill a bookmaker. Nick had told the agents he saw Infelice, standing in a hallway, and that he believed he was at a restaurant after the killings.

The thing was, on June 14, 1986, federal agents happened to be tapping the phone in the home Infelice shared with his wife in River Forest, west of Chicago. And Infelice was on and off it virtually the whole day. Marcello's lawyers had the monitoring log and clips of conversations for the jury to hear. There was no way Infelice could have been there. In Nick's testimony, prosecutors asked him about Infelice, and he had said he only thought he saw Infelice.

But Tom Breen was going to drive the point home. Any opening to cast doubt on what Nick had said needed to be fully exploited. The lawyers pointed to nearly thirty calls to and from the Infelice house that day. Calls came in from friends talking about dinner reservations, and calls went out as Infelice, who dealt in bookmaking, apparently called a sports hot line to get the latest scores and horse-racing results.

As August was drawing to a close, jurors had been hearing evidence for most of the summer, and they had listened to more than one hundred witnesses in all. The trial had covered decades of Outfit dirty work, assigning blame in some of the most high-profile mob murders in Chicago during the last thirty years of the 1900s. Nick Calabrese had taken his place among the most significant witnesses anywhere in the United States to turn his back on his former life and testify against organized crime.

Nick had been most damaging to his brother, but he had blamed every man on trial for something. So with closing arguments ready to begin, all expected the defense to take a final stab at discrediting him and to color the government's star cooperator as a prolific killer who had woven a detailed string of lies together in a final effort to shed as much blame as he could. The defense attorneys would do as much as possible to show that Nick, when his own back was to the wall, had lied to give the government the kind of information it needed to solve more than a dozen hits. Once Nick's DNA was found on the gloves in the Fecarotta murder, they would argue, this is what he had concocted in an effort to once again draw breath outside the walls of a federal prison.

Some of the men had never met before Nick brought them together. Lombardo at one early court date had given Doyle a puzzled look and asked, "Who are you?" as if he were an intruder. By the end of the trial the defendants regularly shook hands or hugged as they came and went from court. It had settled into its own routine. Jurors came and went and took notes and ate together, then passed one another peppermints in a plastic cup while in the jury box. A group of regular court watchers took up their favorite seats. Reporters chatted about the Cubs or did crossword puzzles as they waited for the proceedings to begin.

Now there would be one last opportunity for the lawyers to tell jurors what all of the evidence had meant.

One last opportunity for prosecutors to stand by Nick as a man who once was mired in the Chicago mob but was being truthful as he broke from his bloody past.

And one last opportunity for the defense lawyers to try to argue their clients out from under the crushing weight of a case destined to take its place among the greatest government efforts of all time against the Chicago Outfit.

19

CLOSING ARGUMENTS

"The truth is somewhere between the clouds."

That's what Joseph Lopez had said when he first addressed the jury in June.

It was seemingly a statement about relativism. The truth is up there someplace, and it's up to each of us to gaze skyward and try to figure it out. Ten people can look up as clouds are rolling by on a breezy day and see ten different things. A camel. A butterfly. A swan. What you see is up to you.

But for Markus Funk and the rest of the prosecution team, that wasn't what the Family Secrets case was about. It was about accountability. It was about the people left behind as the Outfit took lives, those who had appeared in court to tell the jury about their loss. It was about Emma Seifert; Michael Cagnoni's widow, Margaret Wenger; and others. Yes, there *was* truth to be found, Funk told the jury as he gave the case's first closing argument.

"The truth in this case is what you heard from this witness stand."

James Marcello. He had suborned perjury and obstructed justice by encouraging his mistress, Connie, to lie to a grand jury. He had paid hush money to Nick and controlled an illegal video poker business with his brother. He had personally been involved in the killings of Nicholas D'Andrea and the Spilotro brothers as well as one attempted murder. The plan had been to interrogate D'Andrea, but his skull had been smashed with the butt of a shotgun in a car Marcello drove. The Spilotro brothers had been lured to their doom with promises of promotions, and Marcello had helped set up their murder and execute it, Funk said. Anthony Spilotro had called Marcello from his brother's dental office. And the jury had heard from Michael Spilotro's wife and daughter about calls from "Jim" and Michael's last day on earth. "No one gave James Marcello the license to decide between life and death."

Joey Lombardo. He had tried to extort Morris Shenker, Funk argued, despite his laughable claim to have only been playacting "like James Cagney." He could plainly be heard threatening Shenker's life if he didn't give the mob its due and promising that he had an army behind him. He had extorted porn shops and massage parlors and even admitted running a dice game. And he had personally orchestrated the "cold-blooded" murder of Daniel Seifert. The message was that you don't cooperate with law enforcement, and the killing had paid off "in a perverse way," Funk noted. The pension fraud case against Lombardo and his cohorts had disintegrated after Seifert was eliminated. "There's nothing funny about the jokester, the Clown, Lombardo."

Frank Calabrese Sr. He ran an expansive juice loan operation that employed agents and collectors and funneled money up the Outfit hierarchy. Frank Sr. had told jurors he never resorted to violence, but he hadn't made millions "just by being a nice guy," Funk told the jury. He was an extortionist and imposed street taxes. "This man right there was involved in the murders of thirteen human beings," Funk said, pointing at the sneering Frank Sr., who sat back in his chair and began to chuckle again as the prosecutor motioned his way. Nick had given the jury a detailed account of many of those killings, and the evidence in the case corroborated him. The hours of recordings in the case made Frank Sr. a liar, Funk said. Frank Sr. was on tape telling his son about murders, and then he outrageously told the jury he was only trying to impress his boy.

Paul Schiro. He was involved in Outfit burglaries. He was the Chicago syndicate's man in Phoenix, an extension of its lucrative Las Vegas arm. He had helped kill his friend, Emil Vaci, who was talking to authorities about missing slot manager Jay Vandermark. "He was spending too much time in the grand jury for the Outfit's liking," Funk said.

Anthony Doyle. He collected on juice loans for Frank Sr. in the 1960s, though he had claimed to have turned down the job. But Doyle could be heard on the tapes of Frank Sr. talking about Ronnie Jarrett and ongoing street operations outside the prison walls. He had been taped joking that Nick needed "shock treatment." He was a corrupt police officer who had looked up information on a murder investigation for the Outfit, and he had passed it to a reputed leader of a violent street crew.

Funk told jurors to think about all they had heard and to compare it with the positions the defense had taken. Marcello's lawyers had called him innocent. Lombardo was supposedly "sort of an affable, funny guy who liked to playact." Frank Sr. was "a family man," and another playactor. Schiro's attorney had said he too had nothing to do with the Outfit. And Doyle had no idea why he was in trouble, even though his exchanges with Frank Sr. had been caught on tape. "He was indicted for buying a ham sandwich for Frank Sr.," Funk said derisively about the defense.

The government had provided accurate information as the jury looked for the truth, Funk continued. And even though members of the panel were about to sift through months of testimony from dozens of witnesses, they had what the prosecutor said was a fairly easy job.

"The evidence makes it clear that these defendants are guilty many times over," Funk told them confidently. "These men are about making money, about accruing power for themselves, about accruing money for the Chicago Outfit."

No one had given the men the right to do the things they did, he went on. His voice was tense, with more than a hint of indignation at the five defendants in the room with him. Who did they think they were? Who said they could just walk into a business and demand money?

"Ask yourself, who are these people?" Funk said. "The reason these people have that kind of power is fear. They know how to instill fear in other human beings."

A few of the jurors took notes as Funk spoke, while most sat upright and just listened, taking in the summary and watching the room. He began walking them through all of the evidence they had heard but stopped first to address some of those the government had called to testify. Many had been players in the world of the Chicago mob—"very bad people"—who wouldn't have been among those whom prosecutors would have chosen to carry their case. Many were crooks themselves, or worse.

Chief among them of course was Nick Calabrese.

"It's pretty hard to come up with someone who's more cold-hearted than that," Funk acknowledged. "We didn't hold a casting call for witnesses."

The fact that some of them were less than saints wasn't the government's fault, he offered; it was the five men on trial who had brought the witnesses to court. Many of those the jury had heard from were the associates of the defendants, people they had recruited and selected for Outfit work. Nick was a troubling person to be sure, but the jury had a lot of other evidence to rely on that corroborated his testimony, Funk told them.

Prosecutors had shown that there was a conspiracy and that the men had been part of it. They had participated in the acts of the conspiracy, agreeing with other members to carry it out. The members had acted with the common purpose of making money and furthering the mob's goals. The jury had heard over and over about the organization and its chain of command. Decisions were made from the top down, with bosses giving orders to soldiers who brutally carried out their directions.

Some of the excuses and explanations and recordings the jury had heard were ridiculous, Funk told them. From Frank Sr., who regretted most of all that he had burned a holy card in his hand, to the hapless Joey Lombardo unwittingly snapped in the "Last Supper" photo. "He just happened in for a sandwich."

Funk explained that to find a defendant guilty, the jurors would have to decide that he had taken part in two or more of the predicate offenses in the conspiracy—murder, gambling, imposing street tax, the collection of juice loans, obstruction of justice. They would need to find that there was a pattern of racketeering and that the defendant had associated with the enterprise and knowingly conspired with others.

There were a few types of murders in the case, Funk told them. Some were Outfit members killed for not following the organization's rules, for example, William "Butch" Petrocelli and the Spilotro brothers. Others were associates or payers of street tax who had run afoul of the mob, such as Michael Cagnoni. And many others were suspected of cooperating—Daniel Seifert, Michael "Hambone" Albergo, and William Dauber, for example. And some were in the wrong place at the wrong time: Charlotte Dauber, Arthur Morawski, and Donald Renno.

Nick probably wasn't someone you'd ask out to lunch, Funk allowed, but you could tell he was telling the truth. Frank Sr., Marcello, and Doyle had all been captured on tape discussing the possibility that Nick could be telling authorities what he knew.

"Ask yourself why are they so concerned about Nick Calabrese if he's just a guy telling stories?" Funk told the jury.

Frank Sr. had even said he would give his blessing for something to happen to Nick if it were discovered that he was in fact helping *"Scarpe Grande."*

"Does that sound like a guy spinning fairy tales for his son?"

Frank Sr. was sitting at his table, watching as Funk spoke to the jury. And he was smiling.

Funk noticed and immediately stopped talking. He gave his own stare back to Frank Sr.

"There's nothing to smile about in this case," he said.

Frank Sr. was staring at Funk, smirking and shaking his head. A juror would later tell prosecutors that a few members of the panel had actually seen him mouth the words *You're a fucking dead man* in Funk's direction, but no one seated near him actually heard him utter it.

Lombardo sat with his head tilted, watching Funk through his tinted glasses. Doyle, Schiro, and Marcello listened with mostly glazed looks as the prosecutor outlined the case against each of them, and Frank Sr. steamed as Funk told the jury that the extraordinary amount of evidence they had heard had been enough for them to reach guilty verdicts "many times over."

"We ask you to find these five men guilty because, ladies and gentlemen, they *are* guilty."

It was clear that the defense lawyers would have to use their closing arguments to attack Nick, and they didn't disappoint. Marc Martin was first, reminding jurors that they were to carefully consider the cooperator's motives, interest, and bias when they weigh his testimony. Nick had told them he had decided to aid investigators in an attempt to avoid the death penalty. Wasn't it clear that he would like to save himself?

"He has spent his adult life lying, cheating, conniving, committing crimes, and getting away with it," Martin said.

Think about the kind of man they were talking about, he said. Vaci had been dragged into a van in a Phoenix parking lot. He had looked into Nick's face and literally begged for his life.

"He responds with a bullet to the head."

Nick had splashed lighter fluid onto the face of a man he had just killed, Martin reminded the jury, referring to the killing of Petrocelli and the attempt to burn his body in his car. What did an oath to tell the truth really mean to this person?

The case had profound implications for Marcello, and the jury was being asked to make a profound decision based on the word of Nick. If he told you it was raining outside, you'd need to go out and check for yourself.

"This is a man that a long time ago decided his life, Nick Calabrese's life, was more valuable than the life of others," Martin said, pacing back and forth before the jury.

The first witness of the trial, the "mobologist" James Wagner, president of the Crime Commission, had testified that top-echelon informants have been known to lie. Nick was simply bringing Marcello, a reputed mob boss, into the case and tying him to high-profile murders to get the best arrangement for himself.

Look at the D'Andrea killing, Martin suggested to the jury. There was much about Nick's version of events that either was not corroborated by the evidence or simply made no sense.

Prosecutors and Nick had talked about D'Andrea's skull being crushed, but an autopsy performed on D'Andrea showed no fractures. Nick had described him as a hulking man who was hard to bring down, but the same autopsy showed D'Andrea was just five foot one. And Nick had said his ankles were tied or taped, but there was no evidence of that, either.

Apparently there was no surveillance or planning of the murder, and Marcello couldn't be linked to it with forensic evidence. Nick said he was just told to show up, Martin stated, and he testified he had met Marcello there for the very first time. Did it make sense to bring strangers, rather than trusted associates, together for a murder? Then four men had been driving on public streets while one of them supposedly beat D'Andrea to death in the backseat.

"You don't think someone would notice something like that?"

Nick needed to put Marcello at the 1981 murder to support his contention that Marcello was at the making ceremony in 1983, an induction that Martin said sounded as if Nick had concocted it from tidbits in books and other places in the public domain. Nick had said there were two qualifications before someone could become a made member: the candidate had to have committed a murder for the mob, and he had to be 100 percent Italian.

As Martin spoke, his points appeared on the overhead screen with a pea green background and decorated with a bright shamrock. Marcello was not full-blooded Italian, Martin reminded the jury as observers in the courtroom laughed quietly at the graphic. The government had stipulated to the Irish descent of his mother.

"You know she was Irish; she had fourteen children," Martin said. The only thing truthful about Nick's claim that Marcello was made "was he made it up."

There was no direct evidence that Marcello had participated in the attempted murder of Nick Sarillo, the man bombed in his van, Martin said. It was just the word of Nick again. Likewise, there was nothing to corroborate Nick's claim that Marcello had bankrolled the effort to murder Vaci in Arizona.

When it came to the Spilotro murders, Nick had more motivation than ever to lie, Martin claimed, and it was another crime with no physical evidence pointing to Marcello. That was the marquee pair of killings in the Family Secrets case, and Nick knew he had to solve it for investigators in order to get his deal. When Patrick Spilotro had secretly taped Nick, he had said he didn't know anything about it.

The plan to kill the brothers had seemingly been put together too quickly if Nick were to be believed, Martin argued. And the plan he talked about had resulted in numerous Outfit members supposedly hanging around a suburban subdivision in broad daylight. Everyone allegedly was wearing gloves, and the brothers didn't notice? Nick had said Michael had come down the stairs to where he was waiting in the basement and had shaken his hand. That would have given away the ploy.

"They would've been running for the back door," Martin said with an incredulous tone. "Michael would have been going for his gun. [Nick] gave them this offense because he felt he had to solve it to get his deal and save his life."

Nick couldn't even point to the house where it had supposedly taken place.

"Of course he couldn't," Martin said. "If he could point out the house, it would be something we could check out."

The autopsies in the case also seemed to contradict Nick, Martin said. Dr. Pless had said the men suffered a mass beating, which Nick didn't seem to see. He had talked about a rope being used, but Pless found no ligature marks on the brothers' necks. Nick had mentioned wiping up one small spot of blood from the floor, when the autopsy showed the brothers had basically drowned in it.

And there was the Rocco Infelice problem. Nick had told the FBI in one of his debriefings that he saw the mobster there, but the government wiretap on Infelice's home phone had proven him wrong. Michelle Spilotro had said her father left their house in Oak Park at 2:00 P.M. to go to his meeting. Infelice could be heard making calls on his phone all afternoon, chatting with friends and listening to sports scores. At 3:12, 3:50, 4:53, Infelice was still at his house.

It all added up to reasonable doubt, Martin said. "Nicholas Calabrese lied."

There were problems with the testimony of the Spilotro family members, too, he argued. When they were interviewed at the time of the killings in 1986, they had said nothing about calls from Marcello. Michelle Spilotro told the FBI her father had not taken any significant calls on the Saturday of his disappearance. And if he had, where were the phone records? The government hadn't produced anything to show a call from Marcello to the home.

All five of the defendants were watching closely as Martin leaned toward the jury and spoke in a low, earnest voice. They seemed very focused and interested in what Martin had to say.

The case was really about a dysfunctional family, the Calabreses, Martin argued. The jury had heard a bunch of babbling and coded nonsense on most of the tapes between Frank Sr. and Frank Jr., and little of it had anything to do with Marcello. And when Marcello was taped talking with his brother about a possible investigation, Martin said, it was only because he did not want to get dragged into anything and falsely implicated.

When he was released from prison, he stayed in the Chicago area, knowing that an investigation was brewing. He lived in the suburbs and went about his business. He had every chance to run, but he stayed home and, yes, took care of Connie.

"And that's it."

For Lombardo, Susan Shatz and Rick Halprin would provide the closing argument as a tag-team. Shatz started off by going back over the evidence related to the work car, the Ford LTD that had been recovered after the Seifert killing.

The man who had sold the car had been unable to identify Lombardo in any photo lineup, as investigators were working to learn the identity of "David Kemp," the name used by the purchaser of the car. And as Lombardo's defense team had been arguing all along,

Lombardo easily could have inadvertently touched the title application that showed his fingerprint if the sheet had been in the office of Irwin Weiner. His secretary was a notary whose name appeared on some of the papers. The dates showed that the documents "would've been lying in Mr. Weiner's office for as long as four days."

Prosecutors had tried to show that Lombardo bought the police scanner that was found in the car, but that too was less than definitive, Shatz argued. One clerk at the store where it was bought, a teenager at the time, was able to point to a photo of Lombardo as the person who had bought it. On the sales receipt was the signature *Savard*, which also appeared on other sales slips from purchases made at the store. It was Weiner who had directed his employees to sign for equipment using that moniker, she said, and it was arguably Weiner who had the most to lose if Seifert had survived to testify. Weiner was the owner of businesses wrapped up in the alleged loan scheme, giving him "enormous motive" to want Seifert silenced.

Shatz had addressed the specific points of evidence against Lombardo, leaving Halprin to pick up the bulk of the argument by turning his attention to the big picture.

"Joey Lombardo could easily have been a member of the Chicago Outfit if he had chosen to be," Halprin began. He had grown up in the old neighborhood, was Italian, and had friends who were linked to organized crime. But Joey had a different idea, he said. Lombardo used his connections to people who were members and money-making associates of the mob to further himself.

Many of the men accused of conspiring along with Lombardo were now dead, Halprin noted, as was the man whom Nick said had named Lombardo as taking part in Seifert's killing. Nick said that Fecarotta had told him at a restaurant that Lombardo had been involved, and no one would be prosecuted for repeating what a dead man had supposedly said.

"Especially if you're the person who killed him," Halprin said.

And there was the testimony of Lombardo himself for Halprin to contend with. The lawyer called him an "agenda-driven defendant" and said he hadn't been completely truthful with the jury. Lombardo hadn't identified Joey "Doves" Aiuppa as a mobster, for example.

"He doesn't trust you," Halprin said. "He's frightened to death of you. He doesn't believe any twelve of you will give him a fair shake."

That was because of his past, Halprin said, which included the two prior convictions for conduct that Lombardo contended was misunderstood by other juries. He was a seventy-eight-year-old man. He had a history and a name. Lombardo was scared to make certain statements because he again assumed he would be punished simply for his associations.

Mars had made Lombardo look like "a ridiculous old fool" in some of the testimony, but the government hadn't provided enough clear evidence to convict Lombardo this time around, Halprin offered. He reminded the panel of his client's "double defense": Lombardo had testified that he didn't kill Seifert and he was not a capo in the Chicago Outfit. But if the jury chose to believe otherwise, they could also decide that Lombardo had withdrawn from any conspiracy upon leaving prison in 1992. His newspaper ad denying any Outfit connections was as good as a public denouncement and withdrawal of his past life.

The jury might think the conversation with Morris Shenker proved Lombardo was in fact a mobster.

"Dead wrong!" Halprin bellowed, grabbing the jury's attention with his echoing voice. Lombardo was associated with men in both camps—the organized crime world and the world of the powerful associate. He hustled his way into relationships with people like Allen Dorfman. The conversation with Shenker was an example of Lombardo helping Dorfman, whose dabblings with the Teamsters were certainly suspect.

Lombardo was trying to get Shenker to honor his debt and wasn't really acting on behalf of the Outfit. He had effectively become a "rent-a-mobster" for Dorfman when he had promised Shenker he would never reach seventy-three. It was all pretend, and the government hadn't proven otherwise, Halprin said, arguing the case was nothing but "rumors, half-assed suspicion, and innuendo."

Lombardo wasn't some Outfit kingpin. He had no cars, no cash, and "no country homes." He was an old man who had hustled himself into prison in the past. He had been reporting a stolen wallet when Seifert was killed, not driving a getaway car or taking part in the shooting itself. Lombardo had done his time, and since 1992 he had done nothing to bring the attention of law enforcement. With all of the government's informants and all of its surveillances, Halprin said, something would have been developed against Lombardo had he been involved at all in the affairs of the Chicago mob after 1992.

It was a well-organized and well-presented case, Halprin said, but it was now up to the jury to decide what to do to Lombardo. Finding Lombardo innocent of the charges in the case would not be redemption, he told the jury.

"Redemption is a judgment that will have to come from a higher power than any court."

The defense arguments had started with a pair of focused attempts to explain away the government's evidence. They had been delivered in classic form by a pair of distinguished, veteran Chicago lawyers. Martin and Halprin were polished attorneys whose closing comments had been controlled and marked by measured and careful arguments centered on the facts at issue. Both men had made specific attacks on the prosecutors' version of events, toning down the trial's circus feel.

And then, once again, it was Joseph Lopez's turn.

Lopez rose from his defense table in a trademark black suit and his pink socks. He wore a black-and-pink checkered tie that seemed designed to induce seizures and to glow with battery power.

"This country was founded by people who rebelled against the government," Lopez told the jury. "Don't forget Valley Forge—where George Washington marched his troops on bleeding feet."

Because of the Constitution and "bloodshed on American soil," we enjoy certain rights, he said. Defendants enjoy a right to a trial by jury, and they are presumed innocent. It's up to a jury to hear the evidence, believe whatever part of it they wish, and put together the truth.

"Just like putting together something from IKEA."

Lopez agreed that the case was actually a family feud. It starred Nick "the Grim Reaper" and "I Cannot Do Time" Frank Jr. And it was peppered with crooks and hustlers and con men. "Rats swim in the sewer," he explained. Prosecutors had handpicked the cast of criminals, he argued, offering immunity to those the government wanted the jury to hear from.

Frank Jr. had written his letter to the FBI to get out of jail, and he had been lying ever since, Lopez said. He was a thief who had stolen from his father—not exactly the kind of person you could trust to deliver the truth. The taped conversation in prison portrayed a lying son and a father who wasn't telling the truth, either, as he tried to impress his wayward kid.

"You have two people trying to out-B.S. each other."

Frank Jr. had driven a wedge between his father and his uncle Nick.

"Junior has destroyed his family. People in this room that never did a darn thing to him," Lopez insisted. Now he gets to "sit in Arizona making pizzas," he continued, drawing a laugh.

Frank Jr. contacted the feds because he wasn't man enough to do time, Lopez charged. He had once bragged about his Outfit connections, and now he was complaining. Frank Sr. had never stuck a gun in Frank Jr.'s mouth, the lawyer promised. The son was just a "cunning and conniving little person," Lopez told the jury.

"Poor Frankie boy; 'Daddy was mean to me,'" Lopez said mockingly.

Don't listen to him; he's a thief and a cocaine addict, Lopez insisted. If you invited him to dinner, he'd steal your silverware.

"He'd probably take the soap out of your bathroom, too, if it was nice enough."

Nick wasn't much better, Lopez said. He had appeared to testify and had sat in the witness chair, unable to look anyone in the eye as he testified. He told lie after lie.

"Nothing but a walking piece of deception is what he is."

Nick had cried like a baby to "Mommy FBI," Lopez said, beginning to find a groove. He was like a preacher winding up, but the only congregation that mattered was in the jury box. Few were taking many notes, choosing instead to watch Lopez and look around the courtroom, wondering what they should be thinking.

Three state's attorneys in several counties had given Nick a pass on a host of murders, Lopez argued, and all because Nick had been caught in his crimes and blamed his brother, a man he obviously hated. Nick had taken no responsibility for his own conduct. Instead, Lopez said, it was Frank made him do this and Frank made him do that. It seemed as if Nick couldn't go to the bathroom without his brother's permission, he told the jury.

"Did Frank tell you to cut the head off a dog?" Lopez asked a Nick who, of course, wasn't there. There was nothing to feel sorry for when it came to Nick, "the Grim Reaper."

"He would shoot you in the head over a cold ravioli."

It was a line that Lopez would later say he had made up on the fly. The next morning, it was stripped across the front page of the *Tribune* with a large courtroom sketch of Lopez in midsentence with his hands in the air.

Nick had run the Chinatown crew with Jimmy LaPietra, Lopez continued. He was a sadist who would cut people's throats, move bodies, and then go have coffee. This was someone the jury should listen to? The jury had heard of man's best friend, he said; well, Nick had beheaded him.

Prosecutors were doing their best not to react to the argument, while those in the gallery continued to chuckle along. Mars sat at the government's table, rocking in his chair with his head tilted back, looking at the ceiling for a few minutes.

Lopez moved finally to some of the specific allegations leveled against his client but continued with his rapid-fire delivery.

James Stolfe of Connie's Pizza was "another liar." Frank Sr. was a partner in a Naperville restaurant venture with him, and they had vacationed together.

The Ortiz and Morawski murders hadn't happened as Nick had said. Lopez said he had presented reliable witnesses who had seen only one shooter. Nick would just paste together stories around published facts to try to make things sound good.

The Albergo murder. Well, for one, there was no evidence he had even been killed, Lopez argued. There was no body where Nick had said Albergo was buried. How did the two brothers manage to dig through packed clay with a hand shovel? How did construction crews not notice a fresh hole in an area where they were supposed to pour a floor?

The making ceremony—it was a concoction from a book, Lopez told the jury. There was no gambling operation, and there was no enterprise. There was only "the Starship *Enterprise*," Lopez said. The entire thing was a myth. *FBI* should stand for "Forever Bothering Italians." What people said in the neighborhood was not evidence.

Even the famous photo of the old mob leaders at the restaurant didn't show anything but a bunch of "grumpy old men drinking Corvo," Lopez said. "The enterprise died with them on the last clam."

There was no sign that Ronnie Jarrett's mother-in-law's garage had been a killing room. In fact, there was no physical evidence linking Frank Sr. to any murder, Lopez said as his client nodded along. There was no DNA, no fingerprints, no hairs, no fibers, no photos, no phone records, and no bloody gloves belonging to Frank Sr. There were no work cars or masks or radios, Lopez said, no guns or anything beyond Nick's word. He could have called plenty of witnesses to rebut the claim that Frank Sr. was a hit man, the defense attorney said, but Nick had killed them all.

If anything, Frank Sr. was a moneymaker. It made no sense for him to be doing the kind of heavy work that Nick described.

"You don't put the earner out on the street to catch the arrow."

Lopez also put up a series of images on the overhead screen. There was a cartoon crying infant when the lawyer said Nick had acted like a baby and a cartoon cut of meat when he said Nick had roasted Frank Sr. like a burned pork chop. The lawyer urged the jury to consider Frank Sr.'s words, both in the recordings and on the witness stand. He had told them that he liked seats in the back of the theater. Frank Sr. worked sixteen hours a day, and none of his loan customers had appeared as a witness to say that he had been violent.

The government hadn't proven him guilty beyond a reasonable doubt, Lopez said. Frank Sr. should be viewed through a veil of innocence.

"Like Casper the Friendly Ghost."

*

The soft-spoken Paul Wagner would have a bit of a tough act to follow. He focused on the specifics of the case against Paul "the Indian" Schiro.

The "evidence" consisted entirely of the words of three people, Wagner said, Nick and former Schiro associates Richard Cleary and Sal Romano. The jury members might remember something their mothers had probably told them, he said: consider the source. And aside from the claims of those three "derelicts of society," the government had presented nothing else.

"These men are walking, talking reasonable doubt."

Again, there was no DNA evidence, no gambling records, and no wiretaps. There was also no mention of "Pauly" or "the Indian" in any of the recordings made of some of the defendants in prison, Wagner pointed out.

Prosecutors had overstated Schiro's importance in connection with the Outfit. Schiro was really just a burglar who counted Anthony Spilotro as a lifelong friend. Markus Funk had gone as far as putting words in a witness's mouth, Wagner said. Michael Spilotro's wife, Ann, had said that her husband had told her Schiro was one of the few people he and Anthony trusted, but Funk had argued that Michelle Spilotro said it as well. It just went to show that prosecutors were willing to be creative with the truth to get the jury to believe their view of the men in the case, Wagner argued.

There was no evidence that Schiro was a mob heavyweight or that he had devised the plan to kill Vaci. Who was in charge of that operation? "The made man, Nick Calabrese."

The victims in the case were his, and now the government was asking the jury to take his word, Wagner said.

"In large part he's a person who has forfeited his claim to live in decent society," he said. "He's a stone-cold killer."

What weight could possibly be given to his account? Nick was a man who had admitted to killing innocent people, such as Arthur Morawski. He was facing no local murder charges and no doubt expected to walk out of prison one day to see his children again.

Schiro was just an add-on and a good one for Nick to come up with because, unlike most of the people he had named as being involved in murders, Schiro was still alive. Nick deserved no sympathy from anyone, yet he had turned the U.S. government into his advocate.

Ralph Meczyk, representing Anthony Doyle, began by telling the jury he imagined they had been asking themselves a question.

"Why does a police officer, a good man, an honest man, visit a convicted felon in prison?"

What had made him do it? He wasn't a made member of the mob following someone's orders, so why had he gone to see Frank Sr. at the federal facility in Milan, Michigan?

The answer went all the way back to Anthony "Twan" Doyle's childhood, Meczyk said. He had grown up in Chinatown, and his roots ran deep. Those who grew up there and became friends were almost like blood relatives, he said. Doyle was a bighearted and compassionate person who never forgot where he came from. He had lived with his mother and raised himself on the mean streets.

"Frank was his brother, and Ronnie Jarrett was his brother," Meczyk said, and those connections to friends from his old neighborhood trumped police rules.

The jury should feel a sense of humanity when thinking about the victims in the case, but Meczyk said Doyle's humanity should be noted, too. When Meczyk had spoken to the jury in his opening statement, he had told them he was proud to be Doyle's lawyer.

"And I still am."

Doyle should be thought of as an "Officer Friendly" character. He was friendly to his colleagues and the public he served as a transit and gang officer. He had always wanted to be a cop, and prosecutors had not proven he was involved in the juice loan business. The police slogan wasn't "We serve and collect," Meczyk said. Doyle had never violated his oath as a police officer.

Nick, "an admitted perjurer," had been the one to tell the jury that Doyle supposedly was a collector of juice loans in the 1960s. He had said Frank Sr. became upset when Doyle was becoming a cop because he didn't want his operation to lose a good man. Well, Doyle hadn't even become a police officer until 1980, Meczyk argued, seemingly putting that claim in doubt. No juice loan customers had appeared and accused Doyle of taking their money.

Doyle had never met Nick, and even on the government tapes Doyle was referred to as an old friend and not a "muscle guy." Doyle had pulled up routine information from a police computer and mentioned it to Frank Sr., someone he had known for years and felt sorry for. When Frank Sr. spoke for hours in code, Doyle was just nodding in agreement to be a listener for his friend. It was the government's evidence, but Doyle had spoken to the jury, too, through the tapes. If they listened, they could tell Doyle was merely playing along and feigning interest.

"Give Doyle the justice he deserves."

Mitch Mars had been fighting a stubborn cough in the latter stages of the trial, but there hadn't been much time for rest or to get it checked out. He was feeling tired and a bit worn out, and there was even some brief talk about having another prosecutor step in to wrap things up.

But not surprisingly, that wasn't going to happen.

If Mars was anything, he was a finisher.

He stepped confidently to the podium for the government in a dark, conservative suit, unrattled by anything he had heard from the defense. He looked at the jurors and spoke to them about what they had heard and seen—not from the other lawyers that day but during their weeks of listening to evidence presented in the landmark trial.

A city had suffered for too long, and they were in position to do something about it.

"As you know," Mars began, "this case involves the history of organized crime in Chicago."

Prosecutors had started with Capone and tracked the Chicago Outfit forward through the men on trial. Jurors had heard about "forty years' worth" of crimes. They had heard about a ruthless criminal organization that had "survived and prospered at the expense of who knows how many victims."

For the Outfit to maintain control of the city's underworld, people had been hurt and people had died.

"These defendants are members of that organization," Mars said. The men on trial had agreed to work together and use the organization to commit crimes, including extortion and murder. There were four men in the room who were professional criminals and killers who had taken lives. "They have done so for the Outfit." The fifth was a rogue police officer who had taken their side.

The defense had worked hard to discredit Nick Calabrese and point out his terrible past, and there could be no doubt that Nick was a criminal of the highest order. But the case wasn't about Nick, Mars said. It was about the enterprise, the entire criminal organization. Witnesses who knew the secrets of the Outfit's dark work were not going to be fine citizens. Nick had been honest about his history and had testified about decades of his own crimes.

You could tell, Mars said, that Nick was being truthful "about a very horrible life." He was no artful speaker, just a man giving his best memory. His demeanor was nothing like that of "the Clown," Lombardo, who was a compelling personality and an artful manipulator. Nick had sat on the witness stand, unable to look at anyone in the courtroom. He was quiet and robotic. Ask yourself, Mars said, "which was the boss and which was the worker."

Nick had been subjected to rigorous and thorough questioning by some of the best lawyers in Chicago, men who had studied the case and knew how to cross-examine a witness. Nick had passed the test.

"They did not catch him in a lie, much to their chagrin."

Nick's crimes were not committed for his personal benefit but to further his organization. He had pleaded guilty, and Judge Zagel, not the U.S. Attorney's Office, would decide what his punishment would be.

There could be no arguing that Nick had offered something in return for whatever leniency he might go on to receive, Mars continued. He had given information on eighteen Outfit murders spanning more than thirty years. Living relatives of many of those victims had now had their long-held questions answered.

"The issue is not whether you like Nicholas Calabrese—that is not why we're here," Mars told the jury, his voice at times sounding as if he was suppressing an anger that was welling up from his gut. "The issue is whether you believe him."

Frank Calabrese Sr. could be heard on the tapes admitting to seven murders, telling his own son what he had done. And his defense was basically twofold: that Nick was lying and making things up, and that Frank Sr., too, was not being truthful; he was just boasting in some bizarre attempt to impress Frank Jr.

The problem with that theory was that both Nick and Frank Sr. had given the same story about murders such as the killing of Richard Ortiz and Arthur Morawski. That meant both men would have had to be lying in exactly the same way and they would have to be doing so when Nick had never even heard the tapes of his brother. It wasn't possible for it to be a coincidence. The brothers could not give details about seven murders "and have it match and it not be true." And if Nick had been truthful about those seven murders, Mars argued, why would he make up the others?

"If he's here to tell the truth, he's here to tell the truth," he said.

Nick was backed up on tape concerning the murder of Anthony and Michael Spilotro, as well, Mars argued. James Marcello had been captured talking to his brother about it. They were worried about Nick's cooperation and knew that the feds' biggest target was what they code-named "Zhivago." James Marcello didn't have anything to fear if he had done nothing wrong, and he had paid money to buy Nick's silence.

Other witnesses had filled in other parts of the picture of the Chicago Outfit, and other tapes had provided insight, as well. There was the tape of Joey Lombardo supposedly "play-acting" when he'd threatened Morris Shenker. "This is not pretend," Mars said. Lombardo could be heard telling Shenker that to take Lombardo out would be to eliminate only one man but there was a force behind him. The case had definitely shown that to be true. Nick hadn't committed his crimes by himself, and neither had Lombardo.

Lombardo's crew had killed Daniel Seifert as a team, he said.

"Daniel Seifert ran afoul of the Outfit code," Mars told the jury. "You don't testify. You don't provide information. You don't cooperate with law enforcement."

The Spilotros also had been killed through teamwork. Outfit members had planned together for months to do them in, with Nick involved in the first preparations for the job in Las Vegas. Then, when their guards were up, the Spilotros were invited for their "promotions" by someone they knew—James Marcello.

Martin had raised the issue of the brothers being tipped off by the men in the basement wearing gloves, but Mars argued it didn't really matter. Once the men reached the basement, they were never leaving. The men waiting for them were on them in seconds.

"They could've worn T-shirts that read WE'RE HERE TO KILL THE SPILOTRO BROTHERS," Mars said. "It wouldn't have mattered."

As far as a rope being used in that crime, Nick had seen Louis Eboli throw a rope over Michael's neck. The autopsy showed abrasions that could have been made by one, even if the rope wasn't the instrument that had caused death.

Marcello's defense had also raised the issue of Nick's belief that Infelice was at the murder—another good point—but, Mars said, Nick had never really been sure, telling the FBI he thought he had seen Infelice out of the corner of his eye. The murder was twenty-one years earlier, possibly making some of the details murky, but it didn't mean Nick wasn't there. The important thing was that he remembered how he had gotten there. Marcello had driven him, a fact he had first omitted from his conversations with the FBI because he was paid to.

Mars offered more than a dozen reasons why the jury could know that Lombardo had killed Seifert, from Lombardo's fingerprint to the purchase of the scanner to Nick saying what John Fecarotta had told him about those who were involved. Seifert was the only witness against Lombardo, and he never got to testify. Seifert was standing in the Outfit's way when it came to continuing to have access to millions of dollars in Teamsters pension funds. Lombardo had supposedly seen the light in more recent years, Mars noted, and was now leading an honest life.

"How do you withdraw if you claim you were never in it?" Mars asked, his voice again shaking with emotion as he stared at Lombardo. "It's bogus story after bogus story."

Lombardo supposedly didn't even know how he had wound up in the "Last Supper" photo. And he had lied about knowing that some of those men were in the Outfit's hierarchy, including some he had been found guilty of committing crimes with in the past.

"How about just coming clean on what you got convicted of?" Mars said, raising his voice again and looking at Lombardo, who looked back with his head tilted to one side. "How about that, Mr. Lombardo?"

And the record was clear on Frank Sr., Mars said; he was a master manipulator. He might be counting on human nature and its frailties to escape blame for what he had done, but don't be fooled, Mars continued. Frank Sr. was a murderer, an extortionist, a loan shark, and a racketeer.

"He should be convicted," Mars said definitively.

Paul Schiro and Anthony Doyle should be convicted, too, he said, repeating the accusations against them. Nick had been truthful when he'd explained their roles.

Doyle was an inside man for the Outfit, Mars said, and his testimony belonged in the trash bin that Meczyk "paraded around at the beginning of this trial." He had been asked to figure out where the Fecarotta investigation was headed and where evidence collected in the investigation was going, and he had delivered. The idea that he didn't know the evidence was headed to the FBI was laughable.

The job of Doyle's unit was to protect such evidence. How could they not know where it went? Don't listen to Doyle's claim that what he told Frank Sr. was no big deal, Mars urged.

"Why do you think a man who has committed thirteen murders wants to know who the snitch is?" he asked. People got hurt for just that reason, and Doyle knew it. He had followed along with the talk of doctors and hospitals and the like. "Let's give the guy a physical," Mars said, quoting Doyle.

Yes, Mars concluded, the case was about the history of the Chicago Outfit, and it was time for an ending to be written. A city held in the grip of men like these was waiting for them to be held accountable. They had gotten away with their crimes for far too long. They were the products of an organization that had done what it wanted for decades, and it was time for justice. It was time for justice for the families of the victims and for the rest of us.

"Criminal cases are about accountability and justice, not only for the defendants but also justice for our system, justice for our society, and justice for the victims," Mars said. "Our system works. It is the greatest system in the world. But it only works when those who should be held accountable are held accountable."

20

END OF A TRIAL, END OF AN ERA

What was it that Joey "the Clown" Lombardo had said to Morris Shenker back in 1979?

He had made a threat while federal agents listened in and had boasted about having an army behind him. His organization was a machine—much bigger than a single operative, he had warned. Remove him from the picture, and it didn't really matter, because there would be another just like him to step in and take his place.

To resist the mob was to fight against the order of things.

"All you can do is send a guy like me to jail—one guy," Lombardo had said. "But you ain't gonna send the system to jail."

Maybe so, but the Family Secrets case would come as close to a blow against the Outfit as a system as Chicago had experienced in the modern era. Prosecutors had put the organization itself in the crosshairs, alleging that the mob existed as a criminal enterprise and calling it the "charged business" in the case. It was driven to preserve itself, they had asserted, thriving through its moneymaking rackets and protecting itself by any means necessary. It had ended hundreds of lives as it kept its ruthless grip, scarring families and leaving an indelible mark on the city's reputation. Even Chicago at the turn of the new millennium, an emerging global city with its eye on the future, would be known as much for its violent history of organized crime as it would be for its gleaming skyscrapers.

The jury would deliberate for a little more than four days before finding on Monday, September 10, 2007, that the five defendants were guilty of racketeering conspiracy.

The men sat virtually frozen as the verdict was read. There were no sighs or outbursts. Marcello didn't flinch. Schiro's jaw was moving but only because he was chewing gum. Frank Sr. didn't have any noticeable reaction, either, before Lopez stuck a file folder in front of his face to shield him from the stares of the media a few rows away. Being found guilty in the conspiracy meant long prison terms that would all but ensure that most of the men would die behind bars.

Frank Sr.'s son, Kurt, arrived to court too late to hear the verdict read, spending a few minutes in the courtroom after it had already been announced before heading back toward a bank of elevators to leave the building. As he pressed the button and waited, he said he had mixed emotions about the case and his father's conviction.

"I feel bad for all of the victims who are here," Kurt said. "I hope they're able to move forward, as torn up as they've been, and I hope my family can go on, as torn up as they've been."

And what about his father? The years of abuse were effectively over. Frank Sr. would never see another day outside a federal prison.

"I don't hate him," Kurt said. "I'm not a hateful person."

And in the case of Frank Sr. and two other defendants, the government would win extra insurance that their days of freedom were at an end.

Following another, shorter round of argument—punctuated by Frank Sr. at one point shouting "Them are lies!" in front of the jury—and several more days of deliberation, the jury would find that the three men were accountable for ten of the murders in the case. It was not a sweep for prosecutors, but it meant Lombardo, Marcello, and Frank Sr. qualified for life sentences.

The jury found that Lombardo was responsible for the murder of Daniel Seifert, whose son Joseph was among those in court to hear the verdict. It was thirty-three years to the day since the killing, and Joseph said he had stared at Lombardo as the verdict was read, hoping to catch his eyes. Lombardo had just leaned over the defense table and rested his chin in his hand.

"For some reason he didn't look my way," he said afterward with a little laugh.

Marcello was blamed by the jury for the murders of the Spilotro brothers, Anthony and Michael, causing Tom Breen to put a hand to his forehead as the decision was read. In the gallery nearby, Patrick Spilotro grabbed the hand of his wife, Kathy, in a moment of silent triumph.

The verdict brought a sense of justice that Patrick was still relishing months later as he sat with Kathy in an Italian restaurant in the downtown area of the suburb of Elmhurst. One of his sons was the executive chef of the handsome place decorated with photos from the golden age of Hollywood. Waitresses and staff greeted the couple, and Patrick took pride as he ordered the specialties of the house.

When Nick had testified, in some ways it was the culmination of years of work for Patrick, too. He had never stopped asking those who might be in the know what had happened to his brothers. Patrick had seen Nick in prison in the late 1990s and had urged him to tell the government all that he knew.

"I told him it was never too late to do what was right," Patrick said.

He said he was hopeful there might be more prosecutions in the future, as more became known about who was responsible for the murders of his brothers. But even so, he said, he was doing his best to put some of what had occurred behind him. As he ate, he took a call on his cell phone from a Las Vegas area code. It was Anthony Spilotro—his nephew—who worked for that city's fire department. Patrick said there were still many misconceptions about his family, and especially his brothers, who, he continued to maintain, were not the monsters the media and others made them out to be.

"We have forty college graduates in our family," Patrick said. "That's what we're about."

But not everyone got the news they had hoped for and prayed to hear for years. On some of the murders the jury found itself deadlocked and unable to reach a decision on assigning guilt. One of those was the killing of Nicholas D'Andrea, the man Nick had testified about hitting with a bat before helping a group of men tackle and eventually kill him.

D'Andrea's son, Bob, who like his father was built like an ox, paced in the hall outside the courtroom, with reddened eyes and a shocked expression on his face. Marcello wouldn't officially be blamed for his father's murder.

"The whole world knows he did it," he said angrily. "I didn't wait twenty-six years to hear this."

Frank Sr. had appeared to be praying before the jury's decision on the killings was announced, and maybe his plea was partly answered. He was found to have been responsible for seven of the murders he had been linked to, but still shook his head as the verdicts were read. In the other six murders, the jury again was unable to reach a unanimous decision.

Those Frank Sr. was blamed for were the Michael Cagnoni killing, the ambush murders of Charlotte and William Dauber, the shootings of Richard Ortiz and Arthur Morawski, the strangling of Michael Albergo, and the death of John Fecarotta.

"Now he can rest in peace after twenty-four years," Richard Ortiz's widow, Ellen Ortiz, said outside of court. "The Lord punishes in many, many ways."

But it wasn't a complete loss for Frank Sr., and Lopez called it a clear victory that the jury could not reach a decision in the killings of Paul Haggerty, Donald Renno and Vincent Moretti, Henry Cosentino, John Mendell, and William Petrocelli.

Charlene Moraveck, who had been married to Haggerty, staggered out of the courtroom on the arm of a victims' services caseworker, who helped her take a seat in a waiting area near a bank of windows on the twenty-fifth floor of the courthouse. She sobbed uncontrollably with a look of pain on her face.

She spoke with news reporters after she was able to compose herself.

"I waited thirty-one years," said Moraveck, who always believed her husband had no mob connections and his murder was a case of mistaken identity.

"That bastard ruined my life," she said of Frank Sr., before turning her anger toward the jury. "They couldn't come to a decision. I could have made a decision in five minutes. Everything was taken from me. It's never in the past."

Anthony Doyle hadn't been accused of any of the murders, and among those who had, only Schiro was able to completely avoid blame for a killing. The jury was unable to reach a verdict in the Arizona hit on Emil Vaci.

The pattern that emerged from the jury decision was that in order to blame a defendant in a killing, at least some on the jury wanted Nick's word to be supported by something else. Whether it was Frank Sr. talking about a murder on tape or Spilotro family members talking about Marcello, it took an extra verification to push the jury over the top. Nick's word had been the only thing linking Schiro to the Vaci murder, for example, and the panel had been unable to agree whether that was enough.

"It seems that they, as in probably most homicide cases, wanted to have some solid corroboration for our main witness, Nicholas Calabrese," Mars said under the glare of television news cameras in the courthouse lobby.

"So, it seems they're broken down along the lines of [Nick's] testimony along with tape-recorded evidence of his brother Frank or forensic evidence such as the fingerprint associated with Joseph Lombardo's participation in the Seifert homicide."

But even without a shutout win, prosecutors still claimed a great victory. Leaders of the U.S. Attorney's Office and the FBI praised the work of those who had put the monster case together and seen it through. Marcello, Lombardo, and Frank Sr. were eligible for life sentences, and Schiro and Doyle could expect long stays in prison, as well.

"It's hard to imagine how much satisfaction you get with a case like this," Mars told reporters. "It certainly is the biggest case I've been involved with."

Lopez agreed that it seemed the jury had not been able to take everything Nick said "as being Gospel." It seemed to him that Frank Sr.'s words on the tape had been the key jurors had used to blame him for many of the murders.

It was going to be impossible for Frank Sr. to get a fair trial no matter what evidence was presented, Lopez said.

"I don't think anybody charged in a case like this could get a fair trial anywhere, because of the publicity prior to trial, because of shows that they make in Hollywood, and because of scripts that they write in Hollywood, and people's perception as they walk into this courthouse," Lopez said.

"You see it all over the place. Al Capone is probably the most famous Chicagoan we have. You go to Paris and ask who John Gotti is, they won't know, but if you ask them about Al Capone, they're going to know who he is."

Several months later Lopez sat in his office, reflecting on the case. On the wall, near the giant sailfish, was a framed front page of the *Chicago Tribune*, one with a larger-than-life courtroom sketch of himself giving his opening statement in the Family Secrets case.

Frank Sr. was still left to be sentenced, but that was mostly a formality. The best hope for the defense was that they could convince Zagel, or an appeals court later, that when jurors had supposedly seen Frank Sr. mouth a threat to Markus Funk during his closing argument, it had unfairly biased the jury against Frank Sr. or other defendants. Most saw it as a long shot that there would be retrials ordered based on that issue.

So, what had worked when the jury heard the case and what had been a failure?

Some of the other defense lawyers in the case blamed the testimony of Lopez's client for bringing everyone down. They believed they had had a chance of keeping their small lifeboat afloat before Frank Sr. had taken the stand and started chopping out the bottom of it with an axe.

Maybe and maybe not, Lopez said. It was Frank Sr.'s right to testify, and there was no way he was going to sit there and let his brother and Frank Jr. speak against him uncontested.

"He was Frank," Lopez said. "That's how Frank is. He always wanted to tell his story. It was more his decision than my decision."

Still, Lopez said he believed Frank Sr. had no hope of winning without taking the stand. The jury already was going to hear his voice on the audiotapes from the prison, and Frank Sr. would need to try to explain them away as best he could. The jury needed Frank Sr. to get up there and deny being involved in any of the murders, and in the end he had escaped a unanimous verdict blaming him for all of them.

And Frank Sr. wasn't the only defendant whose testimony hadn't gone well.

"What about Lombardo? Didn't we all get dinged by Lombardo, too?" Lopez asked. "He was no better than Frank. In fact, he was probably worse."

Frank Sr. at least had admitted he was involved in organized crime, Lopez said, while Lombardo had offered a seemingly contradictory defense of claiming that he was never in the mob and also that he later withdrew from the conspiracy.

What might have hurt Frank Sr. the most was the evidence on his own plea agreement in his earlier case, which he had fought under relentless questioning by Scully by arguing that he was illiterate and couldn't read it.

If the jury believed what was in the plea agreement, they were halfway to convicting Frank Sr. of the conspiracy anyway.

Lopez said he believed Frank Sr. would be left most bitter by what his own family members had done to him. They had painted him as an abusive father and a bad brother, which Frank Sr. would forever say was untrue. He had given his sons a good life, with clothes and cars and vacations, and hadn't physically harmed them, Lopez said.

"He thinks about all the Thanksgivings and Christmases he's had with these people and now they turn on him," Lopez said. "His son, especially."

Lopez would go on with his own defense practice, handling a long police misconduct case and the criminal trial of an alleged Latin Kings gang leader after Family Secrets ended. He said he expected to continue representing organized crime figures in the future but wasn't sure what those cases would look like.

Certainly in his mind there would be nothing to rival the case of the Calabreses, which held Chicago's attention throughout the summer of 2007.

"You'll never see anything like this again," he said, leaning back in the chair behind his desk. "That era is done—the Outfit is dead. What is it now, a few bookies?"

Ralph Meczyk said he thought his client, Anthony Doyle, had simply been lost in the mix. He had held up well enough on the stand, believing that he too had to testify to explain what the jury was already going to hear from him on the recordings made at Milan.

If he could have separated himself from the other defendants, maybe he would have had a better chance. Instead the jury had seen a former Chicago police officer sitting in a room with the likes of Joey "the Clown" Lombardo and listened to "a tidal wave" of evidence.

He thought the verdict against his client was a contradictory one. Nick, "a known liar," had been the only person to say Doyle had been a Calabrese collector. So if jurors had decided they needed to corroborate everything Nick had said, why had they convicted Doyle on his word?

Halprin said his strategy had been knocked off track when Frank Sr. decided to testify. He had spent a year preparing Lombardo to take the stand, believing he could set his client apart and have him explain his position in the case in his oddly funny and likable way, a true Chicago character fighting for the few years he had remaining in this life.

Frank Sr. had testified just after Lombardo and tried to copy Joey's charm, failing as he argued with the judge about what parts of his past he could go over. "He dragged everyone down," Halprin said, calling Frank Sr.'s testimony ridiculous in every way.

As for Family Secrets as a whole, it was "a time warp case," he said, and one that showed how far the Chicago mob had fallen.

The Outfit had once ruled most of the western United States, and by the start of the trial, it had been reduced to "four hundred gambling machines in Cicero."

The men on trial were relics and dinosaurs, the remnants of the Chicago syndicate of the 1920s. Their convictions heralded the end of the mob of the last century, men who had been links on the Outfit's chain from Capone to Accardo to Aiuppa. Those men were Lombardo's mentors and the leaders of the mob that Frank Sr. and Marcello had risen up in.

Halprin called the case the final chapter of *Captive City*, the landmark 1969 book by Ovid Demaris that chronicled what Demaris called "the omniscient Outfit." The mob in the Demaris book was a complex entity with tentacles reaching into government, business, and law enforcement to secretly control Chicago.

That was the worldview of the men in the case, Halprin said. They were fossils, literally from another era, with minds that were operating in the city of decades ago.

"That's why they killed all these people," Halprin said. "Now they wind up in the twenty-first century, with all of these rules. And they have no idea what's going on."

For men such as agents John Mallul and Michael Maseth and prosecutor Markus Funk, there was still work to do.

Even in its weakened condition, the Chicago Outfit was still seen as attempting to make inroads into labor unions and the legalized casinos that had been allowed to open in Illinois. And the mob continued in its core rackets, most notably sports bookmaking and juice loans, and was still known to be branching into legitimate businesses and collecting street taxes from strip clubs and adult video stores.

It was a slimmer operation, with its six street crews of the past merging into four. By 2008, the working crews were Elmwood Park, Twenty-Sixth Street, Cicero, and Grand Avenue, with the FBI estimating there were about one hundred active members of the Chicago Outfit. The mob left in the wake of Family Secrets was leaner, with fewer top bosses and fewer internal disputes.

There were still murders and disappearances to investigate. Anthony Chiaramonti's 2001 murder was officially unsolved, and Anthony Zizzo, mentioned several times during the course of the trial, disappeared in the months after the Family Secrets indictment was handed down. He was believed to be among the leaders of the Cicero street crew when he vanished. The seventy-one-year-old's Jeep

Laredo was found abandoned in the parking lot of a Melrose Park restaurant. Some speculated that the fact that he wasn't indicted along with men like Marcello had raised the wrong red flags inside the mob's hierarchy and led to speculation that he too could have been cooperating.

In 2001, Bruno and Frank "Toots" Caruso and their cousin Leo were ousted from the Laborers International Union of North America for their alleged Outfit ties following a push by the union and the U.S. Justice Department to root out mob influence. The Chicago Crime Commission believed the Caruso family was running the Twenty-Sixth Street crew.

Allegations that the mob intended to have influence at the Emerald Casino in suburban Rosemont were widely publicized, and questions about some of its investors' possible Outfit ties eventually doomed the project. In September 2005, Mallul testified at a public hearing that led to the Illinois Gaming Board stripping the casino of its gambling license, a decision affirmed by an administrative law judge. Mallul told the panel that during the Family Secrets investigation, James and Michael Marcello were secretly recorded, in one of their prison talks, discussing in their coded language the Outfit's goal of getting a piece of the action in Rosemont.

"Are we gonna be in there at all?" James Marcello could be heard asking his brother on the tape.

But whatever future investigations looked like, they would happen without John Scully and Mitch Mars, the longtime leaders of mob investigations in the U.S. Attorney's Office in Chicago.

Scully retired just as the trial was ending, leaving the Organized Crime Division without his steadying influence amid a time when the amount of resources being directed toward Outfit investigations was being reduced.

And in February, about five months after the Family Secrets trial ended, Scully gave a eulogy at a funeral for Mars.

With the jury verdict in hand, Mars had gone to the doctor about the cough he had been fighting as the trial ended and had received the worst possible news. He had lung cancer, a stunning diagnosis for a man in his midfifties who wasn't a smoker.

He left the office that fall to rest in private, hoping through the holidays to recover and make it back to work as his section's chief in 2008. Updates on his condition were few, even in his own office, since he didn't go out of his way to trouble others for sympathy.

And even though he had been sick, his death on February 19, 2008, still came as a shock to many who knew him, and many who didn't. His passing so close to the end of the trial made news in the city he had worked so hard to rid of organized crime.

Chicago's U.S. attorney Patrick Fitzgerald said the impact Mars had on organized crime in Chicago couldn't be overstated. He had been a tireless enemy of the Outfit, a respected adversary of defense lawyers, and a good friend to many.

"The Chicago legal community will note that it lost a great and accomplished trial lawyer," Fitzgerald said in announcing the death of Mars. "The world of law enforcement will note that it lost a committed and savvy investigator of organized crime who every few years accomplished time and again what others would hope to accomplish in a lifetime—with Mitch, of course, giving 100 percent of the credit to the agents and trial partners he worked with and none to himself.

"But we would do a disservice to remember Mitch only by what he accomplished as a prosecutor in the courtroom. Mitch personified the word *public servant*. He came to work every day and served the citizens. He worked extremely hard and was quite talented and sought nothing in return except the feeling that he was part of doing something good," Fitzgerald said.

"We will best remember Mitch as the most decent of persons: honest, to a fault; committed, beyond a doubt, to his wife, his friends, and his country; and a team player who assumed all responsibility but took no credit. Anyone who knew Mitch as a person knew that he was also quite funny, laughing as often about himself as about others and all too happy to enlist others to join in as well."

Mallul and Maseth were deeply saddened to lose a man they considered a friend in addition to a leader in their work lives. They called him smart and motivated but remembered him as humble, too.

"He didn't walk around like somebody owed him a debt of gratitude or like somebody should put him on a pedestal," Mallul said in a phone call from his office the day Mitch's death was announced. "He did this job to do the right thing."

Even the lawyers who had been Mitch's opponents in the Family Secrets trial had nothing but positive things to say about him and the way he had conducted his investigations and the trial. Rick Halprin was distraught, saying he regretted he had never had the chance to have dinner with his courtroom opponent as the men had planned to do once the trial ended. He called Mars the driving genius behind Family Secrets and said he was "of the old school." He was tough but fair and self-effacing. And when he made a promise—even in the heat of a high-profile investigation or trial—"you could take it to the bank."

Of course, one of those hit the hardest by Mitch's passing was Scully. He had spent more than twenty-five years working beside his good friend, and he found himself challenged to remember him at the funeral and summarize his life in just a few moments.

In his remarks before those gathered to pay their last respects, Scully described Mitch as one of the best federal prosecutors in America but said he was so much more. He was a good husband, son, and friend. Scully remembered him as a true South Sider—the product of Catholic grammar school and a White Sox fan, proud of his Polish heritage. He was the jokester in the office and one of its best storytellers.

He had found his professional calling in prosecuting organized crime cases, with his work marked by his humility and sense of fairness, Scully said. He loved literature and Civil War history. He loved golf and poker and traveling with his wife, Jennifer. At Christmas parties he was the guy at the microphone making everyone laugh.

Family Secrets had been a crowning achievement for him, but he hadn't sought out the limelight or boasted about any of his success, Scully said. Instead, Mitch took his greatest sense of accomplishment from knowing that he hadn't let down the families of the victims in the case.

"Maybe the ultimate testament to Mitch came yesterday," Scully said, describing the hundreds of people who had come to Mitch's wake.

"His mom told me of the six or seven people who came up to her," Scully continued. They had said how sorry they were, and Mitch's mother had asked whether they worked with her son. "They said, no, they were just members of the general public and that they wanted to come and to thank her for raising such a fine man and to relate how appreciative they were of him, as he had done so much for them. Most of them were citizens from Cicero."

It was certainly a fitting tribute, and Scully said he was finished.

"I'll end this how I think Mitch would," he said. "Your Honor, the prosecution rests. May he rest in peace."

What reaction Nick Calabrese might have had to the death of Mars would remain unknown. He was awaiting sentencing at an undisclosed federal prison, his whereabouts closely held for his own safety. His ultimate future would be up to Judge Zagel, who would decide how much leniency Nick's unprecedented cooperation should earn him. The judge would have to strike a balance between adequately punishing someone who had admitted to so many murders and also giving him enough of a break that future Nick Calabreses would have some incentive to come clean and spill their secrets, too.

In his first sentencing after the trial, Zagel seemed to be feeling at least somewhat lenient. He sentenced Mickey Marcello in March 2008 after listening to his son, Sam, talk about what Mickey meant to his family. Sam said his father was sorry for what he had done.

"He's a decent man, he's remorseful, and he's very conscious of his actions," Sam Marcello was quoted in the *Tribune* as saying. "He always insisted I conduct myself with principle."

Zagel acknowledged that Marcello was loyal. It was hard to argue that point. He had remained dedicated to his brother, James, sticking by his blood even after James was sent to prison. The judge also said, however, that Marcello was loyal to a fault, telling Marcello he had been led down a "disastrous path."

"Maybe one of your principles is one of your problems," Zagel told Marcello. "Maybe you were too good of a brother."

Zagel said he had planned to give Marcello more than nine years in prison, but after hearing Sam speak, he decided to send him away for eight and a half.

No matter what sentence Nick received, it remained a possibility that he could be brought to the witness stand again in future trials. One of those trials, however, would not be for Frank "the German" Schweihs, who died in custody due to complications of cancer in July 2008. Schweihs was angry and threatening to the last, spitting insults at prosecutors during his final appearance before Zagel and leaving some in the courtroom wondering how Schweihs could have been quieted long enough for a trial anyway. Once, when Schweihs was talking loudly to his lawyer in court, Funk had glanced in his direction.

"You makin' eyes at me?" a hunched Schweihs snarled from a wheelchair. "Do I look like a fag to you or something?"

Whether or not Nick would testify again—against the Caruso family or others—he had already filled in many more gaps for the FBI than his testimony had covered. In his extensive interviews with FBI agents, he provided information on a number of murders that were not a part of Family Secrets, mostly because Nick had learned the details of killings through a third party and not directly.

Among the other murders Nick mentioned was the killing of Manny Skar, who was involved in mob gambling and about to flip before he was shot outside his Lake Shore Drive building in 1965. Nick told authorities that John Fecarotta had once told him Joey Lombardo and Anthony Spilotro were responsible and the murder had qualified Lombardo to be made.

Nick said a man named Dickie D'Angelo was the one who shot his brother's onetime juice loan partner Larry Stubich. Angelo LaPietra had never given Frank Sr. permission to kill D'Angelo in response.

Lombardo has long been suspected of being involved in the 1973 murder of Richard Cain, the corrupt police officer and mobster, at the Grand Avenue sandwich shop, but Nick didn't name him in that murder. Nick informed the FBI that Johnny "Apes" Monteleone had told him the LaPietra brothers, Fecarotta, Turk Torello, and Aiuppa were to blame.

One of the most notorious unsolved mob killings in Chicago history was the shooting of Sam "Momo" Giancana, a boss who led the mob beginning in the late 1950s. He was shot while making Italian sausage in his home in Oak Park in 1975. Nick told the FBI he knew that Anthony Accardo had been part of the killing and that Angelo LaPietra had disposed of the gun. The weapon used to shoot Giancana was equipped with a silencer that Frank Sr. and Ronnie Jarrett had made, Nick said.

Allen Dorfman, shot outside a suburban hotel in 1983, also was on Nick's list. Fecarotta had told him that he and Frank Schweihs were responsible.

Jasper Campise and John Gattusso were killed in 1983 after they botched a hit on Ken Eto, a man known as "Tokyo Joe," who was to be sentenced in a gambling case. Nick told the FBI that Jimmy DiForti and Sam Carlisi were involved in the murders of the men, who were found stabbed in a car trunk.

Most of the murders Nick described are old, and those he blamed are long dead themselves, but there were a few exceptions. The most notable had actually been aired in the trial, when Nick had said that John DiFronzo, a man he knew as "Johnny Bananas," was involved in the killing of the Spilotros.

At the end of 2007, law enforcement and experts still believed DiFronzo had an active, leading role in the Outfit. DiFronzo had risen through the mob's ranks in juice loans, had moved into legitimate business, and had connections to waste hauling. He was convicted of racketeering in the 1990s for trying to infiltrate an Indian casino in California, but by late 2008 he had not faced any charges based on Nick's account of the Spilotro murders.

Law enforcement would have to work to corroborate Nick's account, a view made clear by the jury's indecision on some of the murders in the Family Secrets case. It was clear that at least some on the jury weren't ready to assign blame for murders based on Nick's word alone.

But that had no effect on what the FBI thought of him.

Both Mallul and Maseth said they remained convinced that Nick, perhaps the most significant mob traitor ever in Chicago, was telling the truth. The agents spent months and years talking to him and said there was too much detail in his account for him to have been lying. In short, they had grown to trust him.

Nick had come to know the seriousness of what he had done, they said, and felt remorse. When he had become upset on the witness stand while talking about how Mrs. Cagnoni and her son had nearly been killed by an Outfit bomb, he wasn't play-acting. The thought of killing those two innocents still eats at him, they said.

He may have rationalized what he did through the knowledge that it wasn't his idea for his victims to be killed and the fact that they would have been killed whether he was there or not. Most were involved with the mob in one way or another. The Outfit had marked them for death, and someone was going to do the job. And Nick knew if he had been assigned a murder and balked, he would have taken their place.

Mallul said that Nick viewed himself as just a soldier living in a kill-or-be-killed world. He was a man who did his job, but emotionally he was left tormented and haunted by his years as a ruthless Outfit killer. In many ways he remained the scared man forced to dig a hole, truly terrified when he and his brother had pushed and pulled that first body off a pile of dirt, dropping it through the South Side clay.

"Does he see people's faces?" Mallul said. "Yeah. I believe he does."

ACKNOWLEDGMENTS

Special thanks to FBI Special Agents John Mallul and Michael Maseth, who made themselves available for interviews, allowed themselves to be quoted, and answered questions about the case. Thanks also to former assistant U.S. attorney John Scully and assistant U.S. attorney Markus Funk, who were kind enough to offer their time to discuss their work.

I'm also very grateful to defense lawyers Rick Halprin, Joseph Lopez, and Ralph Meczyk, who, even though they didn't always see eye to eye in court, certainly supported this project and were generous with their time. Rick, especially, is a wonderful dinner companion.

Thank you also to Patrick and Kathy Spilotro, who sat across a table from me to discuss the investigation, the trial, and their family's history.

Thanks also to the tireless Randall Samborn of the U.S. Attorney's Office in Chicago and Ross Rice of the FBI, who helped provide access, make records available, and answer questions.

Behind the book from the outset was *Tribune* colleague Rick Kogan, who pushed me to do it and brought the right people together. And thanks to Sue Betz and Lisa Reardon of Chicago Review Press for their work with me as a first-time author.

Always in my corner are my coworkers and editors at the *Tribune*, especially editors Matt O'Connor and Peter Kendall, who guided the trial coverage at the paper. Thank you to *Tribune* photographer Alex Garcia, as well, who took time out of his busy schedule to shoot the author photo for this book. And thanks to reporter Liam Ford, who was more than a capable backup for me during Family Secrets.

Personal thanks to all of my friends and neighbors who provided support throughout the writing of this book. Thanks to the Smiths for warm meals on some cold writing nights, and of course to members of "the String," who always have my back.

I'm grateful for the encouragement from my parents, Doug and Kathy Coen, and from my other parents, Mike and Sharon Marsalis.

And always I am thankful for Michelle, Meredith, and Liam, who put up with a working husband and dad who came home from a busy job only to sit in front of a computer and write, and then spent weekends and vacation days writing some more. All of it is, of course, for you.

KEY FIGURES

NICHOLAS CALABRESE
The key mob turncoat in the Family Secrets case. He was a former member of the Twenty-Sixth Street, or Chinatown, crew who rose to become a trusted Outfit hit man.

FRANK CALABRESE SR.
Nick's brother and a onetime "street boss" in the Chinatown crew. He was reputed to be Chicago's leading loan shark and was linked to multiple murders in the Family Secrets case.

JOEY "THE CLOWN" LOMBARDO
The wisecracking overseer of the Chicago Outfit. He was accused of being a capo of the Grand Avenue crew, and his past crimes included the attempted bribing of a U.S. senator.

JAMES "JIMMY LIGHT" MARCELLO
The reputed boss of the Chicago Outfit at the time of his arrest in the Family Secrets case. The FBI and IRS believe he made millions controlling video gambling machines in the Chicago area.

PAUL "THE INDIAN" SCHIRO

A reputed mob enforcer for the western arm of the Chicago Outfit. He was linked to a mob murder in Arizona.

ANTHONY "TWAN" DOYLE

A former Chicago police officer accused of leaking information to Frank Calabrese Sr. during the Family Secrets investigation. He had access to data on one of the killings and was taped passing that data to Calabrese in a federal prison.

FRANK "THE GERMAN" SCHWEIHS

A feared hit man who acted as the muscle for Lombardo and the Grand Avenue crew for decades. He was too sick with cancer to stand trial with the others in the summer of 2007 and died the following year.

OTHER KEY OUTFIT MEMBERS

ANGELO AND JAMES "JIMMY" LAPIETRA

Leaders of the Chinatown crew while the Calabrese brothers were involved in gambling and juice loans. They are believed to have ordered many of the hits in the Family Secrets case.

RONNIE JARRETT

An Outfit associate who acted as a soldier under Frank Calabrese Sr. and was accused of taking part in many of the murders in the case.

FRANK "GUMBA" SALADINO

An enforcer who worked in the Calabrese organization. He was known for his intimidating size.

ANTHONY "BIG TUNA" ACCARDO

The reputed boss, or "old man," of the Outfit for many of the years covered in the Family Secrets case.

JOEY "DOVES" AIUPPA

Accardo's successor as the Outfit's number one.

JIMMY "POKER" DIFORTI

A made member of the mob who allegedly took part with the Calabreses in some of the killings in the case.

JOHN "NO NOSE" DIFRONZO, A.K.A. "JOHNNY BANANAS"

A reputed mob leader accused by Nicholas Calabrese of taking part in the murders of the Spilotro brothers.

VICTIMS

ANTHONY "THE ANT" AND MICHAEL SPILOTRO

Brothers killed in 1986 after being lured to a suburban basement with the promise of mob promotions. Anthony Spilotro ran the Outfit's operations in Las Vegas and was taken out for bringing too much heat to the organization there.

DANIEL SEIFERT

The owner of a suburban plastics firm gunned down in front of his family in 1974, just before he could testify against Lombardo and others accused of defrauding a Teamsters pension fund.

MICHAEL CAGNONI

A suburban businessman whose car was bombed in 1981 on a Chicago area tollway after he apparently rethought his promises to have his lucrative shipping firm pay heavy street tax to the Outfit.

WILLIAM "BUTCH" PETROCELLI

A mobster who was a member of the crew known as "the Wild Bunch." An alleged partner of noted mob hit man Harry Aleman, he was killed in 1980 for being too flamboyant and outspoken about his goal to lead the Outfit.

MICHAEL "HAMBONE" ALBERGO

An associate of the Calabreses who was subpoenaed to testify about juice loans and made the mistake of promising to take others with him if he was ever sent to prison. His killing in 1970 was the first murder in the case.

HENRY COSENTINO
A mob associate allegedly killed in 1977 after fighting with "Gumba" Saladino and shooting him in the leg.

PAUL HAGGERTY
Killed in Chicago in 1976 by mobsters looking for information about a robbery.

JOHN MENDELL
A skilled burglar killed in 1978 in retaliation for breaking into the home of mob boss Anthony Accardo to resteal jewels Mendell had first stolen from a business with ties to Accardo.

VINCENT MORETTI AND DONALD RENNO
Moretti also was killed in 1978 as part of a violent statement made by the mob after the Accardo break-in. Renno, Moretti's friend, was just in the wrong place at the wrong time.

WILLIAM AND CHARLOTTE DAUBER
Bill Dauber was a noted mob hit man believed to have been responsible for more than two dozen killings, and he was part of the Outfit's valuable chop-shop operations in Chicago's south suburbs. After word got out that he was cooperating with federal agents, Dauber and his wife were gunned down in 1980 while driving home from a court date.

NICHOLAS D'ANDREA
A mob associate beaten to death in 1981 during "questioning" over the shooting of a south suburban crime boss.

RICHARD ORTIZ AND ARTHUR MORAWSKI
Two men shot to death in a car outside Ortiz's bar in 1983. Ortiz was a mob associate suspected in an unsanctioned hit.

EMIL VACI
A federal grand jury witness the Outfit believed could testify against mob leaders involved in the killing of Jay Vandermark, who had cheated the Outfit out of some of its Las Vegas skim.

JOHN FECAROTTA

A mob hit man who ran afoul of the Calabreses and Outfit leaders. His was the last killing (1986) in Family Secrets and the one that provided the key lead that broke the case.

ATTORNEYS

RICK HALPRIN

A veteran of the federal courthouse in Chicago and the lawyer for Joey "the Clown" Lombardo. It was his original plan to set Lombardo apart by having him be the only defendant to testify.

JOSEPH "THE SHARK" LOPEZ

A lawyer, known for his flashy dress and energetic argument, who counted some mobsters among his friends. He represented Frank Calabrese Sr., whom he sometimes had trouble controlling in court.

RALPH MECZYK

Lawyer for Anthony "Twan" Doyle, a defendant Meczyk grew to trust and like.

MARC MARTIN AND TOM BREEN

Lawyers for reputed mob boss James Marcello. A pair of experienced attorneys, they have worked on many high-profile cases in Chicago.

PAUL WAGNER

Attorney for Paul "the Indian" Schiro.

MITCHELL MARS

Head of the Organized Crime Division of the U.S. Attorney's Office in Chicago and a deputy chief in the original antimob strike force in the city. Mars was the architect of the strategy to attack the Outfit itself as an enterprise in the Family Secrets case. Mars led the prosecution, questioned Nicholas Calabrese for the jury, cross-examined Lombardo, and gave the rebuttal argument.

JOHN SCULLY

Like Mars, a career prosecutor who rose in the ranks of the U.S. Attorney's Office making major cases against the mob. He gave the opening statement in Family Secrets and cross-examined Frank Calabrese Sr.

MARKUS FUNK

An up-and-coming prosecutor who rounded out the Family Secrets team and went on to be a key prosecutor in Chicago mob cases in the wake of Family Secrets. He cross-examined Doyle and gave the closing argument in the case.

CHRONOLOGY

OCTOBER 1969

Nick Calabrese asks his brother, Frank Calabrese Sr., for a role in his juice loan operation. Nick begins keeping the books on debtors and gamblers.

AUGUST 1970

Drawn much further into Outfit life than he intended, Nick commits his first murder with his brother. Michael "Hambone" Albergo of the Calabrese ring is killed after being subpoenaed to testify about loan sharking and after promising that if he ever went to prison, he would not go alone.

SEPTEMBER 27, 1974

After agreeing to testify against Joey "the Clown" Lombardo and others about the theft of Teamsters pension funds, Daniel Seifert is ambushed and gunned down, in front of his wife and son, outside his Bensenville plastics business.

JUNE 24, 1976

Paul Haggerty is taken to a garage owned by the mother-in-law of mobster and Calabrese associate Ronnie Jarrett. His body is dumped in the trunk of a stolen car.

MARCH 15, 1977
Henry Cosentino is killed, allegedly by Frank Sr.

JANUARY 16, 1978
Burglar John Mendell is killed as revenge for breaking into the River Forest home of Tony Accardo, the Chicago Outfit's "Number One." Nick helps Frank Sr. strangle him and cut his throat.

JANUARY 31, 1978
Donald Renno and Vincent Moretti are lured to a closed Cicero restaurant and killed by Nick, his brother, and a group of Outfit members.

JULY 2, 1980
William Dauber, a mob hit man, and his wife, Charlotte, are chased down and shot as they drive home from a court date in Joliet. Dauber, a chop shop kingpin, had begun cooperating against Chicago Heights mob leaders.

DECEMBER 30, 1980
William "Butch" Petrocelli is killed for partying too much and bragging that he's going to run the Chicago mob. His body is left in his car on a Cicero side street after a botched attempt by Nick to burn the vehicle.

JUNE 24, 1981
A bomb tears through Michael Cagnoni's sedan as he heads onto a suburban tollway to work at his shipping business. A hit crew worked for weeks to build the remotely activated explosive that killed him. Cagnoni had begun resisting paying the mob a hefty street tax.

SEPTEMBER 13, 1981
Nicholas D'Andrea is beaten to death by a hit team in Chicago Heights during "questioning" about the shooting of a mob boss.

JULY 23, 1983
Nick and his brother are part of a three-man team that guns down Richard Ortiz outside his bar on a Cicero street. His friend Arthur Morawski dies too in a hail of bullets.

OCTOBER 9, 1983

Nick becomes a "made" member of the Chicago Outfit, welcomed into the inner circle of the syndicate by its leaders in a secret ceremony involving the burning of holy cards and a promise of allegiance until death.

JUNE 6, 1986

Grand jury witness Emil Vaci, a potential threat to the mob's Las Vegas empire, is killed in Arizona. Nick is the gunman who shoots Vaci in the back of a van and dumps his body in a gulley.

JUNE 14, 1986

Anthony and Michael Spilotro are lured to a suburban home with promises of Outfit promotions. Both are attacked and beaten to death by Nick and a group of Outfit members. Their bodies are discovered buried in an Indiana farm field.

SEPTEMBER 14, 1986

Nick betrays one of his closest friends, tricking John Fecarotta and shooting him to death on the Northwest Side.

MARCH 1997

Nick, Frank Sr., and Frank's sons, Frank Jr. and Kurt, plead guilty in a racketeering case in federal court in Chicago. All are sentenced to prison, and the case brings tensions between Frank Sr. and Frank Jr. to a boil.

JULY 27, 1998

Frank Jr. writes a letter from the federal penitentiary in Milan, Michigan, offering his cooperation to the FBI in Chicago. He writes the case agent who handled the racketeering investigation against his family, indicating he will work with the FBI against his father and uncle.

FEBRUARY 1999

Frank Jr. begins taping his father, who is incarcerated with him at Milan. Operation Family Secrets is launched.

JANUARY 2000

Nick is told that a DNA sample taken from him links him to the shooting of Fecarotta; he begins contemplating cooperating against his brother.

JANUARY 2002

Nick has his first meeting with FBI agents and Mitch Mars of the U.S. Attorney's Office. He begins to describe his life in the Chicago Outfit, pulling back a curtain on years of unsolved mob murders.

JANUARY 2003

The FBI begins taping James Marcello and his brother Michael when Michael visits the Milan penitentiary. The Marcellos are captured talking about their gambling operation and the ongoing investigation involving Nick.

APRIL 2005

The investigation comes to a head as prosecutors and the FBI announce the landmark Family Secrets indictment against the Chicago mob, charging the Outfit as a criminal enterprise that protected itself through decades of violence and murder. Some of the most infamous gangland killings in Chicago history are declared solved, and organized crime leaders including James Marcello and Joey "the Clown" Lombardo are charged. Frank Calabrese Sr. is indicted as well and accused of murder including the killings of Albergo, the Daubers, Petrocelli, and Ortiz and Morawski.

JANUARY 2006

After he had gone into hiding with the indictment announcement, Lombardo is arrested in the Chicago suburbs in the company of an old friend who had helped him avoid the FBI. He is turned in by Patrick Spilotro, his dentist and a brother to mobsters Anthony and Michael Spilotro, whose murders have been linked to James Marcello in Family Secrets.

JUNE 2007

The trial begins in U.S. District Court in Chicago. After a series of defendants plead guilty, five who are charged in the conspiracy remain: Lombardo, Frank Sr., James Marcello, Paul "the Indian" Schiro, and crooked cop Anthony "Twan" Doyle.

JULY 2007

Nick takes the witness stand for a week of historic testimony, turning against his brother and the organization he swore to be loyal to above all else.

SEPTEMBER 2007

The Family Secrets jury convicts the five men in the case of broad conspiracy charges. They are able to assign blame in ten of the murders, including blaming Marcello for the Spilotros killing, Lombardo for the Seifert murder, and Frank Sr. for a number of long-unsolved slayings. The jury was unable to reach a unanimous decision on whether Schiro was to blame for helping to kill Emil Vaci.

Elk Grove
Village

11

6

selle

Wood
Dale

Bensenville

Schiller
Park

Norridge

Lake
Michigan

Franklin
Park

8

ndale
eights

Addison

Elmwood
Park

River Forest

13

15

Villa
Park

Elmhurst

Melrose
Park

len
lyn

Bellwood

Maywood

Oak Park

1

Chicago

Lombard

10

Forest
Park

9

Cicero

7

2

Hillside

Berwyn

4

14

Brookfield

3

La Grange

Lyons

Summit

Downers
Grove

sle

Burbank

Woodridge

Darien

Burr
Ridge

Hickory
Hills

Evergreen
Park

olingbrook

Lemont

Palos
Hills

Chicago
Ridge

Alsip

Blue
Island

Riverdale

Calumet
City

Goodings
Grove

Palos
Heights

Crestwood

Oak
Forest

Harvey

Orland
Park

Lockport

Tinley
Park

Markham

South
Holland

Lansing

Country
Club Hills

Mokena

Chicago
Heights

Matteson

5

New
Lenox

Richton
Park

Park
Forest

Sauk
Village

D

Frankfort

Manhattan

12

1.25 2.5   5 Miles

1 2820 South Lowe Avenue, Chicago
Location of the garage of a home owned by Ronnie Jarrett's mother-in-law where Paul Haggerty and John Mendell were killed.

2 West Thirty-Third Street and South Shields Avenue, Chicago
Believed to be approximately the spot where Michael Albergo was killed and buried. This is the location Nick Calabrese led the FBI to for an unsuccessful excavation in 2003.

3 Ogden ramp to southbound Tri-State Tollway (I-294)
Location of the bombing of Michael Cagnoni's car.

4 4300 block of West Twenty-Fifth Street, Cicero
Location where William Petrocelli's body was found in his car.

5 Chicago Heights
Location of Nicholas D'Andrea murder; exact address unknown.

6 810 Foster Avenue, Bensenville
Location of Daniel Seifert murder.

7 5100 West Cermak, Cicero
Location of Richard Ortiz and Arthur Morawski shooting.

8 North Austin and West Belmont avenues, Chicago
Site of the John Fecarotta killing.

9 West Twenty-Second Place and South Laramie Avenue, Cicero
Site of the closed restaurant where Donald Renno and Vincent Moretti were killed.

10 Roosevelt Road just west of South Mannheim Road, Hillside
Site of the restaurant where Nick Calabrese described being part of a "making" ceremony that marked his induction as a full member of the Chicago Outfit.

11 Somewhere off Illinois Route 83, Bensenville
The home where Anthony and Michael Spilotro were killed in a basement.

12 Monee-Manhattan Road, four miles east of the town of Manhattan
Site of William and Charlotte Dauber killings.

13 4600 West Division Street
Site of auto pound where Henry Cosentino's body was discovered in the trunk of a car.

14 The Bridgeport neighborhood, Chicago
Home to the Twenty-Sixth Street, or Chinatown, crew.

15 West Grand and North Ogden avenues
Chicago Old West Side neighborhood nicknamed "the Patch," the original Chicago home of many of the men in the case.

INDEX

421